FRIENDLY FIRE

To Francesca and Alice

FRIENDLY FIRE

THE SECRET WAR BETWEEN THE ALLIES

LYNN PICKNETT, CLIVE PRINCE
AND STEPHEN PRIOR
with additional historical research by Robert Brydon

MAINSTREAM
PUBLISHING
EDINBURGH AND LONDON

This edition, 2005

First published in Great Britain in 2005 by
MAINSTREAM PUBLISHING COMPANY (EDINBURGH) LTD
7 Albany Street
Edinburgh EH1 3UG

ISBN 1 84018 996 7

A catalogue record for this book is available from the British Library

Typeset in Baskerville
Printed and bound in Great Britain by
Antony Rowe Ltd, Chippenham, Wiltshire

Acknowledgements

Our special thanks to:

Francesca Prior; Michelle Norton; Joanne Norton; Alice Prior; Ben Prior; Stephen J.W. Prior; Stephanie Prior; Lyndsay Brydon; Mike Wallington; and our agent Jeffrey Simmons.

For kindly sharing their information and expertise: Michael 'Tim' Buckmaster; Anthony Cave Brown; Charles Destrée; Ralph de Toledano; Willie Henderson; Madeleine Masson Rayner; George P. Morse; Scott Newton; the late Walter Pforzheimer; Pierre Raynaud; Keith Prince; Andrew Rosthorn; Howard Sartori; James C. de C. Scott; Eric Taylor; John Taylor; John H. Waller.

For their valued help and support: David Bell; Debbie Benstead; Clementina Bentine; Yvan Cartwright; Leon Ellenport; Carina Fearnley; Nigel Foster; Iain Gray; Mary Neilson; Jim Naples; Mark Naples; Craig Oakley; Lily and David Prince; Richard Taylor; Sheila Taylor; Sue and Tony Young.

The staff of the following libraries and archives: British Library and British Newspaper Library; Cambridge University Library; Edinburgh City Library; Georgetown University Library; House of Lords Record Office; Imperial War Museum; Institute of Contemporary History and Wiener Library; National Archives of Scotland; National Library of Scotland; Sikorski Museum and Historical Archive; UK National Archive (Public Record Office); US National Archive (Washington DC and Maryland).

Contents

Stephen Prior 1947–2003

As this book was largely Stephen's idea, it is a matter of great sadness to us and his family that he was never able to see it published. It will come as no surprise to those who knew him that his enthusiasm for this project endured – even in his last days in hospital he was full of ideas and insisted on correcting the typescript.

An extraordinary man, we miss his insights, knowledge and resourcefulness, besides his astonishing capacity for hospitality and hilarity. He made our joint three-book career enormous fun.

Lynn, Clive
and Robert

INTRODUCTION

The More Things Change . . .

Friendly Fire arose because we wanted to explore in detail some of the issues we had raised in *Double Standards: The Rudolf Hess Cover-Up* (2001), which examined the mystery of the Deputy Führer's flight to Britain in May 1941. The intriguing and deliberately obscured background to the Hess affair begged for follow-ups. The project that became *War of the Windsors* (2002), which began by investigating the clandestine involvement of members of the British Royal Family in peace moves during the Second World War, evolved into the 'secret history' of the House of Windsor. Our other main line of research, which led to this book, was the complex relationship between the wartime Allies, particularly the three leaders: Churchill, Roosevelt and Stalin.

We presented proposals for both books to our publishers in summer 2001, but as the following year was the Queen's Golden Jubilee we were asked for the Windsor book first. By the time we knuckled down to *Friendly Fire*, the world had become a darker, considerably more edgy place because of the terrorist attacks on the Twin Towers in New York and the Pentagon in Washington, propelling the West into a 'War on Terror'. Once again, the United States and the United Kingdom were Allies, and subsequent events – such as the invasion of Afghanistan – plunged the 'special relationship' back into the spotlight. Suddenly our research into the special relationship's origins in the Second World War – after all, it was Winston Churchill himself who coined the phrase – had a sharper relevance.

During the process of writing, the book became increasingly topical, as, under the American initiative, the focus of the War on Terror moved to the rather less obvious target of Saddam Hussein's Iraq. As *Friendly Fire* took shape during the months of diplomatic tumult over seeking the United Nations' backing for the invasion of Iraq, and then the Second Gulf War itself (not to mention its aftermath), the similarities between what we saw every day on the news and what we were writing about became uncanny. And perhaps the strangest thing is that most people have absolutely no idea that, in many significant ways, history is repeating itself.

The Second World War and the Second Gulf War are seen as vastly different, the latter enmeshed from the first in raging controversy, allegations of conspiracy and cover-up. Many suspect that there was a hidden agenda behind the Bush administration's enthusiasm to send US forces into Iraq; others believe that it was both illegal and immoral; certainly questions were asked about the justification for invading another sovereign country, however atrocious the regime, without the UN's backing. Yet the motives and legality for fighting the Second World War are rarely questioned. To do so is to risk being shouted down as ill informed – or even pro-Fascist. After all, everyone knows it was a just war, with the single noble aim of destroying Hitler and his evil regime, and absolutely no ulterior motives . . .

In reality, the same questions asked about the war on Iraq *should* have been posed about the Second World War, but in the late 1930s the public was far less well informed – or perhaps still had to learn how to be cynical – and the system easily allowed those in power to mislead the people.

The parallels are striking. There is growing evidence that President George W. Bush and his administration deliberately misled

Introduction

the world – including their fellow Americans – about their real reasons for wanting to overthrow Saddam Hussein and occupy Iraq, using the pretext of seeking his weapons of mass destruction (WMD) and links with al-Qaeda. Critics point out that key members of Bush's administration had been calling for an American-led invasion of Iraq for some five years before the attacks of 11 September 2001, fuelling suspicions that the tragedy was simply used as an excuse. Similarly, despite the portrayal of the Second World War as a moral crusade against Nazism and Japanese imperialism, even before the United States joined the conflict President Franklin D. Roosevelt took advantage of the war in Europe to further certain long-held ambitions – establishing military bases on British-owned territory and boosting American overseas trade at Britain's expense.

The media have examined in detail the various allegations of spin and 'sexing up' of intelligence dossiers to persuade the British and American publics that Saddam Hussein was a clear and present danger to the West. Yet Winston Churchill's famous warnings during his 'wilderness years' about the threat posed by Nazi Germany relied upon information leaked to him by MI6, and exaggerated the size of the Luftwaffe sixfold. And in 1940, he first exaggerated the threat of invasion, then deliberately withheld from Roosevelt and his own ministers evidence that Hitler had abandoned plans to invade Britain. It suited Churchill for them to believe that invasion was imminent: not only would Roosevelt continue to supply aid but the threat of invasion also kept Churchill's own position secure – powerful parliamentary opponents were poised to challenge his war leadership once the invasion threat was over – and the public would unhesitatingly continue to make the sacrifices he demanded.

Across the Atlantic, President Roosevelt lied even more blatantly, for example telling Congressmen in 1938 that US intelligence had evidence of a plan by Germany, Japan and Italy for joint offensives against the West – a plan that was non-existent. In the run-up to America's entry into the war, Roosevelt also presented his country with versions of events – such as U-boat attacks on US shipping – that were more fiction than fact. But they worked: the American mood shifted towards joining the conflict.

The role of the intelligence agencies is also under scrutiny as never before. Did they exaggerate the evidence for Iraq's weapons of mass destruction because that is what their governments wanted to hear? Yet there is no question that in 1941 British intelligence passed off fake 'Nazi documents' to the US President, which he used to persuade Congress to bring America ever closer to direct engagement. There is even persuasive evidence that British agents finally tricked Hitler into declaring war on the United States, giving Roosevelt no option but to take America into the European conflict. And, incredibly, British intelligence also interfered in the American elections to ensure that Roosevelt won his unprecedented third term.

Conspiracy theories abound about recent events, notably the 'LIHOP' ('[They] Let it Happen on Purpose') theory about 11 September 2001: that US intelligence knew in advance, but they, or the government, deliberately did nothing to prevent the attacks because the atrocities would provide the perfect excuse for invading Iraq – recalling similar theories about Pearl Harbor, that other indelible scar on the American psyche.

In February 2004, during the furore over the failure to find Saddam's WMD and accusations that Tony Blair had knowingly exaggerated their threat, one Cabinet minister ill-advisedly compared Blair to Winston Churchill, causing outrage for daring to utter the two names in the same breath: things were done differently, and more honourably, in Winston's day. *He* would never have misled people or twisted the facts. Churchill's grandson, Nicholas Soames – the Conservative MP and former Minister of Defence – declared icily: 'My grandfather . . . would have regarded it as his solemn duty as Prime Minister to have ensured that the reasons for going to war were detailed, valid, legal and honourable, and above all accurate. Blair and the No. 10 machine were so obsessed with spin and hype that they were ignorant of, and disinterested in, the hard military realities.'[1] Tough words in the family tradition, but the facts, we contend, are somewhat different . . .

Even the volatile relationship between the American and French governments that boiled over in the months before the Second Gulf War has its origins in the tussle between General de Gaulle and President Roosevelt, and the latter's attempts to oust France from the 'premier league' of nations.

Introduction

The major difference between then and now is that it is no longer possible for governments to get away with blatant manipulation and cover-ups quite so easily. The media and public may be far wiser to their tricks than in the past – but it would be a mistake to think that such stratagems were never played before. In the mid-twentieth century, lies and guilty secrets could be made to disappear simply through falsifying the 'official' history: Churchill's blatantly 'spun' account of events in his six-volume *The Second World War* can still take the breath away.

Although, inevitably, we will be accused of rewriting history, of being selective, our intention is rather to *return* history to what it should have been – stripped of the layers of wartime propaganda that became the official story. It gives us no pleasure to revisit the great legends such as Churchill and Roosevelt so iconoclastically: we are simply reporting what others have ignored or, in our view, misinterpreted. And because of our heavy criticism of Roosevelt and members of his administration, we will probably be condemned as 'anti-American'. However, our criticisms are levelled at the US *administration* of the time and, in any case, most of FDR's deceptions were visited on his own people. And there is no question that Churchill tried to use Roosevelt in the way Roosevelt used him – it was just that FDR held all the aces.

Most studies of the Grand Alliance concentrate on its common goal: the defeat of the Axis powers. However, it is now apparent that the Allies were fighting a second war, just as desperately – *with each other*. The relationship between the Allies – and therefore wartime strategy itself – was largely shaped by each country's determination to be ahead of the others economically and politically when the war ended.

The true nature of the Alliance can be seen from the relative status of the 'Big Three' in 1945. The United States and the Soviet Union emerged stronger and more powerful than before, but had actively colluded to emasculate Great Britain. As we will see, if there was any 'special relationship' in the Second World War, it was between Roosevelt's America and Stalin's Russia.

Certainly towards the end of hostilities, this jostling for position was more obvious, even overshadowing the push to defeat Germany and Japan. These unholy behind-the-scenes tussles included the dirtiest kind of espionage, sabotage and betrayals, effectively prolonging the war and costing many thousands of lives. This is why this book is entitled – with even more than the usual irony – *Friendly Fire*.

CHAPTER ONE

The Hess Predictions

'Only history can relate the full story. And I shall write
the history.'

Winston S. Churchill, *c.* 1941[1]

During negotiations with British representatives in June 1941,
Hitler's Deputy Rudolf Hess predicted two major consequences for
Britain if it did not make a compromise peace with Germany:
Britain would lose both independence and empire to the United
States, and victory would ensure the domination of Europe by the
Soviet Union.

On 10 May 1941, almost the last person one would expect to
arrive in Britain had unceremoniously crashed to the ground in a
Scottish field. Hess had flown single-handedly to Britain, being
forced to parachute out of his Messerschmitt fighter-bomber south of
Glasgow. Arrested by the Home Guard, the architect of the
Nuremberg rallies and the Führer's right-hand man was handed over
to the army. It was with this incongruous humiliation that Hitler's
closest confidant, and the second most important figure in the Third
Reich, began his clandestine – but hugely significant – life as a
prisoner of the British. In practice, however, this meant Hess was at
the mercy of Winston Churchill, who used his plight for his own

agenda. As the Hess factor is essential background for *Friendly Fire* – the exposé of the Allies' infighting – a summary will set it in context.

Unravelling the myths

Hess told his captors he came to make peace, intending to land on the private airstrip at Dungavel House, the estate of the Duke of Hamilton, Scotland's premier peer and the King's representative north of the border, who was sympathetic to the idea of a negotiated settlement. Hamilton swiftly denied any foreknowledge of Hess's mission – indeed, officially, *nobody* in Britain knew anything about it.

Hitler hastily announced that a delusional Hess had stolen the plane in a valiant but misguided attempt to end the war – a scenario with which the British government basically agreed. But oddly, beyond suggesting to the press that the flight to Scotland revealed trouble within the Nazi regime, the British failed to capitalise on Hess's arrival. The silence was deafening and perplexing: even the public, naturally agog to know all about the drama, never had their curiosity satisfied. Behind a wall of silence, Hess lived out the rest of the war as a prisoner, all access to him strictly controlled by Churchill, before being sentenced to life imprisonment at the Nuremberg war crimes trials.[2]

The accepted interpretation, carefully fostered by successive British governments, is that Hess acted alone, without even confiding his plan to Hitler, believing insanely that a powerful British faction urgently sought to end the war by overthrowing Churchill and initiating peace talks. Such was the largely unchallenged myth for 60 years.

However, in *Double Standards* – based on newly released or leaked official records and witness testimonies – we concluded that far from being the inconsequential act of a lone madman, Hess's flight was one of the pivotal moments of the Second World War. Hitler *had* known of Hess's mission – although making it clear he would be disowned if the plan failed. There *was* a substantial and powerful 'peace party' in Britain who believed the nation should find a way out of a war it was losing disastrously: in fact, it included many in the top stratum of the British Establishment, even enjoying the support of George VI himself and his indomitable mother Queen Mary. This group *did* know that Hess was arriving; his flight – the last stage of a plan already months old – was intended to prove the German offer genuine. The group's 'welcoming committee' was waiting for Hess at Dungavel House, but he became lost and baled out of his plane eight miles away, hoping to find his way to Hamilton's residence. Among those waiting for him was George, Duke of Kent – no less than the King's youngest brother.

Since the publication of *Double Standards*, that scenario has been corroborated by Martin Allen's discovery of certain documents in the Public Record Office, Kew. A memorandum from an agent of the secret wartime propaganda service SO1 reveals that the morning after Hess's capture the Duke of Kent was driving a car that collided with a coal lorry on the Douglas–Lanark road, which runs past Dungavel House. Kent's passenger was the Duke of Buccleuch, who, we discovered, was deeply implicated in the Hess plot.[3]

Others involved included the Polish government-in-exile (as the invasion of Poland began the war, any deal to end it would obviously require their agreement) and the Special Intelligence Service, SIS, usually known as MI6. Many researchers believe the involvement of British intelligence proves that the Deputy Führer was lured to Britain as part of an elaborate deception operation. However, we found that MI6's upper echelons, including its Director, Sir Stewart Menzies ('C'), supported the idea of negotiations, believing that the continuation of the war could only benefit what was perceived as the real enemy, the Soviet Union. MI6 was involved in the Hess plan because they wanted it to succeed.

It aimed to oust Winston Churchill as Prime Minister and replace his government with one more amenable to negotiations with the Nazis. Despite the impression created by post-war history, such politicians were not difficult to find in 1941. Many MPs and peers opposed the continuation of the war, intensifying their calls for a change of policy, if not of government, immediately before Hess's flight. Just three days before, a shaken Churchill had faced a sustained attack in the House of Commons led by David Lloyd George, who had been Prime Minister during the First World War. Churchill's future – and the fate of millions – teetered on a knife-edge.

We now know Hess brought with him detailed proposals intended as the framework for serious peace talks: several reliable witnesses saw the document. However, the proposals were unilaterally rejected by Churchill. Not only were they never put to the British people (perhaps understandably), but neither were they ever shown to their elected representatives – or, incredibly, even to the War Cabinet. Yet surely the issue is not whether the terms should have been accepted in 1941, but whether it is right in a democracy (and in the middle of a war being fought for democratic freedom) that one individual should have the power not only to reject an offer to end that war, but also to cover up its very existence. Because the document has never been made public – officially it never even existed – its precise terms remain unknown. But the general principles are agreed even by 'official-line' historians. Hess himself repeated them often enough to his British questioners: if Britain left Europe to Germany, Germany would leave Britain to its Empire. Churchill himself acknowledged this in the draft of a speech he intended giving to the Commons two days after Hess's capture. Although persuaded by the Foreign Secretary, Anthony Eden, and others that it would be better to keep the Germans guessing by saying nothing, the draft still survives, including the statement that Hess believed he could make peace 'on the basis that Great Britain and the British Empire should be left intact, apart from the return of the German Colonies [seized at the end of the First World War], and that Germany under Herr Hitler should become unquestioned master of Europe'.[4]

This was Hitler's position even before he came to power; he had offered peace talks on the same basis throughout the war. As veteran American war journalist Quincy Howe noted in *Ashes of Victory* (1972), 'What Hitler put forward in 1940 as a serious bid for peace with Britain, Goebbels called hallucination when Hess proclaimed it in 1941.'[5]

Briefly, the message was that Britain was in a no-win situation, about to lose the war, so might as well cut its losses. But even victory might prove as damaging as defeat because of the concomitant financial ruin and the calamitous effects on the country's independence, not to mention the fortunes of its Empire.

Despite the official version of events, in which Hess was barely even interrogated during his imprisonment, it is clear that he *was* involved in negotiations – or, more accurately, a stage-managed *pretence* of peace talks. At least twice during his captivity in the heavily guarded Mytchett Place, near Aldershot, Hess was visited by government representatives, first by Lord Simon, the Lord Chancellor, and later by Lord Beaverbrook, the powerful Canadian financier and owner of the *Daily Express*, who exerted considerable influence over governments and prime ministers for a staggering five decades. Before the outbreak of hostilities, both spearheaded opposition to war with Germany, and Beaverbrook continued to actively seek an end to the conflict even after it had broken out.

Although Lord Simon's visit is usually dismissed as a question-and-answer session, designed to elicit information from Hess about German strategy (particularly Hitler's intentions towards Russia), official papers reveal it was presented to the Deputy Führer as the preliminary to serious negotiation with the British government. The ruse involved persuading Hess that the War Cabinet knew about their meeting – but that it had been kept from both Churchill and his loyal Foreign Secretary Anthony Eden, implying a rift between government and Prime Minister. In fact, the reverse was true: only Churchill, Eden and senior Foreign Office official Sir Alexander Cadogan knew about the clandestine talks.[6]

As a former Home Secretary and Chancellor of the Exchequer, Lord Simon, having met Hitler and Hess in pre-war Berlin, was sufficiently important to impress the Deputy Führer, who recognised his status in the anti-war lobby. Clearly Hess believed them to be serious peace talks: even the official, but secret, memos refer to it as a 'conference', and Simon as the 'negotiator'. Although Simon's real identity was withheld from the guards, Hess himself was informed in advance whom to expect. One of the guards recorded in his diary that he had inadvertently learned Simon's name from the prisoner! Minutes were even taken, Hess duly receiving his copy.[7]

Hess declared that the Germans had no plans to invade Britain. There was simply no need. A blockade by U-boats, and strategic Luftwaffe raids, would eventually starve it into submission. But, he said, such suffering was unnecessary: a deal would maintain Britain's independence and Empire, provided it recognised Germany's mastery of Continental Europe.[8]

Friendly Fire

In custody, Hess wrote the 32-page report 'Germany–England from the Viewpoint of War with the Soviet Union', which he handed to Beaverbrook in September 1941.[9] (About to be sent by Churchill to Moscow for talks, Beaverbrook was keen to discover Hess's view on the Russian situation.) To Hess, 'a victory for England would be a victory for Bolshevism', arguing that if Germany were to be defeated, the Soviet presence in Europe would increase significantly, as would its ideological influence even in countries not under its direct control. This would strengthen the extreme left in Britain, besides encouraging communist-inspired nationalist movements across the Empire.

Hess also argued that, win or lose, 'the longer the war lasts, the more will the balance of power between England and America move in favour of the latter'. On his arrival he had declared, in the words of the first government official to question him, that 'the avaricious Americans had fell designs on the Empire' and 'If [you] made peace now, America would be furious. America really wanted to inherit the British Empire.'[10] Many politicians, civil servants, leading industrialists and financiers had made the same predictions even before the war started: the coming conflict would ruin the country and destroy the Empire, ultimately benefiting only America and Russia – precisely Beaverbrook's earlier reasons for opposing Britain's entry into the war.

Of course, such predictions were accurate: the USSR gained nearly 50 years' domination of half of Europe, while Britain was ruined by the war, lost its Empire, and was forced into a dependence on the United States that continues to this day. Today, all that is seen as an unfortunate but essentially unpredictable consequence of Britain's declaration of war and of Churchill's firm resolve to keep fighting even when all appeared lost.

Although it was largely the political and economic realities behind Hess's warnings that enticed us into delving deeper into the *unofficial* intricacies of the Second World War, we were also intrigued by another way in which the affair lifts the lid on what we contend was the real relationship among the Allies. Because the Hess mission is usually dismissed as irrelevant, its consequences are rarely considered; yet, they are remarkably revealing – especially

Churchill's handling of the affair in order to radically change Britain's fortunes in the war.

Britain cornered

At the time of the Hess mission, Britain was fighting alone against a seemingly invincible enemy. The Blitz was annihilating large swathes of London and other major cities, while U-boats sank desperately needed supply ships. The proud British people, possessors of a mighty empire, believed they were not many months – perhaps merely weeks – away from starvation, invasion and slavery under the Nazi jackboot. In 20 months of war, everything that could go wrong had gone wrong.

Although Britain and France had declared war on 3 September 1939 in response to Germany's invasion of Poland two days earlier, hostilities only began in earnest on 10 May 1940. Despite their promises to come to the Poles' aid, beyond declaring war the British and French had done nothing to stop the Germans occupying Poland. The next eight months had seen the nerve-racking 'phoney war', when, apart from some action at sea and strategic bombing raids, and a humiliating defeat for Britain and France in Norway, very little had happened. Then, on 10 May 1940, Hitler unleashed his *blitzkrieg* on the Netherlands, Belgium and Luxembourg, smashing through them as a curtain-raiser for the defeat of France, which he hated so virulently. The combined French and British forces were forced back to the northern coast of France, famously evacuating from Dunkirk. On 22 June, the French government signed an armistice with Hitler, leaving Britain isolated across the Channel. Four weeks later, Hitler made his 'last appeal to reason', an offer of peace talks to Britain, now at its lowest point.

By a strange coincidence, 10 May 1940 also saw another historic change: the appointment, by a very reluctant George VI, of Winston Churchill to succeed Neville Chamberlain as Prime Minister. Clearly, the Nazi strategy for the swift defeat of France and the ultimatum to Britain was based on the expectation that Chamberlain would still be Prime Minister, in which case Hitler's offer of peace talks would have met with a very different response. But now Hitler's opponent was the uncompromisingly bellicose 'bulldog' Churchill, and the offer was rejected. However, as we will see, the new Prime Minister faced stiff opposition from members of his War Cabinet, and even he was not entirely opposed to the idea of a settlement with Germany – in the right circumstances.

Although the barrier of the English Channel and the North Sea protected against the German advance, it also meant that Britain was penned in, unable to launch an effective counter-attack. Desperate contingency plans were made in anticipation of a Nazi invasion. Although plans for Operation Sea Lion were indeed drawn up, from German documents captured after the war, we and others argue that it was primarily a deception to divert attention from the more serious preparations for Hitler's real next target: the Soviet Union. (Others argue that Sea Lion began as a serious operation, but was abandoned as impractical after three months. But, significantly, Hitler allowed the world to *believe* he intended to invade Britain to cover preparations for Operation Barbarossa, the offensive against Russia.[11])

The rationale behind the deception hypothesis is that a risky invasion across the Channel was completely unnecessary. Germany now had control of the European coast from Scandinavia to the border of Spain. As Hess pointed out, all that was needed was a U-boat blockade that would starve the island into submission. And it nearly happened.

The Battle of Britain began on 10 July, when the Luftwaffe bombed airfields, ports and armaments factories to prevent the RAF mounting cross-Channel raids. In September, the Nazis switched to the terror-bombing of London and other major cities, intending to browbeat the people into suing for peace.

Why should they fail? Britain's position seemed hopeless: with no Allies, already dependent on the USA for munitions and food, and unable to mount a counter-offensive across the Channel. The Nazis assumed victory would be a foregone conclusion. After all, it had taken them just 36 days to bring Poland to its knees. In April 1940, the British and French attempt to expel them from Norway was effectively over within a month. Just six weeks elapsed from the blitzkrieg on the Low Countries to the capitulation of France. When the war moved into the Balkans at the beginning of April 1941,

Yugoslavia surrendered after 11 days and the British forces in Greece had been expelled by the end of the month.

By the time of Hess's flight, the German Army, the *Wehrmacht*, only needed to fight for 20 weeks to capture the whole of Western Europe and the Balkans. Who could possibly beat them? Wherever British forces had encountered the Wehrmacht, their ignominious retreat became such a byword that escaping without wholesale capture, as at Dunkirk, is still portrayed almost as victory. British successes against Italy in North Africa and Greece evaporated as soon as Germany came in to reinforce Mussolini's troops.

Not surprisingly, there was deep pessimism in the corridors of power. A wholehearted supporter of the war against Nazism, even Sir Alexander Cadogan wrote about the reverses in Greece: 'Evacuation going fairly well. That's all we're really good at! . . . Our soldiers are the most pathetic amateurs, pitted against professionals . . . Tired, depressed and defeatist!'[12] Small wonder that others were taking what steps they could to save their country, as they saw it.

Despite Churchill's defiant rhetoric, to an outside observer there seemed no question that Britain would eventually have to ask for terms. Staggered at the delay, the German leader was impatient for a resolution before embarking on Operation Barbarossa unhindered.

Churchill's game

By the end of 1941, however, the situation had changed dramatically. After the onset of Barbarossa in June, Russia was now an Ally – and the Nazi war machine that would have targeted Britain was tied up on Soviet soil. From that point onwards, Britain was unlikely to lose the war. And America, after the Japanese attack on Pearl Harbor in December, had now willingly joined the conflict. The Triple Alliance – what Churchill called the Grand Alliance – was now in place. Britain could now *win*.

In *Double Standards*, we argue that this change in fortune was largely due to Churchill's skilful exploitation of the failure of the Hess mission, using it to strengthen both his own hand and Britain's strategic position. Initially, Churchill exploited it in order to neutralise 'peace group' opposition against him at home. Although history – first written by Churchill himself in his six-volume *The*

Second World War – acknowledges no such concerted hostility, the evidence tells quite another story.[13]

Churchill's first year in office was hardly an unqualified success. Forced to work with a War Cabinet in which the 'appeasement' element was still influential, he often faced opposition. Although his position had been strengthened by Chamberlain's death in November 1940, and he had also used the opportunity created by the unexpected demise of Britain's Ambassador to the United States to remove the troublesome Foreign Secretary, Lord Halifax, by appointing him to that post, he was still not in complete command.

Criticisms in Parliament of his war management and even his competence were never far below the surface, and in May 1941 the pre-war 'peace group' was trying to force matters to a head. As we have seen, he had to endure Lloyd George's frontal attack just three days before Hess's flight, gambling everything on a vote of confidence. However, two months later, on 20 July, Churchill carried out what the British historian Andrew Roberts terms a 'Churchillian Night of the Long Knives', when he finally purged his government of all 'Chamberlainite' elements. He encountered no serious political opposition for the rest of the war:

> The 20th of July reconstruction . . . represents the final victory in a long *sotto voce* war of attrition fought between Churchill and the Chamberlainite Tory Establishment, and proves that the Prime Minister at last felt secure enough to model his coalition according to his own tastes.[14]

The more extreme pro-peace element behind the British end of the Hess plan appears to have been in disarray, and – apart from a desperate final attempt to overthrow Churchill in August 1942, which ended in the Duke of Kent's mysterious death in Caithness[15] – to have been neutralised as a serious threat. But how did Churchill manage this incredible turnaround?

There was the threat of Regulation 18b, the draconian wartime law that allowed the detention without trial of anyone deemed by the government – meaning Churchill – to be a threat to the war effort. Within weeks of Churchill coming to power, the British Fascist leader

Sir Oswald Mosley and 149 others were imprisoned under 18b for the duration. Such action could be taken against anyone found to 'have or have had associations with any persons concerned in the government of . . . any Power with which his Majesty is at war'.[16] No wonder those who had actively conspired with the Deputy Führer were quaking in their shoes.

Churchill also adopted a subtler approach, for example managing to persuade the 'peace group' that he was following their agenda, albeit covertly. The fake Hess negotiations indicated to the peace group that the Prime Minister was at least keeping his options open, and that perhaps a deal was not completely out of the question. The fact that two of their number, Lords Simon and Beaverbrook, had been permitted to meet with Hess was no doubt taken as encouragement.

Very few of that coalition of vested interests were actively sympathetic to Nazism or Fascism, simply believing it was in Britain's interests and – a factor largely forgotten today – those of its Empire, to reach a compromise with Hitler, and that Churchill's obsession with fighting on to certain victory or defeat was condemned to disaster. To them, Russia was the greater threat. And from the first stirrings of the Nazi menace many had advocated staying out of any war altogether and forcing Germany and the USSR into conflict, dealing with both problems simultaneously. This was the position of the Duke of Kent, Chamberlain – and MI6's Sir Stewart Menzies. And by exploiting the imprisoned Deputy Führer, Churchill appeared to be fulfilling that strategy.

The secret protocol

Although at the time of the Hess affair Germany and Russia were allies, inevitably, for geopolitical and ideological reasons, Hitler and Stalin would sooner or later become embroiled in a titanic struggle to the death.

The single most important trigger for the outbreak of war was undoubtedly the Nazi–Soviet Non-Aggression Pact of 23 August 1939. This seemingly impossible, and supremely unholy, alliance threw into disarray all diplomatic efforts to avert war, ending any hope of containing Hitler by setting up a coalition of nations that even he (and more importantly, his military commanders) would hesitate to challenge. Once the Pact was signed, war between Britain/France and Germany became inevitable. Unpalatable though it may be to certain ideological schools, the blunt fact is that Stalin – who within two years would be welcomed as an ally of Britain and the US – was as much to blame for starting the war as Hitler.

What was – apparently – not known at that time, and only emerged after the war, was that the Pact also included a 'supplementary secret protocol' in which Hitler and Stalin agreed to divide Poland. With supreme irony, Russian judges at Nuremberg condemned the surviving Nazi leaders and their regime for 'conspiracy to wage war', a crime of which their own government was clearly just as guilty. (Hess's defence tried to introduce the existence of the secret protocol for this very reason, but the tribunal hastily ruled it inadmissible.) As we will see, there is some evidence – although not absolutely conclusive – that the other Allies *did* know about the secret protocol even before Russia joined them; but if so, it would have to be buried deep. It might raise far too many awkward questions about why, after starting the war by violating Poland, the Soviet Union should suddenly be acceptable as an equal partner with the democracies.

At the time, a leading diplomatic historian summed up reaction to the signing of the Pact: 'It scarcely seemed possible that both Germany and Soviet Russia should simultaneously renounce the whole ideological basis on which their policy for the past six years had been ostensibly based.'[17] Churchill called it simply an 'unnatural act'.[18]

The Nazi Party had been born out of opposition to a short-lived but dramatic Bolshevik takeover in Bavaria, which was even briefly declared a Soviet republic. Hitler swept to power largely because he promised to smash Bolshevism both in Germany and its motherland, the Soviet Union. Meanwhile, Stalin had presented Communism as the natural enemy of Fascism and Nazism for a decade. How could two such megalomaniac fanatics abruptly agree to be allies? (The suddenness of this bizarre alliance is highlighted by the fact that the swastika flags hurriedly displayed at Moscow airport to greet Joachim von Ribbentrop, the Nazi Foreign Minister, when he arrived to sign the Pact were props from an anti-Nazi propaganda film.[19])

Stalin had gained time by ensuring that Hitler dealt first with Britain and France in the west – just as Menzies and others in Britain had advocated that Stalin should be made to fight Hitler. But nobody – least of all Stalin – imagined that this marriage of convenience would last. A bitter divorce was inevitable; but when would Hitler strike? By 1941, Stalin was afraid that the British would settle with the Nazi leader, leaving Hitler free to attack the Soviet Union.

Unquestionably there was a direct connection between Hess's mission and the onset of Operation Barbarossa just six weeks later: the whole point of the Deputy Führer's flight was to end the war between Britain and Germany so Hitler would only have to concentrate on one enemy. That is why Hitler *had* to disown his Deputy and oldest friend: if he had admitted that Hess was on an *official* peace mission, Stalin would have realised this meant Russia was next.

From the intercepted Enigma codes (kept secret even from his own Cabinet) Churchill already knew that Germany planned to attack Russia soon. Pretending to negotiate with Hess encouraged Hitler to think something might be salvaged from the wreckage. On 22 June 1941, the very day that Operation Barbarossa began, Goebbels recorded: 'The Führer has high hopes of the peace party in England. Otherwise, he claims, the Hess affair would not have been so systematically killed by silence.'[20] It is hard to be plainer.

By encouraging Hitler to believe peace was still possible, Churchill was effectively pointing him in the direction of the USSR. This also kept members of the British peace party happy – such as MI6 boss Menzies – believing even Churchill to be a convert to their cause. But there is another, extraordinary, possibility. Churchill's masterly use of Hess may even have led to a de facto ceasefire between Britain and Germany – in the words of one of our informants a 'virtual armistice', which lasted until the summer of 1942.

Although the very idea of Churchill tacitly doing a deal with the Nazis appears to be outrageous and unthinkable, the facts are suggestive. Hess's flight coincided with the last (and heaviest) night of the London Blitz, and the Luftwaffe's terror-bombing on all British cities ended six days later. Although the connection was noted even then, today's histories explain it away as a side-effect of Hitler turning his attention to Russia. But even if this is correct, as Barbarossa's fate hung directly on Hess's mission, how could Hitler possibly feel secure enough to turn his back on his enemies in the west? (The 'secret truce' scenario will be explored more fully in a later chapter.)

Churchill and Hitler did not necessarily make a formal clandestine agreement or even communicate directly in any way. With a shrewd grasp of each other's psychology, both realised that while the Hess proposals were (apparently) still on the table, direct conflict between their countries could be minimised. Maintaining the illusion that Hess was still being taken seriously was the foundation stone of Churchill's supremely skilful bluff: at least, by encouraging the Nazis to turn eastwards, buying war-weary Britain a breathing space.

Exploiting American anxiety

The other way in which Churchill exploited the captive Hess, using him as a building block in the construction of his Grand Alliance, was by playing on American fears that the mission heralded the start of peace negotiations. An end to the war was the worst possible scenario for America, already gearing up for all-out arms and munitions production to meet Britain's demands.

Two months before Hess flew to Britain, Congress passed the Lend-Lease Act, removing any pretence of American neutrality and agreeing to supply Britain with much-needed weapons and equipment. Although this allowed Britain to remain a player in the war, there was a terrible price to pay – literally. For Britons, such as Beaverbrook, their worst nightmare had come: the country was rapidly disappearing under a mountain of debt to America that could never be repaid.

Just over a month after Hess's capture, the British Consul in New York reported to London that the British government's silence about why Hess had come or what had happened to him, as well as events such as a hasty visit to Washington by the US Ambassador in London, had 'combined in the public mind to create out of the Hess case a series of steps towards a negotiated peace'. The report described the 'feeling of apprehension and uncertainty' that these rumours were causing throughout US industry and warned that:

'The most serious result has been the introduction into the minds of some industrialists the doubts of the advisability of vast plant expansion lest this rumoured peace negotiation prove a reality.'[21] 'Apprehension' – at the thought of *peace*!

President Roosevelt had been scheduled to give an important speech on Pan-American Day, 14 May 1941, but two days before – and two days after Hess's arrival – he abruptly cancelled. (Roosevelt was always suspicious about Hess's flight, musing, 'I wonder what is *really* behind this story?'[22])

Meanwhile, Churchill continued to send the President carefully worded signals. When, a week after Hess's arrival, Roosevelt was keen to know what he was saying, the Prime Minister provided a summary, telling him that Hess had offered the choice of immediate peace or several more years of war, hinting that some in Britain would be receptive to the first idea: 'If he is to be believed, he expected to contact members of a "peace movement" in England whom he would help to oust the present government.' Churchill added that Hess had made 'some rather disparaging remarks about your country and the degree of assistance that you will be able to furnish us'.[23]

Roosevelt finally made his landmark speech on 27 May, declaring an 'unlimited national emergency' that gave him sweeping powers, although short of declaring war, which Congress must approve. (He had declared a 'limited' state of emergency when war broke out in 1939.) The day before his speech, he told a press conference that the US had fought many 'undeclared wars' in the past – effectively declaring a new undeclared war. He also stated that as the Nazis would attack America once Europe was conquered, it made sense for America to support Great Britain. Quite suddenly, Roosevelt gave in to Churchill on issues he had been resisting for months, such as providing US Navy cover for convoys. The only conceivable reason for such a reversal was Hess's arrival – nothing else would explain it – and the only possible motive was anxiety that the European war was about to end. Roosevelt had to whip up American support, and, bluntly, encourage Churchill to carry on fighting – in order to keep America solvent.

Clearly, these reactions demonstrate that business considerations played at least some part in the American decision to support Britain. Having been encouraged by their President to gear up for war production, many industrialists and investors faced disaster if the war they were supplying suddenly stopped. As we will see, the American economy was in such a precarious position at that time that only the orders for war material from Britain were preventing it sliding into a recession that threatened to be worse than the Great Depression. Undeniably, in the short term the war in Europe kept the American economy afloat, and in the long term enabled the United States to overturn the British Empire's pre-war economic supremacy and replace it as the world's greatest financial power.

But was this simply a lucky consequence of the ideological struggle against Nazism or, as Hess alleged, part of a conscious design by Roosevelt and his administration? This is one of the key questions that underpinned our investigations.

With friends like these . . .

Churchill skilfully used the Hess affair to send completely contradictory signals to his future Allies. He assured Stalin that the arrival of the Deputy Führer in Scotland did not presage a British–German peace deal. (Maxim Litvinov, Soviet Ambassador to Washington, confided to Lord Halifax that when he first heard of the Nazi attack on Russia he believed it was the result of a deal between Churchill and Hitler via Hess.[24]) But the Prime Minister also deliberately led Roosevelt to believe it *did* mean that peace was possible.

Having successfully diverted the Nazis towards Russia, Churchill was effectively allowing the Red Army to fight Britain's war, at least for a time. He also played on the President's fear of economic ruin if the European war stopped, setting Roosevelt on a course that would, eventually, draw his fellow Americans into the war.

But these future Allies were already mired in profound self-interest and long-standing prejudice. Indeed, their bitter infighting had begun well before Hitler's war.

CHAPTER TWO

The Unthinkable

'No doubt it is quite right in the interests of peace to go on talking about war with the United States being "unthinkable". Everyone knows this is not true . . .'

Winston S. Churchill, 1927[1]

By the mid 1920s, antagonism among the future Allies was already festering. The First World War had left them unequal – and either hungry for more power or desperate to cling on to what they had. Many of the old regimes had been swept away, the peace settlement creating a new Europe: new states, such as Poland and Czechoslovakia, were cobbled together from the defeated Austro-Hungarian and Ottoman Empires and former Tsarist Russia. This cauldron of hate would eventually bubble over.

The 1917 Russian Revolution raised a new spectre to haunt the old order: international Communism, which regarded the working classes of all nations as its allies and the ruling classes its enemies, and aspired to convert the rest of the world. Russia's mission was nothing less than global revolution – and world domination.

The First World War had also given centre stage to America and Japan: suddenly the world was bedevilled with new rivalries, new enmities and dreadful new possibilities.

33

The American legacy

The seeds of the Second World War were sown in the settlement that ended the First. The victors' manifestly unjust, punitive and vindictive treatment towards Germany was bound to breed resentment, discontent and a burning hunger to recapture its former greatness – especially with one-eighth of its territory and one-tenth of its population 'confiscated'. One of the inevitable territorial disputes happened almost immediately, with Russia and Poland battling over the Ukraine in 1920. However, few realise that all this was largely an *American* initiative – which they virtually forced upon their European allies.

Although the USA was wealthy because of its size and natural resources, it had had little effect on the global balance of power. The great republic remained aloof, its isolationism dating to George Washington's urging the new nation to stay clear of 'foreign entanglements'. This principle became the mainstay of the 1823 Monroe Doctrine, which shaped US foreign policy up to the Second World War. President James Monroe had declared: '. . . the American continents [*sic*], by the free and independent condition which they have assumed and maintain, are henceforth not to be considered as subjects for future colonization by any European powers.'[2] Although not spelt out, the converse – that the USA would not interfere in European affairs – was implicit. Largely self-sufficient, why should they concern themselves with foreigners? Consequently, the US hung back from the First World War until 1917 – even then becoming embroiled only reluctantly because it had traded freely with all the warring nations (although the Royal Navy's blockade of Germany meant most American supplies went to Britain and France).

When, in April 1917, Germany began to attack American ships, President Woodrow Wilson sombrely sided with the Allies. (Ironically, because tentative peace negotiations had just started in Europe, this probably extended hostilities.) At first, the Americans were largely confined to naval action; their troops only arrived in Europe in large numbers in the summer of 1918, tipping the balance against Germany. Even so, the US was careful to define itself not as an Ally but an 'Associated Power' – an important difference. The

The Unthinkable

Allies were all in it together, but as an Associated Power the United States reserved the right to withdraw at any time, or make its own peace with Germany, without even consulting the other nations.

The final peace settlement was based on President Wilson's 'Fourteen Points', first set out before Congress in January 1918 (later also outlining his 'Four Ends' – general principles for good government and international relations), encapsulating his vision of the post-war order and defining what America was fighting for. Some principles affected all nations, such as the right of a people to self-determination, while others were more specific: for example, the Thirteenth Point called for the resurrection of Poland, absorbed into the Russian Empire in 1791. Wilson's greatest pride was the Fourteenth Point, the creation of a 'general association of nations' to safeguard the sovereignty of all states and resolve disputes.

In October 1918, the doomed Germans approached President Wilson – not the British or French – for an armistice, through neutral Switzerland. He replied that his terms – for both Germany and the Allies – were encapsulated in his Fourteen Points. After three weeks of intense communication between the two governments, he dispatched his most trusted adviser, Colonel Edward M. House, to the Allies to make sure that they, too, would agree to peace on his terms.

Although originally Wilson told them that the Fourteen Points were provisional and could be debated, he had always intended to make peace only on that basis, telling House that if they refused his terms, economic pressure would compel them to agree. Just a few months after America had entered the war, he told him, 'We can force them to our way of thinking.'[3]

House ruthlessly informed the Allied governments that any reluctance to accept the Fourteen Points might mean a separate American peace with Germany. He had with him a cable from the President threatening to go public about any disagreement – powerful moral blackmail as, worn out by war, the British and French people would undoubtedly have put intense pressure on their governments to accept the American terms. In the event, House had no need of the cable – the Allies got the message clear and strong anyway.[4]

Friendly Fire

On 4 November 1918, they formally accepted Wilson's Fourteen Points with two conditions: the British (as the greatest maritime nation) were unhappy about conceding absolute freedom of the seas, although prepared to discuss the issue, and the French insisted that Germany should pay for the ruin it had spread throughout Europe. A week later, the armistice was declared. Wilson had successfully imposed his Fourteen Points on the Allies, which were enshrined in the Treaty of Versailles, formally ending the First World War.

The Fourteen Points may have been presented as a set of principles reflecting President Wilson's vision of a just, peaceful and stable world order, but as British Cabinet Office historian Basil Collier points out, there is a subtle subtext. Whether deliberately or unconsciously, Wilson's Fourteen Points all worked to the economic and political betterment of the United States. Essentially, they would reinforce the nations that the US sought to strengthen – or undermine its greatest competitors.[5] Reviving Poland was intended to weaken Russia by driving a wedge between it and Germany. Italy would be strengthened by being given territory (mostly taken away from Germany). Britain's sea power would be curbed, allowing the US greater access to world trade markets. France would be strengthened (but not too much). Germany would be weakened, as Wilson's insistence on removing the Kaiser would break Prussia's hold over the rest of Germany, which was based on the Prussian monarchy's constitutional role in the German Empire. Even the right of a people to self-determination had a subtext, being aimed at the ethnic minorities within the powerful Habsburg empire: applying the principle would create a patchwork of new nation states while destroying the empire as an independent entity.

The problem for the Democrat Wilson was that he was not only out of touch with the American people's traditional isolationism, but also with his own government. In November 1918, just as the war was ending, elections gave control of both chambers of Congress to the Republicans. At the Paris Peace Conference, although in a dominant position, Wilson negotiated without consulting Congress – even though it would have to ratify any agreement he made.

Although the Treaty of Versailles is usually described as emerging from the 'Paris Peace Conference', all that actually took place was the

The Unthinkable

Preliminary Peace Conference in which the Allies and the USA thrashed out the application of the Fourteen Points. This took so long – six months, until May 1919 – that there was no time for the peace conference itself. Meanwhile, since a state of war still officially existed, neither the US nor the Allies could trade with Germany, which meant that the blockade continued to cause massive hardship. The French economy reached the point of collapse and survived only because of an emergency loan from Britain.[6]

Prolonging this situation by negotiating with Germany would only have made the situation worse, so even though it had been promised talks, all that actually happened was that its delegation was handed the proposals, told there would be no discussion, and given a deadline by which to submit proposed modifications – which the Allies/US would accept or reject. (Lloyd George was aghast, wanting face-to-face discussions with the Germans, but was out-voted.)

Under Wilson, the conference also agreed to establish the League of Nations in accordance with his Fourteenth Point: he even insisted that its Covenant was part of the Treaty of Versailles, although this backfired. Seeing membership of the League as incompatible with America's traditional isolationism, Congress refused to ratify the Treaty because of the Covenant. (The US concluded its own peace with the Treaty of Berlin in August 1921.) Ironically, the American President virtually blackmailed Europe into accepting not only a settlement but also the League of Nations, for which they had no desire – and to which America refused to sign up. Undoubtedly, had he the power, Wilson would have signed up to both Treaty and League, but it did mean that the US took no responsibility for a situation in Europe that its President had largely created. And the effectiveness of the League of Nations was hampered by the absence of the USA.

With the war over, the American people mostly reverted to isolationism, wondering why they ever became embroiled in a European war, which they regarded as a mistake. Many even believed they had been dragged into it by their own bankers and arms manufacturers – a belief that shaped Americans' attitudes to the looming Second World War.

A crippling burden

The other major bone of contention between Europe and the US after the First World War was war debts. During hostilities, the US had loaned vast amounts to the Allies – mainly Britain. Now it was repayment time. Many Europeans resented the fact that, even though America had prospered because of the war, it still expected them to pay their debts. In response, the British – in a transparent move to blame the Americans for European hardship – announced that they only wanted from their Allies what they were obliged to pay the US, implying that if America would cancel Britain's debt, Britain would cancel those of its Allies. This caused great resentment in the USA.[7]

A sullen fiscal dance ensued, with Britain reducing the debts from France, Italy, Romania, Yugoslavia, Greece and Portugal by 60–80 per cent, and then the US reducing Britain's by 30 per cent. After negotiation, in January 1923, the British agreed to pay off its debt to the US in 62 annual instalments (i.e. up to 1985) of £33 million. As everything Britain received from its Allies was paid over to the US, Britain made no profit from the First World War.

German reparation payments were extremely convoluted. Due in annual instalments – until 1983 – the US government loaned Germany the money so it could afford them. The loan was then paid over to, say, Britain or France, who used it to repay its own war debt to the US Treasury. In effect, America was getting its own money back, while Germany was plunging even further into debt. This also meant that if the US stopped advancing loans and credit to Germany, the entire economy of Europe would be weakened, if not collapse. This prospect ensured the continuation of American credit, as a devastated European economy would have an adverse effect on American exports to Europe. The system's fatal flaw would be exposed ten years later, by the world recession sparked off by the Wall Street Crash of 1929.

A rising sun

The First World War also saw the rise of another new world player with imperial ambitions – Japan, which posed a challenge to Europe's colonial powers in the Far East and China, where they had enjoyed a monopoly on exploitation. Japan emerged as a force to be reckoned with after fighting and winning a war with Tsarist Russia in 1904–5, after which it basically took over the Chinese province of Manchuria. (Officially, Manchuria's sovereignty was restored by the peace settlement, but Japan was allowed to keep troops there to protect its interests.) The Manchurian–Siberian border would remain an area of international tension – between Japan and first imperial Russia and then the USSR – until the Second World War.

Prosperity in East Asia meant access to China's vast resources, the country struggling to keep its independence while the European empires (and to a lesser extent the USA), with long-established trading colonies, wanted to increase their share. Seeking to emulate the Europeans' economic expansion, the Japanese needed to increase their presence in China. They split the opposition by allying with Britain, signing a series of Anglo-Japanese alliances, in which the two agreed to cooperate to protect each other's interests. Because of this, Japan declared war on Germany in the First World War, patrolling the Mediterranean and joining British forces against German trading colonies in China.

Because the German and Russian navies had been destroyed, Japan emerged as the world's third greatest naval power. During the Paris Conference, Japan was regarded as one of the 'Big Five' nations, and even gained from the Versailles settlement by being given German trading colonies in China (for which China refused to sign). But despite their elevation, the Japanese soon realised that they were only included on sufferance – mainly because they were not white-skinned. When they sought to enshrine the principle of racial equality in the League of Nations Charter, Australia and the USA led the ensuing outcry, and Britain was lukewarm on the subject. So it was dropped.[8]

In 1922, during trade negotiations with the US and Europe, Japan was pressed into giving back to China the former German-owned territory it had won at Versailles, increasing its sense of isolation and inequality – and at the same time, Britain was persuaded by the USA, Canada and Australia to terminate the Anglo-Japanese Alliance. Also in 1922, the US Supreme Court ruled that no Japanese could become American citizens, then in 1924 Congress passed an Exclusion Act preventing any Asiatics from being accepted as immigrants.[9]

Friendly Fire

The Japanese realised they were only welcome on the international scene if they confined themselves to the Far East (where they were squeezed by the European empires and the USA), whereas the Europeans and Americans could operate unhindered wherever they liked. They consequently decided to become the *dominant* power in Asia.

With scant natural resources, Japan could only succeed in becoming a major world power by becoming one giant factory – importing raw materials to manufacture goods and exporting the finished products – and its economy therefore depended on access to raw materials and foreign markets. As the historian Guy Wint writes of Japanese thinking at the beginning of the 1930s: 'If Japan were able to conquer the adjacent territory from which raw materials could be produced – such as Manchuria – and if it could obtain military control of the markets for buying Japanese exports, it could breathe at peace.'[10]

As the 1930s progressed, Japan's role in international affairs increased, to the world's alarm. In September 1931, when a conspiracy by Japanese army officers to provoke hostilities led to the occupation of Manchuria, the Japanese government resigned in favour of one that supported the army's actions, and which declared Manchuria ('Manchukuo') an 'independent' state. Fighting between Japan and China continued until early 1932, when there was an armistice. But Manchuria was only the first step in the Japanese plan – they aimed to control the whole of China.

Under the 1922 Washington Treaty, both the US and Britain should have gone to China's aid, but neither did anything other than condemn Japan – not even imposing sanctions. In *An Ocean Apart*, David Dimbleby and David Reynolds argue that America had too little at stake in the region, and Britain too much.[11] Similarly, when Japan attacked Shanghai early in 1932, the League of Nations condemned Japan but nobody wanted to risk war by threatening sanctions. (Japan left the League in protest anyway.)

By expanding in the region, Japan directly threatened three major power groups: the European colonial powers (Britain, France and the Netherlands), the USSR on the long-standing powder keg of the Manchuria–Siberia border, and the USA's trade and economic interests. It was therefore in a very powerful position.

The rise of Nazi Germany complicated matters. With no interests in the Far East, the Third Reich could put pressure on nations that had possessions there by acting in concert with Japan. For example, the vast landmass of the USSR now had potential threats on two fronts: Germany in Europe, and Japan in Siberia. Likewise, it was to Japan's advantage to foster closer links with Germany, which put pressure on the USSR and the European imperialists, predominantly Britain. Japan was also concerned about Chinese leader Chiang Kai-shek's growing accord with the Communist leaders – and because of a Japanese initiative, Germany and Japan signed the Anti-Comintern Pact in Berlin in November 1936. Events in the Far East seemed like a four-way chess game, but with Japan in a key position.

Britain versus America

Although almost never mentioned in these days of the 'special relationship', in the years after the First World War, the greatest international tension – and most likely potential for war – was between Britain and the USA. This was recognised by Colonel House, who reported to President Wilson just after the Versailles conference:

> While the British Empire vastly exceeds the United States in area and population and while their aggregate wealth is perhaps greater than ours, yet our position is much more favourable. It is because of this that the relations between the two countries are beginning to assume the same character as that between England and Germany before the war.[12]

The sources of the rivalry were simple: access to natural resources and markets for international trade were more or less completely controlled by Britain. Although the United States had largely relapsed into isolationism, some Americans had no wish to return to such a lonely position. As the First World War had uniquely stimulated American manufacturing, allowing unprecedented access to world markets, expansion was their industries' new watchword. However, as the world market was largely carved up among the

Europeans – especially Britain, whose control of maritime trade was so tight that until the First World War the US had to negotiate with the British government to export to *anywhere* in Europe. The British Empire was a 'closed shop', the dominions and colonies keeping other countries out by levying heavy tariffs and duties. Sterling, the world's strongest currency, also gave Britain a huge commercial advantage.

Britain had been the world's greatest economic power and the leading creditor nation, but the war ended this pre-eminence. Until 1914, it was simply too rich to worry about a foreign economic policy or bother much about the world outside the Empire – an arrogance described as 'splendid isolation'. But after the First World War it had to acknowledge it had competition.

Britain's might had always resided in the Royal Navy, the size of which, before 1914, had been dictated by the 'two-power standard' – it should always be a match for the next two strongest navies combined. After the war it could no longer afford such a luxury, and the Admiralty soon recognised that it would be particularly difficult to fight a war in the Far East, given the threat from Japan.

In 1919, Lloyd George's government adopted the 'ten-year rule', meaning that future military spending was based on the assumption that the British Empire would not be involved in a major war for ten years – a pious hope, as there was simply no money to do so. (When the period was up, the government adopted a 'rolling' ten years. In the words of the naval historian John Gallagher, 'Every morning, a new ten years began.'[13]) This had serious consequences for the Empire: when, in 1925, the government decided to upgrade the naval base in Singapore because of the Japanese threat, the ten-year rule meant the work was continually postponed. It was only in 1932, after Japan had actually attacked China, that the government ordered it to go ahead. (Ironically, Churchill championed the ten-year rule.[14])

In July 1915, when the USA set out to build a navy that would be the equal of any other nation (i.e. Britain), the Admiralty realised that if the Americans maintained their rate of production, the US fleet would outstrip the Royal Navy within ten years. In December 1920, Lloyd George asked the Committee of Imperial Defence to consider Britain's response, impressing upon them that this was the most

important and difficult question they had ever faced because –
incredible though it may seem – it could even lead to war with the
USA.[15] Britain's options were stark: surrender its traditional naval
superiority, engage in a financially crippling arms race to stay ahead,
or try to reach an agreement on the balance of power. The last two
options ran the risk of war.

Anglo-American relations sank to their lowest at the beginning and
end of the 1920s. The first crisis was calmed by the Washington
Agreements of 1921 and 1922, signed by the major maritime powers,
which agreed spheres of influence and access to trade and fixed the
number of capital ships for each navy. Britain and the USA were
allowed to possess an equal number, Japan a fleet 60 per cent the size
of Britain's and America's, and France and Italy 35 per cent. All five
nations agreed not to build any battleships for ten years, while
Britain and the USA had to scrap some of theirs.

Humiliatingly, Britannia no longer ruled the waves – and now
America was Britain's equal. E.H. Carr, the leading historian of
diplomacy whose background in the inter-war Foreign Office gave
him a special insight into Britain's foreign policy, wrote in 1939: 'The
two-Power standard of the pre-War period had been replaced, as the
corner-stone of British policy, by the one-Power standard *plus*
perpetual peace with the United States.'[16]

The advent of the first Labour government led by Ramsay
MacDonald in 1924 helped Anglo-American relations: US politicians
found it easier to deal with Labour, seeing Britain's ruling classes as
arrogant and untrustworthy. However, that government lasted only a
year before Stanley Baldwin's Conservatives returned. As the
historian Donald Cameron Watt writes: 'The second Baldwin
government were [*sic*] nevertheless to begin by doing their best to
cultivate good relations with the United States, and to end in an
almost total breakdown of Anglo-American relations, accompanied
by back-stage anxieties about the probability of an Anglo-American
war.'[17]

Despite Carr's assertion that the Washington Agreements
constrained the British Empire to 'perpetual peace' with the USA, by
the end of the decade relations were again so strained that an Anglo-
American war seemed unavoidable. The diplomat Sir John Wheeler-

Bennett wrote in 1932: 'In both countries men of goodwill declared war between them to be "unthinkable", a sure sign that they had already begun to think about it.'[18]

The immediate cause of this breakdown was the failure of yet another naval conference. As the earlier agreements had not covered cruisers (escort ships), in 1926 the US Navy set out to match the number of British cruisers – resulting in the General Naval Conference in Geneva the following year, at which Britain, the USA and Japan attempted to reach agreement on permitted numbers. But the chief US delegate described the event as not 'negotiations at all, but merely a form of hostilities'[19] – especially between Britain and America. The breakdown of the conference led to a downward spiral in Anglo-American relations, which hit rock bottom a year later.[20]

The USA began to encroach on areas that Britain regarded as its own, signing a treaty with Egypt which, although a nominally independent country, was firmly under British influence. The Americans also established unofficial diplomatic contact with the governments of Canada and Australia, conducting business without involving London. As tension increased, to add to British indignation, America began to make overtures to France – it even looked for a time as if France was going to be America's preferred 'point of contact' in Europe.[21]

One of those who foresaw an imminent American war was Winston Churchill, then Chancellor of the Exchequer. In July 1927 – during the Geneva Conference – he sent a memorandum to the Cabinet, including the quotation at the beginning of this chapter, arguing that the alternative of war was 'the only basis upon which the naval discussions at Geneva are proceeding'.

In November 1927, the British diplomat Sir Robert Craigie stated bluntly, 'War is not unthinkable between the two countries.'[22] A Foreign Office memo essentially agreed: 'Hitherto, it seems to me, we have been inclined to deal with the United States from a wrong angle. We have treated them too much as blood relatives, not sufficiently as a foreign country.'[23] And Sir Maurice Hankey, the Cabinet Secretary – the most senior civil servant in Britain – expressed his exasperation in October 1928:

The Unthinkable

> We played up to America over the Covenant of the League,
> abandonment of the Japanese Alliance, Washington Treaties,
> debt settlement, Irish settlement . . . always making concessions
> and always being told that the next step would change their
> attitude. Yet they are, as the result [sic], more overbearing and
> suspicious against us than ever.[24]

As it happened, Anglo-American tension was reduced by changes
of government on both sides of the Atlantic, with the election of
the pro-Anglo-American-cooperation Herbert Hoover as President
and the return of Ramsay MacDonald as Prime Minister. Despite
his predecessor, Stanley Baldwin, warning that: 'The American
money power is trying to get hold of the natural resources of the
Empire',[25] MacDonald made a priority of restoring good relations
with the US – even visiting America in October 1929, the first
British Prime Minister to do so while in office, where he was a
great success. At the London Naval Conference a year later, the
British (Labour) delegation made concessions to the USA that
defused the tension.

However, an unlikely factor in resolving the Anglo-American
dispute – and avoiding what seemed inevitable conflict – was the
Wall Street Crash of 1929, which plunged first America, and then the
world, into recession. The disaster effectively wiped out America as
a major economic force in Europe for the next decade – until the
onset of the Second World War. In Europe, investment money
started to flow into the Bank of Paris rather than the banking houses
of New York.[26] (Of all the European nations, France weathered the
storm best – while Britain's unemployment peaked at 2.8 million,
and Germany's over 5.5 million, it never climbed much beyond
400,000 in France.[27])

The situation had reversed so dramatically that by the mid-1930s,
Britain's foreign policy, particularly its capabilities for war, had
become *dependent* on American cooperation and approval. Baldwin
(Prime Minister again in 1935) declared that the Royal Navy would
never undertake a blockade without American support.[28] In 1939,
E.H. Carr commented: 'Not only can Britain never contemplate war
with the United States, but she could never contemplate any war

with a first-class Power in which she could not count on the benevolent neutrality of the United States.'[29]

On the other hand, while acknowledging that its waging war depended on American support (or at least a lack of American opposition), Britain took a series of 'imperial preference' measures, enshrined in the Ottawa Agreement of 1932, effectively pricing America out of Empire markets, in which sterling still held sway. Successive American administrations, particularly Roosevelt's, were determined to destroy this barrier.

Unexpected bedfellows

Britain and the United States as enemies may seem ridiculous at first, but equally startling is the fact that so soon after the First World War, Britain's greatest potential ally was Germany.

The Treaty of Versailles had exacted a heavy toll on Germany. One-eighth of its European territory – and 10 per cent of its pre-war population – had been excised, as well as all its overseas colonies. Most of its iron, steel and shipping had also been seized, and the important industrial areas of the Rhineland and Saar placed under French control. The air force had been disbanded, and the army limited to 100,000 men, serving for at least 12 years to prevent amassing too many reservists. The navy's limit was 15,000 men. Then there were the punitive reparation payments . . . As memories of the war dimmed, even many in other countries saw all this as unfair and uncivilised. And the desire to reverse these humiliations and restore Germany to a world power created a situation that was only too ripe for exploitation by new nationalistic political movements, such as the Nazis.

In fact, the Nazis' control of Germany was another consequence of the Wall Street Crash. After attracting mass support from the disenchanted and impoverished in the mid-1920s, Hitler's following *declined* as the country recovered from the First World War. But the economic ruin of Germany following the 1929 crash – crippling inflation and rising unemployment – recreated the conditions and discontent on which the Nazi Party fed. In the July 1932 elections it became the largest party in the Reichstag, and Hitler was appointed Chancellor on 30 January 1933. Following new elections at the beginning of March, the Reichstag granted Hitler dictatorial powers.

He was quick to exploit them, passing the first of the infamous laws that stripped Germany's Jews of their rights: by the end of 1935, they were no longer even citizens. On 10 May 1933 came the notorious bonfires of books by authors such as Einstein, Thomas Mann, Proust, Zola and other 'degenerate' writers. In June, all other political parties were banned, trade unions following a month later. In October, Germany left the League of Nations.

This was the immediate result of the Nazis' triumph, but there should be no mystery about Hitler's long-term ambitions, as he had made them clear from the outset in *Mein Kampf* (actually co-written by Rudolf Hess[30]), published in 1925. First, Germany was to be restored as a major power, by reversing the Treaty of Versailles – recovering the ethnically and linguistically German territories from other states, predominantly Czechoslovakia and Poland, and removing the limits of its armed forces. Hilter sought a 'Greater Germany' – a unified country of German-speaking peoples – primarily through a union with Austria. (This had been expressly forbidden by Versailles, particularly enraging the Germans. Where was *their* right of self-determination?)

Rather than compete for colonies in Africa and Asia, the Third Reich would take its dependent territories – *Lebensraum* ('living space') – from Central and Eastern Europe. Indeed, Hitler argued that Germany's attempt to compete directly with the British Empire, leading to the First World War, had been a great folly. Eastward expansion would also bring a confrontation with the Nazis' natural enemy, the Soviet Union. Not content with seeking to eradicate Communism in Germany, they looked forward to destroying it at its source.

Hitler saw no reason for his Germany to cross Britain; he had a great personal respect for the British – largely because of the two individuals who influenced him most. The racial theorist Alfred Rosenberg argued that, being largely Anglo-Saxon, the English were part of the Aryan 'master race', while geopolitician Professor General Karl Haushofer (whose ideas reached Hitler via Hess), who devised the concept of Lebensraum, believed that the British Empire played a vital role in world stability, complementing, rather than conflicting with, the Third Reich's interests.

Friendly Fire

Hitler and Hess's attitude was straightforward: if Britain did not interfere with Nazi Germany's ambitions for mastery of Europe, Germany would leave the British Empire alone. As Anthony Cave Brown writes, 'As was evident in *Mein Kampf,* Hitler believed that Germany could only become a world power again through an alliance with Great Britain or Italy or both.'[31] The increasing tension between Britain and the US also significantly influenced Hitler: commenting on the unpublished 'sequel' to *Mein Kampf* (written in 1928) – one chapter entitled 'England as an Ally' – Brigadier-General Telford Taylor, Chief Counsel at the Nuremberg Trials, wrote, 'The rising power of America is . . . the factor on which Hitler most relies as a stimulant to a British alliance with Germany.'[32]

Like it or not, Britain had to come to terms with the new German regime and its implications for the balance of power in Europe and the world. While many were disturbed by the removal of Jewish rights and the book burnings, some vested interests considered the new regime a challenge – and yet others a golden opportunity.

Even before Hitler came to power, there was a general feeling among British financial circles – even in the Foreign Office – that Germany had been over-harshly treated. It seemed reasonable that Germany should be allowed to regain some of its former territories and boost its armed forces. It was this attitude that led to the Anglo-German Naval Agreement of July 1935, which allowed Germany a fleet up to 35 per cent of the size of the Royal Navy. By signing, Hitler signalled that he had no intention of challenging the British Empire, which in any case he had explicitly foresworn in *Mein Kampf.*

As is now recognised, a large and extremely important section of the British Establishment regarded the Nazi regime more as an opportunity than a threat for two reasons. An economically strong Germany provided a good excuse for severing Britain's increasingly tight ties with the United States, and many in the Establishment in any case regarded the Soviet Union as by far the greater enemy because of its anti-capitalist ideology. They saw Germany as a useful bulwark against Bolshevism, enthusiastically following the progress of the Nazi Party.

The Director-General of the BBC, John (later Lord) Reith, said after the 'Night of the Long Knives' in July 1934 – the purging of the

The Unthinkable

SA (*Sturmabteilung*, usually known as 'Brownshirts'), in which dozens were killed, including 50 of its leaders – 'I really admire the drastic actions taken . . . '[33] (Many agreed, believing that Hitler was purging the party of the bully-boy element, and turning in a more moderate direction.) In December 1934, Hitler hosted a dinner party whose guests included *Daily Mail* owner Lord Rothermere and his son Esmond Harmsworth, chairman of the Newspaper Proprietors Association. (Of the British Union of Fascists, a headline in the *Daily Mail* – written by Rothermere himself – on 8 January 1934 declared 'Thank God for the Blackshirts!'[34] That month, another of his newspapers, the *Daily Mirror*, ran a campaign encouraging its readers to sign up to Oswald Mosley's movement.[35]) In September 1936, the elder statesman – and great Liberal – Lloyd George was also entertained by Hitler, declaring him to be 'the greatest German of the age'.[36]

The famed financial district of London's City favoured strong economic ties with Germany, all the more because of the Nazis' hatred of Bolshevism. E.H. Carr, writing on the eve of the war, defended the City against allegations of pro-Nazi leanings, pointing out that it was equally pro-German before Hitler's ascendancy[37] – implying, however, that the City *remained* pro-German when the Nazis came to power.

The British historian Scott Newton argues that the most powerful force in British politics between the wars was a group made up of the Treasury, the City of London, the Bank of England, the Conservative Party and Liberals of the Lloyd George school, being 'committed to the defence of free enterprise and the limited state against the internal threat of socialism and the external menace of Bolshevism'.[38] According to Newton, the policy of appeasement towards Germany followed by successive governments in the 1930s was a natural consequence of this. Strong economic ties already existed between the two countries – ironically, largely because of Germany's defeat in the First World War, as British industry and banks moved in to invest heavily in rebuilding Germany.

However, there was also a growing groundswell of opinion in favour of establishing an Anglo-German axis for both economic and political reasons – although this is usually conveniently forgotten today. Astonishingly, what was proposed was an economic partnership that aimed at almost uniting the two countries' economies. The key figure behind this radical notion was Montagu Norman, the hugely influential Governor of the Bank of England – controlling Britain's monetary policy – from 1920 to 1944. (The *Wall Street Journal* called him the 'Currency Dictator of Europe'.[39]) Norman believed not only that it was in Britain's financial interests to link Britain and Germany economically but also that this would offer protection against the threat posed by the Soviet Union: a thriving and prosperous Germany would provide both a physical and ideological barrier, also challenging the growing financial might of the USA and France. Consequently, under Norman, investment in Germany became a matter of policy for the Bank of England, which actively encouraged British banks to do so.[40]

Although inevitably labelled a 'crypto-Fascist',[41] Norman's belief in linking the British and German economies predated the Nazis' rise – but he did seem remarkably oblivious to the unfolding story of Nazi atrocities. He was a close colleague and friend of the formidable economist and President of the Reichsbank, Hjalmar Schacht ('Hitler's banker'), becoming godfather to Schacht's son, whose middle name was Montagu.

Despite a clash of philosophy with Nazi economists (who advocated that Germany should adopt a system of economic self-sufficiency – 'autarchy' – in keeping with their racial and geopolitical concepts), Norman welcomed the new regime because of its fanatical anti-Communist commitment. As early as September 1933, he decided that the Bank of England should back the Nazis, specifically to ensure their regime's stability.[42]

Norman also worked to persuade the Prime Minister, Stanley Baldwin, that Stalin posed the greater threat. Though unsuccessful, he did win over several other Cabinet ministers, most significantly Sir John (later Lord) Simon (Foreign then Home Secretary, later chosen by Churchill to lead the pseudo-negotiations with Rudolf Hess) and Neville Chamberlain, then Chancellor of the Exchequer but later Baldwin's successor as Prime Minister.[43]

As a result of Norman's policy, by 1938 Germany was Britain's largest export market outside the Empire, and its fifth largest even including the Empire.[44] (The USA was Britain's second-largest non-Empire market.) Dividing up the world markets was crucial: to avoid wasteful competition, Britain and Germany would agree which countries to target for exports, an unprecedented degree of collaboration between two nations. Even by March 1939 – when Hitler reneged on the Munich Agreement and annexed the remainder of Czechoslovakia – 'the prospect of an Anglo-German industrial partnership did not seem too far fetched.'[45] And even during the Polish crisis, Norman continued to encourage Anglo-German economic cooperation.[46]

This putative Anglo-German union was viewed with alarm in America, so much so that it became a major factor in key decisions taken by President Roosevelt in the run-up to the war. Indeed, conflict between those two countries would be a heaven-sent blessing for America.

CHAPTER THREE

New Orders

'Megalomania is the only form of sanity.'
Winston S. Churchill, 1911[1]

If the Nazis represented the Devil, then the Soviet Union was certainly the 'deep blue sea'. Now ruled (at least theoretically) by its people, it was seen as a new and largely terrifying phenomenon that aimed to spread its creed across the globe.

After an uprising forced Tsar Nicolas II to abdicate in March 1917, a liberal-led provisional government was installed. But at the end of October, the Bolshevik ('Majority', then 'Communist') Party led by Lenin (the assumed name of Vladimir Ilich Ulyanov) seized power, immediately declaring an armistice with Germany. Initially absorbed with a civil war (in which British and French troops became embroiled) until October 1920, the Bolsheviks then attacked the newly created Poland, expecting to be welcomed by the people as liberators but instead finding themselves halted outside Warsaw. The Poles not only drove the Red Army back but also ended up capturing territory from Russia.

The USSR caused widespread alarm across Europe, and it was only in 1924, when Britain's Labour government formally recognised this rough and fanatical new nation, that any major power established diplomatic relations with the new regime.

Ironically – given the later paranoia about 'Reds under the bed' – the United States welcomed the new Russia as a vast improvement on the former despotic regime. One of Wilson's Fourteen Points called for all nations to embrace the USSR – 'and more than a welcome, assistance of every kind that she may need and may herself desire'.[2]

On 2 March 1923, a few days before the stroke that was to kill him, Lenin wrote his 'testament' for *Pravda*, setting world revolution at the heart of Soviet ambitions, via the Third Communist International, known as the Comintern. A committee of representatives of national Communist parties, its annual congress decided on international policies, while its permanent Executive Committee of expatriate foreign Communists made the day-to-day decisions. The second annual congress, in 1920, adopted Lenin's 21 conditions, anticipating world revolution through subversion among workers and even within the armed forces, stating, 'The work by Communists will for the most part have to be conducted illegally.'[3] This did little to endear Communism to other nations.

Originally, the Comintern was intended to control both domestic and world Communism – but as it wanted the blood of capitalist governments, while the Russian government needed their goodwill, the Comintern rapidly became a tool of the Soviet government. The changes in the Comintern's policies are therefore a fairly accurate barometer of Soviet thinking. Realising that Europe's workers were not, as expected, spontaneously rising up against their capitalist bosses, the Comintern turned to promoting Communism as the 'only real alternative' to Fascism – which became a very real dilemma after the Nazi–Soviet Pact. As they could hardly denounce Stalin, but equally could not approve of Hitler, they just ignored it, instead attacking other left-wing groups and the imperialist powers.

Enter Stalin

Stalin ('steel'), born Iosif Vissarionovich Dzhugashvili in Georgia, trained for the Orthodox priesthood before embracing Marxism. Emerging as a major player in the Politburo (the USSR's policy-making body), he was a fervent Russian nationalist – causing bitterness between himself and the internationalist Lenin. After Lenin's death, Stalin became supreme leader of the Soviet Union and global Communism, dominating the USSR for 25 years. With a ruthless focus of which the more tyrannical Tsars would have been proud, he eliminated his rivals first on the left (such as Leon Trotsky), then the right. By 1930, he stood alone.

Stalin reversed Lenin's priorities, being more concerned about controlling the USSR than world revolution, expelling Trotsky from the Party in 1927 (and later from the country). Stalin considered Lenin's policies had isolated the fledgling Soviet Union; the USSR would have to deal with foreigners if it was to thrive. While never abandoning his dream of global Communism, he appeared genial to the outside world, fostering the illusion that Russia would be less of a threat, appointing the pro-Western Maxim Litvinov as Foreign Commissar in 1930 – and even joining the League of Nations in 1934.

In March 1921, Lenin had introduced the New Economic Policy, which owed surprisingly little to Marxist principles: while the peasants had to supply a quota of food for the state, they could sell any surplus for profit. From 1922, when peasants were given security of land tenure, many became rich. However, Stalin decided to replace the old agrarian society with modern industry, initiating the first of his Five Year Plans in October 1928 – resulting in an even more totalitarian regime than Lenin's. Farming now existed purely to supply urban needs, requiring collectivisation. The land Lenin had given to the peasants (*kulaks*) was taken by the state. Naturally, they resisted, so food for the towns was seized with the utmost brutality. By the end of the first Five Year Plan, at least 5 million people had died, disappeared or ended up in forced labour camps – the notorious *gulags* – while half of Russia's livestock had been lost. But while other industrialised nations' output fell drastically following the Wall Street Crash, the USSR's had doubled by 1932.[4]

Despite his avuncular image, with psychopathic ruthlessness Stalin turned Russia into the model for all police states, claiming the country needed to protect itself from 'capitalist encirclement' and the 'danger of foreign military attack'[5] – true up to a point: Hitler and Japan's encroachments in China posed real threats to the USSR.

New Orders

Stalin's domestic reign of terror excised all the original Bolshevik element. In March 1938, he presided over the first Party Congress for 4 years: of the 2,000 delegates of 1934, only 35 were still there in 1938; in the intervening years 1,100 had been arrested, imprisoned or executed, for 'counter-revolutionary crimes'. Of the 139 members of the Party's Central Committee only 27 remained; the others had been shot. Lenin's Politburo was cleaned out, mostly with trumped-up charges of betraying the revolution or of spying for a foreign government – usually Britain or Japan – followed by show trials ending in execution or transportation to the gulags. The worst years of Stalin's increasingly paranoid Great Purge were 1936–8 when 54 major party figures 'confessed' to having connections with Trotsky or foreign governments. All were executed or died in prison.[6]

The Red Army also suffered. Between 1936 and 1938, 60 per cent of officers above the rank of colonel were purged, including 3 of the 5 marshals, 75 of the 80 members of the Supreme Military Council and the entire district military command. This loss of experience weakened Soviet armed forces just as another European war was looming.[7]

By the outbreak of war, nearly all the Comintern (formally dissolved in 1943) had also gone. The task of subversion in the west had passed from the national Communist parties controlled by Comintern to the Soviet intelligence organisations.

In the early 1930s, the USSR infiltrated foreign government departments and intelligence agencies, largely through the NKVD (People's Commissariat for Internal Affairs[8]) and the Fourth Department (later the GRU). Officially, the NKVD gathered political, and the Fourth Department military, intelligence, but it was a fine line. The NKVD began to recruit young fellow travellers, as in the notorious Cambridge spy ring – Philby, Burgess, Maclean and Blunt.

However, Russia's traditional enemy was Japan, prompting Stalin's unlikely partnership with the ultimate capitalist nation – the USA. For its part, America saw closer cooperation with the USSR as, in the words of William C. Bullitt, Roosevelt's adviser on Soviet affairs, a 'bulwark against the aggressive tendencies . . . developing in Japan'.[9] It was this mutual fear of Japan that finally led the new

Roosevelt administration to recognise the Soviet Union. Stalin sent Litvinov to Washington in November 1933 to announce the end of anti-American propaganda and religious freedom for Americans in Russia. In return, the US officially recognised the Soviet Union.[10]

Stalin's terror

In October 2003, German President Johannes Rau caused outrage by stating that the Allies – specifically the Russians – should accept their share of the responsibility for the horrors of the Second World War. Although the Soviets' wartime brutality and Stalin's domestic depredations makes them at least the equal of Hitler's regime, it has never been 'politically correct' to acknowledge as much. Today, even asking why Soviet war crimes went unpunished runs the risk of being tarred with the 'neo-Nazi' brush, as if anyone who highlights Stalin's crimes is somehow trying to excuse Hitler's. Of course, this is arrant – and dangerous – nonsense.

Max Hastings acknowledged in response to Rau: 'Today, we can see that Stalin was morally indistinguishable from Hitler – indeed, Stalin could even boast of having murdered even more people.'[11] And yet the great heroes of the West – and champions of freedom – Churchill and Roosevelt, happily accepted Stalin as an equal partner in the fight against Germany. Why? Indeed, when the British and Americans accepted Stalin as ally, he was a monster of grosser proportions than Hitler.

Bolshevik terrorism reached new proportions under Stalin, its main instrument the forced labour camps, or gulags. Concentration camps, like those of the Nazis, they housed the regime's actual or potential opponents – built, as historian and journalist Anne Applebaum notes in *Gulag: A History of the Soviet Camps* (2003), to 'incarcerate people not for what they had done, but for who they were'.[12] The Russian camps differed from the Nazi counterpart during the 1930s mainly in that their inmates were forced to work. (The Nazis did not introduce this until the eve of the war.)

Although the Tsars and Lenin used forced labour, under Stalin's NKVD the gulags mushroomed, as his paranoid purges uncovered yet more 'enemies of the people' to provide labour for his industrialisation programme. Most gulags were in sub-zero, remote regions – Siberia the classic example – many actually within the Arctic Circle, to exploit valuable raw materials, such as timber or coal. Criminals and political prisoners, including those who had foolishly joked about Stalin, ended up in the gulags. Settlements were also established for internal exiles in remote areas such as the desert of Kazakhstan – not technically prisons, but communities for dissidents and others: about six million people passed through this system during Stalin's rule.

Stalin's first massive purge began in the early 1930s as a result of the first Five Year Plan – the switch from agriculture to industry – requiring the wholesale moving of populations, or 'dekulakisation'. How many people were forcibly relocated is unknown – but clearly the Politburo's official figure of between five and six million is too low (some estimates double this figure).[13] Disruption to the food supply and mass relocation caused widespread starvation, especially in the Ukraine. Between three and four million died during transportation or of exposure: most of the survivors ended up in the gulags.[14]

As Stalin's paranoia spiralled, the gulag system extended exponentially: whole regions became one massive camp complex, the most notorious being Kolyma, in the extreme north-east where temperatures fall to -45⁰C. Here, the prisoners mined gold to be sold to the West, later mining uranium with minimal protection from radiation.

Each gulag aimed to be self-supporting. Some were farms, some mines, while in others thousands died building railways. Prisoners were fed according to their output: the weak were immediately doomed. As camp commanders were punished if death rates were excessive, prisoners on the point of death were 'released'. Often deaths went unrecorded. Even today, thaws in frozen regions reveal secret mass graves.

In major cities such as Moscow and Leningrad, new convicts arrived at the train stations in lorries painted with the name of innocuous goods, such as 'bread'. The overcrowded human cargo was caged, holes in the floor for sanitation. Food was minimal, water sometimes given just three times in a month-long journey. Many died horribly before they reached the camps.

Originally, the gulags were only incidentally brutal, usually through bad organisation, individual sadism and Moscow's indifference. However, during Stalin's Great Purge of 1936–8, 'the Soviet camps temporarily transformed themselves from indifferently managed prisons in which people died by accident, into genuinely deadly camps where prisoners were deliberately worked to death, or actually murdered, in far larger numbers than they had been in the past.'[15] Stalin had the gulags removed from maps and their locations became a state secret. NKVD documents employed chilling euphemisms (like the Nazis' later labelling of Jews as 'merchandise'): male prisoners were 'Accounts', women with children 'Receipts' and pregnant women 'Books'. From that time, spouses of 'enemies of the people' were also imprisoned, children removed to state orphanages.

In 1937, in one of the most Kafkaesque parodies of justice, Stalin issued quotas to regional NKVD chiefs for 'first-category' punishment – execution – and 'second-category' – gulag imprisonment for at least eight years. To appear enthusiastic, local officials asked for increased quotas: in Armenia, where the quota was 500 first-category and 1,000 second-category arrests, the NKVD petitioned Stalin for permission to execute an extra 700.

Perhaps due to overcrowding, in the same year the NKVD issued camp commanders with quotas of prisoners to execute, by category. Thousands died; the exact figure will never be known. Stalin curtly informed the Communist Party Congress in March 1939 that 'more mistakes than might have been expected' had occurred in this programme, ordering the execution of those responsible for the executions. But the reason for this volte-face was economic, not humanitarian: the newly appointed head of the NKVD, Lavrenty Beria, ordered camp commanders to improve their survival rates to wring the last drop of work out of the prisoners, now 'units of labour'. The threat of diminished productivity also reversed the possibility of early release for good behaviour (the minimum sentence being 8 years, the maximum 25), in June 1939. In wartime, political prisoners were not released even after completing their sentence.

Stalin's gulag victimisation reached a peak in the early 1950s, the last years of his life. The camps remained in use nearly as long as the Soviet regime – being dissolved as late as 1987, on the order of Mikhail Gorbachev (whose grandfather was an inmate).

According to Anne Applebaum's *Gulag*, during the years of Stalin's regime some 18 million people passed through the system, not including the exile villagers or prisoners of war forced to work. She estimates the total number of Stalin's forced labourers as just under 30 million, admitting that figure is, if anything, too low.[16]

The only available statistics on the number of deaths in the gulags are the annual counts compiled by the NKVD, some 1.6 million between 1930 and 1953, but this does not include those who died during transportation, or 'special exiles' (and camp commanders often under-reported deaths). Estimates of the total number of Stalin's victims – those who starved to death under the Five Year Plans, died in the gulags or were executed in his purges – vary from 10 to 20 million. Nobody knows.

At the beginning of the war, the gulag system dwarfed the Nazis' concentration camps. (Constructed from 1933 for political opponents, these are often confused with death camps, such as Auschwitz, used to implement the 'Final Solution' from 1942.) In June 1935, the total population of Germany's five concentration camps was about 3,500, principally Communists. Then the camps – including five new ones – also took 'anti-social' elements such as gypsies and homosexuals. After Kristallnacht, the orchestrated anti-Jewish riots of November 1938, the total population briefly peaked at over 50,000, although by April 1939 it had dropped back to just over 20,000.[17] (Unlike the NKVD, the German authorities kept meticulous records.) During the same period, the gulag population averaged about 2 million – 40 times the German total at its maximum.

When considering the human cost of the two economic and social policies, Stalin once again emerges as the greater evil. On the eve of the war, Hitler's Germany had – as yet – nothing to compare with the mass deaths of 'dekulakisation'. The Führer's 'Night of the Long Knives' in 1934 had claimed fewer than a hundred victims; Stalin's ran into thousands. Alan Bullock, in *Hitler and Stalin: Parallel Lives* (1991), estimates that (excluding war casualties) Stalin was responsible for twice as many deaths as Hitler.[18] So why have Nazi excesses become the embodiment of twentieth-century evil, while Stalin's are routinely excused as an aberration?

Some argue that there was at least some kind of twisted logic behind Stalin's ruthlessness – paranoia about 'enemies of the state' and the pursuit of social and economic transformation – while the Nazi genocide was the result of irrational race-hate. That, and the clinical way in which the annihilation of an entire people was organised, is why the Holocaust is uniquely atrocious.

However, even the primarily political gulags were tainted with ethnic cleansing, as Anne Applebaum notes:

> In Nazi Germany, the first targets were the crippled and the retarded. Later, the Nazis concentrated on Gypsies, homosexuals and, above all, on the Jews. In the USSR, the victims were, at first, the 'former people' – alleged supporters of the old regime – and later the 'enemies of the people', an ill-defined term which would come to include not only alleged political opponents of the regime, but also particular national groups and ethnicities, if they seemed (for equally ill-defined reasons) to threaten the Soviet state or Stalin's power. At different times Stalin conducted mass arrests of Poles, Balts, Chechens, Tartars and – on the eve of his death – Jews.[19]

During the war, Stalin sent various ethnic groups he suspected of pro-German sympathies to the camps en masse just in case. First, he homed in on the Volga Germans – a million-strong community whose ancestors had settled from Germany in the eighteenth century (few of whom still spoke German). Then he turned to other communities, eventually ordering the forced deportation of over two million people, including the Chechens, nearly 80,000 of whom died in 1944. They were allowed to return to their homeland after Stalin's death, but the resentment still festers today.

Applebaum writes: 'For the first time, Stalin had decided to eliminate not just members of particular, suspect nationalities, or categories of political "enemies", but entire nations – men, women, children, grandparents – and wipe them off the map.'[20] He aimed at 'cultural genocide' – erasing these cultures, while providing new workers for the Soviet state.

The final irony is that, after the war, Stalin's paranoia turned to Russia's Jews, whom he believed to be part of an international Jewish conspiracy that underpinned capitalism. This was the same as Hitler's delusion – except he blamed it for the rise of Communism and Stalin. From 1948, the Soviet tyrant actively repressed the Jews: it was only his death in March 1953 that prevented Soviet Jewry from following the Chechens and the Tartars into the gulags.[21]

But how much did the West know of Stalin's horrors when he was welcomed as an Ally? The existence and scale of the gulags was certainly known, largely due to escapees and refugees at the end of the 1920s. Much had been written about the camps, particularly in the left-wing press. Initially, the main concern was humanitarian – the British Anti-Slavery Society launched an investigation – but the focus was soon the economic threat posed by Soviet slave labour. In 1930, the US briefly banned goods produced by 'convict labour' and in 1931 a series of high-profile articles appeared in *The Times* on conditions in the Soviet camps.[22]

'What camps?' was the Kremlin's response, as some were hastily eradicated, thousands dying during transportation. Show camps, in which prisoners were kept in relative luxury, were exhibited to visiting delegations from foreign Communist Parties. Although none of this fooled the West, it provided a good excuse to ignore what was going on in Stalin's Russia.

Neither were the purges a secret, or the Five Year Plans' depredations. So what prompted the British and Americans to stand shoulder to shoulder with Stalin and annihilate Hitler and his regime? Did they simply need Soviet might to defeat Germany? Was it just a case of 'my enemy's enemy is my friend'? Or were Roosevelt and Churchill's double standards concerned less with fighting evil and more with political ambition?

Saviour of America

During the 1930s, America was frantically endeavouring to re-establish economic viability. The Wall Street Crash and ensuing Depression had taken such a toll that by mid-1932 production was down by nearly 50 per cent, and in the winter of 1932–3 unemployment reached an estimated 15 (some estimate 17) million – roughly 25 per cent of the workforce. Between 1929 and 1932, over 100,000 businesses failed, farming profits dropping from $11 billion to $5 billion. When Franklin Delano Roosevelt took office in March 1933, some 50 million Americans were on the breadline.[23]

In November 1932, President Hoover's wait-and-see handling of the crisis ensured a landslide victory for his Democrat opponent, securing Roosevelt 57 per cent of the popular vote and an electoral vote of 472 to 59. As the American constitution then required a long handover period between administrations (during which Roosevelt survived an assassination attempt), his inauguration finally took place on 4 March 1933. In his inaugural address, he coined the phrase (later much repeated), 'the only thing we have to fear is fear itself'. With great historical synchronicity, the election that gave Hitler undisputed mastery of Germany took place the day after Roosevelt's inauguration.

Roosevelt ('FDR') became the longest-serving President in the history of the United States, from 1933 to 1945, the only one daring to stand for more than two terms in office. A precedent had been set when George Washington had declined a third term because it would allow one individual too much power. Only someone who believed himself to be of equal or greater ability to the legendary Washington could have challenged this custom; only someone with the supreme political skill of Roosevelt could have won that challenge. (After Roosevelt's patrician reign, in 1951 the US Constitution was changed to make it impossible for anyone to repeat the feat: one man had indeed accumulated too much power.)

All subsequent US Presidents have lived in Roosevelt's shadow – he is the benchmark by which they have been judged and by which they judge themselves. Not only did he have to grapple in rapid succession with America's two greatest post-Civil War crises – the Great Depression and the Second World War – but he also redefined the American Presidency, extending its powers at the expense of Congress and weakening many of the founding fathers' checks and balances.

As with Churchill, such was Roosevelt's stature that for many years after his death his legend prevented any objective assessment of his career – although some attempted to redress the balance, most notably Washington political columnist John T. Flynn's *The Roosevelt Myth* (1948). Fortunately, time has encouraged more critical analyses such as Michael Simpson's *Franklin D. Roosevelt* (1982). Another British historian, Donald Cameron Watt, puts it this way:

> . . . Roosevelt's ability to lead America so successfully for three and a quarter terms of office stemmed from his technique of dominating those he led by a mixture of the authority which any Presidential candidate inherits at the moment of his election, the strength of his own personality and the secrecy which underlay his ability to be all things to all the disparate elements which made up his coalition.[24]

A shrewd, ruthless politician who fully exploited intelligence-gathering, Roosevelt carefully fostered the image of an ordinary Joe. To a journalist, he summed up his political philosophy: 'Philosophy? I am a Christian and a Democrat. That's all.'[25] Rex Tugwell of the 'Brains Trust' of unelected personal advisers with whom Roosevelt surrounded himself said, 'He had a trick of seeming to listen, and to agree or to differ partly and pleasantly which was flattering . . . Finally no one could tell what he was *thinking*, to say nothing of what he was *feeling*.'[26]

Like all legends, the human being was distinctly flawed. Even his leading biographer – and admirer – Arthur M. Schlesinger, writes of FDR's 'thin streak of sadism', quoting Attorney General Francis Biddle: 'However genial his teasing, it was often . . . pointed with a prick of cruelty', given 'to wound[ing] those who loved him'.[27]

Perhaps the key to understanding Roosevelt's personality and style of leadership is to remember that it was said that the only things that ever kept him up past midnight were election nights, Pearl Harbor – and a tense game of poker. Bluffing, the poker face and playing his cards close to his chest were his trademarks. He relied on personal advisers, confidants and unofficial envoys working outside the usual machinery of government and diplomacy, often going over the heads of his officials and ambassadors. In 1942, he confided to his Secretary of the Treasury, Henry J. Morgenthau, Jr:

Friendly Fire

> You know I am a juggler, and I never let my right hand know
> what my left hand does . . . I may have one policy for Europe
> and one diametrically opposed for North and South America.
> I may be entirely inconsistent, and furthermore I am perfectly
> willing to mislead and tell untruths if it will help win the war.[28]

Of course, such Machiavellian characteristics are not only excusable
but a positive asset to a president or prime minister in times of
national crisis. Actions that would normally lead to impeachment are
shrugged off as necessary 'white lies'. But Roosevelt's words to
Morgenthau also described his pre-war presidency, particularly from
his second term in 1936.

Roosevelt was one of the first world leaders to use the medium of
radio to explain his plans to the public and win them over. But while
Churchill and Hitler, in their different ways, also memorably used the
'wireless', only he spoke quietly and intimately straight into family
homes. A week into his presidency, he held the first of his 'fireside
chats'. Beginning, 'My friends . . . ', he would explain complex economic
and political issues (or his own angle on them) in simple, homely
analogies. The people warmed to Roosevelt because he spoke their
language – describing his vision for a more affluent America by saying
he wanted 'a chicken in every pot'.

But there was a darker side to Roosevelt's unparalleled success.
His presidential power had been achieved and maintained largely
through unofficial, clandestine influences. Even Roosevelt was not
above dirty tricks, pursuing his aims through subterfuge – back-door
channels, secret deals and the judicious withholding of information
from (or even blatant lying to) Congress and the people. Indeed, this
happened repeatedly throughout the Second World War. Roosevelt
defined the presidency of today and his modus operandi – and the
standards of presidential behaviour he made acceptable – can be
traced to Watergate and the Iran-Contra affair.

Roosevelt was the first President to exploit the FBI, digging up dirt
on his opponents, but also forcing it to halt investigations into his
supporters and friends, as in the case of Undersecretary of State
Sumner Welles, under FBI investigation for homosexuality.[29] He was
also the first President to routinely use phone-tapping and bugging,

even against his own administration.[30] However, as we will see, FDR was the only President to use a *foreign* intelligence service – the British – against both political opponents and fellow Americans.

Robert Dallek argues that Roosevelt set the precedent for the American President using 'national security' as a justification for misleading the people.[31] As historian Patrick J. Maney, author of *The Roosevelt Presence* (1992), writes, 'It was a short step . . . from the exaggerations and distortions of fact that accompanied Roosevelt's efforts to aid Britain before Pearl Harbor to the systematic deception of the American public that occurred throughout the war in Vietnam', and that Roosevelt made it 'easier for future presidents to abuse their power in the interests of national security'.[32]

In his second term, Roosevelt became a 'political royalist', causing allegations of favouritism, nepotism and even – in the case of his family if not himself – corruption. Both his sons exploited his status: Jimmy's insurance company traded on his White House connections to win major contracts with US corporations. Elliott made fortunes from the sales of military aircraft and radio stations. FDR himself often personally phoned the heads of companies to encourage them to close deals with his sons.[33]

Roosevelt came from the outer reaches of a rich and influential clan descended on his father's side from Dutch immigrants who settled in New York in the seventeenth century and on his mother's from Huguenot refugees, the de la Noyes (which became 'Delano', FDR's middle name). The dynasty had already produced one President – the Republican Theodore Roosevelt (1901–9), FDR's fifth cousin.

Born in 1882, the only child of an alcoholic, semi-invalid father and a domineering mother, FDR 'learned stoicism in the face of injury or disappointment, telling his parents what they wanted to hear and hiding his true feelings. In escaping from his formidable mother's control, he became devious.'[34]

Every summer, the family visited Europe, giving the future President an understanding of foreign countries often lacking in American statesmen, and he even became fluent in French and German. When his father stayed at Bad Nauheim in Hesse-Darmstadt, the young Roosevelt was enrolled for several weeks in a

German school, imprinting an indelible impression of the national character that eventually shaped the way he ran the war. To him, all Germans – not just Nazis – were naturally belligerent and militaristic, enemies of world peace.

Biographers usually dismiss Roosevelt's German schooling as a mere biographical blip. However, Roosevelt wrote in 1940 to his friend, the Scottish railway magnate Sir Arthur Murray (later Lord Elibank, whom Roosevelt had known when he was Assistant Military Attaché to the British Embassy in Washington during the First World War):

> . . . remember that I, too, went to school – a village school – in Germany and, indeed, spent almost every summer there until I was fourteen years old.
>
> In those early nineties I gained the distinct impression that education and outlook under the old Kaiser and under Frederick was quickly and almost suddenly changed when Wilhelm, II, [*sic*] came to the throne. When I was eleven in 1893, I think it was, my class was started on the study of 'Heimatkunde' – geography lessons . . . The following year we were taught all about . . . what we would see on the way to the French border . . . the class was 'conducted' to France – all the roads leading into Paris.
>
> The talk among us children became stronger each year toward an objective – the inevitable war with France and the building up of the Reich into the greatest world power. Even then we were taught to have no respect for Englishmen, and we were taught that Americans were mere barbarians, most of whom were millionaires.[35]

From the age of 14, FDR attended Groton, a Massachusetts version of an English public school, before studying law at Harvard, ambitions supercharged by having a President in the family. In 1903, he became engaged to Theodore's niece, the bright but undeniably plain Eleanor Roosevelt, probably more to bask in reflected presidential glory than from love. (Although they produced six children, one of whom died in infancy, Eleanor demanded a separate bed in 1916, not realising that he was already three years into an affair with her social secretary, Lucy Mercer. When she found out in 1918, she offered FDR a divorce, but as this would have ended his political career – and because his mother threatened to cut him off financially – he declined, but told Lucy that Eleanor had refused *his* offer of a divorce. After this, their marriage became a partnership. After her husband's death, Eleanor wrote: 'I was one of those who served his purpose.'[36])

After briefly working for a Wall Street legal practice, he entered politics, becoming Senator for New York State in 1910. In March 1913, he landed his first Washington job as Assistant Secretary of the Navy, where 'In crises with Japan and Mexico in 1913, he manifested an ill-considered belligerence.'[37] When hostilities broke out in Europe, he was immediately in favour of American involvement.[38]

In 1920, as the Democrats' vice-presidential candidate (to James M. Cox), FDR was heavily defeated. The following August, he was struck down with polio. Although recovery was slow, he dealt with the setback courageously, eventually teaching himself to stand for long periods with steel leg braces, and to walk with support. When he re-emerged from the political wilderness to become Governor of New York State in 1928, and then President, the press corps agreed never to print photos of him in his wheelchair or being carried (as he often was getting out of cars or going up stairs).

FDR's world order

During his tortuous recovery, Roosevelt formulated a detailed plan for a world order that, he believed, would ensure peace and stability. He advocated the creation of a 'Society of Nations' to settle international disputes, consisting of a policy-making Assembly and an Executive Committee in which the 'big five' – the USA, Britain, France, Italy and Japan – would have permanent seats while six more would be elected by the Assembly. Although Roosevelt was to modify the details of his 'Grand Design', it eventually became the United Nations.[39]

Roosevelt believed that world security should be entrusted to powerful nations acting as 'world policemen', only the 'policemen' being allowed to possess weapons and armed forces. All other nations were to be disarmed, forcibly if necessary. If any nation rearmed, it would be 'quarantined' by trade sanctions; if this failed, it would be bombed; finally, it would be invaded.[40]

Although, obviously, one 'policeman' would be the USA, Roosevelt's ideas about the others changed: initially ideally restricting them to the English-speaking nations (i.e. the USA, Britain and its major dominions of Canada, Australia, New Zealand and South Africa). As we will see, he modified this idea during the war, and it became the basis of the United Nations Security Council.

Donald Cameron Watt writes: 'He was, in fact, a moral imperialist on a super-Wilsonian scale, determined . . . to make as much of the world over into the American image as was possible.'[41] Roosevelt drew his own geopolitical ideas largely from the nineteenth-century theories of Admiral Alfred Thayer Mahan, which he duly expanded. According to Willard Range in *Roosevelt's World Order* (1959), FDR believed that the world order had broken down, partly due to 'a decline in the moral and spiritual fibre of the world's peoples, particularly the people of Europe'.[42] As for America's position in the world, Range explains:

> He looked upon the United States as a nation whose international morality was superior to that of most states and as the only great power free enough from power politics to take a disinterested view of world affairs, and with a moral reputation adequate to provide leadership in mobilizing the moral force of men elsewhere. Only the United States could be the conscience of the state system.[43]

Roosevelt believed that it was the USA's destiny to lead the world – another idea that he took from Admiral Mahan. Range goes on:

> Another reason for United States leadership of the world, in Roosevelt's mind, was his belief that as Europe disintegrated into chaos, Western culture might disappear unless the United States preserved it and assumed leadership in perpetuating and restoring it.[44]

Like most Americans, Roosevelt was strongly opposed to colonialism:

it was his initiative to give the Philippines – effectively an American colony since 1899 – its independence. A constant source of antagonism between him and Churchill was his belief that British colonies should become independent. Roosevelt was to take advantage of the unique wartime circumstances to try to make this happen.

However, there was a dichotomy, as FDR, believing that the English-speaking nations shared common interests, advocated an Anglo-American alliance:[45] essentially, he wanted the US to ally with Britain but not its Empire, over which, as far as he was concerned, the sun could hardly set fast enough – not just because of his anti-colonialism but because of its stranglehold on world trade.

With his prejudice against Germany he was virtually alone among statesmen in considering that the terms of the Treaty of Versailles had been too soft.[46] Roosevelt also adopted Mahan's bias against Japan's 'yellow peril'. Range explains:

> Alfred Thayer Mahan had written much about this at the turn of the century, arguing that by sheer force of numbers the yellow races could engulf and destroy Western society if they ever went on the rampage; and Mahan appealed to the West to take hold of these awakening peoples, guide them, and do the utmost to imbue them with Western-Christian-liberal principles so that when they became strong and fully awake they would behave as civilized people rather than the barbarians Mahan then thought them to be.[47]

From his youth, Roosevelt had been hostile towards the Japanese, 'the Prussians of the East',[48] hence his choice of the USSR as partner in the four-cornered diplomatic game in the Far East, and shortly after coming to office, his official recognition of the USSR – which also suited Stalin.

Roosevelt's attitude to the Soviet Union also depended on the same nineteenth-century geopolitical theories. The idea that the massive and resource-rich USA and Russia would inevitably become the two dominant powers in the world had gained considerable ground, although then Russia was still under the Tsars. In 1835, the influential French political theorist Alexis de Tocqueville wrote that one day America and Russia would each 'hold in its hands the destinies of half the world'.[49] The Tsar's demise did little to shake Roosevelt's belief in the destiny of the two major powers. (To him, even a bad Communist regime was still preferable to the one it replaced.) This belief in the inevitability of Russian ascendancy underpinned many of his decisions in the war – including his acceptance of Stalin as an Ally.

The world stage

As an internationalist, Roosevelt had always favoured American involvement in world affairs, but to become President he did a deal with powerful press baron – and staunch isolationist – William Randolph Hearst. In return for Hearst's support during his election campaign, Roosevelt would keep the US off the world stage.[50] As a result, for most of his first five years in office he paid little attention to foreign affairs, declaring his administration's foreign policy somewhat airily as being a 'good neighbour' to other nations.

In fact, at first Roosevelt seemed determined for the USA to go it alone, as at the World Economic Conference in London in June and July 1933, where delegates from 64 countries sought solutions to the post-Crash recession, particularly by stabilising world currencies. As the US had been committed to attend by Hoover, Roosevelt sent a delegation, headed by his Secretary of State, Cordell Hull, who was willing to compromise on the currency issue. But a month into the conference, Roosevelt sent a Treasury official to defend America's preference for flexible currencies, thereby undermining his own delegation. He also sent the infamous 'bombshell message', effectively terminating the conference – a 'gratuitous insult'.[51]

This caused the final rupture between the USA and Europe over First World War debts. The Europeans' hardship after the Wall Street Crash had hampered their repayments, resulting in President Hoover granting a one-year moratorium in 1931. A month before it expired, a conference of the European nations in Lausanne agreed that all war debts between them should be cancelled, and German reparations settled by a single payment of £150 million. When the moratorium was up, Britain made just token payments to the USA in 1932 and 1933; France and other European debtor nations defaulted completely when the moratorium expired. To the British, the 'final insult'[52] was the passing of the Johnson Act in 1934, which Roosevelt publicly supported and which forbade the US government or American banks from granting loans to any country that defaulted on its war debt.

After the Act, Britain did default – as Germany had stopped paying reparations, the British government considered the US's demand for continued payment to be unreasonable. After this, Roosevelt regarded the current British government as obstinately uncooperative, and waited for a change of administration. In any case, the domestic economic crisis was a much greater priority.

The New Deal

In his acceptance speech for presidential nomination in Chicago in July 1932, Roosevelt declared, 'I pledge you, I pledge myself, a new deal for the American people.' The press picked up on the soundbite, and the 'New Deal' was born.

Enshrined in a series of laws rapidly passed through Congress in a special session known as the 'Hundred Days', from March to June 1933, essentially the New Deal used federal money to relieve the economic and humanitarian effects of the Depression, to prop up the nation's economy and try to spend America out of recession. The British historian David Arnold explains:

> The activities of banks and the Stock Exchange were regulated. The gold standard was abandoned and the dollar devalued. Pensions and the salaries of government officials and employees were cut. An organisation was established to provide relief for the aged, the infirm, and the unemployed. Loans were given to farmers and householders to prevent foreclosures on mortgages, and financial measures were taken to restore health to the country's agriculture. The railways were reorganised. A body was set up to plan and organise the development of the Tennessee Valley. The Civilian Conservation Corps was established to provide work for a quarter of a million young men in projects such as flood control. And above all there was passed the National

71

> Industrial Recovery Act, which sought to regulate pay and
> conditions and hours of work, and which arranged for federal
> expenditure on projects such as building roads, bridges, dams,
> and airports.[53]

The New Deal marked an unprecedented encroachment of the
federal government into the lives of its citizens and over the powers
of the individual states.

Traditionally, poor relief was the responsibility of individual states;
in practice, it was usually taken on by charities or wealthy
benefactors. However, within a year the New Deal's relief agencies
were reaching 20 per cent of the population – nearly 20 million
Americans dependent on federal relief – a situation that could hardly
last forever.[54]

Such radical 'socialist' upheaval prompted many right-wingers to
wonder what was coming next, some denouncing Roosevelt as a
class traitor. Some businessmen feared this paved the way for
Communism. One Republican described the use of federal funds to
develop the poor region of Tennessee Valley as 'patterned closely
after one of the soviet [*sic*] dreams' – which Michael Simpson
acknowledges as 'not without a grain of truth'.[55] At least some of the
New Deal projects were inspired by the first of Stalin's Five Year
Plans – although Roosevelt's New Deal also strikingly echoed
Hitler's current New Plan, which harnessed state funds to stimulate
the economy and alleviate the effects of recession.

Yet as Arthur M. Schlesinger explains: 'The New Dealers, after all,
believed in capitalism. They wanted to reform the system, not
destroy it. Their social faith was in private ownership tempered by
government control.'[56] However, it did present Communists – and
ultimately Moscow – with a golden opportunity to infiltrate into the
very heart of the United States government. They weren't slow to
grasp it.

Several new agencies administered the New Deal, offering
unprecedented advancement. One such employee rapidly becomes a
key player in our story – and arguably the single most significant
figure among the Allies in the Second World War – the now barely
known, but highly influential, *éminence grise*, Harry L. Hopkins.

The 'Iowan Machiavelli'

Harry Lloyd Hopkins frequently expressed amazement that the son of an Iowan harness-maker and one-time gold-prospector should end up as not only the intimate adviser of the President of the United States but also on close terms with such monumental figures as Churchill and Stalin, and a dinner guest of King George VI.

From being Roosevelt's 'Chief Apostle' of the New Deal,[57] Hopkins became his most trusted adviser on all matters of policy, with an unprecedented degree of influence. During the war, he even became virtually co-President (some say President in all but name), from his White House base. Many of the great decisions that shaped the course of the war – and the post-war world – were taken by Roosevelt and Hopkins together.

Hopkins' friend and biographer, Hollywood screenwriter and one of Roosevelt's speech writers, Robert E. Sherwood, expresses the image of Hopkins shared by both Roosevelt's opponents and his own administration as 'a sinister figure, a backstairs intriguer, an Iowan combination of Machiavelli, Svengali and Rasputin'.[58] A more critical commentator of the Roosevelt administration, John T. Flynn, writes, 'This curious person, operating in the shadows, became, next to the President himself, the most powerful person in the United States',[59] while the important financier Bernard M. Baruch (of whom more later) wrote that 'Harry Hopkins was the Colonel House of Franklin Roosevelt's Administrations, and like House, was a trusted, tireless worker who wielded extraordinary behind-the-scenes power.'[60]

Sherwood, one of the writers of Roosevelt's historic speech in the wake of Hess's mission, revealed that it was Hopkins who specifically requested the inclusion of the declaration of a state of 'unlimited national emergency', claiming the President had asked for it. However, checking the draft, Roosevelt stopped in surprise at this passage, asking, 'Hasn't someone been taking some liberties?' But when Sherwood anxiously explained that it came from Hopkins, Roosevelt just shrugged – and kept it in.[61]

Hopkins was born in Sioux City, Iowa, in 1890. His college education (as a below-average student), in Grinnell, Iowa, opened him up to surprising influences for such a relative backwater. One of his most admired tutors was the Quaker Jesse Macy, an early convert to Darwinism, who preached a 'United States of the World' and the democratisation of all nations. Living for many years in London, Macy was an intimate of the left-wing Fabian Society.

Another important influence on the young Hopkins was Dr Edward A. Steiner, a Czechoslovakian Jewish émigré (and friend of Tolstoy's), who taught Applied Christianity – embryonic Sociology – Hopkins' only 'A'-grade subject.[62]

After graduation in 1912, it was Steiner who inspired Hopkins' career in social work for various poor relief and child welfare organisations in New York City, his rare flair for administration ensuring swift advancement. In the 1917 city elections, Hopkins supported the Socialist candidate and, as he reluctantly admitted to a Senate Committee in 1938, he was for a time a member of the Socialist Party.[63]

When America entered the First World War, he was rejected for military service because of a detached retina, instead becoming director of the Red Cross in Alabama. In 1921, he returned to New York as Executive Director of the New York Tuberculosis Association. When, as New York's governor, Roosevelt introduced unemployment measures after the Wall Street Crash, Hopkins became Chairman of his Temporary Emergency Relief Agency, a precursor of the federal New Deal agencies.

His personal life was chequered: he married Ethel Gross in 1914 and they had three sons, but in 1927 began an affair with one of his co-workers at the Tuberculosis Association, Barbara Duncan. When Ethel divorced him in 1931, he married Barbara a month later. Even his admirers disapprove of his behaviour towards his first wife, whom he left penniless to bring up their three sons.[64]

Even his own mother admitted: 'I can't make Harry out. He never tells me anything about what he's really thinking.'[65] The American historian George McJimsey sums him up as 'a wise-cracking chain-smoker who tossed off sarcastic one-liners and delivered rough judgements aimed at deflating lofty ideals and puncturing pompous egos'.[66] The usual quoted assessment is that of Joseph E. Davies, the US Ambassador to the USSR in the 1930s: 'He had the purity of St Francis of Assisi combined with the sharp shrewdness of a race-track tout.'[67]

His attitude to money – whether personal or the billions of dollars of federal funds he controlled – was bizarre. He worked for peanuts and, despite his extraordinary power, died while still of relatively modest means, seemingly indifferent to material comfort, although he also possessed a self-indulgent streak. He loved racing – placing modest bets – nightclubs and the theatre. One of his associates during his New Deal years commented, 'Hopkins was a man's man and he loved the flesh pot [sic].'[68]

Chaotic and unsavoury in dress and appearance, Hopkins was described by Dr Jacob Goldberg, Secretary of the Tuberculosis Association in the late 1920s: 'He was intense, seeming to be in a perpetual nervous ferment – a chain smoker and black-coffee drinker . . . He would wear the same shirt three or four days in a row.'[69] In 1939, during one of the frequent bouts of ill health that bedevilled Hopkins' period of greatest influence, his Mayo Clinic physician commented wryly: 'If we can get our distinguished patient to give us a little more co-operation with respect to a more hygienic mode of living this would pay big future dividends.'[70]

Even during dire illness, Hopkins remained an inveterate womaniser, his name being linked with Marguerite 'Missy' LeHand, Roosevelt's trusted and indispensable secretary, and Betsy Cushing Roosevelt, the estranged wife of Roosevelt's eldest son.[71]

The perfect career move

Implementing the New Deal was a vast undertaking, needing a skilled administrator. Roosevelt called Hopkins to Washington just two months into his presidency, putting him in charge of the Federal Emergency Relief Administration (FERA) – which Hopkins himself had persuaded him to set up to distribute New Deal funds. In his first two hours, Hopkins approved the spending of $5 million; by the time it was closed down in December 1935, FERA had spent $4 billion.[72]

In the winter of 1933–4, Hopkins persuaded FDR to initiate a massive work programme, creating four million jobs in 30 days, despite opposition from the unions. The Civil Works Administration was created, spending nearly $1 billion in its first four months.[73]

Hopkins – known to FDR affectionately as 'Harry the Hop' – became a member of the 'inner cabinet' around the President that made the real decisions. While the others changed over the years, Hopkins alone remained throughout, soon displaying 'a weakness for palace intrigue'.[74]

In summer 1934, suffering from the effects of overwork, at Roosevelt's urging Hopkins toured Europe to examine social projects in Britain, Germany, Austria and Italy. But Roosevelt also entrusted him to clandestinely evaluate the diplomats in the US Embassies.[75] This was Hopkins' first tentative foray into the world of foreign policy, a role that would consume him from the onset of the war – as Roosevelt's 'personal representative capable of bypassing the State Department and the scrutiny of Congress'.[76]

Hopkins was in Europe during the 'Night of the Long Knives' and the abortive Nazi coup in Austria. After meeting Mussolini, he wrote: 'I was not prepared for the contempt which he expressed of Hitler's murders or his stupidity.'[77] When Hitler cancelled a meeting at the last minute, Hopkins was 'rather glad'.[78] Back home, Hopkins was dismissive of the social plans he had seen in Nazi Germany, Fascist Italy and Stanley Baldwin's Britain, saying: 'It is clear that we have to do this in an American way . . . Instead of copying foreign schemes we will have to devise our own.'[79]

The mid-term elections of 1934 overwhelmingly backed the New Deal, encouraging Roosevelt to extend it. Next came the significant Worker Relief Bill, handing control of the New Deal billions directly to the White House administration – causing anxiety even among many fellow Democrats, who opposed the bill. The Works Progress (later Project) Administration was established under Hopkins' control, extending beyond assistance for factory workers and farmers to white-collar workers, even the arts. The WPA's Federal Theater Project supported John Huston and Orson Welles, while its National Youth Administration found part-time jobs for two million students, including a young Richard Nixon.

As his first term progressed, many became concerned at Roosevelt's cavalier attitude to the presidency's constitutional limits, often exploiting loopholes or using his powers in unintended ways. For example, while the Constitution allowed him to 'regulate Commerce with foreign nations and among the several states', Roosevelt used the last part to justify imposing controls on industry.[80]

New Orders

Although rarely discussed today, many of Roosevelt's measures were declared unconstitutional or illegal by the Supreme Court, such as his attempt to use taxation to regulate industries, not simply to raise revenue. In ten such cases put before the Supreme Court in 1935 and 1936, Roosevelt lost eight.[81] Even so, the New Deal was unequivocally perceived as a success by the grateful American public, and Roosevelt was re-elected for a second term in 1936 by an even bigger landslide – an all-time record popular vote of just over 60 per cent, carrying 46 of the 48 states. Because of Roosevelt's personal success, the Democrats also won large majorities in the Senate and the House.

But the straight-talking, homely Joe was losing his grip on the ordinariness he sought to personify. Michael Simpson sums up FDR's second term: 'Arrogance, deviousness, incompetence and obstinacy marked his course to defeat; the triumph of 1936 seemed to have gone to his head, and he became a "political royalist".'[82] In the early months of 1937, he attempted to take on the Supreme Court that had continually found against him in constitutional matters by trying to pack the Court with his own appointees and supporters. As even he was powerless to sack the judges, and the number was fixed at nine, he proposed to change the law to add one new judge for each existing one over the age of 70 who refused to retire – increasing the number to 15. He told the public it would inject younger blood into the Supreme Court, enabling it to catch up with its backlog – which, as critics quickly pointed out, didn't actually exist. M.J. Heale, in *Franklin D. Roosevelt: The New Deal and the War* (1999), calls it 'a flimsy case for his real objective of placing a liberal majority in the Supreme Court'.[83] Roosevelt's blatant ploy failed – although the Court hastily became noticeably pro-New Deal – and so transparent were his motives that even previously diehard supporters deserted him.

Roosevelt also tried to reorganise the government to gain more power. Eventually, after over a year's struggle, Congress also defeated these measures in March 1938 (although a watered-down version became law a year later). But the most notorious of these acts was his attempt to 'purge' the party of Senators who opposed him during the Democrats' primary elections in mid-1938, by eliminating the conservative wing of the party. This turned into 'an embarrassment', a 'disaster'.[84] Yet the real force behind the attempted purge was Harry Hopkins, who assembled a group – including James Roosevelt – to organise the replacement of conservatives and 'obstructionists' with liberals as they came up for re-election. This 'Elimination Committee', as it was dubbed, was intended not only to shift the Democrats to the left, but to keep a tighter rein on party discipline and control the nomination of the 1940 presidential candidate.[85] This was convenient for Hopkins – who was to be that candidate.[86]

However, his personal life was going badly: his second wife, Barbara, died of cancer in October 1937. Then stomach cancer struck him. Two-thirds of his stomach was successfully removed, although he remained seriously ill for the rest of his life.

In December 1938, Roosevelt appointed Hopkins Secretary of Commerce – his only official government post – the first step towards nomination in 1940.[87] However, although FDR had begun to groom Hopkins as his successor during his second term, another bout of severe illness spelt the end of the latter's presidential ambitions. Trusting nobody else, FDR defied convention, going for a third term. Nevertheless, it seems that he regarded Hopkins as the 'rightful' President, cheated out of office by ill health, and allowed him unprecedented influence over some of the most important decisions ever made by a head of state. Effectively, Hopkins was the real, but unelected, President of the war years.

Where democracy and accountability are concerned, surely this is dubious enough. But there is another reason to scrutinise Hopkins' influence over Roosevelt and the Allied war effort. There is now considerable evidence that Hopkins harboured a dark secret: that he was, all along, a Soviet agent.

Soviet spies at the White House

New Deal 'socialism' was attacked by the right, and Roosevelt labelled as a crypto-Communist. During his second-term campaign, the Republicans even claimed his administration was under Communist control. By 1938, when Republican fortunes revived, the House of Representatives created its Committee for the Investigation of Un-American Activities, later notorious for over-zealousness in the post-war McCarthyite period. Originally set up to investigate Communist influence on New Deal agencies, as their 'Chief Apostle', Hopkins was singled out. In 1938, the Chairman of the Committee, Martin Dies, denounced him, along with others in FDR's administration, as 'Communists and fellow travellers'.[88]

The accusations reached as far as the First Lady – perhaps with some justification. Deeply involved in social issues, Eleanor Roosevelt's policies were distinctly left-wing, including her patronage of the American Youth Congress, whose members and leadership openly included Communists. On the other hand, she always maintained that the social benefits of the New Deal would *prevent* Communism taking hold in America, by removing the causes of discontent that nourished it, roundly denouncing US Communist Party leaders as unpatriotic.[89]

Although extreme-right Republicans would automatically regard anyone with liberal views as 'Bolshevik', it is still true that the New Deal agencies drew their employees from those with social welfare experience, who tended to be from the left. Because of such criticisms, Roosevelt felt it necessary to declare: 'I have not sought, I do not seek, I repudiate the support of any advocate of Communism or any other alien "ism" which would by fair means or foul change our American democracy.'[90] As he later addressed a Youth Rally in February 1940:

> More than twenty years ago, while most of you were very young children, I had the utmost sympathy for the Russian people. In the early days of Communism, I recognised that many leaders in Russia were bringing education and better health and, above all, better opportunity to millions who had been kept in ignorance and serfdom under the imperial régime. I disliked the regimentation under Communism. I abhorred the indiscriminate killings of thousands of innocent victims . . .
>
> I, with many of you, hoped that Russia would work out its own problems, and that its government would eventually become a peace-loving, popular government with a free ballot, which would not interfere with the integrity of its neighbours.

Friendly Fire

That hope is today either shattered or put away in storage
against some better day.[91]

During Roosevelt's presidency, Communist membership in America
rose from 10,000 to perhaps as many as 100,000 by the end of the
war – not many, given America's population. But the tiny number of
'reds' were outstripped by far more 'pinks', and many left-wing
organisations or pressure groups, while numbering just a few
committed party members, came directly under Communist control
– and, ultimately, that of Moscow. Known Communists, or those
closely affiliated, even had regular access to the White House.[92]

Seeking to put extra pressure on Japan, Roosevelt's policy of
cooperation with the USSR also meant his administration was
dominated by pro-Soviets – in turn also facilitating Communist and
Soviet penetration. As A.J.P. Taylor notes, 'more Communists were
to be found in the State Department than in the Ford automobile
works, if anyone had looked for them'.[93]

Although in the post-war world we are used to the idea that British
intelligence organisations were the most thoroughly penetrated by
the Soviet Union – through notorious figures such as Philby, Burgess,
Maclean and Blunt – before the war it was *American* government
institutions that were riddled with Russian spies. By the mid-1930s,
Soviet intelligence had only managed to infiltrate one British
government ministry, whereas in Washington its agents had
footholds throughout the Roosevelt administration – despite the fact
that Moscow considered the US government a much less important
target than the British.[94]

One fellow traveller who saw the Nazi–Soviet Pact as an act of
betrayal was the American journalist Whittaker Chambers.
Although working for Soviet intelligence since the early 1930s, he
was increasingly disenchanted with Stalin's regime. After training in
Moscow in 1933, he had recruited a ten-strong cell of Communist
agents in several government departments, which was in contact with
the Comintern, and – through himself – the Fourth Department, the
Soviet military intelligence organisation. The day after the German
invasion of Poland, Chambers confessed all to Adolf Berle, who was
both Assistant Secretary of State and Roosevelt's adviser on internal

security, naming members of his cell and other contacts – some 30 spies.[95]

Some names should have rung alarm bells – especially Alger Hiss and Harry Dexter White, then important in government departments. Hiss (codename 'Ales') worked his way up from the Department of Agriculture to the Justice Department, finally becoming a political adviser in the State Department's Far Eastern Division. He also served on the Nye Committee that formulated America's neutrality legislation. Harry Dexter White was an economist in the Treasury Department who advised on monetary policy to the Treasury Secretary, Henry Morgenthau, and who had an enormous influence over the post-war global economy. Chambers stated that Hiss was the USSR's 'number one source' in the State Department and White the number one source in the Treasury.[96] Adolf Berle, for – in the words of intelligence historian and former CIA officer Hayden B. Peake – 'reasons he never explained satisfactorily',[97] failed to bring Chambers' confession to the attention of the FBI or the State or War departments. But he did report it to Roosevelt, who, astoundingly, 'was not interested. He seems simply to have dismissed the whole idea of espionage within his administration as absurd',[98] which suggests that Berle failed to report the matter to the relevant agencies because the President told him not to.

Chambers' confession was no secret in Washington's top political circles: others, including William Bullitt and labour leader David Dubinsky, also brought it to Roosevelt's attention and were utterly amazed when he just waved it aside. It was fully two years later that Berle investigated Alger Hiss – only to dismiss the allegations on the advice of those in Roosevelt's administration who considered him beyond reproach. The FBI finally requested a copy of Chambers' confession in 1943. Even then, Roosevelt allowed Hiss and White to advance in their influential careers unhindered, enormously influencing the Second World War and even the shaping of the post-war world.

Chambers' cell was one of many run by the Fourth Department and the NKVD. Other Soviet agents included Laughlin Currie, an economic adviser to Roosevelt, and Duncan Chaplain Lee, Personal

Assistant to 'Wild Bill' Donovan, head of America's wartime intelligence organisation, the Office of Strategic Services (OSS).[99] By America's entry into the war in December 1941, the NKVD controlled ten senior officials in Roosevelt's administration.[100] By 1943 (with the USSR an ally, cooperation was even greater), Soviet intelligence had penetrated every major branch of the Roosevelt administration.[101]

Remarkably, the only one of this important group of spies who was ever prosecuted was Alger Hiss – and even then not for treason or espionage. Although named as a Soviet agent by the Un-American Activities Committee, as the statute of limitations had expired he could no longer be charged with treason, only with perjury. After two trials, he was sentenced to five years' imprisonment, of which he served four. (The senator who hit the headlines by leading the case against him was Richard Nixon.)

Of course, this is astounding: the President of the United States deliberately blocking investigation into alleged traitors to America. But why? Was it – as most historians have assumed – because he was so arrogant he simply could not comprehend that the Russians could penetrate his administration? (Whittaker Chambers commented to the intelligence writer Ralph de Toledano in 1951: 'We cannot possibly begin to write the history of our time until the simple fact is recognised that Franklin Roosevelt was an extraordinarily stupid man.'[102]) Was he taking advice from other trusted aides, also under Soviet control? Or did he even know and approve of these people passing information to Moscow for his own complicated agenda?

Questions have even been asked about the ultimate loyalties of Eleanor Roosevelt. Although cynics suggest her left-wing sympathies were a front to win the 'pink vote' for her husband, the First Lady was closely associated with individuals known to have been under Moscow's control, potentially enabling the Russians to influence both her and even the President. For example, Anna Louise Strong, with whom she and the President lunched at the White House, has been described as an 'indefatigable propagandist for Soviet Communism'.[103]

Eleanor – and through her, FDR – also maintained a discreet channel of communication with the leader of the Communist Party

of the USA, Earl Browder.[104] He would write to the artist Josephine
Truslow Adams (a descendant of President John Adams), who
included his comments in letters to Eleanor, who in turn would show
them to her husband. This channel appears to have been opened in
late 1943 (after Browder's release from prison for passport fraud, a
sentence that Roosevelt had reduced by executive order), FDR
asking Eleanor to show him all of Josephine Adams' letters. Some of
the correspondence makes extraordinary reading.

On 28 August 1939 – just five days after the signing of the
Nazi–Soviet Pact – Eleanor wrote to Strong denouncing Stalin's
action but including the remark, 'Of course, it seems quite possible
that there may be in addition to this some secret agreement by which
Russia will take her share of any particular country she is interested
in controlling.'[105] As we now know, there *was* such a secret protocol,
in which Stalin and Hitler agreed to carve up Poland between them,
and that Germany would not interfere with Soviet efforts to annex
the Baltic states.

Could intelligence have reached the White House about the secret
protocol? If so, what was the First Lady doing mentioning it in her
letter to a known contact of Moscow? Was she possibly trying to tip
off Stalin that his secret was out? Or, given FDR's close interest in
her letters to Communists, did he ask her to include it, using her as
a 'back-channel' contact to Stalin, passing information unofficially to
him? Did the President want Stalin to know that Washington was
aware of his game, without using official channels? But surely this
was terribly risky. If it came out, it might be asked why, if they knew
about the secret protocol, didn't the Roosevelts expose it?

But even if Eleanor Roosevelt was a Communist agent, her
influence over her husband was by that time minimal; much more
serious is the suggestion that someone with a considerably greater
hold over Roosevelt was working for the Kremlin – Harry Hopkins.

This bombshell was dropped by KGB Colonel Oleg Gordievsky,
who defected to the West in 1985. The ramifications are so
astounding that Western historians have been in denial, reluctant
even to consider them, precisely because of how it would change the
neatly set-in-stone history of the Second World War and the origins
of the Cold War. Not only did Hopkins know all the secrets of the

US government, but during the war he also earned Churchill's trust, influencing many key decisions made individually and jointly by the President and Prime Minister. Hopkins personally controlled wartime supplies from the USA to the USSR, also playing a vital role in decisions affecting the post-war balance of power between East and West. If Hopkins was passing information to the USSR, and influencing Roosevelt and Churchill on Moscow's orders, nothing less than a wholesale rewriting of key aspects of twentieth-century history would be called for. But what is the evidence?

Not long after joining the KGB in 1962, Gordievsky attended a lecture by Iskhak Akhmerov, head of NKVD operations in the US during the 1930s and 1940s, and Alger Hiss's controller. Momentously, the subject of his talk was Harry Hopkins, 'the most important of all Soviet war-time agents in the United States'.[106] But was Hopkins knowingly an NKVD or GRU agent, or – as Gordievsky came to believe – an unwitting agent, an 'agent of influence', through over-enthusiasm, naivety or being cleverly played by Soviet agents, revealing sensitive information or influencing the Allies' war effort in Russia's favour? Given Hopkins' position, even this would be bad enough.

Most intelligence historians have since accepted Hopkins as an agent of influence, although usually more out of fear of examining the implications of his being a conscious agent than because of the evidence. On the other hand, political and diplomatic historians have ignored this new information completely. As United States Air Force historian Eduard Mark points out, since Gordievsky's revelation, not one of the publications about Hopkins or US foreign policy has taken it into account.[107] But if Hopkins was a Russian spy, it changes everything.

In fact, while not absolutely conclusive, the evidence points to his being an out-and-out red-dyed-in-the-wool conscious agent. Although Hopkins and Akhmerov had occasional meetings, we only know about them from the latter; there are no references to them in Hopkins' papers.[108] If he had no idea that Akhmerov was an NKVD agent, why keep silent about him? On the other hand, if he did know, why did he meet him?

Other activities of Hopkins are also suspicious. KGB files that reached the West in the late 1990s reveal that in 1943, Hopkins tipped off the Soviet Ambassador that one of his officials had been seen passing money to a Communist underground leader in California, having learned of this from FBI chief J. Edgar Hoover.[109] It really is difficult to see this as anything other than a treasonable act to warn Soviet intelligence that the FBI was onto them.

Other compelling evidence of Hopkins' value to Stalin comes from the famous 'Venona intercepts'. It was not until 1996 that the US National Security Agency (NSA) finally declassified these wartime cables to and from Soviet intelligence networks in the United States, intercepted by US intelligence. One was dated 29 May 1943, during the important Trident Conference in Washington, at which Roosevelt and Churchill decided to defer a cross-Channel invasion – an issue of paramount importance for Stalin – in favour of a campaign in Sicily. The message was sent to Moscow by agent 'Mer' ('Mayor'), almost certainly Akhmerov. Mer informs Moscow that he learned from a high-level contact at the conference – 'source 19' – about this decision. '19' also supplied details of the debate that led to the decision, including those who supported the idea and who opposed it – all vital information for Stalin.

In the journal *Intelligence and National Security* in 1998, Eduard Mark analysed the cable minutely, comparing its information about '19' to the movements of all the delegates of the Trident Conference: demonstrably the information could only have come from Harry Hopkins. This is hard to reconcile with a mere 'agent of influence': after all, '19' immediately passed on to Akhmerov the most important details of the conference. He knew what he was doing.

However, there is another possibility: was Roosevelt using Hopkins as a back channel to Stalin? In this scenario, Hopkins knew full well that Akhmerov was an NKVD agent, but he passed information that Roosevelt *wanted* to reach Stalin. Hopkins' 1943 tip-off may have been because Roosevelt had no wish for a spy scandal to blow up in America while the USSR and USA were on the same side against Germany, and considered that an off-the-record warning from his right-hand man would be more effective than official action.

If so, then this raises important questions about the President's relationships with the Soviet leader and his Western Allies. Why did

FDR want Stalin informed not only of Trident's decisions (which he would learn officially from Roosevelt six days later[110]) but also – behind Churchill's back – who supported and who opposed his strategy?

There are two possibilities: Hopkins was a knowing agent of the Fourth Department or NKVD[111] – a traitor passing on his nation's most sensitive secrets, presumably as a former Socialist, for ideological reasons. Or he acted as a back channel to Stalin, and his dealings with Moscow were sanctioned by Roosevelt. Although most historians avoid the question completely, knowing which possibility is correct is vitally important for understanding the relationships between the Allied leaders. Therefore, as our story unfolds, Hopkins will remain in the spotlight as we search for clues to enable us to answer this question, which becomes all the more important because as war loomed he entered the period of his greatest influence over Roosevelt, the United States – and, indeed, the world.

.

CHAPTER FOUR

War

'Although no subsequent political action can condone wrong deeds, history is replete with examples of men who have risen to power by employing stern, grim, and even frightful methods, but who, nevertheless, have been regarded as great figures whose lives have enriched the story of mankind. So may it be with Hitler.'

Winston S. Churchill, 1935[1]

On 12 September 1938, Roosevelt and Harry Hopkins sat in the presidential train at Rochester, listening intently to Hitler's broadcast from that year's Nuremberg rally, in which he demanded the return of the German-speaking part of Czechoslovakia, the Sudetenland. If not handed over immediately, it would be taken by force.

Hitler was out to provoke. Under the Treaty of Versailles, the Germans were specifically forbidden a military presence in the important strategic area of the Rhineland, to prevent them defending themselves in the future. When Hitler tested the former Allies by seizing control in March 1936, neither the British nor French did anything more than protest. More significantly, his *Anschluss* – the enforced union of Germany and Austria (opposed by the Austrian government but supported by most of its people) – of March 1938 was by no means greeted with howls of horror. But Hitler's demand for the restoration of the Sudetenland was different: the area was a part of the Republic of Czechoslovakia, another sovereign nation. The ensuing crisis sent panic flooding across Europe.

On that train, the German-speaking Roosevelt understood Hitler's broadcast very well – and immediately despatched Hopkins to carry out a secret survey of the aircraft industry to assess its capability for war production.[2] Hopkins was also tasked to find a way of diverting New Deal funds to build factories and aircraft, channelled through his Works Progress Administration.[3] Accompanied on his tour of the west-coast aircraft factories by local WPA Director Colonel Conolly, in his final report – drafted by the liaison officer between the Army General Staff and the WPA, Colonel Arthur Wilson – Hopkins proposed building eight to ten factories in areas of high unemployment.[4]

Obviously at that point nobody had a clear idea of how many – if *any* – planes might be needed. (By the time Hopkins finished his survey, the Czechoslovakian crisis had passed, following the false reassurance of the Munich Agreement, giving Hitler what he wanted without a shot being fired.) Therefore, Hopkins' recommendations must have been based on another factor. Clearly, rather than asking: 'This is what Britain and France need; how can we supply it?' he was actually thinking: 'This is how much we can supply; how can we make sure they need it?'

And what Roosevelt and Hopkins were planning was, in fact, illegal: the original New Deal legislation had specifically prohibited using the funds for military purposes. Hopkins' report even tacitly admitted as much, advocating using New Deal funds from the next relief bill for armaments and aircraft industries 'without regard to the present rules'.[5] There was, in fact, already a considerable tie-up between Hopkins' WPA and the military – for example, army engineers often managed the WPA's civil engineering projects. In order to sidestep Congress, New Deal workers were used on projects that – while not strictly military – had strategic importance, such as building airports, army training centres, docks and bridges.[6]

War

Before the war, apart from its navy, the United States' armed forces were relatively tiny; in 1939 the army was 19th in terms of manpower – behind Belgium and Greece.[7] Accordingly, the budget allocated by Congress was small, and so the funds diverted by stealth from the New Deal were particularly important – indeed, they effectively doubled the War Department's annual budget.[8]

More New Deal funds were clandestinely switched to military projects shortly after the Czechoslovakian crisis, when Hopkins had a meeting with the US Army's Deputy Chief of Staff, Brigadier-General George C. Marshall. After the war, Colonel Wilson wrote:

> You may know that after his meeting with Harry Hopkins several millions of dollars of W.P.A. funds were transferred (secretly) to start making machine tools for the manufacture of small-arms ammunition. This was before Hitler declared war in Europe; and this one move put the production of small-arms ammunition at least a year ahead when England went into the war and started to place orders in this country for the manufacture of small-arms ammunition.[9]

In 1939 – on Hopkins' recommendation – Marshall was appointed Chief of Staff for the duration of the war. Until at least 1942, Marshall's channel of communication with the White House was Hopkins.[10]

Once again, however, the legend of FDR dazzles. Even though his actions were illegal, he has been forgiven because the outcome was favourable. Roosevelt's supporters, such as Robert Sherwood, even praise his farsightedness as the only statesman to recognise even in 1938 that a German war was inevitable. And wasn't he marvellous to crank up US war production to meet the challenge – even if it meant breaking the law?

According to his apologists, FDR's use of New Deal money to boost defence production was a ruse: while pretending his primary concern was unemployment and the economy, his *real* motive was defeating Nazism; using New Deal funds was merely a convenient way of hiding his plan from the isolationists in Congress. Ironically, although Roosevelt consistently told Congress he was primarily motivated by economic considerations, history claims he was really driven by idealism. In other words, the preferred option today is that FDR was *lying*! However, when it is realised exactly how precarious a state the American economy was in at that time, it becomes apparent that he was telling the unvarnished truth.

Midway through Roosevelt's second term, the New Deal began to run out of steam – there was only so much money for so many bottomless relief programmes. Despite a steady global recovery from the 1929 crash, the second half of 1937 saw America sliding back into recession. Again, the consequences looked serious for the rest of the world.

The 'Roosevelt Recession' was largely the President's own fault. In the summer of 1937, in an attempt to balance the budget, he slashed federal expenditure, expecting business to fill the gap. It didn't, resulting in an economic downturn that began in August, then 19 October's 'Black Tuesday' saw an even worse Stock Market crash than 1929. By the spring of 1938, unemployment had shot up again by 4 million to 11 million, and to around 20 per cent of the workforce in 1939.[11]

As the recession began to bite during the winter of 1937–8, Roosevelt indecisively adopted a policy of 'fiscal conservatism' – the very opposite of the New Deal. Significantly, this coincided with Hopkins being out of action following his cancer operation; as soon as he had recovered, he persuaded Roosevelt to reverse his 'conservative aberration' and return to the principles of the New Deal.[12] A second big fall on the stock market in March 1938 persuaded FDR to take Hopkins' advice. This meant continuing to use federal funds to spend the country out of recession – like a desperate gambler throwing good money after bad. But what could the government spend money on now?

Historians generally agree that the American economy was rescued by the Second World War; as Michael Simpson, for example, writes:

> If the acid test of anti-depression policies is the extent to which they reduce unemployment, then the New Deal rates five marks out of ten; almost eighteen million were jobless in 1933,

and nine million were still unemployed in 1939. Moreover, at any given time, the New Deal assisted only a third of the workless, while, as thousands of blacks, senior citizens and sharecroppers could testify, the 'forgotten man' often remained forgotten. Other economic indicators recorded better gains, but the economy as a whole remained sluggish until rescued by war.[13]

John T. Flynn puts it more colourfully:

> Here now was a gift from the gods – and from the gods of war at that. Here was the chance to spend. Here now was something the federal government could really spend money on – military and naval preparations.[14]

Although the link between war and recovery is usually ascribed to luck, perhaps there was more to it than that. In *The Roosevelt Myth*, Flynn describes his conversation in January 1938 with one of Roosevelt's 'most intimate advisers' (almost certainly Hopkins):

> I asked him if the President knew that we were in a depression. He said that of course he did. I asked what the President proposed to do. He answered: 'Resume spending.' I then suggested he would find difficulty in getting objects on which the federal government could spend. He said he knew that. What then, I asked, will the President spend on? He laughed and replied in a single word: 'Battleships.' I asked why. He said: 'You know we are going to have a war.' And when I asked whom we were going to fight, he said 'Japan' and when I asked where and what about, he said 'in South America.' 'Well,' I said, 'you are moving logically there. If your only hope is spending and the only thing you have to spend on is national defense, then you have got to have an enemy to defend against and a war in prospect.'[15]

More recently, another critic, Robert Shogan, writes: 'The cause of freedom, intertwined with patriotism, could serve as surrogate for the domestic goals of the early New Deal and kindle the intellectual and emotional spark needed to revitalize his presidency.'[16]

Given Roosevelt's and Hopkins' diversion of New Deal money into arms production, it is hard to disagree that this was no accident. Ironically, Hopkins' inspiration originated in a conversation with German embassy official Rudolf Leitner, who explained how Hitler had solved two problems by using the unemployed to build military facilities and armaments.[17]

Although Flynn's conversation, at the beginning of 1938, related to Japan, as the year unfolded a European war offered a new possibility – which had the added advantage of halting the growing threat to American trade and investment posed by Britain's system of imperial preference and a resurgent Germany.

Roosevelt and many in his administration believed that Britain and Germany had 'a propensity to get together to the detriment of the United States'.[18] Roosevelt also thought that Neville Chamberlain was trying to secure Anglo-German agreements specifically to exclude the US from Europe, Africa and South America, and Sumner Welles saw a real danger of an Anglo-German economic coalition, a fear shared by FDR's leading adviser on foreign policy, William Bullitt.[19] As British political analyst Robert Shepherd writes: 'The British were suspicious of American isolationism, while the Americans were suspicious that Britain's imperial interests might lead her to make an economic agreement with Germany.'[20] FDR said to his son Elliott on the eve of the first wartime summit with Winston Churchill in August 1941:

> The British Empire is at stake here. It's something that's not generally known, but British bankers and German bankers have had world trade pretty well sewn up in their pockets for a long time. Despite the fact that Germany lost, in the last war. Well, now, that's not so good for American trade, is it? If in the past German and British interests have operated to exclude us from world trade, kept our merchant shipping down, closed us out of this or that market, and now Germany and Britain are at war, what should we do?[21]

Post-war historians on both sides of the Atlantic, while acknowledging that Roosevelt and his key advisers *feared* the Anglo-German threat, hastily point out that such fears were 'baloney'.[22] However, as has been mentioned, there *was* a concerted move, adopted as policy by the Bank of England, for economic cooperation between the two nations – and in any case, the Americans' *belief* in such cooperation would have influenced their decisions.

A 'closed shop' British Empire and Anglo-German collaboration would have spelt disaster for the US, especially as America teetered on the brink of a new depression. According to Flynn, at the beginning of 1938 Roosevelt was banking on propping up the economy with a Japanese war – but not one fought on US soil. By September, however, Hitler was creating a less risky alternative: a far away war that need not involve the US at all, while offering the same opportunities for supplying the warring sides – if they could get round the Neutrality Act. Roosevelt would have something else to spend New Deal money on, and a new market for American arms.

It was risky: if such a war didn't happen they could be stuck with warehouses full of unwanted goods – facing financial ruin. As the crisis over Czechoslovakia abated after the now-infamous Munich Agreement, America seemed to be staring downfall in the face. What would they do with all that ammunition and those shiny new planes if the European war failed to materialise?

Fanning the flames

Unquestionably, Roosevelt lied, cheated and deceived during the preliminary sabre-rattling and the first two years of the Second World War, especially to circumvent the law to supply war material to Britain and France. In any other circumstances, he would have been impeached: he abused the office of President, flouted both law and constitution – and deliberately misrepresented the facts to Congress and the American people. He also encouraged Britain and France to take up arms against Hitler and, once the war in Europe had ignited, did his utmost to ensure it continued. Surprisingly, no contemporary historian of Roosevelt's foreign policy – British or American – would dispute any of that: the only outstanding questions concern his motive and aims.

Roosevelt and his supporters have always claimed he acted for moral reasons – which has become the generally accepted view. He wanted to rid the world of Nazism and Japanese imperialism, even if it meant betraying his oath of office: if an isolationist Congress refused to allow him to support those who stood up to the aggressors, he would do it anyway, because it was right. History has largely forgiven him his transgressions because he was vindicated. To many, FDR is even more of a hero by risking personal disgrace for the greater good – although surely it is ironic when an American head of state defends democracy by adopting some of the methods of the dictator. Others are more cynical: never mind principles, he simply wrapped himself in the stars and stripes in order to save the American economy and, along with it, his own skin as President.

But what were FDR's aims, beyond supplying Britain and France with weapons? Some argue that he ultimately wanted to let the British and French do the fighting, as an extension of his policy of 'defence at a distance': to 'contain Hitler by proxy',[23] using American weapons but non-American combatants. It was only when Japan joined the fray that it proved impossible for him to keep the US out of direct involvement. Others, including Flynn, Shogan and the American historian Charles Callan Tansill, believe that FDR always wanted America in the war, but he had to move stealthily to win the support of Congress and the public; discouraging the European Allies from making an early peace was intended to keep the enemy at bay until he could achieve this.

The most cynical motive and most self-serving aim ascribed to Roosevelt is that he sought to save the American economy, the New Deal, his presidency and his place in history by supplying Britain and France with US-made war material, while keeping out of the war altogether. He did this not only to rescue the American economy but also to make America rich and all-powerful. Indeed, by 1945 production had trebled and the USA was the most affluent country on earth. But its emergence from war as a fabulously rich superpower was only partly due to a stimulated industry: the war had also wiped out its competitors, particularly Germany and the British Empire.

Most researchers agree that, for whatever reason, Roosevelt

wanted the European war to start and then to continue until there was a clear victory – not a compromise peace. During the crises of 1938 and 1939, while contributing little to peace initiatives, in secret the President encouraged the British and the French to take a tough line with Hitler, even if it meant war.

Roosevelt's pro-war stance emphatically marked a complete policy reversal: when the first war clouds gathered in Europe in 1935 he was anxious because it might 'threaten the recovery of America and all that he was trying to do through the New Deal'.[24] However, by 1938 he was in favour of the war. What had changed? Perhaps having foreseen the inevitable showdown with Germany, he thought it best to get stuck in as soon as possible. However, there is another explanation for the volte-face: after the new Depression of 1937–8, war in Europe was more likely to benefit, rather than harm, the US economy.

Post-war mythology has it that the Neutrality Acts, which hampered Roosevelt's efforts to aid Britain and delayed America's entry into the war, were forced upon him by an isolationist Congress. Roosevelt and Hopkins' great supporter Robert Sherwood wrote that FDR signed the legislation 'with reluctance'[25] (although Roosevelt took the credit for it in his 1940 election campaign[26]). Yet, during his first term he actively supported the isolationists and actually *initiated* the first Neutrality Act – a classic example of FDR changing his spots then convincing posterity he had been wearing the new ones all the time.[27]

Britain, particularly, regards the Neutrality Acts as evidence of America's naive and knee-jerk parochialism between the wars. In fact, they were not a manifestation of Americans not giving a damn about the outside world but rather the opposite. Many were appalled at the profits reaped by US companies and banks from the carnage of the First World War, and there was a widespread suspicion that American arms manufacturers and bankers had been responsible for involvement in a war they may even have incited. Americans were determined it should never happen again.[28]

As a result of public pressure, in April 1934 the Senate approved Republican Senator Gerald P. Nye's Special Senate Committee Investigating the Munitions Industry, the 'Nye Committee'.

Roosevelt urged the Senate to grant the Committee adequate funds and made no attempt to influence it in any way.[29] It found that US businesses had indeed profited from the war (some by 800 per cent between 1916 and 1917) but not that they had incited it. But even the scale of profits shocked the American public, who felt such profiteering was immoral.[30]

The first suggestion to the Committee that American neutrality in future wars should be enshrined in law came from Roosevelt himself, in March 1935.[31] Flynn, an adviser to the Committee, writes:

> Yet for years writers dealing with this subject have referred to the Neutrality Acts as if they were something that had been imposed on the President against his better judgement and for the purpose of hamstringing him in the conduct of foreign affairs. The whole policy of the Neutrality Acts has been referred to as the 'neutrality blunder' as if it were the blunder of the President's critics instead of one in which he had not only shared but which he had actually initiated.[32]

Although Roosevelt asked for the discretion to impose an arms embargo on aggressors, Congress modified the bill, taking the decision away from him and stipulating that the President *must* declare an embargo on all countries involved in a war. On the other hand, he had wanted the authority to embargo all trade, not just armaments – going further than most isolationists. Congress refused. Then, in December 1936, Roosevelt announced that he would ask for *permanent* neutrality legislation in the New Year session of Congress (the existing laws having to be renewed annually), although in the event pushing through the embargo on Spain became a higher priority.[33]

The first test of the Neutrality Act came with the Italian invasion of Abyssinia (now Ethiopia) at the beginning of October 1935. As required, Roosevelt imposed an immediate arms embargo on Italy. However, as the Act failed to cover the supply of materials needed for war but not actually armaments, such as oil, coal and metals, American companies could continue to supply these. Accordingly, the Act was amended in February 1936: American companies, including banks, were banned from supplying anything to countries at war. (However, the amendment specifically exempted other American republics; clearly, Congress wanted the US to reserve the right to supply warring countries – excluding the British dominion Canada and European possessions in Central and South America – but only on the American continent. Isolationism should not be confused with pacifism.)

It was only after the 'Roosevelt recession' of 1937–8 that FDR tried to circumvent, rather than increase, the curbs on American trade. He had implemented the required embargo against Italy in 1935, and Spain during its Civil War in 1936 – even though as a civil war it was outside the Act and he had to ask Congress to pass a special law.[34] This was not the result of pressure by isolationists, but a policy 'deliberately initiated' by the President.[35] (Because denying arms to the Spanish government worked to the benefit of the rebels, the victorious dictator Franco declared it 'a gesture we Nationalists will never forget'.[36])

Meanwhile, in autumn 1937, war once again erupted between Japan and China. Since the armistice five years before, tensions had simmered away in Japanese-controlled Manchuria, with sporadic fighting after provocation, real or imagined, by both sides. In July 1937, hostilities near Peking spread to many other areas (against the wishes of the governments and military commanders on both sides, neither being ready for open conflict). At the end of August, the Japanese gave up trying to contain the situation and poured forces into China. On 13 December, the Chinese capital fell, the ensuing 'Rape of Nanking' – the Japanese conscripts' orgy of massacres, torture and rape – leaving between 100,000 and a quarter of a million Chinese dead. Japanese officers elsewhere wept openly at the news. By January 1938, some three-quarters of a million Chinese soldiers had been killed against about 50,000 Japanese. Although the fighting segued into the Second World War, by winter 1938 there was an uneasy hiatus, if only because Japan considered the remaining areas of China not worth conquering.

Roosevelt argued that as neither side had formally declared war, he was under no obligation to apply the Neutrality Act embargo (in fact, the Act simply stipulated that a state of war had to exist) and

American companies continued to trade with both China and Japan. This is normally excused as Roosevelt showing 'back-door' support for China against Japanese aggression. However, in 1938, after he declined to invoke the embargo, the US exported roughly equal amounts of arms and equipment to both sides. And, if Roosevelt *had* declared an embargo, Japan would have been the loser, its ability to wage war in China severely, perhaps terminally, restricted.[37]

The only difference between Roosevelt's over-zealous application of the Act in relation to Spain in 1936 and his sophistry at the end of 1937 was that America had started to slide into a new depression. As soon as the recession began to bite, he made much more of foreign policy and the possibility of war, as in his famous speech in Chicago on 5 October 1937 in which he suggested that the 'peace-loving nations' should 'quarantine' belligerent countries – a marked change from isolationism. Perhaps he wanted to test public reaction to the idea of greater American involvement in international affairs. Most reactions were hostile.[38]

The Chicago speech represented a tentative suggestion that the United States might become involved in wars outside the 'Monroe Doctrine' area. 'Quarantine' clearly meant sanctions, backed up by military blockade – but at the same time Roosevelt refused to invoke them against Japan. On the very day of the speech, Sumner Welles officially informed the British that the USA had no intention of intervening militarily in the Sino-Japanese conflict.[39]

Public versus private

Roosevelt's public and private attitudes to the looming war in Europe were very different.

During the Czechoslovakia crisis, President Edvard Beneš asked Roosevelt to publicly urge Britain and France to support his nation. Although FDR suggested to Hitler holding a conference of the relevant nations in a neutral country, he also assured him that 'The Government of the United States has no political involvement in Europe, and will assume no obligations in the conduct of the present negotiations'[40] – almost the opposite to Beneš's actual request. The day afterwards, when he learned that Chamberlain was to go to Munich, FDR ambiguously cabled him: 'Good man.'[41]

Chamberlain's flight infamously resulted in the Munich Agreement that gave Hitler the Czechoslovakian territory he wanted. But six months later, the Führer reneged and the Nazis took over the whole of Czechoslovakia. Hitler justified this by Slovakia's 'volunteering' to become a German protectorate following the post-division implosion of Czechoslovakia, while Chamberlain and French Prime Minister Edouard Daladier argued that since Czechoslovakia no longer existed as a sovereign nation, their guarantee to protect it no longer applied.

Surrendering to public opinion, Roosevelt asked Hitler and Mussolini to guarantee they harboured no aggressive intentions towards any of 31 named states, although he admitted the chances of this defusing the tension were slim. But his effort simply to 'put the dictators on the spot' descended into farce, even presenting the Nazis with a propaganda coup. When von Ribbentrop innocently asked each of the nations if they felt threatened by Germany, unsurprisingly none said they did (powerful nations being too proud to admit it, weak nations too scared). The Germans and Italians also mocked the Americans for asking countries under British and French control and including the Irish Republic as part of the United Kingdom. Mussolini commented that Roosevelt 'is not very well up on his geography'.[42]

In the last days of peace, Chamberlain asked Roosevelt to put pressure on the Polish government to settle with Germany. From Paris, William Bullitt (then Ambassador to France) urged the same. However, FDR contented himself with simply urging Hitler, Poland's President Ignacy Moszczynski and King Victor Emmanuel III of Italy to try to find a peaceful solution through direct negotiation.[43]

From London, Ambassador Kennedy cabled Roosevelt a week after the declaration of war suggesting he mediate between Britain and Germany, following a meeting with George VI, Queen Elizabeth and Sir Samuel Hoare, then the Lord Privy Seal and a leading figure in the anti-war movement. Hoare anticipated that Hitler would seek peace after conquering Poland, arguing that Britain should accept because of the economic ruin war would bring, win or lose. Four hours later, Cordell Hull responded, 'The President desires me to inform you . . . that this Government, so long as present European conditions continue, sees no opportunity or occasion for any peace moves to be initiated by the President of the United States.'[44]

Clearly, Roosevelt's few intercessions in 1938 and 1939 were at best half-hearted. He himself explained privately they were only intended to establish Hitler and Mussolini as the aggressors by not responding favourably to his overtures – but of course they equally put *him* on record as the putative peacemaker, even though the wording of his proposals ensured they would be refused.

The result can be seen in Hitler's changing attitude to the USA in the year between the Czech and Polish crises. During the first, he was very concerned about America's reaction: would it throw its weight behind Britain? Would it simply flex its immense financial muscle (bad enough for Germany) or would it commit militarily? But in summer 1939, he felt safe in ignoring the USA, apparently certain that America would refuse to aid Britain and France.[45] What had made him so sure?

This sea change in Hitler's attitude is generally explained by the mixed signals from Washington during 1939, and isolationist successes in Congress – yet the Neutrality Act was in force, and Congress just as isolationist, a year earlier. (In fact, the Act of 1938 was *tighter* than in September 1939, as Roosevelt had persuaded Congress to relax some of the restrictions on supplying warring nations.) Hitler was reassured by the fact that the President never publicly supported Britain and France, confining himself to gentle appeals to reason: enough to present him in the right light to the American people, but without any real commitment.

This was a stark contrast to his *private* words and actions. On 19 September 1938, as the Czech crisis climaxed, Roosevelt summoned the British Ambassador Sir Ronald Lindsay to announce two contingency plans, depending on the outcome. Lindsay cabled the details to London, ungrammatically stressing the secrecy and sensitivity of his meeting:

> This is the secret part of his communication and it must not be known to anyone that he has ever breathed a suggestion. If it transpired he would almost [certainly] be impeached and the suggestion would be hopelessly prejudiced.[46]

War

The first contingency was that if war was averted Roosevelt would propose a world peace conference, which he would attend provided it was outside Europe. (When war *was* averted this was conveniently forgotten.) However, if Hitler sent his troops into Czechoslovakia, Britain and France should simply blockade Germany – while *not* declaring war. Employing the same logic he used for the Chinese war, he could then avoid invoking the Neutrality Act, and American firms would be free to supply them.

Lindsay reported that Roosevelt was adamant the blockade 'must be based on [the] loftiest humanitarian grounds' – i.e. not presented as an act of war – because the American people would approve 'if its humanitarian purpose were strongly emphasized'. Clearly, the President was suggesting that he and Britain should *pretend* to act out of humanitarian motives. Lindsay reported:

> Several times in the course of the conversation the President showed himself quite alive to the possibility that somehow or other in indefinable circumstances the United States might again find themselves in a European War. In that case he regarded it as almost inconceivable that it would be possible for him to send any American troops across the Atlantic even if his prestige were as high as it had been just after the 1936 elections. But it was just possible that if Germany were able to invade Great Britain with a considerable force, such a wave of emotion might arise, that an American army might be sent overseas.

William Bullitt cabled on 17 September 1938, 'I know of nothing more dishonourable than to urge another nation to go to war, if one is determined not to go to war on the side of that nation.'[47] Clearly, the well-informed Bullitt – one of Roosevelt's closest confidants – believed this was exactly what the US government *was* doing.

After the Munich Agreement, Roosevelt changed tack. In October 1938, he asked his old friend Sir Arthur Murray to accept the role of secret intermediary to Chamberlain, bypassing the normal diplomatic channels. His message for the Prime Minister was: 'In so far as he, the President, was able to achieve it, in the event of war with the dictators, he had the industrial resources of the American nation behind him.' This promise was kept secret from the British Embassy, the US Embassy in London, Congress – and even FDR's own Cabinet.[48] The subtext was clear: the next time Hitler played up, Chamberlain could act tough, counting on American support. But with his apparent commitment to the Neutrality Act, how on earth could Roosevelt be sure he could keep his promise?

In June 1939, he invited George VI and Queen Elizabeth – who welcomed the opportunity to lobby for American support – on a state visit to Washington. The King recorded – his note of the conversation never left his side during the war – a pledge made by Roosevelt:

> He showed me his naval patrols in greater detail, about which he is terribly keen. If he saw a U-boat he would sink her at once & wait for the consequences.
>
> If London was bombed USA would come in. Offensive air warfare was better than defensive & he hoped we should do the same on Berlin.[49]

Of course, when war did come, Roosevelt ordered his navy *not* to engage with U-boats. When London was bombed, America's support was suddenly conspicuous by its absence. He knew all along that he would never be able, or even be allowed, to keep those promises. So why lie to the King? Clearly to encourage Britain to be tough with Hitler – increasing the risk of war.

Other people's money

How much the French and British might spend in America in the event of war was uppermost in Roosevelt's mind during the Czech crisis. In its early stages, he asked Henry Morgenthau to work out the logistics of setting up a special fund for their gold – 'just for safekeeping' – and draw up plans to facilitate their spending on arms.[50]

Hopkins' survey of the US aircraft industry was timely: the following month, a French delegation arrived in Washington in strict secrecy, looking to buy 1,000 fighters and fighter-bombers.

Recession-hit America being unable to supply such a large number, the French reduced the order to 555 – all that could be supplied in time. To meet future orders, the White House told the French that *they* would have to fund the new factories required.[51]

With war looming, in order to circumvent the neutrality laws Hopkins proposed that the aircraft parts should be shipped to Canada to be assembled in factories – to be built by the French government – just over the border, convenient for American workers. When the French announced that too much of their money was tied up abroad to do this, Morgenthau suggested they require its citizens – on pain of imprisonment – to return their money to France (so it could be used to build factories to employ American workers and to buy American materials). The French Finance Minister resigned, and his replacement, Paul Reynaud (soon Prime Minister), opposed the plan, which came to nothing.[52]

After the French team arrived, FDR convened a meeting to discuss increasing aircraft production. Only certain trusted people were invited – not including Secretary of War, Harry H. Woodring, because of his outspoken opposition to American involvement in a European war.[53] According to privileged attendee Morgenthau, Roosevelt warned that the United States faced German attack, and that 'this demanded our providing immediately a huge airforce so that we do not need to have a huge army to follow that airforce. He considered that sending a large army abroad was undesirable and politically out of the question.'[54]

Roosevelt's reasons for stepping up warplane production are ambiguous: he clearly anticipated sales to France and Britain, although carefully asserting to his administration that a strong US Army Air Force was essential. Was he covering up the foreign sales he omitted to tell Congress about, or was he also looking for the reflationary rewards of manufacturing for the domestic market? Either way, the French could pay.

What Morgenthau failed to record was that, at Roosevelt's request, he was already engaged in secret negotiations with the French delegation. However, when they found out about the French team, Woodring and the army chiefs pointed out that, under US law, no aircraft could be supplied to a foreign country until America's own military production targets were met. Moreover, the deal involved new types of aircraft – and under no circumstances could military secrets be given to another country.

Roosevelt displayed characteristic finesse at circumventing these inconveniences, allowing the French to inspect prototypes that the USAAF had yet to accept for service, therefore not technically secret – but the army demanded an official written order before agreeing to let the French observers in. The secret deal was blown in January 1939 when a Douglas bomber crashed in California, injuring one of the French observers. When this reached the Senate Military Affairs Committee, it was about to launch an immediate investigation, but the day before it met, FDR told the press about the plan to sell aircraft to France.[55]

Roosevelt told the Committee that since 1936 his government had possessed proof that Germany, Japan and Italy had formed an alliance to 'move simultaneously or take turns' at attacking other nations. This was patently untrue: their only agreement was the Anti-Comintern Pact; the 'Pact of Steel' between Germany and Italy would not be signed until May 1939, and Japan would even refuse to sign that.[56]

FDR also told the Committee that if Germany conquered Europe, America would lose that continent as a market, and Latin America would also fall under German domination: so US policy should prevent the defeat of America's 'first line of defence' – Europe and the Mediterranean. One of the senators leaked the story to the press, prompting headlines that the President had decided that the new American frontier was the Rhine![57]

When in January 1939 the French government took options on another 1,500 aircraft a year beginning from 1940, it was asked for the necessary investment to expand the industry. By the time France fell 18 months later, its government had invested more in the US aircraft industry than the American government. The British also decided to invest, to ensure that they too could call on the US aircraft industry (as they did once war was declared). By the summer of 1940, Britain and France had invested over $60 million – 70 per cent from France.[58] But these funds were also used to step up production for America's own armed forces, even enabling American companies to develop new models (sometimes with the help of British and French designers). Although Congress forbade new models going to foreigners, Morgenthau sent the full bill – $7 million – to the British and French. In other words, the US military offloaded obsolete planes, replacing them with new models at virtually no cost – and avoiding the necessity for Roosevelt's administration having to ask Congress for money to develop new aircraft. When the British and French pointed out they were effectively paying for America's defence, Morgenthau said he wouldn't let them 'come and weep on my shoulder' – but if they did, 'I'll get rough'. By the time France fell, British and French orders had quadrupled US aircraft manufacture and greatly decreased production times. Between 1938 and the spring of 1940, the number of workers employed in the US aircraft industry rose from 55,000 to 120,000.[59]

The 'ultimate potential enemy'

Of course, the Roosevelt administration's policies were just one of a number of factors in the complex series of events that led to the outbreak of the Second World War. Behind what seems with hindsight a straightforward sequence of events building to conflict lay a complex interplay of political and economic interests. An alliance formed or declined, a treaty signed or broken, even by those not directly involved – most obviously the USA, whose financial and industrial muscle made it a vital factor in the European leaders' decisions – would sooner or later affect every nation. Behind all this was the knowledge that, if they failed to hold, there would be 'total war' – an eventuality uppermost in Chamberlain's mind.

Although today 'appeasement' is an insult, implying cowardice and submission, before the war it merely meant 'to bring peace', and was Chamberlain's own preferred description of his policy throughout Europe: only in Eastern Europe did he consider it necessary to make concessions to Hitler's Germany.[60]

Chamberlain and, to a lesser extent, his predecessor, Baldwin, have been vilified for letting Hitler literally get away with murder before drawing a line in the sand far too late in the day. But recent documents reveal that, although they had a very good reason for 'appeasing' Germany, it was essential to keep it secret. These papers were only released in the 1980s: but by then, of course, history had already been written – and who had the courage to rewrite it? So even though the documents show Chamberlain's motives as considerably more understandable, the underlying reason for his attitude to Hitler remains largely unknown and is seldom explored even by war historians. That reason was Japan.

It was as late as 1982 that the first researcher treated the Japan factor seriously – J.A. Gallagher, Professor of Imperial and Naval History at the University of Cambridge, in *The Decline, Revival and Fall of the British Empire* (1982). As the British war historian Peter Calvocoressi writes in *Total War* (rev. edn, 1989), 'What the official records show is that the British cabinet was genuinely concerned about a factor which has not received its due prominence – the danger to British interests and British obligations from Japan.'[61]

Both Baldwin's and Chamberlain's governments knew that Britain had no hope of fighting on both the European and Pacific fronts, but with Germany and Japan threatening British interests, that nightmare scenario looked increasingly likely.

As early as 1932, a review of the Empire's defences noted gloomily: 'The situation is about as bad as it could be . . . the whole of our territory in the Far East, as well as the coastline of India and the Dominions and our vast trade and shipping, lies open to attack.'[62] Even then, the government realised that at least where the navy was concerned, it would have to choose between Europe and the Far East. And as Japan posed a greater direct threat to Britain's *economic* well-being, it chose the Far East. As this was before Hitler's rise to power, and there seemed little prospect of a conflict in Europe that would involve Britain, it was not seen as too much of a problem.

But because of the Nazi regime, and Japan's incursions into Manchuria, at the end of 1933 the government convened the important Defence Requirements Committee to assess Britain's preparedness to deal with both these challenges, having finally realised that the ten-year rule had eroded the country's ability to defend itself and its Empire. Chaired by the Cabinet Secretary, Maurice Hankey, and consisting of the Chiefs of Staffs, Sir Robert Vansittart of the Foreign Office and Sir Warren Fisher of the Treasury, it identified Germany as the 'ultimate potential enemy', with Japan a close second. Japan posed the more immediate danger to Britain's *imperial* (i.e. economic) interests but no direct threat to the British Isles. However, Germany – while not challenging Britain's economic interests – *was* able to strike directly. If Germany's belligerence dragged Britain into war, Japan would certainly take advantage of the situation, and so Britain would almost certainly end up fighting Japan as well.[63]

The Defence Requirements Committee recommended, on the one hand, building up the armed forces to war-ready standards by 1938 (hoping it would frighten Hitler off) and, on the other, developing better diplomatic relations with Japan – even if it offended the United States.

Almost as soon as Hitler became dictator, Winston Churchill began to warn loudly about the Nazi threat, severely criticising Baldwin's dithering in impassioned speeches in the Commons. However, he was fully aware of the reasons for first Baldwin's, and then Chamberlain's, vacillations – capitalising on the fact that they could hardly make the 'Japan factor' public. Because it took the focus off the German menace, Churchill played down the Japanese threat – even roundly denying they were capable of taking Singapore.[64] (When war between the Empire and Japan broke out, Singapore fell in just eight weeks.)

Japan's significance can hardly be overestimated: on 2 August 1939 – a month away from war – the Foreign Secretary, Lord Halifax, told the Cabinet that the situation in the Far East was causing him 'more anxiety than the position in any other part of the world'.[65]

While Britain could have contained the Japanese threat with American assistance, it was soon obvious that might never be forthcoming. The USA had chosen another partner, Stalin's Russia, in that complicated chess-game, and could only benefit from the diminution of Britain and the other European imperialists' influence in the region. As Chamberlain lamented in 1937: 'In the present state of European affairs with two dictators in a thoroughly nasty temper, we simply cannot afford to quarrel with Japan, and I very much fear . . . that after a lot of ballyhoo the Americans will somehow fade out and leave us to carry all the blame and the odium.'[66]

Roosevelt actively intervened to prevent Britain employing its only other option, fostering closer relations with Japan. In November 1934, Roosevelt instructed the State Department to tell the MacDonald government that, 'if Great Britain is even suspected of preferring to play with Japan to playing with us, I shall be compelled, in the interest of American security, to approach public sentiment in Canada, Australia, New Zealand and South Africa in a definite effort to make these Dominions understand clearly that their future security is linked with us in the United States.' It worked. MacDonald and his Foreign Secretary, Sir John Simon, disavowed any intention of making an agreement with Japan.[67]

When hostilities between Japan and China reignited in 1937, Germany, Britain, France and Italy offered to mediate: of the Western powers with interests in the region, only the USA was reluctant to act as peacemakers.[68] The State Department's justification for not becoming embroiled in British peace initiatives was that it had no wish for the Japanese to think that 'there is any form of collusion' between Britain and the USA – called by one historian a 'lame excuse'.[69]

On several occasions during 1937 and 1938, the British almost sent the fleet to Singapore, but hung back each time because Roosevelt refused to support them. In December 1937, on the Yangtse, the Japanese attacked two Royal Navy ships, accidentally sinking an American warship, the USS *Panay*, killing two crewmen and injuring eleven. Chamberlain considered using force in retaliation, but Roosevelt refused to become involved and – unilaterally and without consulting the Prime Minister – accepted Japanese apologies and compensation of $2 million.[70] A month later, when two British policemen were killed by Japanese soldiers in Shanghai, Chamberlain wanted to send in the fleet, but again Washington refused to back him.[71] This contrasts starkly with Roosevelt's eagerness to cooperate with the USSR over Japan, allowing American shipbuilders to build battleships for the Soviet Pacific fleet – although this was eventually blocked by the US Navy, which threatened to blacklist shipyards that took the contract.[72]

American support was also an important factor in Baldwin's and Chamberlain's policies towards Germany. In 1939, the Treasury told the Cabinet that, 'unless, when the time comes, the United States are prepared either to lend or give us money as required, the prospects of a long war become exceedingly grim'.[73] However, because of the Johnson and Neutrality Acts, they knew if they went to war Britain would be denied American financial and industrial support. (Although, as we have seen, Roosevelt played on Britain's neediness by promising it – unofficially.)

The German resistance

Most people believe that for all its horrors and devastation, the Second World War was justified on the grounds that the unthinkable alternative would have been to allow Hitler and Nazism to remain in power. This is usually the excuse for Roosevelt's cunning and blackmail that brought Britain and Germany into conflict: FDR recognised that making peace only really meant delaying war, and that the longer it was delayed the stronger Hitler would become. From that perspective, his actions may indeed seem reasonable.

Of course, this assumes that Hitler, or at least his regime, was there to stay, but this was far from certain – arguably the war even *kept* him in power. There was a great deal of opposition in Germany to him and his Nazis, notably from Germany's old ruling elite – right-wing (although neither Fascist nor Nazi) aristocrats and conservatives, mostly within the German General Staff. The generals tolerated Hitler's regime because their ambitions to rebuild Germany as a major world power coincided with the Nazis', but they still refused to accept his 'New Order'. Some generals believed that they should let Hitler revivify Germany then dispose of him and his retinue, returning the nation to the conservative, monarchist rule of before the First World War. The anti-Hitler military also anticipated a future Anglo-German alliance, wooing their counterparts in Britain as early as 1935. After all, they shared a common enemy, the USSR. The German military attaché to London, Major General Geyr von Schweppenburg, reported to the conspirators in Berlin that 'Britain's military leaders are prepared to give us a fair chance, agreeing that a conflict between Britain and Germany would only result in a victory for Moscow.'[74]

Friendly Fire

In 1935, during an official visit to the German General Staff in Berlin, a British military delegation led by General Sir John Dill, Deputy Chief of the Imperial Defence Staff, and Major General Sir Bernard Paget, the Director of Military Intelligence, had secret meetings with the anti-Hitler generals, who already had detailed plans for a coup. This – but not the details – was revealed to the visiting British delegation, who were asked to obtain at least the tacit support of their government.[75]

The anti-Hitler conspirators remained in close contact with London: the day before the signing of the Nazi–Soviet Pact was announced, Hitler informed his generals of his imminent alliance with Stalin, setting the date for the attack on Poland as 26 August 1939. This information went immediately to the Foreign Office.[76]

The anti-Hitler opposition was no small and powerless clique, but like the British 'peace party' it was a loose coalition of varying agendas, united by the common aim of the removal of Hitler – although differing about the lengths to which they should go to achieve it. The group of conspirators within the German General Staff, called by the Gestapo the '*Schwarze Kapelle*' – the Black Chapel – was centred on Colonel-General Ludwig Beck, Chief of the General Staff of the army until 1938, and Carl Friedrich Goerdeler, the former mayor of Leipzig. Beck resigned because his disagreement with Hitler's policies was too apparent for him not to attract suspicion, although he remained the 'spiritual leader' of the anti-Hitler conspiracy.[77]

Although rarely mentioned, the Munich Agreement actually wrecked a plot to overthrow Hitler. The German General Staff were unanimously against his plan to invade Czechoslovakia, because it could well embroil Germany in an unnecessary war with Britain and France for which their army was insufficiently equipped. It was time to ditch Hitler, but, given his popularity, arresting him out of the blue would be disastrous. They determined to wait for him to order the troops into Czechoslovakia, then seize and declare him insane – a 'feasible and well thought out' plan.[78]

They aimed for 14 September, but that was when Chamberlain offered to make the first of his three trips to Germany for talks with Hitler, defusing the tension. The plan was rescheduled for

28 September – but on that day Hitler finally agreed to the Munich Conference.

It would have helped the plotters enormously to have the British roused to extreme belligerence – to create the right climate of opinion for the coup: General Beck *urged* them to threaten war if Hitler continued with his Sudetenland demands.[79] This message reached Chamberlain and the Foreign Secretary, Lord Halifax, through several routes: Theodor Kordt, from von Ribbentrop's office, held a secret meeting with Chamberlain's close adviser Sir Horace Wilson, while another leading conspirator, Baron Ernst von Weizsäcker, contacted Sir Alexander Cadogan. The wealthy landowner Ewald von Kleist-Schmenzin met Sir Robert Vansittart in London to tell him of Hitler's secret directives and timetable for invasion. Von Kleist-Schmenzin, who was escorted by MI6 officers throughout his stay, also had a meeting with Winston Churchill, who told him, 'You can have everything, but first bring us Hitler's head' and also gave him a letter of support for the German opposition.[80] (It proved to be von Kleist-Schmenzin's death warrant: he was executed when it was found following the July 1944 bomb plot.)

The conspiracy failed because the Munich Agreement gave Hitler what he wanted without necessitating the mobilisation of the German Army. However, the generals and others continued to plot throughout the war, finally being rounded up after the failed attempt to assassinate Hitler in 1944. The Allies' critical failure to use them will be examined in more detail later, but the 1938 plot reveals not only that the British government maintained secret communications with the influential conspirators but also that Churchill had his own contacts in the group, even before he returned to government office.

Another major anti-Hitler plotter was no less than Admiral Wilhelm Canaris, head of the German military intelligence and counter-intelligence organisation, the *Abwehr* – a supremely important position. He had been its head since January 1934, with the task of turning it into something resembling Britain's MI6 – in Hitler's words 'an Order, doing its work with passion'.[81] A shrewd spymaster, Canaris had accordingly built the Abwehr into an effective intelligence organisation. Although not a member of the Nazi Party, in the early days Canaris was a trusted confidant of

Hitler's, but he turned against him after the 'Night of the Long Knives' in 1934 when he realised the Führer's ambitions would be the ruin of Germany. He then joined General Beck's conspiracy.

Staggeringly, on the day that war broke out, Canaris told his closest subordinates that because, win or lose, the war would be a disaster for Germany, the Abwehr would do nothing to prolong it by a single day. On the same day, he informed the British military attaché (their diplomats were leaving Berlin) that a line of communication would be opened via the Vatican.[82]

When he appointed Canaris, Hitler instructed him not merely to refrain from any activity in Britain that might obstruct his hoped-for alliance, but also to open covert channels to his British counterparts. Canaris singled out Sir Stewart Menzies, then Assistant Director of MI6, presumably because they agreed that Communism was the real enemy. In 1935, he sent agents to Britain to cultivate the future 'C' – one even joining the local hunt to stay close to him. In any case, Canaris's own Swiss-based mistress, Halina Szymanski, was an MI6 agent – with his full knowledge.[83]

Throughout the war, Canaris deliberately did as little as possible, and ensured that what he did do was as inefficient as possible, doing the least damage to the British war effort. Later, he even passed the British details of top-secret military developments that might otherwise have given Hitler the edge.

For obvious reasons, Menzies' and Canaris's communication was known only at the highest levels. At the time of the Operation Torch landings in French North Africa in November 1942, Canaris visited the Abwehr station at Algeciras, the nearest Spanish town to Gibraltar. The MI6 team there proposed to London that they kidnap him, but were warned off, on the grounds that Canaris was more valuable to MI6 where he was. As one of the MI6 officers said later, London didn't *exactly* say 'Leave our man alone', but it was understood.[84]

Clearly, Canaris was extremely important, demonstrating the existence of a link between the Schwarze Kapelle and MI6 – and that Menzies, at least, was aware of its activities. Exactly what passed between the two spymasters is still shrouded in secrecy, although it is obvious that something significant is being hidden. Also uncertain is how much Churchill knew – presumably Menzies told him something, but, characteristically, certainly not everything.

The US was also well aware of the anti-Hitler movement in Germany. The British industrialist A.P. Young passed documents from Goerdeler to the State Department, establishing direct contact with the leader of the conspiracy in February 1939. Other contacts were made by the Oxford-educated Adam von Trott zu Solz during visits to the US, and Helmuth von Moltke via American Embassy officials in Berlin.[85]

Poland – and after

When President Roosevelt denounced the Nazi invasion of Poland, he described that nation, with characteristic disdain for the facts, as 'a neighbour which seeks only to live at peace as a democracy, and a liberal, forward-looking democracy at that'.[86] Although Poland was literally Germany's neighbour, the homely description is wrong in every other respect. Poland had ceased to be a democracy in all but name after a military coup in 1926, after which it was ruled by a military junta (the *Sanacja* – 'health' – regime). Elections were only tolerated provided the regime won: opponents were routinely interned in specially built concentration camps. And the Poles were hardly peace-loving, having fought six wars in the few years since the country's resurrection in 1919, most of which they started to fulfil their own territorial ambitions. Unlike Hitler, Poland had no desire simply to turn the clock back to 1914, but set out to win back all the Polish land lost since the eighteenth century – the reason they went to war with the fledgling USSR in 1920–1. And the Polish government (despite its non-aggression pact with Hitler) seriously considered attacking Nazi Germany first, in 1934, but was persuaded not to by the British and French.[87]

It is often forgotten that Poland's deeply ingrained anti-Semitism up to the onset of the Second World War matched the more infamous pogroms in pre-war Nazi Germany. The eminent economist John Maynard Keynes wrote of Poland in his denunciation of the Versailles settlement, *The Economic Consequences of the Peace* (1920):

> She is to be strong, Catholic, militarist, and faithful, the
> consort, or at least the favourite, of victorious France,
> prosperous and magnificent between the ashes of Russia and
> the ruin of Germany . . . Yet, unless her great neighbours are
> prosperous and orderly, Poland is an economic impossibility
> with no industry but Jew-baiting.[88]

It was only in 2003 that the Polish government finally acknowledged
what many had known for years, that some of the wartime massacres
of Polish Jews, blamed for 60 years on the Nazi occupiers, were
actually carried out by Poles.

Their other common ground with the Nazis was hatred of
Communist Russia. Although the Poles knew that Hitler's Germany
would cause them problems, not even the onset of war changed their
view. Poland's President, Marshal Józef Piłsudski, was the first to sign
a non-aggression pact with the Nazi government (in October 1933)
welcoming such a vehemently anti-Soviet regime, despite the
potential conflict over territory. As the Polish Prime Minister Marshal
Edward Smigly-Rydz said on the very eve of war: 'With the Germans
we risk losing our liberty; with the Russians we lose our soul.'[89]

Hitler demanded the return of the German-speaking parts of
Poland, specifically the port of Danzig (today's Gdansk) and the
'Polish corridor' – a strip of land leading to the Baltic that cut East
Prussia off from the rest of Germany, created to accord with one of
President Wilson's Fourteen Points, that landlocked Poland should
have 'free and secure access' to the sea. Even though Danzig's
population was 90 per cent German, it had been declared a 'free city'
under the protection of the League of Nations. Many regarded
Hitler's demand as reasonable – including the British Ambassador in
Berlin, Sir Nevile Henderson, and many members of the
Chamberlain government. However, after the occupation of Prague,
the major question was whether Hitler would honour any negotiated
settlement – or simply drive further into Poland? In Britain, hostility
towards Germany and support for a war exploded following the fall
of Prague.

Although Chamberlain's government promised to intercede if
Poland was attacked, at the time Britain had no particular interests in

that country (far more of its assets were tied up in Germany), and as Hitler's ambitions obviously lay to the east, they were unworried he would turn on them. But as one of the guarantors at Versailles, politically Chamberlain's government could hardly ignore the issue.

In any case, British movers and shakers continued to believe that the red menace was far greater than the Nazis'. As A.J.P. Taylor recalled of the mid-1930s:

> The National Government were in their acts more anti-Communist than anti-Nazi, as indeed they remained until the outbreak of war, and perhaps even after it . . . I believed that if Great Britain were involved in war it would be on Hitler's side against Russia.[90]

But why not let the two problem nations fight each other, taking the heat off the rest of Europe? As Baldwin said in 1936: 'If there is any fighting in Europe, I should like to see the Bolshies and Nazis doing it.'[91]

Neville Chamberlain believed – with total justification – that Stalin was trying to engineer war between Britain, France and Germany because the weakened warring nations would provide Russia with the perfect opportunity for expansion.[92]

Throughout summer 1939 the British led attempts to resolve the Danzig crisis – endeavouring to persuade the Polish and German governments to talk – including several 'private' initiatives by businessmen with vested interests in preventing war (many with the unofficial blessing of Chamberlain and Lord Halifax). The nations also strove to form alliances that would strengthen their position or deter their opponents. Stalin's Russia was in a key position: if it sided with either of the two opposing blocs, the other would think twice before pushing ahead.

Meanwhile, the equally grave (but less famous) Tientsin crisis that began in June 1939 intensified in the Far East. The British authorities in Tientsin had refused to hand over suspected Chinese 'terrorists' to the Japanese, who responded by blockading the town. Their body-searches of everybody who went in and out included British women – to the horror of the British officials. To the alarm of their government and military commanders – faced with the nightmare scenario of simultaneous wars against Germany and Japan – outraged Britons demanded retribution against Japan. The tense situation continued for several weeks. Lord Ismay, Secretary of the Committee of Imperial Defence, wrote, 'For the moment all our eyes are on Tientsin instead of Danzig.'[93]

With such impeccably bad timing, the Tientsin crisis took its toll on the European situation. Hitler seized the opportunity to 'accelerate his tempo' over Danzig, and also tried – unsuccessfully – to persuade Japan to make a military alliance. Nazi propagandists seized on the crisis as evidence of an increasingly emasculated British Empire.[94]

The ending of the Tientsin affair is also enlightening. The USSR had the upper hand in the latest skirmish with Japan on the Manchuria–Siberia border, and at the same time Roosevelt gave the Japanese six months' notice of terminating their commercial treaty – a very serious outlook for Japan. As it was hardly the perfect time also to confront the British Empire, the Japanese backed down over Tientsin.

Hitler was furious, ranting about what he called Japan's 'defection'.[95] After Tientsin, he decided on a pact with Stalin instead of Japan, and the resulting Nazi–Soviet Pact stunned the world – particularly Japan. After all, Germany and Japan had signed the Anti-Comintern Pact, and the USSR was Japan's greatest enemy. There was a bitter rift between Tokyo and Berlin, the collapse of the Japanese government and its replacement by a more pro-British one – and, of course, the end of immediate danger of war between Britain and Japan.

As the Polish crisis quickened, the British and French also tried to ally with Stalin – after all, such a combination of forces would make even Hitler think twice. Indeed, a joint Anglo-French delegation was trying to negotiate such a deal in Moscow even as von Ribbentrop arrived to sign the pact. But Stalin was too suspicious of Britain and France, especially since they had rebuffed his own offers of an alliance.

During the Czechoslovakian crisis, Litvinov had proposed to the League of Nations that the USSR should discuss with the other

European countries the possibility of an alliance that would halt Hitler. But Chamberlain and Halifax were so prejudiced against the Russians that they refused to allow the Cabinet even to discuss the proposal.[96] Then, in the early days of the Polish crisis, following a French initiative, Stalin offered a three-way defence pact to Britain and France: if Germany attacked Poland, all three would declare war on Germany. When the Soviet Ambassador Ivan Maisky put this to Lord Halifax, he received a lukewarm response, and the British Ambassador in Moscow, Sir William Seeds, also greeted the suggestion less than enthusiastically.[97]

Stalin had long believed that the Western powers' hidden agenda was to force Germany and the USSR into conflict while they themselves sat on the sidelines, largely because it was precisely what he would do in their place. When they snubbed his offer, it only confirmed his suspicions. Stalin sacked the pro-Western Litvinov, replacing him with uncompromising comrade Vyacheslav Molotov.

The Russian leader was even more suspicious when Britain and France approached *him* about such an alliance little more than three months later. The wily old peasant and his intelligence service knew full well about the ongoing communication between the anti-Hitler generals and the British, recognising that a secret deal to replace Hitler's regime with a non-Nazi but equally anti-Soviet government was a possibility. Concluding that the British and French only pretended to want an alliance in order to put pressure on Hitler, the Russian dictator shrewdly turned the tables – making a deal that ensured that *his* enemies, the Nazis and the Western imperialist powers, fought each other. In fact, he had declared this intention in his address to the Soviet Communist Party Congress in March 1938, stating that the capitalist countries were poised to wage war for economic dominance and that the USSR would be happy to watch them annihilate each other – and might even 'encourage them surreptitiously in this, to allow them to weaken and exhaust each other'.[98]

Of course, what the world did not know (although Eleanor Roosevelt seems to have been aware of it) was that the secret protocol set out the division of spoils from the coming war, most significantly the carving up of Poland – euphemistically 'a territorial and political rearrangement of the areas belonging to the Polish state'. Most ominously, the secret protocol left open 'the question of whether the interests of both parties make desirable the maintenance of an independent Polish state', but agreed it should be settled by a 'friendly agreement' between the USSR and Germany.[99]

From Stalin's point of view, the secret agreement was intended to recover the 60,000 square miles of White Russia (the western Ukraine) handed over to Poland by the treaty that ended the 1920–1 war. But the Pact also recognised Russian mastery over Finland and the Baltic states (formerly part of Tsarist Russia, they became independent during the revolution, but now Stalin wanted them back).

Chamberlain responded to the Nazi–Soviet Pact by signing a formal alliance with Poland on 25 August 1939. Hitler had ordered the attack on Poland for the following day, but when he heard about the Anglo-Polish alliance he cancelled it – hastily offering Britain a non-aggression pact. The anti-Hitler faction in Germany were jubilant: Admiral Canaris tempted providence by enthusing that peace was guaranteed in Europe for 20 years.[100]

Donald Cameron Watt argues that Hitler's offer was aimed not at the Chamberlain government – the Führer's advisers predicted its collapse after the Polish crisis – but at the British Establishment that would influence its successor. Watt argues it was intended to give the British a guarantee against the USA, on the grounds that it was fundamentally hostile to their Empire.[101] But Poland's fate was sealed: when Chamberlain refused the offer, Hitler ordered a new attack for 1 September 1939.

The knife-edge situation was hardly helped by the intransigence of the Polish government. Up to the moment war was declared, they were in euphoric denial: surely Hitler was bluffing – and in any case, their army would be more than a match for the Nazis. On 31 August, when the British Ambassador visited his Polish counterpart in Berlin, Jozef Lipski – then winding down the Embassy – the Pole declared bombastically 'the Polish Army would probably arrive in Berlin in triumph'.[102]

The Polish over-confidence bolstered their stubborn refusal to negotiate over the Danzig corridor, which may, in turn, have contributed to the outbreak of war. The question has to be asked: was the Polish government itself partly responsible for causing the Second World War?

Undeniably, the Poles barely lifted a finger to resolve the crisis. After Hitler broke off negotiations in the early summer, it was left to Britain and France to act as middlemen, talking to each side separately. In the final days of peace, the British made strenuous efforts to broker direct negotiations – by then the only hope of avoiding war.

On 29 August, against the advice of the British and French, the Polish government declared a general mobilisation, the prelude to war. The same day, Hitler finally responded positively to the British about direct talks, as long as the Polish negotiator, Foreign Minister Józef Beck, presented himself in Berlin within 24 hours – difficult, but not impossible. Incredibly, despite urgent pleas from Britain and France, Beck refused to go.

On 1 September – the day the German invasion began – Sir Nevile Henderson told the US chargé d'affaires in Berlin that 'if the Polish Government had agreed to direct negotiations and had appointed a plenipotentiary, precipitate action by Germany might have been prevented or at least delayed'.[103] But although after Czechoslovakia the Poles could be forgiven for doubting Hitler's word, as cataclysm hung over so many other countries, surely they should have done *something*. (Their attitude was even more peculiar now they were caught between the Wehrmacht and Luftwaffe on one side, and the Red Army on the other.) It seems that the Poles believed they had something up their sleeve – but what?

Roosevelt the warmonger?

Both the Baldwin and Chamberlain governments admitted that Britain could only fight a war with American aid – which the Neutrality Acts forbade. However, Roosevelt secretly encouraged the British and French governments to believe that the US cavalry *would* save them, just as in the movies. Apparently, Chamberlain had no great hope of FDR's promises, but as he knew from the Treasury that American aid was Britain's only chance, he had to *assume* the President would deliver. Undoubtedly, Roosevelt's secret promises boosted Chamberlain's courage in taking a tougher line with the Nazis over Poland, but as Charles Tansill notes in *Back Door to War*:

> . . . in 1939 it appeared as though Neville Chamberlain was assuming the role of the Mad Hatter when he could not send even token assistance to the hard-pressed Poles. Nowadays it seems evident that the real Mad Hatter was Franklin D. Roosevelt who pressed Chamberlain to give promises to the Poles when there was no possibility of fulfilling them.[104]

While working on his book in 1951, Tansill received a letter from Verne Marshall, a retired newspaper editor, claiming that in summer 1939:

> President Roosevelt wrote a note to William Bullitt, then Ambassador to France, directing him to advise the French Government that if, in the event of a Nazi attack upon Poland, France and England did not go to Poland's aid, those countries could expect no help from America if a general war developed. On the other hand, if France and England immediately declared war on Germany, they could expect 'all aid' from the United States.[105]

According to Marshall, FDR also instructed Bullitt to get this message to the British and Polish governments through Joseph Kennedy in London and Anthony Biddle in Warsaw. Marshall claimed his information came anonymously from someone who had seen the note in the US Embassy in Berlin in October 1939. Marshall hints heavily at blackmail: if those governments failed to comply with Roosevelt's demands and ended up at war, they would receive nothing from America. Bullitt and Kennedy both denied to Tansill that they had received any such instruction from the President – although of course they had every incentive to do so, since it would mean that Roosevelt had actually incited the war.

In December 1945, the US Secretary of the Navy (later Secretary of Defense), James Forrestal, noted an off-record conversation with Joseph Kennedy:

Kennedy's view: that Hitler would have fought Russia without any later conflict with England if it had not been for Bullitt's urging on Roosevelt in the summer of 1939 that the Germans must be faced down about Poland; neither the French nor the British would have made Poland a case for war if it had not been for the constant needling from Washington. Bullitt, he said, kept telling Roosevelt that the Germans wouldn't fight, Kennedy that they would, and that they would overrun Europe . . .

What Kennedy told me in this conversation agrees substantially with the remarks Clarence Dillon had made to me already, to the general effect that Roosevelt had asked him in some manner to communicate privately with the British to the end that Chamberlain should have greater firmness in his dealings with Germany. Dillon told me that at Roosevelt's request he had talked with Lord Lothian in the same general sense as Kennedy reported Roosevelt having urged him to do with Chamberlain. Lothian was presumably to communicate to Chamberlain the gist of his conversation with Dillon.[106]

Here we have yet another private and unofficial overture from Roosevelt to the British government, this time via two distinguished diplomats, Clarence Dillon (a prominent Wall Street investment banker, later Ambassador to France and Treasury Secretary under John F. Kennedy) and Lord Lothian (Sir Ronald Lindsay's replacement as Ambassador less than a month before war began), again signalling that Britain could count on US aid when it needed it most.

While acknowledging in 1945 that the immediate source of the 'needling' was Washington (i.e. Roosevelt), Joseph Kennedy blamed Bullitt for persuading the President to adopt this approach. This is debatable: a year earlier Bullitt had complained about just such a strategy during the Czech crisis, and Kennedy would vilify Bullitt given half the chance as they loathed each other. Indeed, in February 1940 they had a furious public row in the State Department.[107] But it is significant that Verne Marshall's story also centres on these two men.

Friendly Fire

William Christian Bullitt was the protégé of Colonel House, who secured him his first job at the State Department. After meeting Lenin during a 1919 Moscow trip, he specialised in Soviet affairs, first in the State Department and then as the first US Ambassador to Moscow. Although vehemently anti-Communist, he believed the USSR was a vital barrier against both German and Japanese expansion in the 1930s. After returning to Washington in 1936 to work on Roosevelt's second-term campaign, he was appointed Ambassador to France.

Breckinridge Long, Assistant Secretary of State, wrote in 1940, 'I look upon Bill Bullitt and Harry Hopkins as the closest to the throne.'[108] As another of FDR's unofficial channels, while in France, Bullitt communicated with the President using a personal code in order to bypass the State Department[109] – clearly the ideal Roosevelt messenger, as alleged by Verne Marshall. Bullitt was often seen as the 'mouthpiece of the President',[110] enhancing his authority in dealings with foreign diplomats.

With Joseph Kennedy, the respect and trust was all on one side. One of Roosevelt's closest supporters and early financial backers, he lobbied for funding from wealthy Democrats and acted as go-between with William Randolph Hearst. However, Roosevelt regarded Kennedy as naive – useful, but to be kept out of his trusted inner circle. Kennedy was even sent to London as a 'practical joke'[111] – because he was Irish-American – but ironically he was a great success, especially with the Royal Family.

Kennedy, the future President's anti-Semitic father, blamed the Jewish lobby in Washington for Roosevelt's failure to 'accommodate' Hitler.[112] In his diary entry of 6 November 1940, Breckinridge Long wrote of Kennedy:

> He does not believe in our present policy. He does not believe in the continuing of democracy. He thinks we will have to assume a Fascist form of government here or something similar to it if we are to survive in a world of concentrated and centralized powers.[113]

By the end of the war, both Bullitt and Kennedy had fallen from grace, but Bullitt, at least, recognised the unmistakable hand of Harry Hopkins behind his eclipse.[114]

Secrets of the *White Book*

Early in the war, the Nazis published their own version of its origins in a series of *White Books*, claiming, predictably, that their 'reluctant' aggression was justified – and that anyway the British, French and Poles were really to blame. The Nazis claimed that one *White Book*, published in March 1940, was based on documents found in Polish government files when Warsaw was captured, which proved that the American government was also partly responsible for the war. These included reports to Warsaw from embassy officials abroad, detailing conversations with American diplomats who had urged the Polish government to stand firm against Hitler because the US would come in – seemingly this was why the Poles refused to negotiate. Although the *White Book* was dismissed as another example of Goebbels's propaganda, the diplomats named in the documents were Bullitt and Kennedy, acting specifically on Roosevelt's orders.[115]

Moreover, Breckinridge Long tells a different story. On 27 March 1940, he attended a meeting with his boss, Cordell Hull, to decide on their response to the *White Book*. It had come at a particularly embarrassing time for the State Department, as just days previously the US minister to Canada, James Cromwell, stated publicly that America was planning 'all-out assistance' to Britain. Hull and Long drafted a public statement denying the claims had the 'slightest credence', but Long adds:

> There is just a sneaking suspicion in our minds that there is more truth than fiction in some of the reported conversations. Not only do they have the ear-marks of authenticity but they indicate actions which are characteristic of both Bullitt and Kennedy.[116]

So what exactly did the *White Book* claim? As it is usually ignored, it can be frustrating to track down, although we were able to unearth a copy in the Official Publications section of the British Library. (The *White Book* consists simply of facsimiles of the original Polish documents with German translations, and virtually no commentary.) It was a revelation.

In November 1938, the Polish Ambassador in Washington, Count Jerzy Potocki, reported a meeting with Bullitt, 'To my question whether the United States would participate in such a war, he [Bullitt] answered: "undoubtedly yes, but only if England and France strike first!"'[117] In January 1939, Potocki reported another long conversation with Bullitt when he was far more specific about Roosevelt's intentions:

> He [Bullitt] leaves with a whole 'trunk' full of instructions and directives from President Roosevelt, the Department of State and the Senate Foreign Affairs Committee.
>
> From the meeting with Bullitt I had the impression that he received full details from President Roosevelt of the view taken by the United States of today's European crisis. He is to use this material when speaking to the Quai d'Orsay [French Foreign Ministry] and is also to make use of it in his conversations with European statesmen. Contents of these directives, which Bullitt gave me in the course of the half-hour meeting, are as follows: 1. A stimulation of foreign policy under the guidance of President Roosevelt, which condemns the totalitarian states sharply and unambiguously. 2. The war preparations of the United States on sea, land and in the air, which are to be carried out at accelerated speed and which will devour the colossal sum of 1,250,000,000 dollars. 3. The decided opinion of the President that France and England must put an end to any policy of compromise with the totalitarian states. They are to enter into no discussion with them which aims at exchanges of territory. 4. A moral insurance that the United States has abandoned isolationist politics and, in the case of war, is ready to actively intervene on the side of England and France. America is ready to place its full resources of finances and raw materials at their disposal.[118]

This is exactly the message that Verne Marshall said Bullitt had taken to Paris on Roosevelt's behalf, and also transmitted to Kennedy in London, supporting the authenticity of the *White Book* documents.

In Paris a month later, Bullitt told Jules Lukasiewicz, the Polish Ambassador to France, that, if war broke out between Britain and France on one side and Germany and Italy on the other, an Axis victory would threaten America's interests, and:

> For this reason one can foresee the participation of the United States in the war on the side of France and England from the beginning. Naturally, only a certain time after the outbreak of the conflict. Ambassador Bullitt expressed it as follows: 'should a war break out, it is not sure that we would participate at the beginning, but we will end it'.[119]

Lukasiewicz's report ends with his assessment of Bullitt's information, saying that, while reserving judgement until he has more details of Roosevelt's intentions, 'One thing however seems certain to me, i.e. that the next time President Roosevelt's policy will be to support France's resistance to the German–Italian pressure and to weaken England's compromise tendencies.'

The *White Book* documents also included a report from the Economic Adviser to the Polish Embassy in London about Kennedy asking him in summer 1939 what Poland wanted from Britain in terms of money and material, promising to urge Chamberlain and Halifax to grant it.[120] Official British papers show that during the Czech crisis, on 10 September 1938, Kennedy told Lord Halifax that if London was bombed, 'the history of the last war would be repeated, leading a good deal more rapidly than in the last war to American intervention'.[121]

Although, of course, no Nazi propaganda should be taken at face value, in the case of the *White Book* the mass of independent testimony suggests that, for once, the Nazis had seized on an authentic story. And according to witnesses of Kennedy's (unpublished) memoirs, he admitted that the documents on which the *White Book* was based 'were not forgeries'.[122] This is all the more significant because they represented the exact opposite of his personal stance: as an 'appeaser' he believed the United States should concentrate on putting pressure on Poland to do a deal with Hitler, and was angered when his suggestions were rebuffed by Washington. He also urged the British to 'put the screws' on Poland.[123] If Kennedy *had* encouraged Poland *not* to deal with Hitler, it can only be because he was instructed to do so, and the evidence suggests strongly that he received Roosevelt's unofficial instructions via Bullitt.

Given its astonishing revelations, why is the *White Book* virtually unknown? Robert Edwin Herzstein, Professor of History at the University of South Carolina – who although a passionate Roosevelt supporter acknowledges the documents' authenticity – admits that FDR persuaded French Prime Minister Edouard Daladier to state in writing that he (the President) had never had any intention of bringing America into the war. Any opponents who tried to cite the evidence of the *White Book* were swiftly silenced by being labelled pro-Nazi.[124]

Citing the *White Book* and the supporting evidence, Tansill concludes that, 'Germany had been baited into a war with Britain and France when she would have preferred a conflict with Russia.'[125] But this is only half the story: Britain, France and Poland had also been 'baited into war'. Through Bullitt and Kennedy, FDR's machinations encouraged Britain, France and Poland to stand up to Hitler on the promise of American material and financial support that he could not be certain of delivering and of military assistance he knew was impossible at that time. It is hard to think of any other description of Roosevelt's behaviour than 'incitement'.

Why war came

When Hitler finally invaded Poland on 1 September 1939, Chamberlain's government had no option but to issue an ultimatum. When the Führer ignored it, it was compelled to declare war. Ironically, both Chamberlain and Hitler had been forced into the opposite of what they wanted: the British Prime Minister sought to avoid a costly war, while the Führer would have preferred Britain as an ally. But the complex web of vested political and economic interests, allegiances and obligations had forced them into a situation that neither could wriggle out of, however much they wanted to.

Many factors contributed to the Second World War, mainly

War

Britain and France's guarantees to Poland, the Poles' refusal to negotiate, and Chamberlain's anti-Soviet prejudice. Even decisions made on the other side of the world, such as in Tokyo and Washington, substantially shaped the course of events. Although the Nazi–Soviet Pact was obviously the immediate trigger, it is impossible to know whether war would have been averted or merely postponed, had any of that summer's decisions gone the other way.

The main underlying cause was, of course, the Nazi hunger for Lebensraum, but Stalin also had his eye on Finland, the Baltic states and half of Poland. The Nazi–Soviet Pact furthered both dictators' ambitions. And yet, of course, within two years Stalin would be welcomed into the Allied camp with open arms and yawning coffers.

Meanwhile, Roosevelt secretly encouraged Britain, France and Poland to take a tough line with Hitler, but although historians rarely argue about his desire to see Germany trounced, they justify his actions by citing his motives: unlike the British and French, he understood that delay would only postpone the inevitable while Hitler grew stronger.[126] But the evidence suggests that his real motives were considerably less idealistic: to find an overseas market ready, willing and able to place massive orders quickly, and to invest in American industry. The only such market was a nation at war.

In responding to Hitler's menace, each government was faced with the terrible consequences of failure. Britain and France's greatest risk was war. Only America's greatest risk lay in there *not* being a European conflict, as Roosevelt diverted New Deal money into war production, expanded the defence industries with French and British investment, and relied on their orders that in turn depended on the outbreak of war.

As the story moves to the very brink of conflagration in Europe, the true motives of the great leaders – especially Roosevelt – emerge from the carnage and the smoke. It will not be comfortable reading for those who prefer the traditional myths. Yet this is the real story of the leadership of the Second World War.

CHAPTER FIVE

The Odd Couple

'No lover ever studied the whims of his mistress as I did those of President Roosevelt.'

Winston S. Churchill[1]

On 11 September 1939 – eight days after the outbreak of war – President Roosevelt wrote to the new First Lord of the Admiralty, Winston Spencer Churchill: 'What I want you and the Prime Minister to know is that I shall at all times welcome it if you will keep me in touch personally with anything you want me to know about. You can always send sealed letters through your [diplomatic] pouch or my pouch.'[2] The War Cabinet approved the arrangement – but it became public knowledge only in Churchill's eulogy for Roosevelt to the House of Commons in April 1945.

Messages were cabled via the American Embassy in utmost secrecy, Churchill signing himself schoolboyishly, 'Naval Person' – as Prime Minister becoming 'Former Naval Person'. Roosevelt was 'POTUS' – President of the United States.

This correspondence is such an integral part of the Second World War – and 'special relationship' – legend that it is hard to appreciate how extraordinary it was. It is still unheard of – indeed, normally not permitted – for a head of state to have direct and unrestricted personal communication with a minister of another nation other than its Foreign Minister. But although these were completely outside normal Foreign Office and State Department channels, not only were Foreign Office objections to the communication overridden by Chamberlain, but Churchill – also with the Prime Minister's backing – refused Lord Halifax's request that the Foreign Office read the draft messages, although Churchill did hand over copies after they had been sent.[3]

Roosevelt kept the correspondence secret even from his Secretary of State, Cordell Hull, who only learned of it in May 1940 when a staff member of the London Embassy with access to it was arrested for spying. Hull confronted Roosevelt, who claimed there were only a few messages, 'obviously . . . related to naval matters'.[4]

But why did Roosevelt favour one particular minister? (Although protocol demanded a similar offer be extended to Chamberlain, he was the only other invitee.) Churchill was 'a relatively minor, if slightly notorious, member of the British Cabinet'[5] – whom the President had only met socially 21 years before and disliked on principle because of his elitist background as a grandson of the Duke of Marlborough. Surely neither their shared interest in naval matters nor Churchill's American mother explains such peculiar favouritism.

As the messages passed through his embassy, it was essential for Joseph Kennedy to be in the picture, but when during Christmas in Washington he demanded to know 'why Churchill?' Roosevelt replied:

> I have always disliked him since the time I went to England in 1918. He acted like a stinker at a dinner I attended, lording it all over us . . . I'm giving him attention now because there is a strong possibility that he will become Prime Minister and I want to get my hand in now.[6]

This is extraordinary prescience: at that time, Churchill was by no means Chamberlain's obvious successor – and there was not even any sign that the Prime Minister was going. But why did Chamberlain and the War Cabinet allow the correspondence, even ignoring Lord Halifax's reasonable objections? Clearly, there was some advantage in this unorthodox communication – but what was it?

The best of enemies?

It is now accepted that Churchill's and Roosevelt's relationship was much rockier than usually portrayed. Richard Lamb writes, 'The friendship between Roosevelt and Churchill has been over-romanticized by historians; they have been seduced by the picture painted by Churchill in his memoirs', and 'the camaraderie masked frequent clashes and continued irritations'.[7] American Warren Kimball agrees: 'In fact, the Churchill–Roosevelt relationship has been much over-romanticized by historians, largely through Winston Churchill's own efforts.'[8] Although Churchill's memoirs flamboyantly describe the future President's 'magnificent presence' at their only pre-war meeting, in 1918 – the one that still rankled with Roosevelt – in 1941 he admitted that he had no memory of him at all.[9]

Roosevelt's real attitude to Churchill is implicit in the private codename 'Moses Smith' he and Harry Hopkins gave him. Smith was one of Roosevelt's tenant farmers who inspired amused condescension locally for his lack of deference to his betters.[10] Churchill's criticism of the New Deal as a 'ruthless war on private enterprise'[11] also stirred resentment, although as a mere backbencher he was too lowly to ruffle FDR's feathers. But it was recalled when Churchill blasted back into power. Their only contact between 1918 and 1939 was Churchill's one-line note in 1933 congratulating Roosevelt on repealing Prohibition – a subject always dear to his heart.[12]

Behind the Churchill myth

Such is Churchill's place in British history – unsurprisingly winning the BBC's recent poll as the 'greatest Briton of all time' – that he is almost untouchable: to criticise him is to be an iconoclastic yahoo. At least, that is, where his war leadership is concerned. Paradoxically, most commentators on Churchill's political life agree that before the mid-1930s, his already long career was mostly a tale of disaster.

The Odd Couple

Churchill tends to be thought of as wrong about everything in his political career *except* the Nazi menace.

However, as with Roosevelt, his reputation has become the subject of increasingly critical scrutiny. Even the admiring Richard Lamb in his *Churchill as War Leader: Right or Wrong?* (1991), while still concluding he mostly did a good job, admits the Great Man was fallible. More critical are John Charmley's *Churchill: End of Glory* (1993) and Clive Ponting's *Churchill* (1994).

Churchill himself never wasted an opportunity to bolster his own myth, especially through his epic speeches – as John F. Kennedy declared when making Churchill an honorary American citizen in 1963, 'He mobilized the English language and sent it into battle'.[13] Churchill ensured his fame, simply by writing the standard histories himself. His six-volume *The Second World War* (1948–54), which masqueraded as objective history, was actually his own story. Because many critical documents would only be released 30 or 50 years into the future, he could present his version of events without too much fear of contradiction. However, as they have gradually emerged into the public domain, we can see for ourselves how shamelessly he twisted the truth – as in his 'special relationship' with Roosevelt.

Many at the time were appalled when Chamberlain recalled Churchill to government at the outbreak of war, after his ten years of backbench 'wilderness years'. The Establishment was largely aghast – particularly Queen Elizabeth and the Royal Family's matriarch Queen Mary[14] – because of his hostility towards appeasement (not to mention his support for Edward VIII during the Abdication crisis). His reappointment as First Lord of the Admiralty caused particular alarm: he had been forced to resign from that post during the First World War after his disastrous Dardanelles campaign with its loss of a quarter of a million Allied lives. (He then commanded an infantry battalion on the Western Front with his usual bravado.)

Churchill is often criticised as a warmonger, although Max Hastings has countered, 'What Churchill was . . . and what many people found equally repugnant, was a warrior. He enjoyed war.'[15] Certainly, the old British bulldog fed on the euphoric heroics of Boy's Own derring-do, confessing to his physician Sir Charles Wilson (later Lord Moran) in June 1945, 'I feel very lonely without a war.'[16] Moran confided to his diary in November 1943:

> War has always fascinated him; he knows in surprising detail about the campaigns of the great captains; he had visited nearly all the battlefields and he can pick out, in a particular battle, the decisive move that turned the day. But he has never given a thought to what was happening in the soldier's mind, he has not tried to share his fears. If a soldier does not do his duty, the P.M. says that he ought to be shot. It is as simple as that.[17]

Although he had seen action in the North-West Frontier and the Boer War, on the Western Front he delighted in night-time forays into no man's land, never flinching under fire, even showing himself above a trench in broad daylight to demonstrate how little risk there was of being shot.[18] He was fundamentally *certain* as only the great, mad or bad can be that he himself would never be harmed. His apparently charmed life seemed proof of a historic destiny.

As Churchill's ultimate ambition was to direct an entire war, he never wasted an opportunity to talk up the possibility of conflict. First, his bogeymen were the Russians – as late as 1930 calling them 'a sub-human generation' – thundering: 'It is by no means certain that, if these forces of soulless barbarism and modern inventions once got us down, we could ever recover or escape.'[19] Then it was the Americans, and then the Germans. His warnings about Nazism seemed to many to simply be the old man crying wolf again.

His jingoistic belief in the glory of war, and unshakeable faith in his own destiny, were there from the first. At 16, he famously declared, 'I see into the future. This country will be subjected to a tremendous invasion, by what means I do not know, but I tell you I shall be in command of the defences of London and I shall save London and England from disaster.'[20] At the age of 23, he wrote to his mother from the North-West Frontier: 'I have faith in my star – that is that I am intended to do something in the world.'[21]

One of those who served with him in India, George Clegg, recalled him declaring: 'Mark my words, I shall be Prime Minister of

The Odd Couple

England before I'm finished' – which caused the usual merriment in the Mess over Winston's flights of fancy.[22] (Churchill finally fulfilled this youthful prophecy at 65, having never lost faith in his near-divine destiny.)

His junior minister at the Admiralty in the First World War called him 'a spoilt child endowed by chance with the brain of a genius'.[23] The Prime Minister, Andrew Bonar Law, summed him up as 'a very unusual intellectual ability [with] an entirely unbalanced mind'[24], and Stanley Baldwin put it this way:

> When Winston was born, lots of fairies swooped down on his cradle with gifts – imagination, eloquence, industry, ability – then came a fairy who said, 'No one person has a right to so many gifts,' and picked him up and gave him such a shake and a twist that with all the gifts he was denied judgement and wisdom. And that is why while we delight to listen to him in the House we do not take his advice.[25]

But because he believed his 'star' dovetailed with the British people's, did he, even subconsciously, ignore or neglect opportunities for peace – easier and less costly ways out of the war – because they would impede his destined glory?

Given his personality, it was hardly surprising his political career was chequered, changing party twice – from Conservative to Liberal in 1904 and back again 20 years later – landing him with the reputation of an unprincipled, self-seeking maverick. Even so, by 1929 he had held the positions of Home Secretary, First Lord of the Admiralty, Minister of Munitions, Secretary of State for War and Air (overseeing Britain's brief intervention in Bolshevik Russia in 1919), Colonial Secretary and Chancellor of the Exchequer. He lost office when the Conservatives were defeated in the 1929 election.

Churchill disagreed so vehemently with his party's Indian policy – even they recognised that the growing demand for greater self-rule could no longer be ignored – that there was no way he could serve in the shadow cabinet. In 1935, he was among 75 Conservative MPs who voted against the Baldwin government over this issue – over which, significantly, he and Roosevelt were to clash seriously.

In principle, he was a fervent monarchist but as Prime Minister he treated George VI with scant regard, often real rudeness, ignoring the King's messages and even summonses to the Palace.[26] Allegedly a champion of democracy, he made unilateral decisions about matters with far-reaching consequences without consulting, or even informing, his ministers, let alone Parliament. A supporter of the then prevalent ideal of firm but, in his view, benevolent dictatorship, he was a particularly fervent admirer of Benito Mussolini: as Chancellor of the Exchequer telling him publicly in Rome in 1927, 'If I had been an Italian, I am sure I would have been with you wholeheartedly from the start . . . your Movement has rendered service to the whole world.'[27] In other words, by his own admission, had Churchill been born in Italy he would happily have become a Fascist! In 1933, he commended Il Duce as a 'Roman genius' and 'the greatest law-giver among men'.[28]

This admiration for other 'men of destiny' even stretched to Hitler – at least for a time. In a 1935 essay included in *Great Contemporaries* (1937) he described the Führer's fight from obscurity to centre stage, presumably thinking of his own 'wilderness years':

> The story of that struggle cannot be read without admiration for the courage, the perseverance, and the vital force which enabled him to challenge, defy, conciliate, or overcome all the authorities and resistances [*sic*] which barred his path.[29]

(His use of 'struggle' – *Kampf* – is interesting, suggesting his current bedtime book.) While being concerned at Hitler's policies – particularly the anti-Jewish laws – he kept an open mind on the dictator's future:

> We cannot tell whether Hitler will be the man who will again let loose upon the world another war in which civilization will irretrievably succumb, or whether he will go down in history as the man who restored honour and peace of mind to the

great Germanic nation and brought it back serene, helpful and
strong, to the forefront of the European family circle.[30]

Everything about Churchill was excessive, from his enthusiasms and
ambitions to his phenomenal capacity for alcohol: even his whisky-
soaked circle felt uneasy with his endless boozing. During the 1930s,
he acquired a reputation as an alcoholic, although C.P. Snow
declared that no alcoholic could drink as much as he did![31]
Essentially, he ran the war while being unfit to drive a car. Anthony
Eden recorded Churchill having the occasional '*stiff* whisky and soda,
at 8.45am'.[32] It was to be a source of constant fascination to post-
Prohibition Americans that the Prime Minister could function so
impressively on so much booze.

Churchill was almost the lone voice raised against the sinister build-
up of Germany's armed forces, basing his speeches on leaked
information from factions within MI6 and the Foreign Office. Leaking
classified information, even to an MP, is very serious: Clive Ponting,
the Foreign Office official, was prosecuted in the mid-1980s for passing
information on the Falklands conflict to a Labour MP to use against the
Thatcher government. (The comparison presumably inspired Ponting's
1940: Myth and Reality and his critical biography of Churchill.)

Churchill's chief sources were Major Desmond Morton, head of
MI6's newly created Industrial Intelligence Centre (IIC) – later his
personal intelligence adviser – and Ralph Wigram, head of the
Foreign Office's Central Department.[33] In October 1934, Wigram
warned of increasing German air power, predicting that once
Germany had reversed Versailles it would turn to Austria and
Central Europe (as set out in *Mein Kampf*). When his superiors
refused to listen, Wigram passed the information via Major Morton
to Churchill, who used it in Commons debates. The government
objected that he was exaggerating – as indeed he was, claiming that
the Luftwaffe was six times larger than it really was.[34]

Wigram would take classified documents to Churchill at
Chartwell in Kent, which then went immediately to his friend,
Professor Frederick Lindemann, who in turn drove to Oxford,
photographed them and drove back (a round trip of six hours), to
return the original to Foreign Office files.[35]

The Nazi–Soviet invasion of Poland

Now about to be tested, British and French assurances to Poland meant nothing: neither rushed to its aid, nor created a diversion by attacking Germany from the west. The British had promised that the RAF would bomb Germany, but it merely dropped leaflets. The French Army, which promised to cross the Maginot Line, did send eleven divisions five miles into the Saar but, despite virtually no resistance, dug in for three weeks – before withdrawing. Meanwhile, the blitzkrieg annihilated the Polish forces in a matter of days, first at Danzig, then Warsaw. (As the Polish army retreated, its countrymen massacred some 7,000 German Poles, simply because of their nationality – being on the wrong side of the line when Europe was redefined at Versailles.[36])

Besides abandoning the Poles, once again a British and French decision effectively allowed Hitler to survive. The anti-Hitler generals' hands were tied, as Britain and Germany were at war in name only.[37]

And, of course, according to the Secret Supplementary Protocol of the Nazi–Soviet Pact, on 17 September 1939 the Red Army moved into eastern Poland. Because of its pact with Poland, was Britain now obliged to declare war on the Soviet Union? Since Hitler had come to power, the British Establishment had been split over whether to go to war with Germany or the USSR and ally with the other; now they faced the possibility of fighting both. Fortunately, Lord Halifax managed to find a solution: the treaty with Poland referred only to attack by European powers, and since the USSR was (of course) Asian, the government was under no obligation to act.[38]

This may have accorded with the letter of the pact, but Chamberlain had declared to Parliament on 31 March 1939:

> In the event of any action which clearly threatened Polish independence and which the Polish government considered it vital to resist with their national forces, His Majesty's government would feel themselves at once bound to lend the Polish government all its support in their power.[39]

The Russian attack clearly met those criteria.

The Odd Couple

The joint invasion was very carefully coordinated – in fact, Hitler's plans *depended* on the Russians. On 10 September, his ambassador in Moscow, Count Friedrich von der Schulenburg, reported that Molotov complained that the Wehrmacht's advance had caught the Kremlin out. Von der Schulenburg stated, 'I explained emphatically to Molotov how crucial speedy action of the Red Army was at this juncture.'[40] (Many other documents captured at the end of the war confirm this coordination.)

It was its invasion of Poland that inspired Churchill's famous description of the USSR as 'a riddle wrapped in a mystery inside an enigma', although he tacitly *supported* the Russians' action, as self-defence against the Nazis.[41] Even arch-anti-Bolshevik Churchill was now in favour of an alliance with the Soviet Union.

By 5 October, the fighting was over and Poland was torn like a bone between two dogs. Germany took 90,000 square miles and 13 million people, setting up a government in Warsaw; the USSR seized 60,000 square miles and 12 million people. The Polish Army's former Chief of the Staff, General Władysław Sikorski, established a government-in-exile in France, which decamped to Britain, together with Polish troops, after the fall of France. Later, the presence of Sikorski and the other Free Polish leaders in Britain became an awkward reminder of the original reasons Britain went to war. Another later source of hostility was the USSR's treatment of the Polish troops – and people – in the Soviet zone.

On 6 October 1939, Hitler offered peace talks with Britain and France – endorsed by Stalin, who branded them warmongers when they refused.[42] (The British Cabinet met four times before replying six days later that Germany should first prove its peaceful intentions.[43])

The Nazis and the USSR agreed on the final partitioning of Poland, pledging to 'tolerate in their territories no Polish agitation which affects the territories of the other party' and that they would 'suppress in their territories all beginnings of such agitation and inform each other concerning suitable measures for this purpose'[44] – i.e. no anti-Nazi activity in the Soviet zone or anti-Communist activity in the Nazi zone. Effectively, Polish Communists in the Soviet sector were silenced about the Nazi rule of the other sector, under pain of internment or worse.

Friendly Fire

The 'communisation' of Soviet-controlled Poland was announced by the secretary of the Ukrainian Communist Party, Nikita Khrushchev. To humour Stalin's paranoia, this first entailed executing the entire leadership of the Polish Communist Party – plus some 50,000 Polish refugees in the Soviet zone. The Russians also handed over to the Gestapo 600 German Communists who had fled to the USSR to escape Nazi persecution.[45]

When the Russians invaded Poland, they took 180,000 prisoners of war, deporting ordinary soldiers to Soviet gulags. Officers, together with officials such as policemen – 15,000 in all – went to three special camps in the western Soviet Union, and in spring 1940 were transported to an unknown destination, after which they simply disappeared. In 1943, after the Nazi invasion, the bodies of 4,400 of these people were discovered in mass graves in Katyń Forest near Smolensk, shot in the back of the head (NKVD style). The Russian government only admitted in 1990 that the NKVD had been responsible, giving locations of two other mass graves where inmates of the other two camps were buried. Stalin had ordered the massacre.[46]

Polish civilians also suffered atrociously in the Soviet controlled zone – as far as they were concerned, there was little to choose between the Russians and the Nazis. As Alan Bullock writes:

> Apart from Jews, the SS and NKVD agreed on the same priority targets for 'elimination'. Variously described in official documents as the Polish intelligentsia, the Polish elite, the former ruling class, it was the political leadership of the nation, local as well as national, which they both set out to destroy.[47]

The Soviet masters of eastern Poland singled out any potential opponent – former government officials, businessmen, intellectuals: 'anyone whose arrest seemed likely to contribute to the psychological breakdown of the inhabitants of eastern Poland'.[48] Those fleeing from the German zone – including many Jewish refugees – were also detained as security threats.

Many of those rounded up were deported to the USSR, although the exact number of Polish deportations is unknown: the Russian historian Aleksandr Guryanov suggests around half a million – nearly 110,000 to gulags and the rest to the exile villages – while others put the number nearer 1.5 million.[49]

Including the Polish Jews who died in the Holocaust, Poland lost about one in six of its population – six million people – during the Second World War, the highest proportion of any nation. Two million died during the 20-month period when it was divided between Germany and the USSR.[50]

In November 1939, the USSR launched an attack on Finland in the 'Winter War'. The small and lightly armed nation proved surprisingly resistant, although the final peace treaty, signed in March 1940, was heavily weighted in Russia's favour. Stalin then went on to annex the Baltic states of Estonia, Latvia and Lithuania.

Cooperation between Nazi Germany and Soviet Russia went as far as intelligence-sharing. The British were aware that the USSR was giving Germany information before Barbarossa – which aided Hitler's success against Britain and France.[51]

British and French strategy

At the outbreak of hostilities, Britain and France decided to use the same command structure as in the First World War: a Supreme War Council made up of Allied Prime Ministers and other senior figures. However, they decided that the Polish government should not be represented – despite the fact that the war was being fought over their country. The Supreme War Council planned for a three-year conflict based on a naval blockade that would either persuade Hitler to seek terms – or turn the German people against him. At that stage, they did not envisage a prolonged fight, largely because Chamberlain believed it would strip Britain of its last vestiges of power.[52]

The blockade strategy failed – because of the USSR. A trade agreement was signed between Germany and Russia in February 1940, and the German Foreign Ministry reported 'the effects of the English blockade will be decisively weakened by the incoming raw materials'.[53]

The period from October 1939 to April 1940 marked the phoney war, as the two sides avoided direct confrontation. The main action took place at sea – Britain blockading Germany from the first day of the war, and U-boats attacking British supply lines. And still Poland suffered alone.

The new Allies' lack of action demonstrates the futility – perhaps even the folly – of their promises to Poland. But why do nothing? It must be remembered that at that stage their overall aim was not to smash Nazism. In fact, as Poland was rapidly conquered, they barely seemed to know what their aims were themselves. Anticipating a long, slow war, Britain and France husbanded their resources carefully. The declaration of war also meant that American supplies were halted because of the Neutrality Act. Roosevelt had privately promised that he would – somehow – find a way around this, but Chamberlain and Daladier could hardly bank on it.

Chamberlain knew that an escalating conflict could well destroy the Empire, resulting in British dependence on America, and a stronger Soviet Union. This is the major difference not only between Churchill and Chamberlain but also between Churchill and every other wartime leader: he focused entirely on smashing the Nazis, without considering the aftermath. Criticism of his tunnel vision dogged him throughout his first year as Premier: he was a self-proclaimed *war* leader who was uninterested in anything else.[54] Although towards the end of the war he began to take a longer view, this fixation was shrewdly exploited by both Roosevelt and Stalin.

While the blockade was in place, Chamberlain's government intended to wait for an opportunity to seek a face-saving peace. His Assistant Private Secretary, John Colville, told Richard Lamb that the Prime Minister believed a real war would fail to materialise and that Germany would have to negotiate because of the blockade – adding that he was prepared to do a deal with anyone except Hitler.[55]

In the early months of the conflict, there were essentially three views in British political and industrial/financial circles: businessmen like Lord Beaverbrook and many Tories believed that as the war threatened to destroy Britain's interests so comprehensively, peace talks should begin immediately. Others, such as Chamberlain and Halifax, who wanted a deal with a Hitler-free Germany – although his regime could remain – made overtures to Göring. The third group believed the whole Nazi regime must go before attempting any settlement, favouring close cooperation with the anti-Hitlerites on the General Staff.

At that stage, not even Churchill advocated the fourth option – that *any* compromise with Germany under *any* leadership was out of the question.[56] The idea that the war should be fought until Germany was crushed was actually anathema to the British, since it would facilitate Soviet domination of Eastern and Central Europe.

Of the many 'phoney war' peace feelers, some were unofficial initiatives of businessmen or neutral countries, but others had the secret backing of Chamberlain and/or Halifax. Other approaches came from the Germans. Within weeks of the outbreak, Halifax wrote to Lothian in Washington, 'Peace feelers come almost every day', and to General Lord Gort, Commander-in-Chief of the British Expeditionary Force: 'A good many peace feelers being put out, all of them tracking to Göring.'[57] This was another reason for not intensifying the conflict.

'I don't need a law'

On the day war was declared, Roosevelt told the American people: 'This nation will remain a neutral nation, but I cannot ask that every American remain neutral in thought as well.' But now that war was a reality in Europe, *could* he keep his promises to Britain, France and Poland?

In spring 1939, he had asked Congress to repeal the Neutrality Act, but was rebuffed. In June, he had persuaded them to modify the arms embargo, allowing weapons and equipment to be supplied to 'non-aggressors', and then only on a 'cash-and-carry' basis – i.e. immediate payment and they picked up the goods themselves. But as Britain and France were technically the aggressors, having declared war, the embargo stood.

In the last days of peace, Roosevelt informed his Cabinet that if war came, he would delay applying the embargo. He asked the State and Justice Departments to prepare the paperwork at a snail's pace, while encouraging all American arms manufacturers to get as much as they could aboard ships or over the border into Canada before he signed the papers. In the event, he managed to delay only until 5 September: after that, the shipment of British and French orders worth $79 million in the pipeline ground to a halt. Although disastrous for them, it was also a massive blow for the USA; the embargo ensured that 'American munitions factories fell idle'.[58]

Having pushed Britain and France into war with his promises, on 20 September Roosevelt petitioned Congress again to repeal the Neutrality Act – his speech, in the words of American historian Willard Range, 'impregnated with subterfuge, never once admitting that his real objective was to aid England and France'.[59] He argued that the embargo was 'most vitally dangerous to American neutrality, American security, and, above all, American peace'.[60] His other major card was that it was in America's financial interests to supply Britain and France.[61] With the backing of Congress, FDR signed the repeal on 4 November, although it applied only to Britain and France, and then only on cash-and-carry terms. But as the French historian Henri Michel writes: 'It was a first infringement of neutrality and acceptable because it kept business turning over; but it was stripping the Allies of their gold reserves.'[62]

Warren Kimball, the leading American historian of Roosevelt's role in Anglo-American relations, points out that the amended Act 'became something that quickly drained France and Britain of much of their liquid capital'. He goes on:

> There is no evidence that Roosevelt's economic strategy aimed at exploiting the European crisis in that way, although Treasury official Harry Dexter White commented in 1938 that Britain would have to accept various economic terms set by the United States 'since she "needs our goodwill much more than we need hers at the present time."' Either way, the economic benefits to the United States were part of the political strategy for gaining public and congressional support.[63]

Unlike many researchers, Kimball does not completely dismiss the notion that Roosevelt exploited the European war to bail America out of its economic crisis, although finding 'no evidence' for it. But Roosevelt repeatedly told Congress and the public that assisting Britain would swell America's coffers – surely his own words count as evidence? And Harry Dexter White, adviser to Morgenthau, had said *in 1938* that if war came, America would be able to dictate economic terms to Britain – which is precisely what happened. If that isn't premeditation, what is? Finally, as White was later unmasked as a Soviet agent, whose interests did he have in mind?

After the embargo was lifted, in the winter of 1939–40, Britain and France bought $50 million worth of arms and equipment from US manufacturers, including ammunition made with New Deal funds diverted over a year earlier. In spring 1940, they ordered 4,600 US aircraft, with more to come – thanks to their own investment.

When Britain and France opened special accounts in the Federal Reserve Bank of New York, Morgenthau proposed that the Neutrality Act should be amended to make it a legal requirement for foreign nations to keep open accounts, Roosevelt merely said airily: 'No. If I want them to do it, I will just tell them to. I don't need a law.'[64]

He also exploited the crisis to extend his presidential powers, in September 1939 establishing the Executive Office of the President, which comprised six departments under his direct control – and taking control of the federal budget from the Treasury Department to the new Bureau of the Budget. After the war began in earnest in May 1940, FDR ensured that the US Treasury, not Wall Street, acted as middleman in Allied purchases. The profiteers in *this* war would be the US government.

After the Russian attack on Finland in November 1939, Roosevelt failed to invoke the required embargo, on the grounds that as neither side had officially declared war, a state of war did not exist, although after the Soviets bombed Finnish cities he did impose a 'moral embargo' on aircraft sales to the Soviet Union, later extended to materials (e.g. aluminium) needed to manufacture aircraft.[65]

Peace: the real bogeyman
Within days of the outbreak of war, Roosevelt instructed Ambassador Kennedy to steer clear of peace negotiations. He went further, actively opposing the British policy to put out 'unofficial' peace feelers to anti-Hitler factions in Germany. At any cost, the war must continue.

Kennedy's opposition to Britain's involvement in the war prompted Roosevelt's virulent outburst to Morgenthau:

> Joe Kennedy . . . has been an appeaser and always will be
> an appeaser . . . If Germany or Italy made a good peace
> offer tomorrow, Joe would start working on the King and
> his friend, the Queen, and from there on down to get
> everybody to accept it . . . He's just a pain in the neck to
> me.[66]

Note 'a *good* peace offer' – not total surrender and subjugation, but a deal that would allow Britain to escape from a war it never wanted with its dignity intact.

Two weeks into hostilities, Roosevelt approved the personal initiative of his financial backer, William Rhodes Davis – who had a lucrative contract to supply oil to Germany – in which he would act as mediator. In Berlin, Davis met Göring, who said: 'You may assure Mr Roosevelt that if he will undertake mediation, Germany will agree to an adjustment whereby a new Polish state and a new Czechoslovakian independent government would come into being.' Astonishingly, Göring agreed in principle to attend a peace conference in Washington, leading Hitler to offer the peace talks on 6 October. But back in Washington, Davis was stunned when Roosevelt refused to see him or even return his calls. Was this complete volte-face due to the unexpected *success* of Davis's mission?[67]

Of the ostensibly unofficial attempts to bring the two sides together, many were actually endorsed by both Neville Chamberlain and Lord Halifax – although they often had to be abandoned because Roosevelt formally reported them to the British government. In November 1939, he informed Chamberlain of a peace move by a 'substantial element of English big business'.[68]

Churchill's finest hour

When in April 1940 the army and Royal Navy retreated after ignominiously failing to prevent the Nazis from occupying Norway, criticism in Parliament of Chamberlain's leadership reached such a crescendo that he realised he would have to form a coalition government. But even when Labour and the Liberals refused to serve under him, and he resigned, it was hardly a foregone conclusion that Churchill would replace him.

The Odd Couple

In 1955, George VI's official biographer, the wartime intelligence officer Sir John Wheeler-Bennett, told Robert Bruce Lockhart:

> . . . George VI did not like W.S.C. He was an admirer of Chamberlain and was one hundred per cent pro-Munich. He disliked W.S.C.'s attitude to Munich, and doubtless his championing of the Duke of Windsor at the time of the Abdication did not commend itself to George VI and his Queen . . . it is on record that he told Roosevelt that only in very exceptional circumstances could he consent to W.S.C.'s being made Prime Minister.[69]

(Interestingly, Churchill as possible leader had clearly been discussed during the state visit in June 1939 – when he was still languishing on the back benches.) In late 1939, only 30 per cent of the public wanted Churchill as Prime Minister, while just over 50 per cent thought Chamberlain should stay. In April 1940, 60 per cent approved of Chamberlain's performance so far in the war.[70]

As there was a coalition there was no general election, but although effectively it was the King's decision whom he called to form the new government, Chamberlain wanted the matter to be finalised before he tendered his resignation at the Palace by ensuring there was only one possible candidate, agreed by all sides. It was either Churchill or Lord Halifax – who was favoured by the Conservatives, the King and outgoing Prime Minister. Although Churchill was the favourite of the Labour and Liberal Parties, and Tory rebels, the Labour and Liberal leaders made it clear to Chamberlain that Halifax was also acceptable. After an intense meeting at 10 Downing Street on 9 May 1940 the shockwaves were palpable when Churchill emerged as the new leader of the country. So how did the scorned, near-alcoholic outsider come to seize the ultimate prize?

Basically, Churchill became Prime Minister because Halifax refused the job, ostensibly on the grounds that as a member of the House of Lords – not entitled to set foot in the Commons – his hands would be tied, especially at such a critical time in Britain's history. Although George VI even suggested suspending his peerage for the duration, Halifax remained 'unpersuadable'.[71]

In his memoirs, Churchill acknowledged that Halifax was given first refusal.[72] Yet his details are suspect – he even misdates this meeting, giving it as 10 May (when he was summoned by the King and took office). One of his researchers, Sir William Deacon, said he was 'hamming [it] up . . . he's being amusing, it's not to be taken seriously'.[73] Halifax's biographer Andrew Roberts suggests that Churchill's account 'ought to be read as literature, rather than a factual account'.[74]

While admitting that Halifax's peerage was not the real problem, Roberts argues that he refused the job because he modestly felt he lacked the qualities to be a successful wartime Prime Minister. This seems unlikely because Halifax continued his efforts to find a compromise peace behind Churchill's back – and becoming head of government would have enabled him to make this official policy.

Halifax's own account makes it clear that he was uncertain that he would be able to exert due control over the war from the House of Lords, and so would become 'more or less an honorary Prime Minister'.[75] But rather than doubting his own abilities, he seems rather to have been afraid that he would not be *allowed* that control: he told Sir Alexander Cadogan immediately after the meeting, 'If I was not in charge of the war (operations) and if I didn't lead in the house, I should be a cipher.'[76]

So who *was* to be in charge of the war? Regardless of who became Prime Minister, the answer most certainly was Winston Spencer Churchill. Chamberlain seems to have wanted a compromise, with Halifax as Prime Minister but with Churchill actually running the war. If Halifax refused these terms, the alternative was for Churchill to run the whole show; handing everything over to Halifax simply wasn't acceptable to Chamberlain, which is odd, since they shared the same war policies – and most decidedly Churchill did not.

Somehow, Churchill held the balance of power. In his diary, John Colville even refers mysteriously to Churchill's 'powers of blackmail' that swung the decision.[77] What blackmail? What did Churchill have that Halifax hadn't? Halifax had the support of the ruling party, the opposition, the King – and the people. Only one person supported Churchill and not Halifax: President Roosevelt.

By instigating the Roosevelt–Churchill correspondence, FDR had effectively given Churchill his blessing, handing him an ace. The President was announcing the identity of his favoured candidate as British leader. Having brought up the subject of Churchill as Prime Minister – then a remote possibility – with a horrified George VI in June 1939, clearly FDR had his eye on his man even then. Then there was his curious statement to Kennedy that he had instigated the correspondence because Churchill might soon be Prime Minister.

As mentioned in the previous chapter, Roosevelt made it clear through private intermediaries that aid would only be forthcoming if the British government took a tough line with Hitler: any further attempts at appeasement would jeopardise assistance. Halifax favoured peace negotiations: therefore only Churchill could bring American support to the table. (Curiously, just a week after war broke out, during a discussion on the neutrality of Egypt – if it remained neutral it could be used as a 'back door' for American supplies – Churchill confidently declared, 'we certainly have no need to keep her neutral for the purpose of war purchases from the United States who will very soon give us all we want direct.'[78] How could he be so sure, when at that stage there was no certainty that Congress would repeal the embargo?)

Originally, Chamberlain appears to have sought to cover all eventualities by making Halifax Prime Minister (to pursue the compromise peace policy) with Churchill in charge of the war effort (in case that compromise peace failed). But when Halifax refused this arrangement, Chamberlain had no choice but to throw his support behind Churchill. No threats or cajoling by either Roosevelt or Churchill was needed – the President's favour was enough.

In this context, FDR's reaction to the news of Chamberlain's resignation is particularly significant. Harold Ickes, Secretary of the Interior, recorded:

> While we were at Cabinet, word was brought in that Chamberlain had resigned. We assumed that Churchill would be charged with the duty of organizing a new Cabinet and the President said that he supposed Churchill was the best man that England had.[79]

(That is the published version. The original adds, '. . . even if he was drunk half of his time. Apparently Churchill is very unreliable when under the influence of drink.'[80]) But why seize on Churchill of all people as the man of the moment – especially when few in Britain saw him in the same light?

Clearly, Roosevelt had decided months in advance that Churchill was his man. But why choose someone he had met only once over 20 years before, and whose background, character and politics – apart from his line on the war – he disliked? Who had briefed him on Churchill? It could hardly have been the anti-war Kennedy, who thoroughly loathed him and all he stood for. (Kennedy wrote: 'Maybe I do him [Churchill] an injustice but I just don't trust him. He always impressed me that he was willing to blow up the American Embassy and say it was the Germans if it would get the United States in.'[81])

A clue may lie in the fact that one man was close to both – the financier and speculator Bernard Mannes Baruch, another immensely wealthy figure who wielded almost unimaginable influence over the seminal moments of the twentieth century. In the First World War, he was perhaps the most powerful man in the United States, being Chairman of the War Industries Board – a position very similar to that of Harry Hopkins in the Second World War. In the early years of Roosevelt's presidency, and before Hopkins' star ascended, Baruch was one of his closest advisers. During the honeymoon period of the New Deal, the press even dubbed him the 'Acting President'.[82]

Churchill had known Baruch since 1919, when the financier was in President Wilson's team at Versailles, and they had subsequently become business partners.[83] When Churchill faced bankruptcy in 1938, even putting his beloved Chartwell up for sale, Baruch was one of two Jewish financiers who bailed him out. (Of course, the fact that Churchill was so heavily indebted to Jewish money was not lost on the Nazis.) Baruch wrote to Churchill in September 1937 asking him to help develop 'an understanding between England and America',[84] and when in summer 1938 Roosevelt sent him to Europe to assess the situation, he sought out Churchill to elicit his views. Churchill said wistfully, 'War is coming very soon. We will be in it and you will be in it. You will be running the show over there, but I will be on the sidelines over here.'[85]

Clearly, Baruch could brief Roosevelt on Churchill's strengths and weaknesses, advising he was the best man to have in power in Britain for his own agenda. Once FDR had chosen him, the unspoken blackmail of American aid would have done the rest – which may explain Churchill's son Randolph's famous account of their conversation in May 1940 as his father shaved:

> After two or three minutes of hacking away, he half turned and said: 'I think I see my way through.' He resumed his shaving.
>
> I was astounded, and said: 'Do you mean that we can avoid defeat? [which seemed incredible] or beat the bastards? [which seemed incredible].'
>
> He flung his Valet razor into the basin, swung around, and said: 'Of course I mean we can beat them.'
>
> Me: 'Well, I'm all for it, but I don't see how you can do it.'
>
> By this time he had dried and sponged his face and turning around to me said with great intensity: 'I shall drag the United States in.'[86]

If it was indeed Roosevelt who made Winston Churchill Prime Minister, then he was soon to repay the favour.

The old man takes over

There was less enthusiasm at home than there was in the White House: '. . . when Churchill first entered the Chamber as Prime Minister, his own benches greeted him in silence. For some months, the only spontaneous cheers for Churchill came from the Labour and Liberal benches.'[87]

As Chamberlain remained Conservative leader, Churchill bizarrely became a Prime Minister with no party. But the new boy wasted no time: besides being Premier and First Lord of the Treasury, Churchill also created the new post of Minister of Defence – and immediately took it himself. He created a five-member War

Cabinet, comprising Chamberlain, Halifax and the Labour Party leader and deputy, Clement Attlee and Arthur Greenwood. It was clearly a compromise cabinet, another sign of Churchill's weak position being the appointment of the anti-war Sir John Simon as Lord Chancellor. The only senior member of Chamberlain's government to be dismissed completely was the pro-peace Quaker Sir Samuel Hoare. Sir Horace Wilson was kept on as head of the Civil Service – another sign of equivocation as he was regarded as the 'Svengali of appeasement'.[88]

Although Chamberlain was far from a spent force, even hoping to return as Prime Minister after the war, within months he was struck down with cancer, dying on 9 November 1940. Only then did Churchill become leader of the Conservative Party.

An historic date

So it was that on 10 May 1940, Winston Churchill finally became Prime Minister – a date of historic importance for two other reasons. At the dawn of that day, the Second World War really began, with the launch of the German blitzkrieg in the Low Countries. Even after Norway, there was still a chance of negotiating an end to hostilities, but once this attack had begun such hopes rapidly faded. (When news of the German offensive filtered through, Chamberlain tried to withdraw his resignation, but it was too late.) The other event took place in Washington.

During the Polish crisis, and most of the phoney war, Roosevelt had had to cope without the advice and support of Harry Hopkins. Months of illness had culminated in his return to the Mayo Clinic in August 1939, just as events in Europe were reaching their climax. Initially, it was feared his cancer had recurred, but it transpired he could no longer digest proteins or fats. As Hopkins had been given only four weeks to live, Roosevelt called in the Surgeon-General of the Navy, Admiral Edward R. Stitt, whose experimental daily injections of nutrients kept Hopkins alive for six more years – otherwise he would have starved to death no matter how much he ate. Confined to bed until March 1940, apart from occasional letters to the President, Hopkins was out of action during almost the entire period of the phoney war. Sherwood writes: 'It was the one crisis in

Roosevelt's career when he was completely at a loss as to what action to take – a period of terrible, stultifying vacuum.'[89]

Despite the treatment, Hopkins was clearly on borrowed time: 'He was to all intents and purposes physically a finished man who might drag out his life for a few years of relative inactivity or who might collapse and die at any time.'[90] Ironically, those six years were his most influential.

Kept ticking over by the injections, on the evening of 10 May 1940 Hopkins was dining at the White House when news flooded in of historic developments in Europe: the Nazis had attacked, and, against the odds, Churchill was now Prime Minister. Because of the crisis, Roosevelt asked his friend and confidant to stay overnight – in fact, the White House was to be Hopkins' home for most of the next five years.

The two men had breakfast and dinner together besides meeting several times each day to discuss new developments in the war. Hopkins even had the best bedroom, formerly Abraham Lincoln's study, which had been allocated to George VI during his state visit. Ironically, once a White House resident he moaned, 'I'm getting sick and tired of having to listen to complaints from those goddam New Dealers!'[91]

With war in Europe, Hopkins helped set up the National Defense Advisory Commission, taking control of war and food production, price controls and the mobilisation of labour. He swiftly gathered expertise in war production, establishing links with the Army Ordnance Department. Roosevelt set up a number of agencies to handle various aspects of the war, without recourse to Congress, on the authority of laws passed in the First World War and even the Civil War.[92] Their directors reported directly to him, forming a 'kind of Government within a Government'.[93]

Hopkins was also instrumental in establishing America's atomic bomb project. In June 1940, when physicist Dr Vannevar Bush enlisted his support for creating a body to oversee and coordinate defence-related research, he secured FDR's approval, and the National Defense Research Council (NDRC) was born. Bush and Hopkins drafted a letter to Bush himself for Roosevelt to sign, authorising the NDRC to cooperate closely with the military authorities, including the instruction, 'Recently I appointed a special committee . . . to study into the possible relationship to national defence of recent discoveries in the field of atomistics, notably the fission of uranium. I will now request that this committee report directly to you [Bush].'[94] But what really lay behind Hopkins' avid interest in the progress of the uranium fission project? Was it patriotism – or was he acting from quite different motives, even as a Soviet agent?

The Tyler Kent scandal

In his biography of Joseph Kennedy, *The Founding Father* (1965), Richard J. Whalen writes that, despite his clash with Roosevelt over war policy, ' . . . in 1940 the Ambassador served as an accomplice in maneuvers designed to deceive the American people as to the ramifications of Roosevelt's foreign policy.'[95] The manoeuvres concerned the repercussions following the arrest of a junior American Embassy official in London, Tyler Gatewood Kent, on 20 May 1940.

The 29-year-old code and cipher clerk was responsible for relaying messages between the US Embassy in London and the State Department, with access to some of the most sensitive material in existence, certainly as far as the British were concerned. A police raid on Kent's flat found a battered suitcase containing copies of some 1,500 confidential documents he had purloined from the Embassy.

Kennedy having waived Kent's diplomatic immunity, he was tried in camera by a British court at the Old Bailey, being found guilty of theft and of violating the Official Secrets Act – although significantly, there was no charge of passing secrets to a foreign power. He was sentenced to seven years in prison – the verdict not being made public until after the American election in November 1940 – and was eventually deported to the United States in December 1945.

The Tyler Kent affair is still perplexing: he seems to have been at the centre of double and triple games of espionage involving MI5, British Nazi sympathisers, anti-Soviet Russian émigrés, the NKVD and German and Italian intelligence – small wonder the whole affair still has to be properly unravelled even after 60 years![96]

For our purposes, the real interest lies in the panic that Kent's arrest caused in the Roosevelt administration, not because he may have been passing information to the Nazis but because it threatened to expose the Churchill–Roosevelt communications to Congress. In his defence, Kent claimed that he was not a foreign agent: he stole the documents to pass to Congress because they revealed that the President was engaged in unconstitutional acts and was deceiving both Congress and the American people.

Robert Shogan argues that the Kent affair was shrouded in secrecy specifically to protect Roosevelt and his secret negotiations with Churchill.[97] Whalen agrees: the fact of their correspondence would have ruined FDR's chances of a third term, and so 'the administration, acting through Kennedy, took extraordinary measures to ensure silence'.[98] But what was so compromising about the messages? Of course, while still expressing 'non-interventionist' views in public and promising to keep America out of the war, Roosevelt's day-to-day communication with the British leader (even when First Lord of the Admiralty) would have been suspicious enough. Also, discussing ways of arming Britain that went beyond what was allowed by the latest version of the Neutrality Act would have been a gift to his opponents in an election year.

Three days after Churchill took office, FDR sent Kennedy to inform the British Government that the US was now prepared 'to go to almost any lengths to help [the] Allies, except to send men'.[99] The new Prime Minister asked Kennedy for 'thirty or forty of our old destroyers' as a stopgap for British production, and for 'whatever planes we could spare'.[100] His cable the next day – his first as 'Former Naval Person' – explained that as he expected Britain to be attacked soon, he asked FDR to proclaim a state of 'non-belligerency' 'which would mean that you would help us with everything short of actually engaging armed forces'. He also asked for the loan of 'forty or fifty of your older destroyers', several hundred warplanes – to be replaced by those Britain had on order – plus anti-aircraft guns and steel, and for cooperation in preventing any Japanese aggression in South-East Asia: 'I am looking to you to keep that Japanese dog quiet in the Pacific, using Singapore in any way convenient.' Churchill added, 'We shall go on paying dollars for as long as we can but I should like to feel reasonably sure that when we can pay no more, you will give us the stuff all the same.'[101] Roosevelt replied that he was unable to provide the destroyers without Congress's approval, and that he was 'doubtful' whether the ships could be spared, as they might soon be needed for America's own defence, but that he would see what he could do about the planes.[102]

This may sound innocuous now, but Churchill had asked for ships, planes and guns from the *US government*. Under international law, the supply of implements of war by a neutral government was considered an act of war. Although the US had long contested this principle, nevertheless it had no option but to comply. For this reason, when the Neutrality Act was amended to allow Britain and France to be supplied on a cash-and-carry basis, it was specifically stated that they could deal only with American arms manufacturers and dealers – i.e. private companies – not with the US government or armed forces.[103]

Under the circumstances, Churchill's request for US ships and aircraft, besides others, such as help in keeping Japan quiet – should have met with an immediate negative from Roosevelt. Even 'seeing what he could do' put him in violation of US and international law, undermining his nation's neutrality. It was tantamount to declaring war – no wonder there was such panic in the State Department.

Because of Kent's swift arrest, none of this came out, but Joseph Kennedy knew about it, and as his relations with Roosevelt broke down, it was something else for the White House to worry about.

Churchill was not to go away empty-handed. Although General Marshall vetoed his request for aircraft and anti-aircraft guns because the US Army needed them, he did agree to the release of 250,000 rifles, 80,000 machine guns, 130 million rounds of ammunition, 900 75mm guns and a million shells – arriving in time to replace equipment lost at Dunkirk – as well as 140 bombers.[104] In Robert Sherwood's words this was 'done by means of more legal manipulation in a "damn the torpedoes" spirit',[105] and – as in many of the subsequent deals – it appears to have been Harry Hopkins who found the loophole: 'It was his convenient conviction that a precedent can almost always be found for a new idea, however revolutionary it may seem, if you really search for it.'[106] The precedent on this occasion was a law from 1919 (when the US scaled down its military) which allowed the army to sell surplus stocks to private manufacturers. The guns, ammunition and bombers were promptly declared 'surplus' and sold off to arms companies, who could then legally sell them on to Britain and France. Some of it demonstrably wasn't truly surplus – the US Navy even sent back 50 Hell Diver bombers, some having only been in service for three months. The US Army had offered to take them, but somehow they ended up in Britain.[107]

'Those bloody Yankees'

In his communications with Roosevelt when still in the Admiralty, Churchill had used the strategy of subtle blackmail and telling Roosevelt what he wanted to hear so the isolationists could be won over. As soon as he became Prime Minister, Churchill began to play on Roosevelt's fears, reassuring Roosevelt that while *he* would never consider negotiating terms (although, as we will see, there were circumstances in which he *might*), he could be replaced by a government that would. Roosevelt was also afraid that if Britain was defeated, its navy might fall under German control – which *did* present a threat to the United States, since America's military strength resided in its fleet, and the combined Anglo-German navy would outstrip it.[108] On 19 May 1940, Churchill told Colville, 'Here's another telegram for those bloody Yankees'[109] – in which he said that, if invasion came, he intended to go down fighting but:

> If members of the present administration were finished and others came in to parley amid the ruins, you must not be blind to the fact that the sole remaining bargaining counter with Germany would be the fleet, and if this country was left by the United States to its fate no one would have the right to blame those then responsible if they made the best terms they could for the surviving inhabitants. Excuse me, Mr President, putting this nightmare bluntly. I could not answer for my successors who in utter despair and helplessness might have to accommodate themselves to the German will.[110]

This was a transparent promise that if Roosevelt sent aid, the fleet would not be turned over to the Germans – besides hinting that some Britons favoured a compromise peace. (The President already knew this – after all, his ambassador took tea with two of them at Buckingham Palace.)

The linking of the fate of the fleet to the assistance Roosevelt could furnish was suggested to Churchill by Lord Lothian in Washington, but the Foreign Office saw it as 'rather like blackmail, and not very good blackmail at that'.[111] In another move to pile pressure onto Roosevelt, on 5 June 1940 Churchill sent a message to the Canadian Prime Minister, Mackenzie King – to be passed privately to the President – declaring that if the US entered the war and Britain was defeated, the fleet would naturally be transferred to them, but 'if America continued neutral, and we were overpowered, I cannot tell what policy might be adopted by a pro-German administration as would undoubtedly be set up'.[112]

Hugh Keenleyside, First Secretary of Canada's Department of External Affairs, was dispatched to Washington specifically to inform the President about this message. Jay Pierrepont Moffat, the US Minister to Canada, recorded in his diary for 10 June 1940:

> This message had disturbed the President considerably, as Mr Churchill had not given specific assurances that the British fleet would under no circumstances be surrendered. He seemed to envisage a possibility that in the event things went wrong, he might have to respond to public pressure, to go to the Palace, and hand over office to a government more sympathetic to the Germans.[113]

Churchill had another delicate balancing task: he had to make Roosevelt aware that Britain was desperately short of arms and equipment (otherwise no aid would be forthcoming) but not so short that they might face defeat (ditto). However, in the event, the 'surplus' Roosevelt authorised in May would be the last for a while. As the British and French forces collapsed, the President waited to see what would happen: after all, what was the point in going out on a limb to help when defeat seemed imminent?[114]

The darkest hour

Within days of Churchill taking office, it seemed that Britain faced utter disaster: just two weeks into the German offensive, the British and French forces had been broken and driven back. The traumatised remnants of the British Expeditionary Force having been momentously evacuated from Dunkirk, it was only a question of when, not if, France would surrender. At that darkest point in British history, *everyone* – including Churchill and his Cabinet – anticipated that if France fell it would simply be impossible for Britain to fight on alone.

Today, most people believe that even with the Nazis beating the British back into the Channel, the solitary figure of Churchill towered above the pessimists (and even the realists), scorning the very notion of a negotiated settlement. However, in reality the new Prime Minister *was* open to the idea provided that the terms were right – although his view of what was right differed from those of his Cabinet. Also, he had to maintain the pretence to Roosevelt that he had no interest in *any* terms, otherwise there would be no further aid.

At that stage, Churchill maintained that negotiations should begin only when Hitler knew it was impossible to defeat Britain: talks had to be conducted with Germany as at least an equal (but preferably weaker) partner. But whereas to him even asking for details of Hitler's terms would be interpreted as a sign of weakness, Halifax's view was that once France fell, Britain had no option but to ask for terms. Churchill, however, did state that if the Führer *offered* terms he would consider them.[115]

Halifax has been slated as a defeatist, an appeaser – even a traitor – but as far as he was concerned, any deal that preserved Britain's sovereign independence was preferable to a defeat that threatened it. He was not prepared to gamble with Britain's independence. But Churchill was. His refusal to negotiate from a position of weakness may even provide an explanation for one of the war's most enduring controversies: Hitler's 'Halt Order' of 24 May 1940. This stopped the German advance for three days – even recalling tank units that had successfully cut off the British retreat – giving the Allies time to set up defences around Dunkirk. Without this three-day delay, there would have been no Dunkirk 'miracle'. Since this was discovered in German documents captured after the war, historians have been at pains to point out that the order came from the German army commanders for (mistaken) tactical reasons. But the order was unequivocally signed by Hitler, who informed his generals that once France was defeated, he intended to offer Britain terms, which would be more likely to be accepted if 'compatible with her honour' – i.e. if the British were not negotiating from a position of weakness because their army was being held hostage.[116]

For many days, it looked as if the British Expeditionary Force was lost – plunging everyone, including Churchill, into the deepest gloom. Surely they would have to make terms. How could Britain fight on without an army? But then, as it became clear that the Dunkirk evacuation was more successful than anyone dared hope, some optimism returned. Matters reached a head in a series of tense War Cabinet meetings on 27 and 28 May, 'probably the most fateful Cabinet meetings of the century.'[117]

The Cabinet was divided. After the meeting on 26 May, Chamberlain recorded in his diary that Churchill declared 'if we could get out of this jam by giving up Malta and Gibraltar & some African colonies [specifically Somaliland, Kenya and Uganda] he would jump at it'.[118] The War Cabinet minutes for the following day reveal that Churchill said 'he [Churchill] would be thankful to get out of our present difficulties on such terms provided we retained the essentials and the elements of our vital strength, even at the cost of some cession of territory'.[119]

Churchill announced he would wait and see how matters stood in two or three months before deciding whether to approach Hitler for terms – but added that he *was* prepared to make concessions then if necessary. Believing that Britain had to seek terms immediately, Halifax disagreed with Churchill so vehemently he even decided to resign but eventually agreed to stay on. Lamb writes, 'It must have been touch and go whether Halifax's or Churchill's view prevailed. If Halifax had had his way, European history would have been very different. On 27 May, he was ready for overtures to Hitler.'[120]

In any case, the situation changed overnight because of breaking news that the Dunkirk evacuation was going better than expected – Britain might still have an army after all. As a result, at the 28 May

The Odd Couple

Cabinet meeting Halifax was isolated because Chamberlain and the Labour members now backed Churchill.

On 4 June 1940 – after the last ships limped away from Dunkirk – Churchill gave one of his classic speeches to the House of Commons, the rousing rhetoric finely tuned to the ordinary people of whom he was demanding such sacrifice – besides his fellow MPs, and even those in his Cabinet who thought Britain should actively be seeking peace. His words were also carefully aimed at foreigners: particularly President Roosevelt, whom he both reassured and presented with a thumbnail sketch of his towering courage – and utterly terrifying expectations:

> We shall fight on the beaches, we shall fight on the landing grounds, we shall fight in the fields and in the streets, we shall fight in the hills; we shall never surrender, and even if, which I do not for a moment believe, this island or a large part of it were subjugated and starving, our Empire beyond the seas, armed and guarded by the British Fleet, would carry on the struggle, until, in God's good time, the new world, with all its power and might, steps forth to the rescue and the liberation of the old.[121]

Even then, a group of 30 MPs and 10 peers, led by Labour MP Richard Stokes, proposed that Lloyd George be made Prime Minister to oversee peace talks – although it must be stressed that they sought peace only when *there was no longer any threat of invasion.*[122] Lloyd George himself took this position[123] – as indeed did Churchill, although his views on acceptable terms were different from Stokes' supporters', a position not precluded by the 'fight on the beaches' speech, with its focus on repelling invasion.

Stokes' group was not an immediate problem for Churchill as long as there was a threat of invasion – as we will see, a period he artificially prolonged by deliberately withholding the news that Hitler had abandoned the idea in September 1940. (It was the Lloyd George/Stokes cabal that orchestrated the pressure on Churchill three days before Hess's arrival, strongly suggesting the two events were coordinated.[124])

'The butchery was Churchill's doing'

Britain was in a precarious position when the German invasion of France began on 5 June 1940. Just eight days later, Paris was declared an open city – the government decamping to Tours then Bordeaux – the first German jackboots echoing in dusty suburban streets that same evening. Three days later, the Reynaud government resigned and the Fascist-friendly First World War hero Marshal Henri Philippe Pétain was asked to form a new government. He immediately sought terms and an armistice was duly signed on 22 June.

In the middle of this, Mussolini saw an opportunity to grab territory from France, declaring war on 10 June. Up until then, Churchill had wanted Italy to stay neutral – largely because of his admiration for Mussolini. While in the Admiralty, he had advocated buying vessels from Italy as an incentive for it to stay neutral, and in early 1940 the British government had even attempted to buy Italian planes, until the deal was blocked by Hitler.[125] On becoming Prime Minister, Churchill urged Mussolini to remain neutral: 'I declare I have never been the enemy of Italian greatness, nor ever at heart the foe of the Italian law-giver.'[126]

On 10 June 1940, Reynaud made a desperate appeal to Roosevelt: 'Tell your people that France is sacrificing everything in the cause of freedom. We desperately need at once every form of material and moral help you can give us short of an expeditionary force.'[127] Although Roosevelt privately urged him to fight on, Churchill suggested he say so publicly to demonstrate his support for the Allies – but FDR was horrified: 'He wanted to say enough to keep the French fighting, but no more.'[128] More practically, by 'some subtle and possibly questionable legal shenanigans worked out by Henry Morgenthau's lawyers at the Treasury Department',[129] Roosevelt got 150 USAAF planes onto a French aircraft carrier in Canada, but it was too late – France had already surrendered. Roosevelt transferred its arms contracts to Britain.

During France's agony, the British considered several plans – now clearly desperate – to keep the fight going. A famous proposal was the formal union of Britain and France – their inhabitants being given joint citizenship (unsurprisingly rejected by the French government).[130] Other initiatives were even more breathtaking. Discussions were held with Irish Prime Minister Eamon de Valera with the offer that, at the end of the war, Northern Ireland should be ceded to the Republic, in return for Eire reversing 'the so-called neutrality of so-called Eire', as Churchill so tactfully put it.[131] The British even got as far as offering a 'firm undertaking' until the stunned Northern Ireland government found out about it.[132] Anxious about the consequences of Franco siding with Hitler, Churchill's Cabinet also considered offering him talks at the end of the war on the vexed subject of the future of Gibraltar, in return for his remaining neutral. (In May, the Cabinet had considered offering Gibraltar to *Mussolini* as an incentive for him to mediate with Hitler.[133]) Franco rejected this because if Britain lost, Spain would get Gibraltar anyway, and he knew that if the British won, they had no intention of keeping their promise.[134] Finally, in need of Argentinian beef and wheat, Churchill also considered leasing the Falkland Islands to Argentina . . .[135]

With the French armistice, Hitler believed the war on the Western Front was over, ordering, on 25 June, ten days of national celebrations. Molotov asked the German Ambassador in Moscow to pass on to the Führer 'the warmest good wishes of the Soviet government on the Wehrmacht's brilliant success'.[136]

Sumner Welles wrote afterwards that Hitler's terms for an armistice with France were 'unexpectedly lenient',[137] although they were traumatic enough. The Führer demanded German control of the Channel and Atlantic coastlines, and two-thirds of the country. In return, the French government was allowed to govern the remainder of the country from the southern spa town of Vichy (originally intended as a temporary seat of government pending a return to Paris). But Hitler *was* lenient about the fate of the French fleet and colonies.

Pétain's Vichy government was allowed to keep its colonies in North and West Africa, and French Indo-China. Hitler was simply not interested: after all, Germany's colonies were to be in Eastern and Central Europe. (However, in September 1940, Japan began a series of military and diplomatic moves to seize the resources of French Indo-China.)

Friendly Fire

Although the British did recognise Pétain's regime as the legitimate government of France, Vichy broke off diplomatic relations with Britain after the notorious Mers-el-Kébir incident. As all French warships were either away or scuttled, there were none for the Germans to capture. Hitler knew that if he demanded the surrender of the remaining fleet, it would probably sail to Britain and keep fighting, so instead he demanded its demobilisation – the armistice 'left the French navy in French hands'.[138] Any French ships in UK ports were taken by the British, most of the others being safely blockaded in France, but a number were docked at Mers-el-Kébir in Algeria. On 3 July 1940, Churchill issued its commander, Admiral Marcel Gensoul, with an ultimatum: join the British fleet (in contravention of the armistice) or scuttle your ships. When this was turned down, the Royal Navy destroyed or disabled all but one, killing 1,300 French sailors. The Allies of less than two weeks before were now legitimate targets – to Churchill. Even Lamb writes: 'The butchery was Churchill's doing . . .'[139]

The ensuing outrage prompted the new Vichy government to break off diplomatic relations with Britain – there were even calls for war to be declared. But Roosevelt welcomed Churchill's ruthlessness: at least those particular ships would not end up sailing under the swastika.

The fall of France brought another 'man of destiny' to the fore – Brigadier-General Charles de Gaulle, appointed Under-Secretary of State for National Defence just ten days before the surrender. Flying to Britain – thanks to Churchill's personal intervention – on 18 June 1940 he made the impassioned broadcast known as *L'Appel* ('The Call'). Appealing to all the French people to gather around him and continue the 'French resistance', he declared:

> France is not alone! She is not alone! She is not alone! Behind her is a vast Empire, and she can make common cause with the British Empire, which commands the seas and is continuing the struggle. Like England, she can draw unreservedly on the immense industrial resources of the United States.[140]

The last sentence may be somewhat optimistic, but it shows how vital American aid was universally considered.

Churchill saw in de Gaulle a fellow '*homme du destin*', recognising him as the 'leader of all free Frenchmen, wherever they may be', agreeing to finance the new Free French forces (which, as most Frenchmen who had been evacuated from Dunkirk elected to return home after the armistice, was just 4,500 soldiers and sailors).

Meanwhile, Lord Halifax doggedly continued to seek peace. During June and July, behind Churchill's back, he put out at least two, possibly four, feelers through Sweden and sympathetic individuals in Washington. Had he become Prime Minister, a compromise peace would undoubtedly have been found in the summer of 1940. Others involved were Halifax's Under-Secretary R.A. 'Rab' Butler and, in Washington, Lord Lothian, whose aim was apparently to persuade Hitler to make an offer. The relevant Cabinet papers remain closed to this day.[141]

Even then, Churchill declared himself open to a deal, as long as Britain had proved to be unconquerable. What he would have found 'acceptable' is unknown, but must have hinged on how much Britain would have to give up to satisfy Hitler (as we know from the Hess proposals, it would have been relatively little).

Was Churchill – not yet in total command – just pretending to be open to peace overtures to circumvent Cabinet opposition? Some of his decisions do suggest that he wanted Britain to fight on in the long term: perhaps understandably, not to be seen as weak, he had forbidden any communication with the Nazi government – but surely it is considerably more puzzling that he also banned contact with the German 'resistance', pre-empting the possibility of ending the war through regime change.

Missed opportunities

Before Churchill took over, contact between the anti-Hitler generals and the British government had continued. After Poland, the Schwarze Kapelle made new plans to remove Hitler with a near-bloodless coup: the army would arrest and charge him with the Polish atrocities, but then declare him mentally unfit to stand trial. Any Nazi leaders who got in the way would be shot and their deaths blamed on the SS. General Beck would be temporary leader pending the restoration of the monarchy, and a ceasefire would be declared as a prelude to an armistice. However, as the conspirators needed to be sure that Britain and France would agree to a ceasefire, Canaris was asked to establish clandestine contact, which he did through the Vatican.[142]

In January and February 1940, the Schwarze Kapelle's overtures were reported to Lord Halifax and discussed by Chamberlain's Cabinet. The conspirators, who were desperate to prevent the war intensifying because they knew Hitler was about to attack the Low Countries, sought the sole condition of a guarantee that the sovereignty of the united Germany and Austria should be respected, while the two conditions on the British side were reparations for the countries attacked by Germany and a guarantee that the wishes of the Austrian people would be respected. This attempt failed, largely because some of the conspirators believed that the plan was too extreme: while they dithered, the Low Countries were invaded – and the uncompromising Churchill became Prime Minister, effectively aborting any new attempt. After this, he ordered that there should be no communication with any German.

Another plan thwarted by Churchill's accession involved J. Lonsdale Bryans, an 'adventurer',[143] who, shortly after war was declared, set out on a mission financed by Lord Brocket – Chamberlain's friend and a major Conservative Party donor – to make contact with the anti-Hitler generals.

Meeting up in Rome with one of General Beck's men, Ulrich von Hassell – the former German Ambassador who believed that ongoing hostilities would lead to Soviet domination of Europe – they evolved a plan to overthrow the Führer and end the war. Back in London in early 1940, Bryans reported to Halifax, who approved the scheme – von Hassell's group would assassinate Hitler only with British backing – even giving him money and a Swiss visa. However, after France fell, the situation changed: 'The secret mission . . . at the start self-appointed, and afterwards Government-sponsored, becomes at this point Government-opposed.'[144]

Halifax told him it was now the government's – i.e. Churchill's – policy not to approve any communication with German nationals –

whatever their attitude to Hitler. Bryans found this bizarre, asking why, if Britain aided resistance movements in the occupied countries, it refused to do so where Germany was concerned.

Hitler's plans for Britain

Hitler was perplexed by the British refusal to ask for terms when the nation was clearly in no position to go on fighting – especially with no clear reason why it *should*, with Poland having been abandoned and its only Ally having come to terms. On 13 July 1940, the Chief of the General Staff, General Franz Halder (one of the anti-Hitler conspirators), wrote in his diary:

> The Führer is most preoccupied with the question of why England does not want to step on the path to peace. Like us, he sees the answer to the question in the hopes which England puts upon Russia. He therefore reckons to have to force England to make peace. But he does not like it very much. Reason: if we smash England militarily, the British Empire will collapse. Germany will not benefit from this. With German blood we would obtain something whose beneficiaries would only be Japan, America and others.[145]

As John Charmley points out, Hitler's obsessions were Jews, Communists and Lebensraum, and in all three instances Eastern Europe offered far more opportunities than the British Isles.[146] And a difficult and costly invasion was hardly the most effective way of defeating Britain – blockade and bombing would be much easier and efficient, as Hitler had recognised as far back as 1938.[147]

Now that Germany controlled the French Channel and Atlantic coasts, the first Luftwaffe raids of the Battle of Britain, on ports, factories and airfields, began on 10 July. (It was only in September, in retaliation for RAF raids on Berlin – themselves revenge for the accidental bombing of London by the Luftwaffe, possibly caused by British counter-measures to confuse the raiders' navigation[148] – that Germany began blitzing civilian targets. But what had happened to Roosevelt's promise to George VI that the United States would come in if London was bombed?) At sea, British shipping, bringing vital supplies to the besieged islands, began to be sunk at an alarming rate – by the end of the year over 3.5 million tons would be lost.[149]

On 19 July 1940, Hitler made his 'last appeal to reason', declaring: 'Mr Churchill ought perhaps for once to believe me when I prophesy that a great empire will be destroyed – an empire it was never my intention to destroy or even harm . . . I see no reason why this war must go on.'[150]

Three days before, he had issued his directive for Operation Sea Lion (perhaps only as misdirection to divert attention from preparations for Barbarossa). What Hitler did not know was that the now-legendary codebreakers of 'Station X' at Bletchley Park, 50 miles outside London, were intercepting German signals transmitted by the Enigma machines. This invaluable intelligence source – codenamed 'Ultra' – was tightly restricted to Churchill and a handful of his most trusted people in London. By October, Churchill – who, despite his 'fight [them] on the beaches' stance, seems to have reasoned shrewdly from the start that Hitler never intended to invade[151] – had learned via Ultra that Hitler had definitely shelved Sea Lion, but nevertheless continued to encourage widespread invasion panic for several months (ironically contributing to Hitler's deception strategy).[152]

There were certain advantages to Churchill's plan: first, it preserved the secret of Ultra. Second, the fear of imminent invasion inspired the beleaguered British with focus, unity and purpose. And if Lloyd George and Stokes' group knew that Hitler had abandoned invasion plans, inevitably they would clamour for terms. Finally, it suited Churchill for Roosevelt to think that Britain was still in imminent danger of Nazi occupation, since – with the threat of its fleet falling into Hitler's hands – it would encourage a steady flow of American arms and equipment.

Churchill bluffed Roosevelt. On 17 September 1940, Bletchley Park decoded a message from the German General Staff ordering airborne troops at Dutch airfields to dismantle their equipment. Although the Prime Minister knew this meant Hitler had abandoned invasion plans, just two days later he cabled Roosevelt about Britain's coming trauma in fighting off the Nazis on native soil.[153]

Even so, while Britain fought alone, the best Churchill could hope for was stalemate. But he had two lifelines: he knew the invasion was abandoned – he was more concerned with the prospect of a U-boat blockade – and that Hitler would soon launch an attack on Stalin's Russia, and when he did, Britain could breathe again.

However, there was a more immediate danger: in November a new US administration was to be elected. Roosevelt's popularity had declined and the Republicans had made great strides in the 1938 mid-term elections. Would FDR stand for an unprecedented third term? Was *any* fellow Democrat capable of winning? If the next President was an isolationist Republican, perhaps even the present level of aid would disappear. Clearly the presidential election would also largely determine Britain's fate – unless Churchill could give it a helping hand.

CHAPTER SIX

Lost Empire

'I have not become the King's First Minister to preside over the liquidation of the British Empire.'
Winston S. Churchill, Nov. 1942[1]

Shortly after – if not *before* – becoming Prime Minister, Churchill initiated another sequence of events that would have far-reaching consequences for Britain, America and the course of the war. This was the mission he entrusted to businessman-turned-MI6 agent William Stephenson (knighted in 1945), now famous as the James Bond-style 'man called Intrepid'. His operation, hidden behind the innocuous-sounding 'British Security Coordination' (BSC),[2] is an episode in Anglo-American relations deemed so sensitive that its true nature has been covered up ever since; only recently have the details even begun to be pieced together.

At the end of the war, the British government compiled an official history, *British Security Coordination (BSC): An Account of Secret Activities in the Western Hemisphere 1940–45* – before burning the organisation's entire archives – which remained classified until 1998, when one of the half-dozen or so surviving copies fell into the hands of a publisher, who put it out in a 'publish and be damned' manner.

Even former member H. Montgomery Hyde's heavily sanitised

account of Stephenson's wartime work, *The Quiet Canadian* (1962), caused waves among the American intelligence community. The CIA's classified in-house journal *Studies in Intelligence* called its publication 'shocking', remarking 'the wisdom of placing it on the public record is extremely questionable'. One of the Americans closely involved with BSC, the lawyer Ernest Cuneo, wrote to Stephenson's former assistant Charles ('Dick') Ellis: 'No great harm came of it, but Montgomery Hyde broke confidences which I was assured were inviolate. They involved newspaper friends of mine who accepted my personal assurances and, indeed, a President for whom I bore deepest affection.'[3] However, Dick Ellis later acknowledged that Hyde's book had actually been written on the instruction of the Ministry of Defence and Foreign Office[4] – many passages taken almost verbatim from the classified official history. After Hyde's death in 1989, his papers were closed by the British government until 2041.[5]

In 1976, another book on Stephenson and BSC appeared: *A Man Called Intrepid* by the confusingly named William Stevenson, but despite Stephenson and Ellis both writing forewords, it is startlingly inaccurate – perhaps a 'spoiler' for Hyde's incomplete, but more-or-less authentic, work. One CIA historian described it as full of 'inaccuracies, distortions, exaggerations, and perversions of facts'.[6] Even Stephenson's famous codename 'Intrepid' was simply his New York cable address. (This is extra-strange, given that William Stevenson too appears to have had access to the official history.)

American intelligence expert Ralph de Toledano drew our attention to *Desperate Deception: British Covert Operations in the United States, 1939–44* (1998) by US historian of diplomacy Thomas E. Mahl, published by Brassey's Intelligence and National Security Library, which explores the extraordinary and – until recently – largely untold story of BSC's subversive operations in the US during the Second World War. Roy Godson, General Editor of Brassey's, explains Mahl's thesis:

> Faced with the growing prospect of war with Germany, the
> British government mounted in 1939 a massive secret political

campaign in the United States (including the use of front groups, agents, collaborators, manipulation of polling data, involvement in election campaigns, etc.) to weaken the isolationists, bring the United States into the war, and influence U.S. war policy in England's favor. This campaign helped change not only the course of World War II but also the face of American politics in succeeding decades.[7]

Mahl himself writes, 'These operations profoundly changed America forever, helping it become the global power we see today – a power whose foreign policy leaders were freed to make, after the war, a multitude of global commitments unhampered by any significant isolationist opposition.'[8] He also defines British intelligence's objective as being to 'move the United States toward World War II and then toward a peace that was in Britain's interest,'[9] calling it 'one of the most important and successful covert operations of history'.[10]

William Stephenson was a Canadian-born millionaire whose European business connections made him ideal for MI6's Industrial Intelligence Centre set up by Major Morton in 1931. In 1938, Stephenson joined MI6's newly formed Section D, in charge of sabotage, subversion and propaganda, headed by Commander Lawrence Grand, which was soon larger than all the rest of MI6 put together. On becoming First Lord of the Admiralty, Churchill put Stephenson in charge of organising sabotage operations in Scandinavia.[11] In July 1940, Churchill removed Section D from MI6, placing it – together with Stephenson – under his new Special Operations Executive (SOE).

In April 1940, MI6 Director Sir Stewart Menzies despatched Stephenson to New York as British intelligence's 'attaché', to liaise with the FBI, which he did with the cooperation of J. Edgar Hoover – and Roosevelt's approval. But as the arrangement took place behind the State Department's back, Hoover was told to avoid 'any unneutral collaboration' with British intelligence.[12]

Hyde describes Stephenson's brief as liaising with American security agencies, working to ensure US aid for Britain, countering Nazi intelligence and subversive operations – and 'eventually to bring the United States into the War . . .'[13] (In the American edition, *Room*

3603, the last part became: 'to promote sympathy for the British cause in the United States'.[14])

Stephenson's role covered the whole of the British intelligence and security community – MI6, MI5, Special Branch, Naval Intelligence, SOE and the Political Warfare Executive (as SOE's propaganda section, SO1, became in 1941) – 'a wide-ranging, full-service, offensive intelligence agency'.[15] It would hardly have been out of place in an enemy country.

There is even some confusion – presumably to obscure anything that would clash with the myth of the 'special relationship' – about who sent Stephenson to Washington and exactly when. Most general accounts of Britain's wartime intelligence activities have him being Menzies' personal representative at the beginning of April 1940. However, Hyde and Stevenson state that Stephenson reported directly to Churchill, bypassing even Menzies, and Stephenson himself later claimed to have been Churchill's 'personal representative' in America.[16] As the evidence (below) is that it was Churchill who selected Stephenson for the American posting in the first place, it seems that even while at the Admiralty he had a strong influence over intelligence matters.

In 1981, Churchill's great supporter John Colville viciously attacked *A Man Called Intrepid* as mostly pure invention, even denying Stephenson and Churchill ever met – admitting only that 'his name may have been mentioned to Churchill'. Colville also writes, 'Foremost among the inventions in this book . . . is the allegation that Sir William provided a secret liaison between the Prime Minister and the President and was in constant communication with Churchill on intelligence and military matters.'[17] As Sir William himself had written a foreword to the book, Colville dismissed him as a self-promoting fantasist (strange for the 'quiet Canadian'), claiming that in all his time with Churchill he never heard Stephenson's name mentioned once, adding that it is conspicuous by its absence in the Churchill–Roosevelt correspondence. Colville's critics point out that the identity of an individual who was a byword for secrecy is hardly likely to be splashed over public records.[18] (Colville was only an Assistant Private Secretary, so hardly Churchill's closest confidant.)

Friendly Fire

CIA officer and historian Thomas F. Troy became intrigued by this controversy – as Stephenson's close friend for 20 years, they had often talked of his special relationship with Churchill. Troy's extensively researched essay of 1970 remained classified until 1987, after which he expanded it into a book, *Wild Bill and Intrepid* (1996), which concluded: 'On balance, I think it [the evidence] favours Sir William's side of the question.'[19]

Although Menzies despatched Stephenson to the United States in 1940, Stephenson was operating *outside* MI6 channels, dealing directly with Churchill himself.[20] In fact, Menzies *opposed* Stephenson's mission for Churchill.[21] (Menzies became head of MI6 in November 1939 – in Troy's words 'despite strong, sustained opposition from Churchill'.[22] In *Double Standards*, we argue this was because Menzies opposed war with Germany, believing that the USSR should be MI6's prime target.) Basically, Stephenson's mission was to undermine isolationism, promote the British cause – by whatever means necessary – and ultimately to fulfil Churchill's wish to drag the United States into the conflict. (Stephenson built on Section D's groundwork: many Anglophile agents had been infiltrated into the US media in 1939, to nudge public opinion in Britain's direction if necessary.)

Ernest Cuneo describes the extraordinary scope of BSC operations:

> Given the time, the situation, and the mood, it is not surprising, however, that BSC also went beyond the legal, the ethical, and the proper. Throughout the neutral Americas, and especially in the US, it ran espionage agents, tampered with the mails, tapped telephones, smuggled propaganda into the country, disrupted public gatherings, covertly subsidized newspapers, radios [*sic*], and organizations, perpetrated forgeries – even palming one off on the President of the United States – violated the aliens registration act, shanghaied sailors numerous times, and possibly murdered one or more persons in this country.[23]

Given Cuneo's intimate knowledge of BSC's operations, his

suggestion that it 'possibly' carried out assassinations on American soil can safely be taken to mean that it *did*.

However, the situation is immensely complicated by the President's knowledge of BSC's activities which, since the organisation supported his policies (and his re-election) while fundamentally undermining his opponents, he tacitly supported. The fact that it was a British operation gave him the ultimate plausible deniability if it was exposed: 'Far from being a dupe, Roosevelt gladly played along with British "dirty tricks" for his own ends.'[24]

Although 'interventionists' were in the minority, many American politicians and businessmen did favour aid – and even full military backing – for Britain. Some believed it to be in America's long-term interests, some were anti-Nazi, others were simply Anglophiles. Mahl describes the links between BSC, the pro-British lobby in America and the White House as 'the three-cornered relationship that made many of these operations a success and moved the United States irrevocably into the international arena'.[25]

Cuneo acted as liaison between BSC and the White House, and other government departments – being effectively to Roosevelt what Stephenson was to Churchill, 'a place for discreet indiscreet exchanges between Churchill and FDR'.[26] In 1988, he wrote to Montgomery Hyde: 'Of course the British were trying to push the US into war. If that be so we were indeed a pushover. It reminds me of that Chaucerian line, "He fell upon her and would have raped her – but for her ready acquiescence."'[27]

Effectively, FDR was using a foreign intelligence service against his opponents and fellow Americans.

In the United States, much of BSC's operation consisted of propaganda promoting the British cause and raising awareness of Hitler's direct threat to America – even if it had to be invented. One aim was to persuade Americans that Hitler had designs on Latin America, although in reality it was unlikely the Nazis would gain a serious foothold there.[28]

BSC covertly funded and controlled – and in some cases created – pro-intervention lobbies, the most famous being the Committee to Defend America by Aiding the Allies (the 'White Committee'), set up after the fall of France by Republican magazine editor William Allen

White. However, as its name suggests, the Committee (which was supported, but not created, by BSC) advocated aiding Britain, not full American involvement in the war. It set out to repeal the Neutrality Act and to ensure that in the coming election both parties nominated candidates who supported aid for Britain. It was superseded by the more extreme interventionist Fight for Freedom Committee, which *did* advocate active US involvement – and which *was* a BSC creation, supported by Roosevelt. Another of their fronts was France Forever, which whipped up support for de Gaulle.[29]

BSC also enlisted the support of sympathetic media folk – journalists and owners of newspapers and radio stations: indeed, some of the most prominent names in American journalism in the war years knowingly worked for BSC's propaganda operation, even the legendary *Herald Tribune* columnist Walter Lippmann.[30] (The *New York Herald Tribune* was the leading BSC-controlled newspaper.) To further confuse the picture, his secretary Mary Watkins Price was an NKVD agent.[31] In fact, the Venona intercepts reveal that through the Americans involved in the operation, Soviet intelligence had thoroughly penetrated BSC.[32] (However, the NKVD only wanted to monitor BSC's activities, not subvert them; despite the fact that the USSR and Third Reich were technically allies, Stalin supported anything that fanned the flames of war in the West.)

Perhaps the most startling name to find among BSC's American agents is Robert E. Sherwood, who came to Hopkins' attention through his work for the White Committee. One of Roosevelt's key speechwriters, he even used to show Stephenson the texts of the President's speeches in advance – and sometimes altered them on Stephenson's instructions.[33]

After Harry Hopkins' death in 1946, Sherwood was selected to write his first – and still standard – biography, having access to his private papers. *Roosevelt and Hopkins: An Intimate History* (1948), published in the UK under the title *The White House Papers of Harry L. Hopkins*, established Hopkins' 'official' image and his role long before more critical researchers were allowed access to the files in 1973. Now we know Sherwood was essentially a British agent, this explains why his book is so clearly 'spun' to fit the Churchillian version of the war.

BSC sponsored books – even cartoons and bogus horoscopes of

Hitler – and infiltrated the arts. The legendary director Alexander Korda was a fully fledged British intelligence agent, his Hollywood office a cover for BSC operations on the west coast. He and others ensured that pro-British and anti-German movies kept rolling out of the studios. *Foreign Correspondent*, produced by BSC-backed Walter Wanger and directed by Alfred Hitchcock, even drew plaudits from Goebbels.[34]

BSC were also heavily involved in lobbying and smear campaigns against prominent isolationist Congressmen, singling out Republican Representative Hamilton Fish, who represented the district that included Roosevelt's home. In 1940, BSC falsely alleged he was in the pay of the Nazis and an anti-Semite. BSC also attacked Senators Burton Wheeler and Gerald Nye (of Neutrality Act fame).[35]

A leading anti-Fish campaigner was Sanford 'Sandy' Griffith, head of the opinion-poll company Market Analysts Inc. In 1940, he listed ways to keep the pressure on him, including rigging local opinion polls (easily managed by someone in his position). In fact, Lieutenant Commander Griffith – who had lived for many years in Europe, including four in London – was agent number G.112 of SO1.[36]

Rigging opinion polls was another vitally important BSC activity – again with Roosevelt's support. Polls had become a significant factor in American (and to a lesser extent European) political life between the wars, but it was only during his presidency that they began to influence the policies and voting habits of the President and Congressmen. They were also vital during the 1938–41 'isolation-versus-intervention' debate. Roosevelt kept a close eye on them as a guide to what America was thinking, in order to tailor his message for maximum popular appeal.

However, as techniques of opinion polls were in their infancy, they were easy to manipulate: asking loaded questions, counting 'don't knows' as for or against, deliberate 'adjustment' of the statistics, even the presentation of results made a difference. Sometimes, simply *not* publishing a poll could affect the result of a Congressional vote.

Thomas Mahl has established that four of America's major opinion polling organisations – including the sacrosanct Gallup – operated under the influence of the Roosevelt administration, BSC, or both.[37] BSC even ran an agent inside Gallup – former advertising executive David Ogilvy. This was one of the revelations that particularly shocked the American intelligence community in 1962, prompting Ogilvy to demand that Hyde remove the reference from future editions – because it was *true*. Through Ogilvy, BSC were able to persuade Gallup not to publish results that went against British policy.[38]

Perhaps more immediately useful to BSC was Sandy Griffith's Market Analysts Inc., which carried out polls at national conventions and rallies to be used to publicise the delegates' views. The headlines they generated (particularly in BSC-friendly newspapers) influenced both public opinion and Senators and Representatives. This practice led to what was probably BSC's greatest success – the hijacking of the 1940 presidential elections.

The British fix US elections

To Churchill, it was imperative that Roosevelt – or at least a like-minded successor – should win the November 1940 election. Besides, he owed FDR a substantial favour for securing *him* his destiny as Prime Minister. To ensure the smooth flow of American aid, and Britain's ability to continue fighting, it was essential that either Roosevelt won, or, if there was a new Republican President, it would be one who agreed with his policies. As a result, Stephenson and BSC went into overdrive, ruthlessly manipulating the election of America's head of state.

The nomination of no-hoper Wendell Willkie as the Republicans' candidate at their Philadelphia convention at the end of June 1940 was so fortuitous – and so odd – that it is called the 'Philadelphia miracle'. History was made when he was swept to victory after the near-hysterical chant 'We want Willkie! We want Willkie!' reverberated round the convention hall, infecting delegates with the excitement.

After the euphoria had died down, a conspiracy theory did the rounds – among both extreme left and extreme right – that Willkie's nomination had been orchestrated by Roosevelt and the British Embassy, in a plot masterminded by Walter Lippmann and banker Thomas W. Lamont. Although there was no hard evidence at the time, from the case constructed by Thomas Mahl it now appears that this picture was correct. Lamont, the 'prime mover' behind Willkie's nomination, was in regular contact with Roosevelt during the run-up to the Republican convention – strange behaviour for a political 'opponent'.[39]

Mahl summarises his case:

> First, the people who created the Willkie candidacy were working closely with Franklin Roosevelt. Second, those who created the Willkie candidacy were working closely with British intelligence and its fronts. Third, Willkie was working closely with British intelligence and its fronts, especially Fight for Freedom, on whose executive board he sat. Fourth, Willkie's close work with his ostensible opponent, Franklin Roosevelt, particularly their joint effort to eliminate members of Willkie's newly adopted Republican Party from office, is a collaboration rare, perhaps even unique, in American political history. Last, the secrecy and compartmentalization of the scheme to promote Willkie are a fundamental attribute of intelligence tradecraft; none of the individual toilers working for Willkie's nomination ever knew enough to be able to see the big picture of the operation.[40]

Willkie was a long-standing Democrat – although anti-New Deal – only switching to the Republicans in mid-January 1940, seven months before becoming their presidential candidate. His candidacy emerged from meetings presided over by Helen Ogden Reid, owner of the BSC-influenced *New York Herald Tribune*. Also involved were the correspondent Vincent Sheean and his British wife Diana; according to recently released Soviet documents, she was a known British agent. Willkie also received strong support from Walter Lippmann.

Strangely for a Republican, Willkie disagreed entirely with the vast majority of his party over the war – but agreed with Roosevelt, supporting aid for Britain (being kept informed of the secret deals made during the presidential campaign) and favouring the draft. Willkie's leading rivals, Thomas E. Dewey and Robert A. Taft, were committed isolationists, and when his candidacy was first announced, some six weeks before the convention, polls showed he had only 3 per cent of Republican support.

Willkie's chances were greatly advanced by the timely death of the organising committee's chairman, Ralph E. Williams, less than a month before the convention. A Taft supporter, the elderly Williams died during a committee meeting, and although there is no solid evidence that it was due to anything but natural causes, it was particularly convenient for the Willkie plotters. (Mahl tried to obtain Williams' autopsy reports, but they had been destroyed long before.) Is it a coincidence that Ernest Cuneo claimed that BSC were 'possibly' involved in assassinations?

Williams' successor, Samuel K. Pryor – later a CIA agent – subsequently admitted to manipulating the convention to favour Willkie by slashing the opposition's ticket allocation, and secretly printing extra to ensure that Willkie supporters swamped the hall. Most breathtaking was his interference in former President Hoover's keynote anti-intervention speech, of which the audience heard not a word – Pryor had arranged for the microphone to be faulty. (Several years later, Hoover obtained a legal deposition confirming this extraordinary scenario.)

In the weeks before the convention, opinion polls – particularly Gallup – showed a steady rise in support for Willkie and a drop for the other four candidates. On the morning of the vote, newspapers reported a 'leaked' Gallup poll showing his triumphant surge to 15 points ahead of his nearest rival, Dewey, claiming he was most Republicans' choice. Then came the convention with its 'We want Willkie!' chant that seemed to confirm it. Many delegates who voted for him later reported their bafflement when they realised that many Republicans back home had never even heard of Wendell Willkie.

Once Willkie began his election campaign, several of his most prominent media supporters such as Lippmann withdrew their support or switched to Roosevelt – as did many financial backers. (One was W. Averell Harriman, the banker who became Lend-Lease Administrator to Britain, who contributed to Willkie's nomination campaign and then to Roosevelt's election campaign. Recently released British documents reveal that Harriman, too, worked closely with SOE.[41])

Willkie's nomination on 28 June 1940 (six days after the French surrender, a particularly grim time for Britain) was of immense importance to Churchill – whoever won the election in November, the American administration would be sympathetic to Britain. Only then, when he was assured of American aid, did the Prime Minister confidently hammer it home that Britain would fight on to victory whatever the odds. Churchillian imagery became much less defensive and more defiantly pugnacious. Mahl writes:

> Without Franklin Roosevelt, or someone similarly interventionist as the president, the British could not possibly win the war. The firm commitment to fight the Germans whatever the odds was not made nearly so early as British propaganda would have had Americans believe. Only in July, after Willkie was nominated and an interventionist president assured, did the British commit themselves, after two cabinet meetings on the topic, to fighting on in the expectation that the United States would rescue them.[42]

Churchill's imagery turned from having to 'fight on the beaches' to outright victory – annihilating Nazism was now presented as a moral duty to civilisation. (Not so with Mussolini – in a broadcast to Italy in September 1940, Churchill still declared, 'That he is a great man I do not deny'.[43])

The President announced to the Democratic Convention in Chicago in July 1940 that he had no desire either to be nominated or to continue in office – although careful not to say that he wouldn't *accept* the nomination. (In fact, members of Roosevelt's administration had known since May or June that he wanted the nomination.[44]) But meanwhile, Hopkins was busy assuring party leaders that if FDR was nominated he would run: when party bosses proposed that he should stand again, the delegates (knowing he was the only candidate with the required charisma or popularity) basically begged him to accept the nomination.[45] FDR declared:

> Lying awake, as I have on many nights, I have asked myself whether I have the right as Commander-in-Chief of the Army and Navy, to call on men and women to serve their country,

or to train themselves to serve, and, at the same time, decline to serve my country in my own personal capacity, if I am called upon to do so by the people of my country.[46]

Joseph Kennedy was so appalled when he heard that Roosevelt wanted a third term that he decided to back Willkie, with maximum publicity.[47] Given that Kennedy was privy to Roosevelt's secret and illegal dealings with Churchill, this was potentially very dangerous.

In 1960, Randolph Churchill told the newspaperman Cyrus L. Sulzberger that his father and MI5 had been responsible for the failure of Kennedy's plan.[48] William Stevenson quoted Randolph, 'We had reached the point of bugging potential traitors and enemies. Joe Kennedy, the American ambassador, came under electronic surveillance'[49] as they amassed evidence of his anti-war and anti-Roosevelt sentiments, and his plan to endorse Willkie. (Even during wartime, phone-tapping the ambassador of a friendly country is a breathtaking breach of diplomatic protocol.) Randolph Churchill told Sulzberger that his father ordered the transcripts to go privately to Harry Hopkins (undoubtedly via Stephenson), who in turn handed them to Roosevelt.

Kennedy was recalled to Washington for a private meeting with Roosevelt – and the next day publicly endorsed Roosevelt for a third term.

'Wild Bill' in London

In July 1940, just before the Chicago convention, Roosevelt dispatched an emissary to London on a twofold mission – William J. ('Wild Bill') Donovan, soon a legend in the world of intelligence as the head of the Office of Strategic Services (OSS, forerunner of the CIA). In 1974, the CIA's Director, William J. Casey, described him as 'a one-man CIA for President Roosevelt',[50] who in turn called him his 'secret legs'.[51] Donovan aimed to gauge Britain's military capability, morale and determination: Roosevelt had to be certain that Britain had the means and the will to survive before deciding whether to go out on a limb with further aid.

Donovan also sought to be fully briefed on British intelligence, as part of William Stephenson's 'educating' American intelligence in subversion and clandestine warfare.[52] Not only had Donovan worked closely with Stephenson and BSC in New York but he had links with British intelligence going back to the First World War. Some even controversially suggest he owed his intelligence training to the British.[53] In any case, he was so Anglophile it often seemed his allegiances lay more with Britain than the United States. Certainly, BSC was largely responsible for his subsequent rise, Stephenson referring to him in secret reports as 'our man'.[54]

Donovan was given VIP treatment – a full briefing on Britain's secret services, including the newly formed SOE – even an audience with the King and Queen during which George VI rather pointedly handed Donovan the intercepted German battle order from Hitler dated 16 July 1940 (three days earlier) authorising Operation Sea Lion, clearly expecting him to report to Roosevelt that Britain was in imminent danger of invasion. Although Ultra remained secret, apparently Donovan guessed that the British had broken the Enigma code.[55] Confident that Britain would survive, Roosevelt decided, after two months of prevaricating, to continue to push for aid for Britain. Now he was to provide 'all aid short of war'.

Destroyers for bases

Although Churchill continued to press for the surplus American destroyers during June and July, it was only after Donovan's report at the beginning of August that the President responded that 'it may be possible' to loan them.[56]

The deal was secretly negotiated during August 1940, involving not just the British Embassy and the British Purchasing Commission but also British Security Coordination, especially Stephenson and Montgomery Hyde, who even wrote pro-deal speeches for major players. The negotiations were kept secret for as long as possible, but during the election campaign Wendell Willkie was kept informed, agreeing not to make the matter a campaign issue, even though his party would have been utterly horrified if they knew it was being discussed. Willkie's only complaint was that it fell short in helping Britain.[57]

However, as Henry Morgenthau said, the problem was: 'It's against the law . . . It's a question of can we do it illegally.'[58] As

Friendly Fire

Sherwood explains: 'Roosevelt never overlooked the fact that his actions might lead to his immediate or eventual impeachment'[59] – but justifies it as a moral imperative. New Deal administrator David Lilienthal recorded that on 2 September 1940 – the day he signed the Executive Order authorisation – Roosevelt 'said twice . . . something to the effect that he might get impeached for what he was about to do'.[60] Ernest Cuneo wrote to Stephenson about a meeting with the Attorney General, Robert Jackson:

> I found him both sad and disturbed. He said he was off to a Cabinet meeting where he had to give the President very disappointing news: the transfer of the 50 destroyers to Britain was unconstitutional. I told him not to feel too badly: that by one o'clock that day he would either reverse himself or he'd be asked for his resignation.[61]

The deal contravened several US laws, including the Neutrality and Espionage Acts, but there were loopholes: for example, although selling American warships built for, or with 'intent to enter the service of', a belligerent nation was illegal, since these ships were originally built for the US Navy, it was technically permissible. Similarly, legal ownership could be transferred to a private American company, which could then give the ships to Britain.[62]

Robert Shogan notes in his *Hard Bargain* (1995):

> Roosevelt's handling of the destroyer deal with the British would set a pernicious precedent. His machinations would give impetus and legitimacy to the efforts of his successors to expand the reach of their powers, overriding constitutional guidelines and political principles, all in the name of national security. This syndrome would be exhibited by post-war chief executives confronted with supposed crises abroad, irrespective of party affiliation, from Harry Truman and the Korean conflict and Lyndon Johnson and the Vietnam War through Ronald Reagan and Nicaragua's Sandinista regime to George Bush and the Iraqi invasion of Kuwait.[63]

182

It would prove a hard bargain for Britain, too.

At the end of June 1940, the Naval Appropriations Bill was amended to prevent naval materiel going abroad unless it was certified as useless for the defence of the US. But as the Navy Chief of Staff, Admiral Harold R. Stark, had testified that the destroyers were still potentially useful, Roosevelt decided that the British should exchange them for land in their Atlantic and Caribbean colonies on which the US could build naval and air bases – he could then argue to Congress that the deal had actually *strengthened* America's defences.[64]

Roosevelt's supporters have argued that this unequal deal was designed to promote the idea to Congress, implying he would have made a gift of the destroyers but *unfortunately* was compelled to ask for something in return to satisfy them. However, there is nothing to support this view – and much against it. For years, both FDR and the US Navy had been desperate for such bases.[65] Since 1918, he had advocated 'defense at a distance', requiring the US to control its territorial waters, defining them in 1939 as 'extend[ing] as far as our interests need'.[66] And by the 1930s, control of the seas also required control of the air space above them, so both naval and air bases in strategic locations outside the American mainland were needed.[67]

Initially, the War Cabinet intended to refuse such a one-sided deal (the value of the land far outweighing that of the destroyers), Churchill complaining to FDR that it amounted to 'a blank cheque on the whole of our trans-Atlantic possessions'.[68] But 'Britain no longer called the tune; she had little choice but to accept aid on whatever terms America proposed.'[69]

Trying not to appear desperate, the British wanted to designate the bases as gifts, but Roosevelt insisted on linking them to the loan of the destroyers in order to placate Congress. (In the end, two bases were officially 'gifts'.) Britain gave the USA 99-year leases on sites in the Caribbean and Newfoundland – a 'stiff price to pay'.[70]

Roosevelt also demanded a public pledge that the British fleet would never surrender to Germany, whatever happened. This, too, was agreed by Churchill and his Cabinet.[71]

The Executive Order authorising the transfer of the destroyers was signed by Roosevelt on 2 September 1940, and announced to

Congress the next day, being 'a virtual act of war – a total abandonment of any pretence of neutrality'.[72]

Ironically, not only were the bases much the more valuable but the ships were also in such poor condition they made minimal difference to Britain's war effort. Only nine of the fifty destroyers were fit for immediate service: by May 1941, twenty were still out of action.[73] In exchange for useless ships, Churchill had parted with land of far greater value, allowed America to gain a foothold in Empire possessions – and even signed away his major bargaining counter, the fate of the British fleet.

The two Frances

Another source of Anglo-American friction was also brewing. Churchill and Roosevelt had to decide how to deal with the two factions claiming to be the legitimate government of France – Pétain's Vichy regime and de Gaulle's Free French.

Marshal Pétain's Vichy was in a tricky position, its survival clearly depending on Hitler's goodwill – but Pétain also had no wish to cross Britain. Despite urgings from his Foreign Minister, Pierre Laval (after the Mers-el-Kébir incident), he wanted to prevent France from fighting alongside Germany. However, Vichy still controlled resources and facilities that were potentially useful to the Nazis – including North African naval bases. On the other hand, this possible collaboration meant that Churchill classed Vichy as an enemy – as Mers-el-Kébir had explicitly demonstrated. Britain's blockade of Vichy France had seriously affected a population swollen by refugees. In October 1940, Pétain ominously promised Hitler Vichy's 'collaboration': already he had banned Jews from government and public office.

Politically and militarily inexperienced, General de Gaulle (a former Pétain aide), initially willing to serve under a French leader who would fight from the colonies, soon realised he himself would have to save the honour of France, declaring famously: 'I am France.' Meanwhile, in his absence, the Vichy government sentenced him to a traitor's death.

At first, de Gaulle aimed at seizing control of Vichy's Central African colonies, mainly to establish a Free French base, but also to deny Germany access to strategically important areas. Aided by British forces, Operation Menace was launched to take Dakar and other French African colonies in September 1940. A complete shambles, Menace was abandoned, although de Gaulle took control of other colonies. In fact, Hitler had not the slightest interest in tying up resources in Africa – the Soviet Union was next.

Menace's failure prompted the Churchill government to make a deal with the Vichy regime that still remains secret and extraordinarily sensitive – the files are closed until 2016, and the relevant documents have even been withdrawn from private archives.[74] However, much of the detail has been reconstructed from other sources.

Although diplomatic relations between Britain and France since the Mers-el-Kébir incident had been non-existent, on 20 October 1940 Churchill authorised the British Ambassador in Madrid, Sir Samuel Hoare, to communicate with his French counterpart. Five days later, Pétain sent an unofficial emissary, Professor Louis Rougier, to London, for talks with Churchill and other officials that lasted until December.

It was agreed that Pétain would not take Hitler's side, support him militarily or make other resources available. He would also resist any German move to seize French colonies, while *not* resisting de Gaulle's similar moves in Central and West Africa. On his side, Churchill agreed to refrain from any military action in Vichy territory – where the naval blockade would also be eased – and to soften his attitude towards Pétain's regime. On the very same day, from Brazzaville in the French Congo, de Gaulle denounced the Vichy government as unconstitutional, declaring himself leader of France.

The secret deal meant that Churchill had to keep de Gaulle – an 'embarrassment' – in check.[75] He also let Pétain know that 'de Gaulle has been of no assistance to the British cause'.[76] But paradoxically, de Gaulle's African operations were useful to Pétain: the implicit threat of the French Empire throwing its weight behind the Free French leader gave him extra leverage in his dealings with Hitler.

Like Roosevelt, Churchill hoped that a French fightback would start in North Africa, after the secret agreement with Pétain urging General Maxime Weygand, the new Delegate-General to French

North Africa (and former Supreme Allied Commander of the British and French forces) to rebel against the Germans.

Meanwhile, the United States continued to recognise the Vichy regime as the legitimate government of France. In *Allies at War* (2001), Simon Berthon writes: 'Curiously, despite Roosevelt's anti-imperialism, there seemed to be one empire in the world which he would do everything to prop up, that of Vichy France.'[77] Recognising that 'Vichy is in a German cage',[78] Roosevelt realised that American support would strengthen Pétain's hand against Hitler, by giving him the option of playing Germany off against the USA. American food aid was sent to Vichy France, but only on the condition that its forces or territory were not used to support the Germans.

FDR appointed an old friend, retired Admiral William D. Leahy – later his Chief of Staff – as Ambassador to Vichy, to 'ingratiate himself with the Vichy leaders'.[79] But Roosevelt had little enthusiasm for de Gaulle and his Free French, despite Churchill's endorsement. Soon after the General had emerged from the French exiles in London, the State Department was uncompromising: 'The de Gaulle pre-war outlook was rightist, with semi-Fascist tendencies in its approach to internal politics, and traditional imperial view of foreign policy.'[80] As far as the President was concerned, Pétain and Weygand were the ones to back, not de Gaulle (ironically, Churchill agreed *secretly* – at that time). The British tried to press Roosevelt to show more support for the Gaullists, but this was irreconcilable with his policy of overt backing for Vichy.

Bankrupt Britain

On 22 August 1940 – 'one of the most significant yet least famous [dates] in British history'[81] – the Chancellor of the Exchequer, Kingsley Wood, submitted a seven-page 'Most Secret' paper to the Cabinet, with the innocuous-sounding title of 'Gold and Exchange Resources'. But its message was stark: Britain's economy was at the point of imminent collapse and no longer able to sustain the war. Within just three months, Britain would either have to surrender to Hitler or admit it was now entirely dependent on the United States.

Some friends rallied: in October, the Czech government-in-exile lent Britain £7.5 million in gold[82] – remarkably generous considering that when the Germans had invaded Czechoslovakia two-and-a-half years earlier, the Bank of England had handed over a large part of the Czech gold reserves to Germany.[83]

Throughout their dealings with Britain, the Roosevelt administration had one eye firmly fixed on its assets in the US, and Morgenthau also kept pressing for Britain to sell overseas assets in order to pay for American supplies. Between August 1940 and March 1941, Britain sold $70 million worth, but still fell short.[84] Until November 1940, Britain had managed to pay for everything from America, but now the cupboard was bare. Morgenthau even suggested that Britain take £200 million in French gold – now the property of the Vichy government – stored in Canada, but this was rejected because of the repercussions following Mers-el-Kébir.[85] (Undoubtedly, Churchill's secret deal with Pétain was also a factor.) And now was not the time to alienate the French-speaking population of Canada. Instead, at the end of December 1940, the Americans took £42 million ($170 million) in British gold held in South Africa, an option *suggested* by the British Treasury, but even they were horrified to discover that Roosevelt had already dispatched an American warship to Cape Town to collect it.[86] Churchill drafted the following angry cable – although it was never sent:

> While we shall do our utmost, and shrink from no proper sacrifice, to make payments across the exchange, I should not myself be willing, even in the height of this struggle, to divest Great Britain of every conceivable saleable asset so that after the victory was won with our blood and sweat, and civilisation saved and the time gained for the United States to be fully armed against all eventualities, we should stand stripped to the bone. Such a course would not be in the moral or economic interest of either of our two countries.[87]

He also likened the Americans to 'a sheriff collecting the last assets of a helpless debtor'. By this time, the US gold reserves were worth $22 billion, while Britain's was under half a billion.[88] John Charmley comments: 'By that stage of the war the Empire was already on the way to liquidation, with the Americans taking the role of receiver to the bankrupt concern.'[89]

Another Roosevelt triumph

The election of 5 November 1940 resulted in a comfortable win for Roosevelt: 54 per cent of the popular vote – 5 million more votes than Willkie – and 449 electoral votes against 82, although it was a closer thing than either of his previous victories. Willkie was at a grave disadvantage, being up against a familiar and trusted leader – while campaigning basically on the same platform.

It was perhaps the most bizarre election in American history. Both Roosevelt and Willkie *proclaimed* moderate isolationist sentiments and promised to keep America out of the war, while advocating that they backed Britain to win. Yet both were privately 'interventionist', willing to join the conflict if necessary. The American voters were faced with two candidates who said exactly the same, but meant the opposite.

Roosevelt's anti-war 'manifesto' stated: 'We will not participate in foreign wars, and we will not send our army, naval, or air forces to fight in foreign lands, outside of the Americas, except in case of attack . . . ' On the campaign trail, he repeatedly pledged: 'I have said this before, but I shall say it again and again and again: Your boys are not going to be sent into any foreign wars.' When 'their boys' were up to their eyes in mud and blood in Europe, his impeccable logic was, 'If someone attacks us, it isn't a foreign war, is it?'

Behind the scenes, with FDR's approval, Hopkins was consolidating his power. With no official status – his only income coming from his nominal post as Director of the Roosevelt Library in Hyde Park – he was actually in charge of organising American rearmament.[90] Such was his influence now that a few days after Roosevelt's re-election, Harold Ickes complained: 'Everything has to seep through Harry Hopkins into the White House.'[91]

The cigar-blue air in Downing Street grew ever more tense. Churchill was worried about the level of Roosevelt's commitment. After FDR's re-election, the Prime Minister had cabled his congratulation, but received no reply.[92] That this was no oversight is revealed by the fact that when, in another unrelated cable ten days later, Churchill nervously added, 'I hope you get [*sic*] my personal telegram of congratulations', Roosevelt replied to all his comments except that one, clearly wanting Churchill to sweat.[93] Having used the resources of British intelligence to get Roosevelt re-elected, would Churchill now be cast aside?

When at the beginning of December Roosevelt took a Caribbean cruise aboard the USS *Tuscaloosa*, his only onboard adviser was Hopkins. As they enjoyed themselves, Churchill sweated in his war-drab office, composing a uniquely important appeal to Roosevelt – nothing less than Britain's future depended on it. The old war-horse was in a truly unenviable position, having to admit that Britain could no longer afford war supplies, throwing himself on Roosevelt's mercy. The message resulted in the very mixed blessing of Lend-Lease. Hopkins said later: '. . . one evening [Roosevelt] suddenly came out with it – the whole programme. He didn't seem to have any clear idea how it could be done legally. But there wasn't a doubt in his mind that he'd find a way to do it.'[94]

The problem was straightforward. Normally, the answer to Britain's cash crisis would have been simply to extend credit, as America had done in the First World War, but as Britain had defaulted on the repayments, the Johnson Act forbade further loans. Roosevelt also wanted to find a way around the Neutrality Act's ban on Britain dealing directly with the US government.

The President's idea was simple: if America could no longer *sell* arms and equipment to Britain, it would *lend* them – but only under specific, uniquely stringent conditions. American companies could continue to supply Britain and the US government (i.e. the American taxpayer) would pick up the tab out of federal funds – therefore technically it was not a loan – then, after the war, Britain would either return or replace what had been supplied. Roosevelt declared he wanted to 'eliminate the dollar sign' where Britain was concerned.

Back in Washington, on 16 December, he called a press conference, using his now-famous, homely analogy: if his neighbour's house caught fire and he had a hose, he would hardly try to sell it to his neighbour – he would happily lend him it. All he would expect once the fire was out was that the hose be returned. However, simple had become simplistic: of course Britain would have to pay up in the end, replacing at its own expense aircraft or ships, and paying (in cash or in kind) for bullets, shells and Spam.

In his fireside chat of 29 December, Roosevelt outlined the general principles of Lend-Lease, beginning: 'My friends, this is not a Fireside Chat on war. It is a talk on national security . . .', explaining that if Britain were defeated the United States would be next. Helping Britain to beat Hitler would not only remove that threat but also keep America out of war. Roosevelt also announced that industry was switching to all-out war production: 'Manufacturers of watches, of farm implements, of linotypes and cash registers and automobiles and sewing machines and lawn mowers and locomotives are now making fuses and bomb packing crates and telescope mounts and shells and pistols and tanks' – with the aim of turning the United States into the 'great arsenal of democracy'.[95] This certainly created the impression that Americans were going to supply – but not engage.

The editors of *FDR's Fireside Chats*, Russell D. Buhite and David W. Levy comment, 'He continued to imply that the way to stay out of the war was to draw it closer.'[96] It was Hopkins who provided the phrase 'great arsenal of democracy', although FDR was unsure about it – as it could be used against him if the scheme was subsequently extended to the Soviet Union (by no stretch of the imagination a democracy).[97] That in December 1940 Roosevelt should be thinking of the possibility of supplying the Soviet Union is more than a little interesting.

Bill 1776

Once again, a convenient legal precedent was found – a minor law passed in 1892, which allowed the Secretary of War to lease army property 'when in his discretion it will be for the public good'.[98] On 3 January 1941, FDR told senators that he was preparing 'a comprehensive plan for all-out aid to Britain "short of war"',[99] while three days later in his New Year address to Congress he outlined the Lend-Lease concept in broad terms. War materiel was to be loaned or leased, paid for temporarily by the American taxpayer, but to be repaid within a 'reasonable time' by products or materials. The Bill that was duly introduced to Congress on 10 January 1941 was something of a mystery. The House and Senate wanted to know who drafted it, in order to question them on the details, but nobody in the administration would take responsibility – and Roosevelt would never say. Cordell Hull, who should have been responsible, denied any knowledge, and Morgenthau denied it was the Treasury.[100] (In 1947, Morgenthau admitted that it *had* been drafted by his legal team, after he and the President had developed the broad outline at a meeting with the head of the British Purchasing Commission.[101])

The Lend-Lease Bill's greatest critic was the Democrat Senator Burton K. Wheeler, who labelled it 'idiotic', saying: 'If it is our war, we ought to have the courage to go over and fight it, but it is not our war.'[102] He denounced it as a 'bill to enable the President to fight an undeclared war on Germany', receiving unexpected backing from White Committee leader Herbert Agar, who actively supported the Bill but agreed – 'There has been too much lying by the supporters of the Lend-Lease bill in the United States Senate and the press . . . Our side kept saying that this is a bill to keep America out of war. That's bunk.'[103]

Officially 'A Bill to Further Promote the Defense of the US and For Other Purposes', Roosevelt called it the 'Aid to Democracies Bill'. But its number is a revelation: H.R. [House of Representatives] 1776, the year the Americans finally freed themselves from Britain. As the previous Bill was 1764, the choice of the number was clearly deliberate, Assistant Enrolling Clerk H. Newton Megill being specifically instructed to give it the number 1776.[104] The obvious interpretation is that it was intended to invoke the spirit of the United States' Declaration of Independence from Britain; Bill 1776 was rubbing salt into Britain's wounds, the once-mighty nation was now humiliatingly completely dependent on its former colony.

Hopkins meets Churchill

Lend-Lease represented an enormous gamble for Roosevelt: if Britain was defeated, the money would never be recouped, and the United States' main market lost. Britain *must* hold out.

Matters became even more difficult. At that time, neither nation had an ambassador to the other. Kennedy had been recalled and his replacement had yet to take up his post, while on 11 December 1940

Lord Lothian died suddenly of blood poisoning. Initially, Churchill wanted Lloyd George as his successor, but he declined on health grounds, so a reluctant Lord Halifax was appointed, partly so Churchill could remove him from the War Cabinet, but also to inveigle his man Anthony Eden into it as Foreign Secretary. However, Halifax had yet to leave for Washington.

Therefore, it fell to Harry Hopkins to cross the Atlantic to start organising Lend-Lease – even though the vote on the Bill had yet to happen – but also to ensure that Britain was willing and able to continue the war.

Hopkins arrived in London in the middle of an air raid. The blacked-out rubble-filled streets, wailing sirens and an atmosphere almost palpably crackling with fear must have come as a rude awakening. He told the American journalist, Ed Murrow, off the record, 'I suppose you could say that I've come here to try to find a way to be a catalytic agent between two prima donnas.'[105]

His first, historic, meeting with one of them came on 10 January 1941.[106] Churchill's anxiety can be gauged by the fact that he produced a copy of the still-unanswered congratulatory telegram he had sent FDR in November, ostensibly to show Hopkins how much he admired Roosevelt, but more likely because he was still smarting at the snub. Churchill admitted to Hopkins that he had been nowhere near as certain as he had pretended that Britain could survive after France fell. However, he was now candid about the cancellation of Sea Lion (having had to acknowledge the existence of Ultra). 'He thinks the invasion will not come,' Hopkins reported, 'Germany cannot invade Britain successfully', and another surprising admission: 'He believes that this war will never see great forces massed against one another.' Clearly to Churchill, bombing, blockade and campaigns of subversion and sabotage were the key to an eventual victory, not full-scale invasion.

In discussing the post-September 1940 campaign against Italy in North Africa, Churchill revealed he was in contact with both Pétain and Weygand: 'He has offered Weygand six divisions – if the former [Italy] strikes – he is in close touch with Pétain on this point – he spoke with no great assurance about it – but it is clear Churchill intends to hold Africa – clean out the Italians and co-operate with Weygand if the opportunity permits.'

At the same time, another of Roosevelt's emissaries, diplomat Robert Murphy, was being given the red-carpet treatment by General Weygand in North Africa. Weygand congratulated the US on the destroyers-for-bases deal, which he said showed that the British Empire was no longer a major player, adding that he was secretly preparing for 'independent military action' against Hitler and Mussolini – with Pétain's approval – and that the policy of collaboration was a pretence. As a result, Murphy recommended that the US supply petrol and oil to French North Africa – but also that Roosevelt dispatch US 'consuls' to ensure the supplies were not diverted to Germany or Vichy, who were actually agents secretly working with sympathetic government contacts with the aim of rising against the Nazis.[107]

Of course, Hopkins' private brief – as with Donovan six months earlier – was to establish whether Britain could hold out against the onslaught of the Blitz, and estimate the chances of Churchill remaining in power. He reported to Roosevelt that the people and the armed forces were behind Churchill, but: 'The politicians and upper crust [only] pretend to like him.'[108]

Churchill soon developed a fondness and respect for Hopkins, whose planned two-week visit stretched to six. By introducing Hopkins to welcoming crowds as 'the personal representative of the President of the United States of America', Churchill also had the opportunity to signal that America stood shoulder to shoulder with Britain. Hopkins met all the key ministers and officials, and twice the King and Queen – once at a private lunch at Buckingham Palace.

Churchill worked on one of his classic speeches while with Hopkins – his first broadcast to the nation for five months.[109] This was the 'give us the tools and we will finish the job' speech given on 9 February 1941, and whether or not it bore Hopkins' stamp, it was certainly aimed at the Americans at the time when the Lend-Lease Bill was passing through Congress: 'We do not need the gallant armies which are forming throughout the American Union.' Churchill was no longer talking of Britain's ability to withstand invasion, but of the complete defeat of Hitler and the Nazis by 'the

British Empire – nay, in a certain sense, the whole English-speaking world'. And speaking of Roosevelt, he ended:

> What is the answer I shall give, in your name, to this great man, the thrice-chosen head of a nation of a hundred and thirty millions? Here is the answer which I will give to President Roosevelt. Put your confidence in us. Give us your faith and your blessing and, under Providence, all will be well.
>
> We shall not fail or falter; we shall not weaken or tire. Neither the sudden shock of battle, nor the longdrawn trials of vigilance and exertion will wear us down. Give us the tools, and we will finish the job.[110]

Besides a long shopping list of ships, aircraft and weapons of all kinds, Hopkins also returned with intelligence and technical secrets to be shared with the US military. One result of an intelligence-sharing agreement – the precise terms of which still remain secret[111] – took place three days before he returned to Washington, when a team of American cryptanalysts arrived at Bletchley Park. In exchange for access to the Japanese diplomatic codes (codenamed 'Purple', their source 'Magic'), broken by the US Navy in September 1940, the Americans were to be given access to Ultra.[112] However, not all Bletchley Park's secrets would be shared – especially the fact that its code-breakers were intercepting and deciphering American communications, and would continue to do so until Pearl Harbor.[113]

Although the cables between Roosevelt and Churchill continued, both leaders now also communicated through Hopkins.[114]

'All aid short of war'

Roosevelt's Bill requested Congress to grant him the power to extend Lend-Lease to 'any country whose defence the President deems vital to the defence of the United States'. Some in his administration urged him to exclude the USSR – or at least make it clear that he would never use his discretionary powers to help Communists – but he refused this compromise.[115] Clearly, he believed it was possible that Stalin would require Lend-Lease and was determined that nothing would prevent it.

The Bill was passed by the Senate on 8 March 1941 by 60 to 31 votes, and three days later by the House of Representatives by 317 to 71. Roosevelt signed it into law immediately. When the vote was announced, Hopkins immediately put a call through to Churchill to tell him the good news.

The Act gave the President enormous discretionary powers. It allowed him to 'manufacture in arsenals, factories, and shipyards under [the US government's] jurisdiction . . . any defense article for the government of any country whose defense the President deems vital to the defense of the United States'. It also specified that: 'The terms and conditions upon which any foreign government receives any aid . . . shall be those which the President deems satisfactory . . . ' the same applying to repayment or benefit given to the US in return. The only check was that he had to report to Congress every 90 days on what had been dispatched ('except such information as he deems incompatible with the public interest to disclose'). As Warren Kimball puts it, 'The only legal limitations were his own judgement, and the need for Congressional appropriations to pay for the goods.'[116]

The only significant change from Roosevelt's draft was that it exempted US Navy vessels from taking part in convoys, and the entry of any US ship, military or civilian, into combat zones. The Act had to be renewed every two years.

Lend-Lease turned the United States into one giant munitions factory. An Industrial Mobilization Plan was drawn up by Bernard Baruch, although not everybody complied – Henry Ford, for example, refused to fulfil orders for the British.[117] Even so, it transformed the economy: by the end of the war, America was supplying 38 countries with Lend-Lease aid, producing more war material than Germany, Japan, Italy and all their conquered territories combined.[118]

Originally, Lend-Lease was to be organised and supervised by a committee of Secretaries from the State, War, Treasury and other Departments. However, Roosevelt decided instead to create the Lend-Lease Administration – under Hopkins' control. In the latter's words, he was now in charge of 'the whole of our aid to Britain programme';[119] 'In effect, it made Hopkins deputy president.'[120] It also gave him control over vast sums: by the end of the war, some $42 billion of federal funds had been spent on Lend-Lease – more than the *total* federal expenditure during the years of the New Deal.[121] And as Lend-Lease now lay at the heart of America's foreign policy, 'As the President's alter ego, Hopkins was drawn more and more into policy and strategy matters.'[122] Yet, despite his incredible power and authority, his annual salary was merely $15,000.

W. Averell Harriman was despatched to London as Lend-Lease Expediter, with the rank of minister: an advocate of America's direct involvement in the war, he was an international banker and FDR's childhood friend. He was also a friend of Hopkins, since they had worked for New Deal agencies. Roosevelt told Harriman: 'I want you to go over to London and recommend everything that we can do, short of war, to keep the British Isles afloat.'[123] Harriman duly arrived on 15 March 1941, to a warm welcome from Churchill, whom he had last met at Bernard Baruch's house in 1929.[124] Although based at the US Embassy, Harriman reported direct to Hopkins through US Navy communications, not the State Department.[125] He saw Churchill at least one day a week and at weekends.

However, recently released documents show that Harriman was also Roosevelt's unofficial liaison with SOE. It was through him, via Hopkins, that the President was kept informed of SOE and BSC operations in America.[126]

'Flayed to the bone'

To the British, Lend-Lease was taken as proof that the US would give them 'the tools to finish the job', but they soon realised that Britain would be very much the long-term loser. In public, Churchill hailed it as 'a new Magna Carta' and 'the most unsordid act in history'. (Surely an odd choice of words – who said it *was* 'sordid'? Was this Churchill's unconscious expression of his real feeling?) He was much more blatantly bitter in private, telling Harold Nicolson of the Ministry of Information that he had thought that: 'we were exchanging a bunch of flowers for a sugar cake. But not at all, the Americans have done a hard business deal.' To the Chancellor of the Exchequer, he was even blunter, saying, 'We are not only to be skinned but flayed to the bone.'[127]

Lost Empire

As with other aspects of FDR's wartime foreign policy, historians find it difficult to understand his precise motives for creating Lend-Lease. Did he really seek to help a needy and desperate Britain? Was he really paving the way for American involvement in the war? Or was he simply intent upon flaying Britain to the bone?

We have seen that although FDR himself always professed American self-interest, historians prefer to believe he was lying. Yet when one isolationist accused him of granting Lend-Lease to save the British Empire, he replied that it had been done for 'purely selfish reasons' and 'what is best for the United States' – adding that the British were under no illusions about this.[128] The true cost to Britain reveals that, again, FDR was telling the unvarnished truth.

When Henry Morgenthau was summoned before the House Foreign Affairs Committee to be questioned about the Lend-Lease Bill, he said that all British assets had been spent or committed by 1 January – only just under $4 million in 'slow assets' remained – and the war was costing Britain $500 million a day. Morgenthau told sceptics bluntly that 'the British financial cow is just about dry'.[129] (Roosevelt himself used the very same words four days later: 'We have been milking the British financial cow which had plenty of money at one time but which had now about become dry.'[130])

Morgenthau also told the Committee, 'Every dollar of property, real property or securities that any English citizen owns in the United States, they have agreed to sell during the next 12 months, in order to raise the money to pay for the orders they have already placed, they are going to sell – every dollar of it.' It was the first the British had heard of it.[131]

Even before Churchill's plea in early December 1940, Morgenthau had already asked the British Treasury representative in Washington, Sir Frederick Phillips, for a list of British holdings in the Americas, ranked according to their liquidity.[132] On 10 March 1941, the day before the final vote on the Bill, with Roosevelt's approval he gave Lord Halifax a 'virtual ultimatum':[133] to show willing, Britain had to agree to sell an important company in the US – the British-owned American Viscose Corporation, a subsidiary of Courtaulds. Churchill stalled, writing later, 'it was impossible for us to continue to make concessions at short notice to meet the exigencies of United

States politics'.[134] But American Viscose was sold in May 1941: 'In the end, the British got about $87 million for a property reasonably worth $125 million.'[135]

At the same time, Morgenthau proposed that US warships pick up more gold from South Africa. Phillips objected, as it had already been allocated to cover other foreign purchases (mainly from Canada). Too late – Roosevelt had already dispatched a ship to pick it up. This time, £30 million in gold was taken.[136]

Not formal conditions of Lend-Lease, the sale of American Viscose and the removal of the South African gold were intended to pay off some of the deficit that had already built up since November 1940. Britain was told this was necessary to 'show willing', if the President were to use his new powers to help them. Even they – and an emergency loan of £60 million in gold from the Belgian government-in-exile – still failed to bridge the gap between what Britain had ordered from America before Lend-Lease and its ability to pay. The British assumed that the new funds could be used to cover this deficit, but in the event this was not allowed, creating a vast crater in their finances. Morgenthau grudgingly arranged relief on some post-Lend-Lease contracts.[137]

Because of the production schedules, there was little appreciable benefit to Britain during 1941 – only 1 per cent of the munitions used that year came from Lend-Lease (as opposed to 84 per cent from home). Until December 1941, most aid was foodstuffs – about 7 per cent of everything eaten in Britain in that year came from America – after that it was military hardware, mainly aircraft and aircraft equipment. By the end of the war, America was supplying about 25 per cent of Britain's military needs.[138]

Throughout 1941, negotiations over the exact terms of Lend-Lease repayments took place in Washington, the British team being headed by the leading economist John Maynard Keynes. The basic principles were straightforward: any unused articles (e.g. ships, vehicles, weapons and/or equipment) would be returned at the end of the war, repaired and made good at Britain's expense; commodities (e.g. ammunition) would be repaid in kind; food and other aid would be 'repaid' in raw materials from the Commonwealth, such as tin and rubber.

But how would it actually *work*? British warships could be repaired in American dockyards, and 8,000 RAF pilots were to be trained in the US – but how could a 'fee' be estimated for such things? And would Britain actually have to *pay*? Roosevelt kept the British government guessing – in 1943 telling Congress that Britain *would not* be expected to pay cash, and a press conference a week later that it *would*.[139]

As negotiations progressed, it became apparent that Lend-Lease had given the US government the leverage it needed to force Britain to reconstruct its economic and trade policies in the United States' favour. The two systems that had locked America out of British Empire markets – imperial preference and the sterling area – were to be scrapped. Once again, as in the case of America's long-standing desire for bases in British territories in the Caribbean and North Atlantic, Britain's plight was being exploited to further the American government's enduring ambitions.

The American diplomat and historian Richard N. Gardner, in *Sterling-Dollar Diplomacy in Current Perspective* (1956, rev. 1980), notes that the Lend-Lease Act had made it solely the President's decision what constituted a 'benefit' to the US, and writes: 'What they [FDR and his advisers] hit upon was the promise by Britain and other aid recipients to co-operate in the post-war reconstruction of multilateral trade.'[140] Roosevelt was later to report to Congress that among the benefits from Lend-Lease was 'an understanding with Britain (and prospectively with others of our allies) as to the shape of future commercial and financial policy'.[141]

Reasonably enough, Britain was not allowed to re-export any Lend-Lease products, but neither could she export any *similar* ones if they might compete with American trade. Another condition – again, in itself reasonable – was that raw materials in short supply in the US that were given or sold to Britain could not be re-exported (with a few special exceptions). But as David Reynolds comments: 'Strictly interpreted, these criteria of "competition" and "short supply" could severely and unfairly restrict Britain's export trade.'[142] Indeed, Britain agreed to reduce *all* exports to 'the minimum necessary to supply or obtain materials essential to the war effort'.[143] Effectively, the real price of Lend-Lease was that Britain would not even be able to attempt to compete with the US in the world market during the war. By the time it ended, America would be so far ahead it would be impossible to catch up.

With no choice, the British government agreed these terms in September 1941. By the end of the war, British exports were just one-third of their pre-war levels, and although not all of this can be blamed on Lend-Lease, the agreement 'did aggravate the decline'.[144] Theodore A. Wilson of the University of Kansas says: 'In effect the British produced a self-denying ordinance that reduced their trade throughout the war and left markets open to American penetration.'[145] Or, more succinctly, 'During the 18 months between Dunkirk and Pearl Harbor, Britain mortgaged its future as a world power.'[146]

The US administration's attitude was summed up by Dean Acheson, Under-Secretary of State, during the 1941 negotiations: 'an effort of the magnitude of the Lend-Lease program on our part imposed upon the British the obligation of continuing goodwill in working out plans for the future'.[147] Roosevelt himself, in January 1942, said that Lend-Lease would 'play a dominant part in weaving the pattern of the post-war policies of the United States'.[148]

From scrapping imperial preference and the sterling area, the US extended 'repayment' for Lend-Lease to concessions on trade in specific commodities (for example, wheat) and even to concessions that looked ahead to *post-war* commerce, such as in civil aviation.

At the root of the American position was a long-standing mistrust of the 'superior' British. As Roosevelt warned Willkie: 'The British are always foxy and you have to be the same with them.'[149] Admiral Stark agreed: 'Never absent from British minds are their post-war interests, commercial and military.'[150] Of course, this wariness was justified: the British negotiators also did their damnedest to twist the situation to their advantage – Roosevelt's aide Adolf Berle complained: 'the British do not propose to pay anything, anywhere at any time.'[151] But they were no longer in a position to be clever. The economic historian Alan P. Dobson sums up the two nations' positions:

> Britain was determined to recapture export markets,

abandoned because of the war, and to accumulate sufficient reserves to facilitate post-war trade and to provide herself with a degree of economic independence: America was equally determined to expand her presence in the international economy and to ensure that Britain was not in a position to hamper that growth. American production quadrupled during the war and as this was before the great consumer society had come into being there were widespread fears in the US business community and government that a depression would ensue if foreign markets were not found for this excess production.[152]

It was dog-eat-dog: pure survival. And as the war progressed, the balance was to shift even more in America's favour.

By the end of the war, Britain had received Lend-Lease worth approximately $27 billion (about £7 billion at 1945 rates). But how can a figure be put on the losses in trade concessions and markets? Roosevelt may not have sold his garden hose to his neighbour, but he went considerably further – even demanding the deeds to his house in 'gratitude'.

It may be argued that Roosevelt was only being shrewd. As since the First World War the British Empire had effectively kept the United States out of international markets, now that America had the chance to reverse the situation, why not take it? There was a fear that Britain regarded the US as, in Roosevelt's words, 'a good-time Charlie who can be used to help the British Empire out of a tight spot, and then be forgotten for ever'.[153] Indeed, Britain could hardly complain, having unashamedly taken unfair advantage for two decades. But surely there is a vast difference between competition in peacetime and exploiting a competitor in the middle of a war – especially a conflict the President had effectively incited.

Lend-Lease has always been portrayed by both sides as an act of unparalleled generosity and self-sacrifice by one nation to the other, idealism rather than economics. But the tough-minded American negotiators made no allowances for Britain's weakened state, or for the fact that – as the President repeatedly told the American people – it was bearing the brunt of Hitler's onslaught in order to preserve

America from attack and to prevent its boys from dying far away in Europe. When it came to economics – and much else – Britain was on its own.

The other possible justification for the US government's vengeful avarice is that whatever it cost Britain was a small price to pay for preserving its freedom from Nazi tyranny. But Roosevelt's own argument for Lend-Lease was based on the opposite idea: that it had to be given so Britain could continue to fight for *America*'s freedom. Surely this makes his cynical use of Lend-Lease for America's economic advantage doubly duplicitous – and seriously challenges the usual interpretation of that particular era in modern American history.

Hopkins' master plan

In April 1941, Hopkins set out his credo in a memorandum entitled 'The New Deal of Mr Roosevelt is the Designate and Invincible Adversary of the New Order of Hitler', arguing that Nazism could never be defeated by the 'old order of democracy', proclaiming:

> But the new order of Hitler can be conclusively defeated by the new order of democracy, which is the New Deal universally extended and supplied.
>
> Just as totalitarianism backs the new order of Hitler, so now the world democracy must back the New Deal of Mr Roosevelt.[154]

Democracy 'must wage total war against totalitarian war. It must exceed the Nazi in fury, ruthlessness and efficiency', although the conflict was not about upholding the old order but creating a new one. The old European-style system must be replaced by the new American democracy. The United States was to be leader of the 'free world'. As Hopkins had declared in a speech entitled 'What is the "American Way"?' in July 1938:

> The 'American Way' is not just a rhetorical phrase. It has deep and significant implications. America was the new land of opportunity to which men came from a tired Old World . . .

an Old World of little land and feudal overlordship and labor surpluses, an Old World of poverty and human resignation.

[. . .]

Democracy is not exclusively an American idea. It goes back to the ideals of the Greek city-states. But we gave it a peculiarly American slant. We gave it a vigor and a reality which the eighteenth- and nineteenth-century democratic revolutions of Europe never approached. Over there the democratic revolutions superimposed a veneer of political equality upon a social system that was antidemocratic through and through, a social system dominated by economic and class inequalities.[155]

In other words, Hopkins believed that European democracy was not authentic. Only the American version counted. He saw the war as an opportunity to impose it not only on the dictatorships of Europe, but also on its democracies.

Hopkins defined his 'new order of democracy' as the 'New Deal universally extended and applied'. For him, Lend-Lease was not solely an economic tool to win the war but also a means to convert the 'old order' – Britain, France and their empires – to that of the brave New World.

CHAPTER SEVEN

Hell

'If Hitler invaded Hell, I would at least make a favourable reference to the Devil in the House of Commons.'

Winston S. Churchill, 22 June 1941[1]

After the triumph of the Lend-Lease Act, Roosevelt unexpectedly fell into such a state of apathy that during April and the first part of May 1941 his administration became anxious about his leadership. FDR was even uncharacteristically cautious about Harry Hopkins' advice. According to Robert Sherwood: 'Hopkins was continually urging bold action and Roosevelt was taking the more moderate, temperate, cautious course.'[2] No one knows for certain why Roosevelt was floundering, but certainly after the birth of Lend-Lease both extreme isolationists and extreme interventionists had piled the pressure on him. Lend-Lease went too far for the isolationists, not far enough for interventionists. Now all sides worried he was against them.

Certainly, Lend-Lease had radically changed the situation. Would Hitler see it as a token of America's increasingly active support for Britain – and therefore an act of war? Would he authorise U-boat attacks on American ships? He had been scrupulous to avoid this – so far.

Hell

Lend-Lease might also cause America to be drawn into the war by accident. By stepping up supplies to Britain, more convoys would be crossing the Atlantic, but if escorted by the US Navy, American ships would soon find themselves fighting off U-boats, which could erupt into war. Congress was careful to ensure that the Act upheld existing laws preventing US vessels from entering war zones. At least publicly, Roosevelt, too, resisted involvement in the convoys, declaring, 'Convoys mean shooting and shooting means war.'[3] On the other hand, at the beginning of April 1941 FDR extended the US neutrality zone, where the navy patrolled, informing the British of any German action, by 900 miles to Greenland and the Azores. Both the Americans and the Germans had orders not to shoot first.

After the first Lend-Lease Act was passed, some members of FDR's administration began to urge that the US should enter the war as combatants. On 12 April 1941, Harold Ickes recorded in his diary:

> So far as I am concerned, I am willing that we should make an open declaration of war, but as I have thought it over since, I still think that I gave the President good advice. He agreed with me and said that probably we would have to wait for a German 'incident'. I suspect that the Germans will avoid at all possible costs any such incident as the President would like to take advantage of.[4]

Already, there had been incidents that could have been used by either side as a pretext for hostilities. On 10 April 1941, the US Navy destroyer *Niblack*, while rescuing survivors from a torpedoed Dutch ship, used depth-charges to drive off a U-boat. Yet neither Roosevelt nor Hitler exploited this to plunge the two countries into war. Although the President later enthusiastically embraced the 'forced incident' idea, at this time he was still nervous of taking it further. At the end of April, William Bullitt wrote to Averell Harriman in London, 'The President is waiting for public opinion to lead and public opinion is waiting for a lead from the President.'[5]

America's 'war by proxy'

Initially, to keep up support for Britain and France, Roosevelt had removed equipment and aircraft from US forces. However, in the summer of 1940, he had persuaded Congress to increase military spending – though apparently merely a contingency for the *defence* of the USA, not offensive action. Broadening his administration – and to circumvent calls for a coalition in the event of American involvement in the war[6] – in mid-June 1940 he appointed two anti-isolationist Republicans, Henry L. Stimson and Frank Knox, as Secretaries of War and the Navy respectively. In September 1940, the Selective Service Bill allowed 900,000 men to be drafted into the army for a maximum of one year's service. His supporters – such as the obsequious Sherwood[7] – cite this as an example of his far-sightedness, but as Patrick J. Maney, in *The Roosevelt Presence* (1992), points out, the Bill was not FDR's own initiative. Congress even voted half a billion dollars more for defence than he asked for.[8]

Roosevelt began to warn about the dangers of U-boats to American shipping and Hitler's intention to attack America, even of the *direct* threat of Nazi bombing – ludicrous scare-mongering: no bomber then could cross the Atlantic and return. Clearly this was part of a softening-up process – but for what? Had he already decided that America *would* go to war, or was this insurance against the possibility that it *might*?

Most researchers agree that the mid-1940 build-up was intended to prevent any offensive action against the US: David Reynolds argues that Roosevelt never envisaged sending troops to Europe, whatever happened, writing, 'Since the autumn of 1938 he had hoped to keep war away from the USA by arming Hitler's opponents, whatever the effect on his own armed forces.'[9] Similarly, Michael Simpson writes of the late 1940/early 1941 period: 'Roosevelt still hoped that all aid short of war would be sufficient to assure an Allied victory, but if America was forced to intervene, he (unlike his staff) believed that her participation could be limited to aerial and maritime warfare.'[10]

Even supporters of the 'back door to war' theory agree that Roosevelt only started to draw America in by stealth once he realised it was no longer possible to keep out of the war. But at what point did this realisation hit him? Opinions differ: John T. Flynn puts it as

October 1940,[11] Willard Range autumn 1941.[12] William Langer and Everett Gleason, authors of an exhaustive study of Roosevelt's war policy for the influential Council on Foreign Relations, point out that:

> It is certainly worth noting that the President at no time prior to Pearl Harbor suggested further increase of the army which, according to the existing program, was designed for national and hemispheric defense rather than overseas operations against Nazi Germany.[13]

('Hemispheric' basically means the whole American continent – i.e. the Monroe Doctrine area.)

The last point is demonstrated by Roosevelt's behaviour in the summer of 1941 when Congress would have to renew the Selective Service Bill for a further year. Although Hopkins, Stimson and General Marshall all recommended that he ask Congress to extend it, apparently he had no stomach for the inevitable fight with the isolationists, and was willing to let the law expire, releasing the new army conscripts. Just four months before Pearl Harbor, the President was contemplating breaking up the US Army. Eventually, Stimson and Marshall (Hopkins was abroad) persuaded him to ask for an extension and got it – by a single vote.[14]

We contend that it is possible to pinpoint Roosevelt's realisation more precisely: between late March and June 1941, months in which three events changed the picture entirely – the ABC-1 plan, the Hess mission and the launch of Operation Barbarossa. The first prompted his dithering about how far to commit America to war, the second shook him out of it by showing him what the consequences would be if he failed to make that commitment, while the third provided hope that American involvement could still be limited.

The ABC plan

Dwight Tuttle writes: 'During Congressional hearings on Lend-Lease, administration spokesmen denied to Congress and the press any intention to convoy or send troops out of the hemisphere – and did so at a time when British–American staff talks were formulating such contingency plans.'[15] These were the preliminary 'ABC staff talks' in London.

The talks proper began in January 1941 in Washington, in strict secrecy (so as not to compromise the passage of the Lend-Lease Bill). While little damage would have been done if these plans had fallen into German or Japanese hands, they would have been wrecked if Congress or the press had got hold of them.[16]

The talks were not Roosevelt's initiative: in November 1940, Admiral Stark had proposed 'Plan Dog' in the event of a two-front war with Germany and Japan: a defensive approach in the Pacific while concentrating first on victory in Europe. Anticipating it would ultimately be necessary 'to send large air and land forces to Europe or Africa, or both, and to participate strongly in this land offensive,'[17] he recommended immediate talks with the British General Staff on contingency plans, which Roosevelt authorised.

Beginning on 14 January 1941, the talks lasted for a month, ending with plan 'ABC-1': if America went in, its top priority would be the defeat of Germany and Italy – which would require US troops on the ground in Europe. A policy of deterrence was to be adopted in respect of Japan, but if that failed, they should be held off until victory in Europe. The Americans failed to understand why Britain wanted to defend Egypt and the eastern Mediterranean, refusing to accept Churchill's strategy of blockade, bombing and subversion on the continent – rather than invasion – but mostly the two sides agreed. The plan was endorsed in principle by Roosevelt and the army chiefs.[18]

The only immediate action required by the Americans was that while keeping the bulk of their fleet at Pearl Harbor, their navy would transfer some ships to the Atlantic to free British warships to sail for Singapore as a deterrent to Japan. But Roosevelt was slow to get this moving.

It must be stressed that as the administration deliberately kept out of these strategic and non-political discussions, they were not influenced by FDR's thinking. Although Roosevelt endorsed the plan (he had little choice) he would have been horrified by the ABC conclusion that the large-scale deployment of American troops in Europe was unavoidable. He had always believed it would never be necessary – and had promised the American people it would never happen. Would he survive if he had to renege on his promise? As members of his administration such as Ickes began to talk up the necessity of direct American involvement, perhaps Roosevelt's indecisiveness after Lend-Lease was due to the gradual realisation that avoiding involvement in Europe might not be realistic. Was even he worried about what he might have unleashed?

Despite officially approving the ABC plan, it was a major blow to Roosevelt, whose real attitude is revealed by the fact that almost immediately he and his administration set about undermining it; as we will see, instead of *deterring* Japan, Roosevelt chose to *provoke*.

Britain, the US and Japan

Another reason for FDR's lack of leadership in April 1941 is that he badly needed to take stock of a highly volatile and rapidly changing situation. The ABC plan shows that neither Britain nor America believed that war with Japan was inevitable, but recognised that Japan might well take advantage of the situation in Europe to extend its influence at the expense of the imperial Europeans – as it had already demonstrated after France's surrender, when it increased its presence in French Indo-China.

During his visit to London in January 1941, as the ABC talks were taking place in Washington, Hopkins had explored the British attitude to Japan. He cabled Roosevelt after a meeting at the Foreign Office:

> Eden told me that he had had a stiff conversation with the Japanese Ambassador here in London yesterday in which he took a very strong line, the main point being that he was asking the Japanese to state what were their real intentions. He informed the Ambassador that the British Government intended to stand for no nonsense in the Far East and British interests there would be protected to the limit if they were attacked. Eden has cabled Halifax about this. He and his colleagues from the foreign office [*sic*] reviewed at length all the various moves major and minor which they think Japan is making. Eden believes that the Japanese consider the presence

of our fleet at Pearl Harbor to be purely a minor matter. He is very anxious that we find a way to emphasize our determination to prevent Japan from making further encroachments. He believes that if we take a positive line towards Japan we might make them pause before attacking Hong Kong. I want to emphasize to you the British belief that Japan, under the influence of Germany, is considering making a positive move against British territory in the near future.[19]

In a later private note to FDR, he added:

Eden asked me repeatedly what our country would do if Japan attacked Singapore or the Dutch East Indies, saying that it was essential to their policy to know. Of course, it was perfectly clear that neither the President nor Hull could give an adequate answer to the British on that point because the declaration of war is up to Congress, and the isolationists and, indeed, a great part of the American people, would not be interested in a war in the Far East merely because Japan attacked the Dutch.[20]

(Contrast Hopkins' response with his answer – below – to Stalin on the same question six months later.)

The ABC-1 report recommended a solution that satisfied both Britain and America, a deterrent – but not appeasing – strategy aimed at avoiding conflict with Japan, at least until Germany and Italy had been seen off.

As soon as American-educated Matsuoka Yosuka became Japanese Foreign Minister in September 1940, one of his first acts had been to sign the Tripartite Pact with Germany and Italy, in order to immobilise the USA. Japan recognised German and Italian leadership in creating the 'New Order' in Europe, while they recognised Japan's leadership in the 'Greater East Asia Co-Prosperity Sphere'. The three undertook 'to assist one another with all political, economic, and military means when one of the three contracting parties is attacked by a power not at present involved in the European war or the Chinese–Japanese conflict'. As the USSR was specifically exempted, clearly the power they really had in mind was the US.

The Japanese Prime Minister, Prince Konoe Fumimaro, was against war (unlike Matsuoka) but thought a German alliance would enable Japan to undermine Britain's position in the Far East.[21] But Japan was also constrained by events in Europe. Although it harboured designs on the Europeans' imperial possessions in South-East Asia, it was nervous that building up its presence there would encourage the USSR to revive hostilities in the north-west – the vexed Manchuria–Siberia border.

After Lend-Lease was announced, Hitler pressed Japan to attack British possessions in the Far East; again, mainly to shift the focus of *American* interest away from Europe. When Japan objected that this would expose them to Soviet attack, von Ribbentrop responded that, if that happened, Germany would attack the USSR. He neglected to mention that plans for Barbarossa were already well advanced.[22]

In spring 1941, Matsuoka visited Italy, Germany and the USSR. Admiring Stalin, he proposed a non-aggression pact with the USSR, which was signed in April – a huge surprise because of the traditional enmity between the two countries. Now that Japan was no longer constrained by fear of the USSR it could move against British colonies. As with the Nazi–Soviet Pact, Stalin's neutrality pact with Japan was a devious move to keep Britain and Germany at war – if Japan weakened Britain by forcing it to divert resources to the Far East, the chances of a German victory would be increased, encouraging Hitler to stay focused on that front for a while longer. Stalin's action was also a severe setback for Roosevelt: for years, the USA and USSR had worked together to restrain Japan. For Hitler, it was a mixed blessing: Japanese action would weaken Britain, but he hoped that Japan would join his attack on the USSR to split Stalin's forces. The winners were Japan and Russia – Stalin had made his nation more secure and weakened the British and American position. And Japan was now free to pursue its imperial ambitions in South-East Asia.

Roosevelt had to consider the ramifications of the pact at home – another reason for dithering during April 1941, postponing moving American ships from Pearl Harbor to the Atlantic, as agreed in the

ABC-1 plan.[23] After the Soviet–Japanese pact, on 24 April he revised his earlier order to prepare for action against the Germans in the western Atlantic: now US ships should *report* German vessels west of Ireland, but not shoot unless shot at.[24]

Roosevelt and Hess

As the increasing likelihood of war – against Germany, Japan or both – seems to have plunged the President into a fog of indecision, he was galvanised into action by the prospect of *peace*, after Rudolf Hess arrived on British soil on 10 May 1941. Peace in Europe at that moment would have spelt disaster for the US.

After steadily building up American armaments from 1938, Roosevelt had now fully mobilised industry as a whole for war – and its only market was the British Empire. Through Lend-Lease, Roosevelt had found a way to continue to supply that market even though it no longer had the means to pay: federal funds were sustaining American industries until Lend-Lease would begin to benefit America. If the Hess mission brought about peace and the removal of Churchill, America would be ruined.

We have seen that FDR's immediate reaction to the Deputy Führer's arrival was to cancel his Pan-American Day speech scheduled for 14 May. He also cancelled Cabinet meetings for three weeks, officially because he was ill with a 'persistent cold', although some claim that it was a debilitating intestinal illness, others a bad attack of haemorrhoids. Sherwood records having a long meeting in the presidential bedroom, afterwards remarking to 'Missy' LeHand, 'The President seems in fine shape to me . . . What is really the matter with him?', to which she replied, 'What he's suffering from most of all is a case of sheer exasperation.'[25] Was his panic over intervention so overwhelming that even he had to take to his sickbed?

There had been considerable speculation about what he was intending to say in his first high-profile speech since Lend-Lease. Would he move America closer to war, or reinforce its neutrality? As we saw in Chapter 1, when he finally made the speech on 27 May, it marked a dramatic reversal in US policy – a definite move in the direction of war. However, we can be reasonably sure that what he said on 27 May was *not* what he had intended to say two weeks earlier.

According to Sherwood, the State Department's original draft merely emphasised 'hemispheric solidarity' – i.e. the continuation of the Monroe Doctrine policy of maintaining the defence of the Americas (which makes sense given the occasion). (One extreme rumour that even found its way into the Washington press was that Roosevelt was about to announce the union of the USA and Britain! Real fear of such a union seems to have partly inspired Hess's mission.[26])

So far, although Roosevelt had been advised that American intervention was now necessary on the pretext of a German 'incident', he had resisted – as, apparently, had Hopkins. It was only now – after Hess brought the spectre of peace – that they embraced the idea. On 14 May, Henry Morgenthau told Harry Hopkins that during the past week he had come round to the view that 'if we are going to save England we would have to get into this war'.[27] A few days later, Roosevelt himself told Morgenthau, 'I am waiting to be pushed into the situation.'[28]

Another significant reversal came on 14 May – the day of the scheduled speech. In mid-April, to the irritation of the British, he had postponed transferring American ships to the Atlantic, as required by ABC-1. Suddenly, he ordered 20 vessels full steam ahead.[29] And on 22 May 1941, he even galvanised the army to prepare for possible pre-emptive strikes against the Azores and the Atlantic islands, in case Vichy allowed the Germans to use or build bases in Africa.[30] Harold Ickes noted on 25 May 1941: 'The President said: "I am not willing to fire the first shot." So it seems that he is still waiting for the Germans to create an "incident".'[31]

Roosevelt had stated that America was to fight an 'undeclared war' on Germany, announcing an 'unlimited national emergency', on the grounds that the Nazis were planning acts of aggression against the United States. But if he had evidence, why not present it to Congress and ask them to declare war? In the event, Roosevelt's speech was, paradoxically, a declaration of undeclared war.

Speech writer Sherwood reveals: 'There were two important prohibitions in this speech. The President would not mention Japan and he would not mention the Soviet Union.'[32] Indeed, a reference to

Finland as one of the victims of unprovoked aggression was struck out of the original draft. Roosevelt was doing his utmost not to cast Stalin's Russia in a bad light.

Delivered at a dinner for ambassadors and diplomats from Latin America, and also broadcast live, the speech stressed that 'aid for democracies would keep the United States out of the war', stating that the 'first and fundamental fact' was that the Nazis sought world domination: Nazi Germany was therefore a threat to the American way of life. He also emphasised the *economic* consequences of a German victory – American workers would have to compete with slave labour and there would be a loss of export markets. On Lend-Lease, he said, 'We have made no pretence about our own self-interest in this aid. Great Britain understands it – and so does Nazi Germany.'[33]

The most potentially provocative statement concerned the US Navy patrols which were helping to supply Britain and that, 'All additional measures necessary to deliver the goods will be taken' – implying the navy would fight off attacks on the convoys. However, at a press conference the next day, he insisted that he did *not* mean that.[34]

The Hess mission had shaken Roosevelt out of his malaise, but he was still in a dilemma, wanting an 'incident', but also shrinking from the consequences; when opportunities arose, he ignored them. On 21 May 1941, an unarmed American merchant ship, *Robin Moor*, was sunk by a U-boat in the south Atlantic, after the passengers and crew had been allowed off in lifeboats. The German captain had acted despite orders not to attack American vessels, and the commander-in-chief of the German Navy, Admiral Erich Raeder, issued an order to prevent a recurrence – which was sanctioned by Hitler.[35] Clearly aware of Roosevelt's private comments, the British Embassy pointed out to Hopkins that the incident would justify the President authorising force.[36] Hopkins in turn urged Roosevelt to instruct the navy that any response was at their discretion[37] – rescinding his previous order not to react at all. Uncharacteristically, Roosevelt declined to follow Hopkins' advice.

Then, on 28 May, FDR told Lord Halifax that he would send US Marines to Iceland – then a Danish possession, which had been occupied by Britain after the German invasion of Denmark – to take over from British forces there and allow them to be deployed elsewhere.[38] In his orders to the commander of the Atlantic Fleet authorising the move, Admiral Stark admitted: 'I realize that this is practically an act of war.'[39]

On 14 June 1941, Roosevelt again stepped up the pressure on Germany and Italy by freezing their assets in the US, and the next day ordered their consulates to be closed.

Whatever Hitler's long-term aims, the claim that at that time he had designs on the United States – and even the rest of the world – is nonsense. His *documented* policy since 1938 had been to avoid any action that would give Roosevelt a pretext for increasing aid to Britain and France (let alone bringing America into the war), for which reason he had forbidden German intelligence from mounting any major operations in the USA.[40] Peter Calvocoressi writes, 'Until the middle of 1941 Hitler had every reason to keep the United States out of the war at almost any cost and he . . . set himself not only to avoid provoking Roosevelt but also to ignore Roosevelt's provocation of him.'[41] FDR's declaration of an undeclared war – and his subsequent actions in Iceland and closure of the German and Italian consulates – certainly constituted extreme provocation. Clearly, he was hoping Hitler would be pushed into declaring war, or at least order attacks on US vessels, taking the decision out of his hands. The fact that the Nazi leader failed to rise to the bait in the face of such clear provocation reveals Roosevelt's claim that Hitler wanted war with America as the resounding falsehood it was.

Secret truce

Churchill not only used the Hess affair to scare Roosevelt out of his apathy, but also to enter into what amounted to a secret ceasefire with Hitler in order to encourage him to attack the Soviet Union. (Remember Churchill had already made a secret deal with Pétain.)

The fact that the last air raid on London coincided with Hess's arrival, and the Blitz on all British cities ended six days later, is normally explained as a consequence of the Luftwaffe being redeployed on Barbarossa. But, even if true, surely it is still significant that Hitler felt secure enough to turn his back on Britain: witness his 'high hopes' of the British 'peace party' on the day Barbarossa was launched.

Although Britain was in no position to land troops in France, Churchill's long-standing plan was that the RAF should launch an 'absolutely devastating, exterminating attack' on Germany when Hitler attacked Russia.[42] But now that Hitler *had* turned east, Churchill suddenly changed his mind – to the astonishment of the RAF commanders. The Chief of the Air Staff, Sir Charles Portal, wrote to the Prime Minister specifically asking why he had changed his policy at such a vital moment.[43]

In fact, air raids on Germany were *scaled down*. (The 'temporary suspension of air-raiding by both sides' was one of the reasons for the post-Hess anxiety in America.) Although at the beginning of July 1941 the Air Staff ordered Bomber Command to concentrate on destroying civilian morale and Germany's transport infrastructure (to disrupt Barbarossa), Churchill overrode them. A review – clearly a delaying tactic – was set up, overseen not by a military strategist but by the economist David Butt, which concluded that the air raids were neither efficient nor accurate enough (even though the whole point of area bombing is that it is not required to be accurate).[44] Even so, in September the Air Staff still insisted that area bombing should be resumed. Churchill then argued that this was not to be implemented until the spring of 1942 in order to conserve resources for a 'big push'.[45] (Although the first of the great thousand-bomber raids, on Cologne – Operation Millennium – took place on 30 May 1942, they remained the exception rather than the rule for another year.)

As with Roosevelt, Churchill's change of heart is a mystery – especially as time was of the essence. If the Germans could take Moscow before the winter, the Soviet Union would be finished; if it could survive the bitter months, at least a stalemate would be likely, if not a Soviet victory. Distracting or piling pressure on the Nazis had to be done immediately. And yet Churchill did nothing. Stalin worried he was simply standing back while Germany and the USSR bled each other dry – as certain Britons had been advocating for years. Could Churchill possibly have *wanted* Hitler to be so confident he could attack Russia unhindered?

Until summer 1942, British and German forces seemed to go out of their way to avoid each other, in what amounts to a second phoney war. Their last face-to-face encounter of 1941 took place in Crete after an airborne offensive launched by Germany ten days after Hess's arrival (and therefore before any 'secret truce'). But after Crete, that was it.

Britons and Germans were fighting face-to-face only in North Africa, where Rommel's Afrika Corps engaged with the Eighth Army (the 'Desert Rats') – but they were fighting for *Italy*, under the direct control of the Italian High Command.[46] Rommel's brief was to help defend Libya and tie up British forces in North Africa – *not* to launch an offensive without direct orders from Berlin. Unfortunately, the maverick Rommel thought he knew better, and launched a successful offensive anyway. (Ironically, his initial success was largely due to Ultra – the British had intercepted Berlin's order not to attack and assumed he would obey it.[47]) Heartened by German successes in Greece and Yugoslavia, Rommel continued to advance, cavalierly disobeying orders as he went.

Rommel was so successful because he was one step ahead. From August 1941, he was able to read the signals sent by the US military attaché in Cairo, Colonel Frank B. Fellers, who routinely sent Washington a full rundown on British plans and movements, as well as troop numbers. In common with all US military attachés, Fellers used the allegedly secure Black Code. However, an Italian agent had managed to steal, photograph and replace a copy from the US Embassy in Rome. After this, all US messages were easily read. It was only in August 1942 that the British discovered this from German documents captured in the Western Desert.

In Iraq, the British were locked in hostilities with a newly installed military government, whom Hitler wanted to woo. Although technically independent, Iraq was effectively a British-controlled territory because of their oilfields there. However, the Prime Minister, Rashid Ali, took advantage of the war to play the British off against the Axis powers. He was replaced as Prime Minister but then successfully staged a military coup, sparking hostilities with the British, and Hitler offered his support. To aid Rashid, the Germans needed access to bases in Syria, then under Vichy French control. This led to the negotiation of the 'Paris Protocols' at the end of May 1941.

Friendly Fire

Admiral François Darlan, former commander of the French Navy – and 'incurably anti-British'[48] – had emerged as an immensely powerful figure in the Vichy government, being simultaneously Vice-Premier and Foreign, Interior and Information ministers, and soon Minister of Defence. Believing Germany would win, to him greater cooperation with Hitler was essential for France's future greatness. He also viewed Britain as finished in Europe, its Empire gradually being subsumed by the US.[49]

On 11 May 1941, Darlan met Hitler at Berchtesgaden, and on the 28th, after negotiations with German diplomats and top brass in Paris, signed the Paris Protocols, agreeing that Germany could use French airbases in Syria (to supply the anti-British Iraqis), the port of Bizerte in Tunisia to supply the Afrika Corps in Libya, and, in principle, the construction of a U-boat base at Dakar in Senegal. In return, France received concessions such as the return of 80,000 prisoners of war and a reduction in the 'occupation costs' demanded by Germany.

In the event, only the Syrian bases were used, temporarily. Hitler neglected to take up the offers of the Tunisian and Dakar bases – potentially useful against the Allies – clearly because he had no wish to do so at that time. The non-application of the Paris Protocols is generally credited to Pétain and Weygand delaying the Vichy government's ratification.[50] But if Hitler had really *wanted* them ratified, surely they would have been – immediately?

In response – again, Ultra had revealed the deal and German plans – in June, a combined force of British, Free French and Australian troops was dispatched to invade Syria and the Lebanon (also a Vichy mandate). Curiously, all German forces were pulled out before the Allies arrived and the only fighting in Syria involved the Vichy French. It was their High Commissioner, General Henri-Fernand Dentz, who decided to resist the Commonwealth and Free French invasion, leading to the ugly scenario of Frenchman fighting Frenchman, until Dentz surrendered on 10 July 1941. (A very generous armistice for the Vichy Army was negotiated and signed by the British without the involvement of a furious de Gaulle.)

Apparently, everything possible was being done to prevent the British from directly confronting the Nazis. Of course, Hitler had no desire to shift resources away from Barbarossa, but what possible reason could Churchill have for avoiding confrontation, when this was precisely the time to *increase* pressure on Germany?

'A wartime deal with Hitler'

In August 1941, in Brazzaville, de Gaulle declared in an interview to the *Chicago Daily News*, 'What in effect England is carrying on is a war-time deal with Hitler in which Vichy serves as go-between.'[51] Indeed, Vichy survived with both Germany and Britain's tacit permission: if Pétain became more actively pro-Hitler, then the British would attack Vichy possessions, and if he grew friendlier towards Britain, then Hitler would seize his territory. So de Gaulle's assertion was true enough about the Vichy situation, but, significantly, it only works in the context of Churchill and Hitler having no desire to actively engage at that time. It was this tacit agreement – the secret 'war-time deal' – that allowed Pétain to play them off against each other.

De Gaulle's remark may have been a memorable soundbite, but he immediately regretted it, desperately cabling the Free French representative in America to stop publication as there was 'a misunderstanding in one sentence which will lead to a misrepresentation of my intentions'.[52]

But it was too late. Churchill was furious – but was it because, as is usually assumed, de Gaulle had falsely and offensively alleged he had done a deal with Hitler? It is now known that Churchill *had* done a secret deal with Vichy. The idea of a similar deal with Hitler may seem unthinkable, but both agreeing to leave Vichy alone reveals their underlying desire not to be dragged into face-to-face confrontation.

When de Gaulle returned to London in September, Churchill instructed: 'No English authority is to have any contact with him when he arrives', ending 'General de Gaulle is to stew in his own juice for a week if necessary.'[53] Only after two weeks did Churchill condescend to see him, but refused to shake hands and insisted on using an interpreter – even though de Gaulle knew his French to be fluent – whom he rather ludicrously made much of correcting. However, the two men then talked alone for an hour – after which they were quite amicable again, de Gaulle accepting one of

Churchill's cigars.[54] Even so, de Gaulle was forced to agree to a French National Committee governing the Free French – a direct snub. (Characteristically, he circumvented this by ensuring that only his loyal supporters were appointed.) And Churchill ordered that de Gaulle was 'on no account to leave the country'.[55]

The 'secret truce' between Churchill and Hitler in the wake of the Hess mission does not necessarily imply any formal contact. There was no need: both would understand the signals – the ending of the Blitz and the lessening of RAF raids on Germany. However, as Sir Stewart Menzies and Admiral Canaris remained in clandestine contact throughout the war, it is possible that messages of reassurance were disguised as intelligence gleaned by Canaris's London agents, telling Hitler he could proceed with Barbarossa without worrying about Britain. (Interestingly, Churchill put Menzies in direct control of Hess, rather than, as would have been expected, the XX – Double Cross – Committee or MI5.)

Equal hells

Before dawn on the shortest night of the year, 22 June 1941, Hitler unleashed Operation Barbarossa.

Stalin, no fool, knew that sooner or later Hitler would attack (as would any casual reader of *Mein Kampf*); the only question was when. However, the Red Army was still recovering from his purges – as the ignominious Winter War against Finland had shown. And Stalin believed he was secure for at least another year, and so thought he had sufficient time during the winter to prepare his defences. This was despite Western intelligence to the contrary – indeed, the British Ambassador in Moscow, Sir Stafford Cripps, had even warned Stalin to expect the invasion on 22 June, six days before Hitler himself decided on that date![56]

Antony Beevor writes in *Stalingrad* (1998): 'Stalin was certain that most warnings had been *"Angliyskaya provokatsiya"* – part of a plot by Winston Churchill, the arch-enemy of the Soviet Union, to start a war between Russia and Germany. Since Hess's flight to Scotland, Stalin had become even more uneasy about it.'[57] In fact, Churchill probably knew about Barbarossa from Ultra – but he had no intention of letting Stalin know that.

Hell

Stalin had also fallen for Nazi misinformation that he was safe until Britain had been defeated or made peace (hence his alarm at Hess's flight) and that Hitler would first make demands before resorting to force. He had also increased trade with Germany, trying to buy time. And surely his neutrality pact with Japan would keep Hitler off his back a little longer . . .

Increasingly paranoid, Stalin tended to reject real information as trickery: in order to undermine Hitler's strategy, the German Ambassador in Moscow, the anti-Hitler conspirator Friedrich von der Schulenburg had warned his Russian counterpart of an impending attack two weeks before, to which Stalin sniffed: 'Disinformation has now reached ambassadorial level.'[58]

Operation Barbarossa involved over three and a half million troops, 3,600 tanks and 2,700 aircraft, attacking along a front stretching from Finland to the Black Sea. Part of the biggest military operation ever mounted aimed for Moscow and Leningrad, the rest for the Ukraine. In 'the greatest battle in history'[59] the usual rules of war disappeared in the mud, guts – and ultimately the bitterest winter winds. Remembering the other's atrocities in Poland, both sides knew there would be no mercy. Hitler specifically exempted German soldiers from prosecution for crimes against Russian troops or civilians, on the grounds that the USSR had never signed up to the Geneva or Hague Conventions. (Some appalled commanders simply neglected to pass this order on.) Both sides operated 'scorched earth' policies, destroying everything, including food supplies.

For the first time, the SS were involved in an offensive, following behind the Wehrmacht and, with the Secret Field Police, executing Soviet officials and other potentially 'troublesome' elements, mostly Jews. This was to evolve into the horrors of the 'Final Solution'.

As always, the civilian population suffered most, caught between the ruthlessness of the invader and the only-too-familiar Soviet regime. In November 1941, Stalin ordered every building and farm for 40 miles behind the lines to be destroyed, to prevent the Germans using them in case of a Russian retreat. 'Never did a population suffer so much from both sides in a war.'[60]

On the day Barbarossa was launched, Stalin immediately offered

Hitler the Ukraine, Belorussia and the Baltic states, but as the Politburo persuaded him victory was possible, on 3 July he took personal command of the 'patriotic war' against Germany, remaining in Moscow, although – because of the Nazis' rapid advance – the rest of the Soviet government was relocated 500 miles deeper into Russia.

If Moscow and Leningrad were taken, it would all be over. The Nazis' plan was to capture Moscow within three months, before the onset of winter – and they almost succeeded. However, although the blitzkrieg successfully drove the Russians back, they simply regrouped and fought on, savagely – undoubtedly spurred on by the certain knowledge that to fail to rise to the challenge would mean being shot by their own side. And the further the Germans advanced into that vast wilderness, the more dangerously they stretched their supply lines.

The Russians desperately hung on until, in October, the brutal Russian winter struck hard. But Hitler refused to countenance the possibility of defeat, despite the bitter historical lesson of Napoleon's retreat. By the first days of November, the invaders could actually see the Kremlin's towers 20 miles away, but a Russian counter-attack pushed them back. Leningrad was besieged, but held out for over two years, although a million inhabitants perished.

In December, when the temperature suddenly dropped to -25⁰C, German casualties from frostbite outnumbered battle wounds. Due to Hitler's increasingly insane urging, the army had made little preparation for a devastating winter war; the Führer believed it would be all over by then. As his generals sought permission to regroup, they were sacked as incompetent. Eventually, he dismissed the Commander-in-Chief Field Marshal Walter von Brauchitsch and, like Stalin, took over as Commander-in-Chief himself.

A moral dilemma

War between Nazi Germany and Soviet Russia created a moral minefield. The USSR's record at that time was even worse than Nazism, and for nearly two years it had adopted a position of 'benevolent neutrality' towards Germany, jointly invaded Poland, aided Hitler against Britain and France, attacked innocent Finland and annexed the Baltic states. Any charge levelled against Hitler could also be levelled – often with more justification – against Stalin. So how should Churchill and Roosevelt react? Patrick Maney sums up the President's dilemma:

> Roosevelt's efforts to depict the battle against the Nazis as a quasi-religious war encountered one embarrassing obstacle: the Soviet Union. In June, after he determined that Russian armies might indeed hold out against Germany, he sought to provide aid to the Soviet Union. As a means of combating Hitler, American aid to the Soviets made perfect sense. True, in a moral sense, there was little difference between Stalin and Hitler; by 1941, Stalin already had the blood of millions of his own countrymen on his hands. True, too, in terms of democratic values there was little difference between Germany and the Soviet Union; both were equally repressive societies.[61]

In a broadcast on the first day of Barbarossa, Churchill stated baldly: 'No one has been a more consistent opponent of Communism than I have in the last 25 years. I will unsay no word I have spoken about it', but: 'Any man or state who fights against Nazism will have our aid.'[62] (He added with breathtaking mendacity that the attack on the USSR was 'no less than the prelude to the invasion of the British Isles'. The people must not be *too* relieved Hitler had turned east.)

At the beginning of July 1941, a Soviet delegation arrived in London to seek assistance, resulting in an agreement that Britain and the USSR would support each other's fight against Germany. Neither would make a separate peace – although Stalin never trusted Churchill to keep his word on this. By the end of August, the British and Red Armies had jointly occupied Iran.

How could the West ignore the fact that Russia had attacked Poland – whose independence was, ostensibly, the very reason that Britain was fighting? But Britain's war aims had undergone a gradual metamorphosis: first it was to defend Poland, then to preserve itself from invasion. Now it was to defeat Nazism.

When Churchill allied with Stalin, not unnaturally General Sikorski of the Free Poles demanded to know what would happen if

Germany was defeated. Would Stalin be allowed to keep the parts of Poland he invaded with Hitler? Or would a Nazi defeat mean Soviet domination of the *whole* of Poland? Sikorski urgently sought reassurance that his frontiers would be restored to their pre-September 1939 situation, creating a dilemma for Churchill, who wanted to postpone the problem until 'easier times'.[63] However, it was to loom larger as the Grand Alliance strengthened.

The immediate signs were not too bad. On 30 July 1941, Sikorski signed a truce with the Soviet ambassador Ivan Maisky, agreeing to the re-establishment of Poland as an independent state – although carefully deferring the question of its borders – and granted an amnesty to all Poles imprisoned in the USSR. But relations between the Free Poles and the Russians soured rapidly.

On 19 July, for the first time Stalin requested the opening of a second front in the form of an attack across the Channel to draw German troops off from the Russian front. He would continue to badger his Allies about this. Their refusal merely fuelled his suspicions that they wanted the Soviet Union and Germany to fight each other to a standstill.

Dollars for Moscow

Harry Hopkins set out again for London on 13 July 1941 to make arrangements for the forthcoming Atlantic Conference between Roosevelt and Churchill, and to review the war, including the new front in Russia.

On 30 June 1941, the USSR had formally requested US aid. As with Britain six months earlier, Hopkins sought to establish whether or not the Soviet Union would survive long enough to receive it – was Stalin worth backing? Finding no answers in London, Hopkins decided to make a quick trip to Moscow to gauge the situation for himself, Roosevelt cabling Stalin: 'I ask you to treat him with the identical confidence you would feel if you were talking directly to me.' He was in Moscow for just two days. It was long enough.

Stalin demanded that the US come into the war immediately, but Hopkins reported: 'I told Stalin that my mission related entirely to matters of supply and that the matter of our joining in the war would be decided largely by Hitler himself and his encroachment on our fundamental interests.'[64]

On one point, Hopkins did manage to reassure the Russian dictator, during a meeting with Molotov, also attended by the US Ambassador, Laurence A. Steinhardt, whose account differs from Hopkins' report to Roosevelt – in one major respect. Hopkins specifically committed the United States to go to the Russians' assistance if they were attacked by Japan. This took Steinhardt's breath away: his own instructions were that no such reassurance should be given.[65]

Stalin asked Hopkins for 20,000 anti-aircraft guns, machine guns, a million rifles, petrol and aluminium for aircraft construction. Another list of requirements presented in Washington, including 6,000 fighters and bombers, totalled almost $2 billion.[66]

Hopkins came to have a great respect for, and confidence in, Stalin, apparently believing that he was the best leader for the USSR. For his part, Stalin's regard for the fragile American is demonstrated by an episode witnessed by Averell Harriman in 1943 during the Teheran Conference with the three Allied leaders:

> Two years later at Teheran, Stalin demonstrated unusual respect for Harry, which I never saw him show to anyone else. When Stalin entered a room, he always waited for others to approach him, but in Teheran, when he saw Harry, Stalin walked halfway across the room to greet him.[67]

Washington was initially sceptical that the Russians could hold out more than a few weeks, but when Hopkins reported back favourably, there was a positive fever to help them. The terms contrast sharply with those imposed on Britain.

Almost immediately after Barbarossa, $9 million worth of non-military supplies were released for the USSR.[68] On 2 August 1941, the USA and USSR signed a 'mutual' aid declaration (although aid only ever went one way). A few days later, Roosevelt personally intervened to speed up the delivery of tools and aircraft.[69] On 18 August 1941, the Russians submitted a second list of requirements, totalling $145 million.[70]

The United States now had a second major customer. Following

Hopkins' fact-finding visit, while waiting for production to rise, the immediate plan was to supply the USSR *at Britain's expense*.[71] When Churchill complained, Roosevelt then gave Russian supplies priority over the US Army – 'throughout the autumn the USA was providing aid to Britain and Russia at the expense of her own armed forces'.[72]

Would the Germans take Moscow before the winter set in? As Roosevelt wanted to see what happened before committing America to Lend-Lease aid, until then the Russians had to pay for the supplies, although Morgenthau extended $100 million credit to tide them over. Roosevelt argued that the Johnson Act didn't apply, as the Russians weren't war debt defaulters – even though they *were*, having inherited debts from the Tsarist and the Provisional governments.[73]

It was only on 7 November 1941 that Roosevelt declared the Soviet Union eligible for Lend-Lease, on the grounds that it was vital to America's own defence. Officially, by the end of the war the US had provided 17 million tons of cargo valued at over $9.5 billion. The 'arsenal of democracy' was now thrown open to a regime that at least matched that of the Nazis.

Although at the beginning of September 1941 Roosevelt had moved Hopkins to more important matters – handing the responsibility for Lend-Lease to Edward R. Stettinius Jr. (later Secretary of State) – he still controlled Russian aid through his chairmanship of the Soviet Protocol Committee, which presided over all aspects of American–Soviet relations during the war.[74]

Hopkins went to breathtaking lengths to please the Russians, even restructuring the State Department, persuading Roosevelt to replace Ambassador Steinhardt, because he failed to inspire Stalin's confidence. When the new Russian Ambassador in Washington, Maxim Litvinov, demanded that the head of the State Department's Soviet desk Loy W. Henderson be removed, Cordell Hull refused. But suddenly Roosevelt himself instructed Hull to move Henderson to another department – clearly thanks to Hopkins,[75] who also had Major Ivan D. Yeaton, the military attaché in Moscow, removed as being anti-Soviet.[76]

Stalin's hold over FDR

Buhite and Levy succinctly explain FDR's war aims: 'The Axis had to be defeated, the British changed, and the Soviets accommodated.'[77] But the lengths Roosevelt happily went to in order to accommodate Stalin were quite astonishing – especially when contrasted with his heavy-handed approach to Britain. He made no attempt to demand anything in return from Stalin.

Harriman explained that Roosevelt was keen to help Stalin out of 'a simple matter of American self-interest' – supporting the Russians meant that if and when the Americans became involved in the war, the Red Army would do the fighting for them on the ground in Europe.[78] However, there were also longer-term considerations. As Buhite and Levy explain: '. . . Roosevelt believed that, because the USSR would play a powerful part in post-war European affairs, Soviet–American relations would be essential to world peace. Nothing should be allowed to interfere with good relations with the Russians.'[79]

Others in the administration also influenced Roosevelt's attitude to the USSR. Beatrice Farnsworth in *William C. Bullitt and the Soviet Union* (1967) says that FDR 'had the feeling . . . that Bolshevik rule, for all its bad features, was an experiment for the improvement of the lot of man'.[80] She attributes this to the influence of Ambassador Joseph E. Davies and Assistant Secretary of State George Messersmith,[81] both of whom told FDR that the Kremlin wanted peace – and that the USSR was *altruistic*. Davies naively believed that Stalin had no desire to impose Communism on the rest of Europe, writing to Roosevelt in January 1939:

> The [Soviet] government is now, at least, devoted to peace. Moreover, for many years its economic necessities will require peace if that is possible.
>
> The leaders of the Soviet government have stated to me that there is only one government in the world that they trust and that is the United States government under your leadership.[82]

Breathtakingly, when in 1941 William Bullitt, a Russian expert and former US Ambassador in Moscow, complained about Stalin's tyranny, the President rebutted:

> Bill, I don't dispute your facts, they are accurate. I don't dispute the logic of your reasoning. I just have a hunch that Stalin is not that kind of man. Harry says he's not . . . and I think that if I can give him everything I possibly can and ask nothing from him in return, *noblesse oblige*, he won't try to annex anything and will work with me for a world of democracy and peace.

When Bullitt called Stalin a 'Caucasian bandit', 'The President showed a trace of irritation: "It's my responsibility and not yours; and I'm going to play my hunch."'[83] Yet Bullitt was the President's expert on the Soviet Union, and Hopkins had met Stalin just once.

Before the President even met Stalin, he told Churchill brutally: 'I think I can personally handle Stalin better than either your foreign office or my State Department. Stalin hates the guts of all your top people. He thinks he likes me better, and I hope he will continue to do so.'[84]

A.J.P. Taylor wrote that Roosevelt was 'ready to accept Soviet Russia as a partner in running the world'.[85] It should be remembered that regardless of the tyrannies of the Soviet regime, Roosevelt – and Hopkins – regarded the Bolsheviks' *principles* as a lesser evil than those of British colonialism and hereditary privilege. Hopkins also sincerely believed that European democracy fell far short of the genuine American article. Yet even while courting the monstrous Stalin, these Americans still stressed that they fought the Nazis and Fascists on *moral* grounds.

The Nazis' inspiration

Roosevelt had claimed that a Nazi-dominated Europe would mean American workers would have to compete with slave labour – both economically undesirable and morally repugnant. In fact, for over a decade, slave labour had been a characteristic of the Soviet regime that he now wanted to cultivate.

The Nazis brought in about a million forced labourers from Poland during 1940, mainly to work on the land. After the fall of France, about another million French prisoners were dispatched to

Germany, although they were paid a little. (By 1944, there were so many 'guest workers' that they accounted for just under a quarter of Germany's workforce – over seven million people.) However, today's image of Nazi slaves, particularly Jews, being forced to work until they dropped in munitions factories and underground rocket complexes comes from a much later stage of the war – and this, as much else, the Nazis modelled on the Soviet system. At the very time Roosevelt condemned Germany's use of slave labour, the conditions under which its Polish prisoners toiled were not nearly as hellish as the gulags. In any case, the numbers of slave labourers in the USSR was vastly greater.

Both regimes were unspeakably and inexcusably evil, but Roosevelt chose to paint a particularly one-sided picture to the American people: deliberately exaggerating Nazi crimes and claiming that Hitler aspired to world domination, while Soviet atrocities – the brutality in Poland, the Katyń Forest massacre and the gulags – and global ambitions were vastly downplayed. But the situation was just as dire in the other countries the USSR swallowed up during Soviet-German détente.

In the Baltic states, the NKVD deported capitalists, army officers, policemen and prison warders, refugees from Poland, members of other political parties – and their families. In Lithuania, the list was extended to 'those frequently travelling abroad, involved in overseas correspondence or coming into contact with representatives of foreign states; Esperantists; philatelists; those working with the Red Cross; refugees; smugglers; those expelled from the Communist Party; priests and active members of religious congregations; the nobility, landowners, wealthy merchants, bankers, industrialists, hotel and restaurant owners'.[86]

The vast majority of those arrested in Poland and the Baltic states were not even granted a show trial, but were subject to 'administrative deportation': the NKVD simply removed them and seized their property. At least 150,000 people – possibly a quarter of a million – were deported from the Baltic states in this way.[87]

The deportations chillingly parallel the later Nazi removal of Jews to the extermination camps – forced-marches to railway stations, overcrowded and insanitary trucks for desperately long journeys to an unknown destination. Descriptions of their nightmare experiences by deportees from the Baltic states are indistinguishable from those of Jews rounded up by the Nazis from the Polish ghettos and elsewhere.

In May 1940, SS chief Heinrich Himmler wrote a secret report to Hitler concerning the handling of the population of Poland, and in particular Polish Jews, in which he stated: 'I hope completely to erase the concept of Jews through the possibility of a great emigration of all Jews to a colony in Africa or elsewhere', going on, '. . . this method is still the mildest and best, if one rejects the Bolshevik method of physical extermination of a people out of inner conviction as un-German and impossible'.[88]

Of course, within two years the 'physical extermination' of the Jews of Europe would be an integral part of the Nazi agenda, the responsibility of Himmler's own SS. His memo suggests that the Nazis had copied the principles and methods of Stalin's regime.

During the German advance into Soviet-occupied Poland and the Ukraine in the first weeks of Barbarossa, as there was no time to evacuate the prison camps, the NKVD and Red Army executed the inmates (although occasionally freeing the non-political prisoners). Some 10,000 were killed in Poland.

During the fighting, under Beria's orders – approved by Stalin – all Russian prisoners of war were to be shot as deserters if they were returned or recaptured: *no* Russian should have any contact with the West without NKVD supervision under *any* circumstances. The US government knew about this, but chose simply to ignore it.[89] Roosevelt also knew about the gulags, and the deportations in Poland and the Baltic states – they were too massive to be hidden. And now that Stalin was desperate for American help, FDR had the perfect lever to force him to reverse human-rights abuses – but he consistently refused to use it.[90] Bullitt urged a quid pro quo with Stalin in return for aid – for example, the return of territory seized in 1939 and a pledge that they would refrain from capturing any more territory. However, 'Roosevelt declined to attach strings to American aid to the Soviet Union.'[91] Clearly, he was prepared to use Lend-Lease as with Britain, as leverage for America's economic advantage, but not for humanity's sake.

Hell

There is another possibility. Given Soviet influence within the administration, was the President's eagerness to help Stalin out – expecting nothing in return – the result of advice from the Kremlin itself? Where exactly did Harry Hopkins' loyalties lie? It was largely his responsibility that the US government threw its support behind the Soviet Union and extended Lend-Lease aid. And, of course, Hopkins intervened to remove government officials and diplomats more or less on the instructions of the Soviet government. As Roosevelt's words to Bullitt demonstrate, his view of Stalin was largely due to his intimate friend and guide, 'Harry the Hop'. Hopkins also ensured he achieved a position that gave him complete control of Soviet–American relations.

As we have seen, over the last 20 years evidence has surfaced that Hopkins was an active agent of the Soviet Union. If true, the President had put himself in the hands of a Soviet agent who totally controlled American supplies to the USSR. The implications are so far-reaching – for twentieth- and, indeed, twenty-first-century history and also, of course, for the reputation of America itself – that most historians choose to ignore this issue entirely. But as we will see, Hopkins' extraordinary career was about to enter an even more influential phase.

CHAPTER EIGHT

Behind the Infamy

'Greater good fortune has rarely happened to the
British Empire than this event . . .'
               Winston S. Churchill on Pearl Harbor[1]

After returning to London from meeting with Stalin, Harry Hopkins
sailed with Churchill across the Atlantic to the Prime Minister's first
momentous top-secret wartime summit ('Riviera') with President
Roosevelt. The setting was carefully chosen: as the US was still
technically neutral, it would not have been proper for the leaders to
meet on either American or British soil, so the two leaders' ships
rendezvoused off Placentia Bay in Newfoundland, where an
American seaplane base was being built under the destroyers deal.
Roosevelt was making a point.[2]

During the four days of the conference (9–12 August), despite the
smiles, the two leaders and their teams battled for their respective
agendas. Although it was the defining moment in Churchill's and
Roosevelt's wartime relationship, each striving to impose his will on the
other face to face, with so few cards to play Churchill could only lose.

The Prime Minister wanted the Americans to join Britain's war,
while surrendering precious little in return. Rightly, Roosevelt was
deeply suspicious that Churchill wanted to exploit American aid not

just to win the war but to maintain – or even increase – the British Empire's strength in the post-war world, reversing the decline of the 1930s. But the President was also seeking to use Britain's neediness to break the Empire's hold on world trade, putting pressure on Churchill over keeping the British Empire a closed shop. He remarked, 'You see, it is along in here somewhere that there is likely to be some disagreement between you, Winston, and me.'[3] Elliott Roosevelt recorded a tired and emotional Churchill's extraordinary after-dinner outburst:

> 'Mr President,' he cried, 'I believe you are trying to do away with the British Empire. Every idea you entertain about the structure of the post-war world demonstrates it. But in spite of that' – and his forefinger waved – 'in spite of that, we know that you constitute our only hope. And' – his voice sank dramatically – '*you* know that we know it. *You* know that *we* know that without America, the Empire won't stand.'[4]

After another long after-dinner session, FDR told Elliott: 'Winnie has one supreme mission in life, but only one. He's a perfect wartime prime minister. His one big job is to see that Britain survives this war.'[5] Churchill refused even to discuss post-war matters, but Roosevelt had no such reluctance.

The President told his son, 'I think I speak as America's President when I say that America won't help England in this war simply so that she will be able to continue to ride roughshod over colonial peoples.'[6] When Churchill asked that Roosevelt declare war on Germany, the President instead proposed a statement of their joint war aims, which, in David Dimbleby's and David Reynolds' words, 'while they confirmed America's determination to see Hitler defeated, exacted a price from Britain in the form of pledges that could imperil the continuance of her empire after the war'.[7]

The result was the Atlantic Charter, setting out their nations' intentions in eight points, the first three being:

> First, their countries seek no aggrandisement, territorial or other;

Second, they desire to see no territorial changes that do not accord with the freely expressed wishes of the people concerned;

Third, they respect the right of all peoples to choose the form of government under which they will live, and they wish to see sovereign rights and self-government restored to those who have been forcibly deprived of them.[8]

The fourth point was hotly debated. The Americans wanted to state that all nations should have equal access to 'markets and raw materials' – diametrically opposed to the Ottawa Agreement's imperial preference system. Churchill insisted that 'markets' was replaced by 'trade'. Despite Sumner Welles' pleas, Roosevelt did concede this (for the time being).[9]

When it was pointed out to Churchill in London that he had virtually signed away the Empire, he airily declared that the Charter referred only to nations liberated from the Nazis,[10] but that wasn't how Roosevelt saw it. Although Churchill claimed ad nauseam that the Charter applied only to Europe, FDR insisted it was global. As late as February 1945, when reporters asked how Churchill's statement about not presiding over the 'liquidation' of the Empire fitted with the Charter's principles, Roosevelt replied that 'dear old Winston will never learn on that point'.[11]

The summit was important for other reasons. Roosevelt and Churchill sent a joint message to Stalin promising material support – an unambiguous signal to Hitler. The Prime Minister also pressed FDR to warn Japan against any further expansion: he should promise – and make known to Tokyo that he had promised – that if Japan attacked the Netherlands East Indies or British Malaya he would ask Congress to declare war. Churchill believed that this would restrain Japan, besides reassuring him that Roosevelt wouldn't abandon Britain in the Pacific. The President refused (although a month before, Hopkins had assured Stalin of American aid in the case of a Japanese attack). In 'practically meaningless'[12] terms, FDR did tell the Japanese Ambassador that any further expansion would mean that 'various steps would have to be taken by the United States notwithstanding the President's realization that the taking of such further measures might result in war between the United States and Japan'.[13]

On the last day of the conference, 12 August 1941, news was received that Congress had extended the draft for another year by just one vote in the House of Representatives: there was no chance that Congress would agree to a declaration of war.[14]

When asked if the Atlantic Conference had moved the United States nearer to conflict, Roosevelt replied he 'would say no'. He also assured Congress that he had made Churchill no new commitments, adding that the major danger was war with Japan.[15]

In September 1941, Ambassador Maisky announced that the Soviet Union agreed to the principles of the Atlantic Charter, despite Stalin's record making it a travesty.

Roosevelt provokes Hitler

Churchill told his Cabinet, 'The President said he wanted a war with Germany, but that he would not declare it. He would instead become more and more provocative. Mr Roosevelt said he would look for an incident which would justify him in opening hostilities.'[16] Via Ultra, the Prime Minister knew Hitler was anxious to avoid any provocative naval incident, so the President duly authorised US Navy ships to escort British convoys as far as Iceland.[17]

On 4 September, USS *Greer* was delivering mail to Iceland when it spotted and pursued a U-boat, reporting its position to the RAF. The U-boat fired on the *Greer*, but missed, as did the US warship's depth-charges. Both ships went on their way unharmed. A week later, the incident surfaced in Roosevelt's broadcast – although as Buhite and Levy comment, 'Deceiving by omission – he omitted the part about the *Greer*'s having initiated action against the submarine – Roosevelt went on to tell his audience that the ship had been attacked by a submarine.'[18] Roosevelt declared it was a 'blunt fact that the German submarine fired first upon this American destroyer without warning, and with deliberate design to sink her'.[19] The US Navy was now to 'shoot on sight' any German or Italian ships and submarines that entered the neutral zone.

On the night of 16–17 October 1941, while going to the aid of a British/Canadian convoy being savaged by a pack of U-boats, the destroyer USS *Kearny* was torpedoed, its 11 dead the first casualties of America's undeclared war. In his Navy Day broadcast, Roosevelt declared 'the shooting has started, and history has recorded who fired the first shot . . . America has been attacked'.[20] Sensationally, he added: 'I have in my possession a secret map, made in Germany by Hitler's Government, by planners of the new world order. It is a map of South America and part of Central America as Hitler proposes to organize it.'[21] Here was serious talk of Hitler at America's back door . . .

The President's version of the *Kearny* episode and the 'secret map' had the desired effect on both public and Congress, which was about to vote on his request to repeal parts of the Neutrality Act that banned the arming of US merchant ships and the entry of US vessels into combat zones. Now Congress readily agreed, virtually spelling the end of the Neutrality Act.

Yet this historic shift was largely due to British skulduggery. The 'secret map' allegedly showing Hitler's designs on America was the brainchild of SOE agent John 'Ivar' Bryce, from BSC's Latin American Affairs section. After approval by William Stephenson, it was created by SOE's forged document unit in Toronto.[22]

Many commentators believe that the President hoped to whip up support *and* goad Hitler into declaring war on America – but it drove the Führer even further away. Four days after FDR's speech, the USS *Reuben Jones* was torpedoed while escorting a convoy, leaving 115 dead. Desperate to avoid war with America, on 13 November Hitler ordered: 'Engagements with American naval or air forces are not to be sought deliberately; they are to be avoided as far as possible . . . If it is observed before a convoy is attacked that it is being escorted by American forces, the attack is not to be carried out.'[23]

Roosevelt may have told Churchill and his own administration that he intended to use these incidents to drag America into the war, but he made no attempt to exploit them to soften up Congress for a declaration of war. He merely furthered his own immediate objectives, such as undermining the Neutrality Act. And, as we will see, when eventually Pearl Harbor handed him the perfect opportunity of declaring war on Germany, he refused to take it.

As Eric Larrabee points out in *Commander in Chief* (1987), although General Marshall and Admiral Stark believed that the United States should mobilise their ground troops if Germany was to be defeated, 'Roosevelt did not approve their plans; he merely did not disapprove them'.[24] He was still hoping that any American involvement could be limited to the air and sea. However, a little more than a month after the sinking of the *Reuben Jones*, America was at war – but not with Germany . . .

Pearl Harbor

'Yesterday, December 7, 1941 – a date that will live in infamy – the United States of America was suddenly and deliberately attacked by naval and air forces of the Empire of Japan.' Thus began President Roosevelt's historic address to Congress the day after the conflagration at Pearl Harbor. Just 33 minutes later, America declared war on Japan.

Shortly before 8 a.m., most of the US Pacific Fleet – some 70 ships – was attacked without warning as it lay at anchor off the Hawaiian island of Oahu. For nearly two hours, the island was pounded by 350 aircraft in two thunderous waves, while 16 submarines and midget submarines attacked from the sea. Eighteen ships had been sunk or seriously damaged, and 200 aircraft destroyed, while 2,403 Americans lay dead, with 1,178 wounded.

The enemy fleet – six aircraft carriers with destroyer escorts and support ships – had left Japan over the week beginning 10 November 1941, assembling off the Kurile Islands, north-east of Japan. On 26 November, it set course for Hawaii, while the submarine force gathered in the central Pacific. It was only when it reached 275 miles north of Hawaii that it launched its blitz. Somehow, it had managed to cross nearly 3,500 miles of ocean without being detected.

The Japanese objective was to eliminate the US from the Pacific for a year, giving themselves time to consolidate their position. But despite the horror, the raid failed, partly because the Americans' aircraft carriers and heavy cruisers were away, and partly because the Japanese commander, Vice-Admiral Nagumo Chuichi, expecting an imminent counter-attack, decided not to send the planned third wave. But even so, coming out of the blue, it was uniquely traumatic to the American psyche. How could such a cataclysm befall the invincible United States?

Friendly Fire

To avoid involving Congress, Roosevelt appointed a five-man board of inquiry under Supreme Court Judge Owen J. Roberts, which charged commander-in-chief of the Pacific Fleet, Admiral Husband E. Kimmel and Hawaii's army commander, Lieutenant-General Walter Short, with dereliction of duty. The Chiefs of Staff, General Marshall and Admiral Stark, were cleared.

Even during the conflict, rumours circulated that Roosevelt knew about the Japanese plan in advance but said nothing because he *wanted* it to happen to achieve his long-held objective of bringing America into the war. In the immediate aftermath of the war, the most prominent historian to make the accusation of FDR's foreknowledge was Charles A. Beard in *President Roosevelt and the Coming of the War* (1948). An ever-increasing library has added to both sides of the controversy, including Robert B. Stinnett's *Day of Deceit* (2000), which Gore Vidal declares:

> shows us that the famous 'surprise' attack was no surprise to our war-minded rulers, and that three thousand American military men killed and wounded one Sunday morning in Hawaii were, to our rulers and their present avatars, a small price to pay for that 'global empire' over which we now preside so ineptly.

A new twist on the 'LIHOP' ('let it happen on purpose') theory emerged in the early 1980s: that it was the *British* who knew the Japanese were gunning for Pearl Harbor, but Churchill avoided warning Roosevelt. The theory received widespread publicity in 1991 in *Betrayal at Pearl Harbor* by James Rusbridger and Eric Nave. A former MI6 officer and controversial intelligence writer, Rusbridger, on researching still-classified British wartime secrets, began to wonder about the secrecy surrounding Ultra material relating to breaking the *Japanese* codes – unlike the German Enigma codes, which are now famous as one of Britain's great triumphs.

Rusbridger's research led him to the Australian Eric Nave OBE, one of the unsung heroes of the Second World War. A brilliant code-breaker – and fluent Japanese-speaker – for the Royal Australian Navy, Nave was seconded to the British Government Code and

Cipher School (GCCS) – the forerunner of Bletchley Park and GCHQ – in 1928. Just before the war, he was assigned to Britain's Far East code-breaking agency, the Far East Combined Bureau (FECB), first in Hong Kong and then in Singapore. He then became the Director of the Australian Security Intelligence Organisation (SIO), where he remained until the mid-1950s. He died in 1993.

The 'LIHOP' theory was long dismissed as the work of diehard isolationists, anti-Roosevelt mischief-makers or patriots in denial that the USA could make such catastrophic mistakes. However, these days it is at least discussed seriously, because certain awkward questions *do* remain – and Roosevelt's penchant for duplicity is at last openly acknowledged. Most significantly, the *motive* imputed to FDR by conspiracy theorists to explain why he would have withheld warnings about the attack is today acknowledged as accurate: he needed Japan to strike the first blow – a clear and unequivocal Japanese provocation that could be contrasted with America's obvious innocence. Indeed, the evidence overwhelmingly shows that Roosevelt set out to *provoke* Japan, essentially the same game he played with Germany in the Atlantic.

A great irony

After China, the Japanese could turn north into Soviet Siberia or south towards the rich European colonies and American possessions in South-East Asia and the South Pacific. China's neighbour to the south was Vichy France's Indo-China, and beyond that neutral Thailand and the British colony of Malaya, with prosperous Singapore on its southernmost tip. They would also provide a gateway to Burma – and India. Stretching across the south of the Pacific Ocean were the rich islands of the Netherlands East Indies – Sumatra, Java, Borneo and New Guinea. Between the Netherlands East Indies and Japan were the Philippines, which the United States had, rather to its embarrassment, owned since the Spanish–American war. At the beginning of 1941, no one knew which way the Japanese would turn.

Ironically, it was Barbarossa that impelled them *not* to take on the Soviet Union. Since the Nazi–Soviet Pact, the Japanese had followed Hitler's lead, softening towards the USSR and signing their own neutrality agreement just two months before Barbarossa. Now Hitler had switched again – without telling Tokyo. Foreign Minister Matsuoka, architect of the neutrality pact, was sacked.

Hitler pressed Japan to join him against the USSR, but Prince Konoe's humiliated government declined. To him, Barbarossa nullified the Tripartite Pact, so he decided to honour Japan's neutrality pact with the USSR, shifting Japan's focus from confrontation with Russia on the Manchuria–Siberia border to the south – and the European possessions. The result was one of the Second World War's great ironies.

Stalin learned of the Japanese decision from GRU master spy Richard Sorge, a German citizen who had joined the Nazi Party in Japan. Until his arrest in October 1941, his intelligence on Japanese-German relations was very valuable: in September, he informed Moscow that the Japanese had decided not to strike against Russia and were turning south. As a result, Stalin dispatched soldiers from the Siberia–Manchuria border to Moscow. It was those troops who saved Moscow in December 1941.[25]

And now Japan . . .

Although Roosevelt morally supported China in its conflict with Japan, he had carefully avoided employing the Neutrality Act embargo when it first flared up in 1937 – but continued to use the *threat* of sanctions to keep Japan in line.

In 1940, 50 per cent of Japan's imports were from, and 40 per cent of its exports to, the United States,[26] so it was worried when, in December, Roosevelt embargoed the export of war materials and scrap iron. Matters intensified in July 1941, after Japan's post-Barbarossa decision to move southwards against European colonies, specifically the oilfields of the Netherlands East Indies – with no oil of its own, and stocks for only two more years, Japan badly needed an alternative source in case America cut off its supply.

When, on 24 July, the Vichy government conceded that the Japanese could occupy strategic bases in Indo-China, Roosevelt demanded that they withdraw, warning that 'an exceedingly serious situation' would result if they attempted to seize the Dutch oilfields. Receiving no response, two days later the President froze Japanese assets in the USA and introduced trade embargoes – traumatic blows to their economy.[27]

Paradoxically, as Patrick Maney observes, 'The embargo on oil served not as a deterrent but a provocation.'[28] Tellingly, six months earlier, the ABC-1 agreement – officially approved by Roosevelt – had urged that a *deterrent* strategy be adopted towards Japan. And yet, as Guy Wint and John Pritchard write: 'Roosevelt steered it [the US] resolutely on a course of economic strangulation so intense and so aggressive that it must result in war or the abject surrender of Japan to America's implacable demands.'[29]

It was the two nations' failure to find a compromise that led to the attack on Pearl Harbor. The negotiations failed because of the Americans' intransigence and provocation – disallowing compromise of any kind: the Japanese government could either roll over or fight. Realistically, there was only ever one possible outcome.

What the Japanese did not know was that the Americans had broken their diplomatic ciphers and were reading messages between Tokyo and the Embassy in Washington. Access to this intelligence source – 'Magic' – was limited to just 15 people, including Roosevelt, Hopkins, Hull, Stimson and Marshall. But even though the Americans discovered that Japan was mobilising for war if the negotiations failed, Roosevelt still tightened the screw.[30] In September 1941, the Japanese military gave its government until mid-October to improve American relations, otherwise it would take action.[31]

The Prime Minister, Prince Konoe, was willing to negotiate – even to consider withdrawing from China and French Indo-China. At the end of September 1941, he proposed that he and Roosevelt meet, offering a non-aggression pact with the US and to repudiate the Tripartite Pact. When Roosevelt turned him down, Konoe and his government resigned.

US Ambassador Joseph C. Grew had specifically warned that if Konoe's government fell, the power of the Japanese military would increase radically, making a surprise attack a distinct possibility.[32] Indeed, former War Minister General Tojo Hideki's new hardline government would never countenance abandoning the Tripartite Alliance.[33] The President knew exactly where his intransigence would lead. To Tojo's government, war was now the only real option, although it allowed the talks to continue until the eleventh hour, even putting the deadline back twice in case of a breakthrough.

On 26 November – after consulting Britain, the Netherlands, China, Australia and New Zealand – Cordell Hull proposed that in return for unfreezing its assets and re-establishing trade, Japan should withdraw from China and Indo-China, recognise Chiang Kai-shek's government and undertake not to honour the Tripartite Pact if America went to war with Germany and Italy. These conditions were unacceptable, as Hull knew they would be.[34] The Japanese task force set sail for Pearl Harbor that same day.

As the deadline approached, special envoy Kurusu Saburo was particularly frustrated by Roosevelt's refusal to engage personally in the talks, having to make do with Cordell Hull and the State Department. Finally, on 2 December, Kurusu appealed to Bernard Baruch to broker a direct meeting with the President, warning that although the Japanese people and the Emperor did not want war, the State Department's intransigence was playing into the hands of an influential military cabal that did. He added that war could be averted if the President personally proposed to Emperor Hirohito urgent talks with Chiang Kai-shek over China, halting Japanese advances in the meantime. As the Emperor would agree, Tojo's government would have to fall into line. Kurusu also suggested that Harry Hopkins should visit Japan as an envoy.[35]

Baruch was unable to arrange the meeting, but later pointed out that Roosevelt did personally appeal to the Emperor on 6 December 1941 (telling a friend ' . . . this son of man had just sent his final message to the Son of God'[36]). However, FDR ignored Kurusu's proposals, simply affirming the Americans' desire for peace and asking the Emperor to, 'Give thought in this definite emergency to a way of dispelling the dark clouds.'[37] As with the Polish crisis, he did *something*, but not enough to prevent war. As Guy Wint and John Pritchard write:

> Above all, it must be stressed that the inevitable consequence of the economic pressures imposed by the United States upon Japan, and of America's failure to pursue its diplomatic negotiations with appropriate vigour, flexibility and

imagination, was that Japan finally had no alternative to the Pacific War other than submission to abject surrender.[38]

In September 1943, Sir Robert Craigie, former British Ambassador in Tokyo, reported that Pearl Harbor was the result of American failings in the negotiations. Churchill responded that his report 'should be most scrupulously kept secret', but added:

> It was however a blessing that Japan attacked the United States and thus brought America whole-heartedly and unitedly into the war. Greater good fortune has rarely happened to the British Empire than this event which had revealed our friends and foes in their true light, and may lead, through the merciless crushing of Japan, to a new relationship of immense benefit to the English-speaking countries and to the world.[39]

There is no doubt that Roosevelt and his administration deliberately set out to provoke Japan into war. An Office of Naval Intelligence (ONI) 'Estimate of the Situation in the Pacific' of 7 October 1940, by the head of ONI's Far Eastern desk and expert on Japan, Lieutenant Commander Arthur H. McCollum, clinches the matter. It identifies the growing Japanese threat to American – and British – interests, while acknowledging that US politics made it difficult for it to declare war. It ends with several recommendations, including deploying extra ships in the Pacific, stepping up aid to China and embargoing all trade with Japan, concluding:

> If by these means Japan could be led to commit an overt act of war, so much the better. At all events we must be fully prepared to meet the threat of war.[40]

The report was sent to ONI Director Captain Walter S. Anderson (with direct access to the President) and naval strategist Captain Dudley W. Knox, who endorsed the recommendations. Although there is no hard evidence that FDR actually saw McCollum's report, Robert Stinnett notes that every one of its eight proposals was implemented on Presidential orders over the following months. In any case, the report shows that the idea of provoking Japan into war was circulating in Washington over a year before Pearl Harbor, and many months before Roosevelt began piling on the pressure. As Stinnett concludes: 'Throughout 1941, it seems, provoking Japan into an overt act of war was the principal policy that guided FDR's actions toward Japan.'[41]

Many people believe Roosevelt was right to force the Japanese into showing their true colours, but the unpalatable fact is that he mendaciously presented Pearl Harbor as an out-of-the-blue atrocity upon a peaceable and unsuspecting US.

The first shot

Stimson recorded the day before the final ultimatum that at a meeting at which he, Hull, Marshall, Knox and Stark were present, Roosevelt remarked, 'The question was how we should maneuver them [the Japanese] into the position of firing the first shot without allowing too much danger to ourselves.'[42] Two days later, US bases in the Pacific (including Pearl Harbor) were warned that due to the breakdown of the talks, hostilities could break out at any moment. However, the next day Admiral Stark revised the wording, including the injunction (repeated twice during the message):

> If hostilities cannot repeat cannot be avoided the United States desires that Japan commit the first overt act.[43]

When the Roberts Inquiry questioned Major-General Leonard T. Gerow, Chief of the War Plans Division, about this, he testified that 'the President had definitely stated that he wanted Japan to commit the first overt act'.[44] But while the principle of letting Japan fire the first shot – firmly establishing the aggressor – is not particularly controversial, when placed in the context of Roosevelt's policy of provocation it becomes decidedly questionable.

On the evening of 6 December, the Japanese government instructed its negotiators in Washington to inform the Americans by 1 p.m. the next day – the time of the attack in Hawaii – that the talks were over. As usual, the message was intercepted by the US Navy who, ironically, deciphered it five hours before the Japanese Embassy.[45] The 'Magic' intercepts were taken to the White House where the officer who delivered them heard Hopkins observe that since war was now inevitable, it was a pity that America couldn't strike the first blow. Image-conscious FDR replied, 'No, we can't do that. We are a democracy and a peaceful people.'[46]

After reading the message, Roosevelt and Hopkins, 'For some reason . . . failed to notify General Marshall, even though he was in his quarters.'[47] (Marshall was told a full 15 hours later.[48]) Roosevelt made no attempt to contact his Chiefs of Staff, all the more remarkable because a sudden Japanese attack had long been anticipated.[49] But as it was supremely important to maintain the fiction of an unexpected assault on US territory, it was important to *react* to the news, not pre-empt it. Everything should look normal in Washington that night.

Where will Japan strike?

Clearly, Roosevelt had a *motive* for withholding information that would otherwise have saved Pearl Harbor, but did he fully grasp that this provocation would end in disaster for the Americans? Or did he think Japan would strike somewhere else?

In fact, few realise today that the first surprise attack by Japan that propelled the Pacific into the conflagration was not at Pearl Harbor, or even at an American target – but on the British Empire. Some two hours before the Hawaii attack, at 1.15 a.m. local time, Japanese warships bombarded the town of Kota Bharu in northern Malaya, before landing ground troops. This was supposed to coincide precisely with the Pearl Harbor strike – to preserve the surprise value of both raids – but the commander of the Malayan task force mistakenly started his operation first.[50]

Even at the time, the fact that the first Japanese attack had been on British Empire territory was played down – in his 'day of infamy' address, Roosevelt acknowledged that, 'Yesterday the Japanese Government also launched an attack against Malaya', but it was almost an afterthought. Yet this happened *first*. Even in contemporary histories, the fact is rarely mentioned, as if only Pearl Harbor is important. (Obscuring the significance is helped by the fact that Kota

Bharu is the other side of the International Date Line, and so officially happened on 8 December.)

In fact, the 'surprise attack' on Pearl Harbor was not surprising *because* it happened, but because of *where* it happened.

Both American and British governments knew full well that Japan was gearing up for war but they carefully kept it from their people to maximise the shock value when it happened. But *everybody*, like Roosevelt himself, 'assumed that Japan would not attack the United States directly but would move against the British and the Dutch'.[51] An attack on America's own interests was not even considered. Indeed, Eric Larrabee argues that Roosevelt thought the fleet at Pearl Harbor would act as a deterrent. The Japanese were expected to reason that if they struck at British or Dutch interests without touching American possessions, Congress would not authorise war. However, the Japanese leaders decided not to take the risk, and to disable the US Pacific Fleet in a pre-emptive strike. Larrabee writes that: 'The President not so much miscalculated as undercalculated, falling short in imagination of that later stage in which the deterrent became the target.'[52]

Unlike the task force heading towards Pearl Harbor, there is no dispute the British and Americans had been tracking the Japanese invasion fleet heading towards Kota Bharu for weeks. When this armada of some 20 destroyers and 25 troop carriers, with escort vessels, left Japan and headed south, Americans and British tracked it with aerial reconnaissance and intercepted radio signals. But where precisely was it heading? Malaya, the Netherlands East Indies or the Philippines? On 26 November – the day of the final ultimatum to the Japanese – the Americans warned the British of an imminent Japanese attack, probably in South-East Asia or the Philippines.[53] Sumner Welles told reporters: 'War is expected, but war aimed only obliquely at us in Southeastern Asia, in Siam, or Malaya, and not directed toward the heart of our power in the Pacific.'[54] John T. Flynn concluded in *The Truth about Pearl Harbor* (1944), the first of the Pearl Harbor 'conspiracy' books:

> . . . the wise men in Washington felt that Japan was going to
> attack somewhere, that she was probably going to attack

Thailand from Indo-China and possibly the Netherlands Indies. They felt there was an outside chance that she might attack Malay. The State Department thought she might attack Malay, Thailand or even the Philippines. But that there would be an attack of any kind on Hawaii did not enter their heads.[55]

General Marshall's reaction to the news of Pearl Harbor was particularly illuminating: it must be a mistake, as surely the Japanese would attack Singapore first![56] Certainly, Roosevelt and his advisers believed their provocation would make the Japanese attack *British* interests. But if they did, where would that leave the United States?

George McJimsey argues that Roosevelt was prepared to go to war alongside Britain if Japan attacked its territory, and that he started to prepare America for this possibility.[57] But if so, FDR was taking a breathtaking risk – Congress might well refuse to approve war in such circumstances. Britain would be left to fight two wars on opposite sides of the world. As Wint and Pritchard point out: 'The American Administration, handcuffed by the Neutrality Act, might have been helpless while its Allies in South-East Asia went down before Japanese attack.'[58]

Roosevelt's manoeuvring also ran completely counter to the British government's own wishes. As events moved inexorably towards Japanese aggression, possibly against British possessions, the British Chiefs of Staff almost panicked. Without American assistance, there was no chance of being able to contain, let alone repel, the Japanese. A terse War Office memorandum on 30 November 1941 set out British policy:

> The effect of war with Japan on our main war effort might be so severe as to prejudice our chances of beating Germany. Our policy must therefore be – and is – avoidance of war with Japan.[59]

Clearly, Roosevelt had other ideas. The poker-playing President may have been taking a huge gamble – but not with American stakes. If Japan had struck against Malaya and Congress did *not* declare war, presumably Roosevelt would have found a way to assist Britain against Japan by some means 'short of war' – perhaps by involving the US Navy in a blockade of Japan.[60] But had he failed, Britain would have had to fight in two widely separated theatres – possibly losing in both – or pull out of the Far East entirely, a not-unwelcome scenario to the US. Alternatively, if Congress did authorise war with Japan, the USA and Britain would act together to neutralise the Japanese threat to American trading ambitions in the Far East.

On the very morning of 7 December, the British Chiefs of Staff told Churchill they were prepared to 'fire the first shot' if the Japanese advanced, *provided* they could be certain of 'US armed support'.[61] The Prime Minister was worried that Britain might be left in the lurch – although he considered war with Japan was to be positively welcomed *if* America became involved. But could Churchill rely on the Americans? Without them, Britain would be finished on two fronts, but with them there would probably be total victory. No wonder he was so nervous. On 6 December, Averell Harriman reported to Hopkins:

> The President should be informed of Churchill's belief that in the event of aggression by the Japanese it would be the policy of the British to postpone taking any action – even though this delay might involve some military sacrifice – until the President has taken such action as, under the circumstances, he considers best. Then Churchill will act 'not within the hour but within the minute'.[62]

Clearly, the British leader was now applying pressure of his own, saying that Britain might not fight Japan alone – which seems to have worked. After receiving Harriman's cable, Roosevelt informed Lord Halifax that on 10 December he intended to announce he would regard a Japanese attack on British or Dutch possessions – or even neutral Thailand – as a hostile act against the United States.[63]

On the morning of 7 December, Churchill cabled his commander-in-chief in the Middle East: 'This is an immense relief as I had long dreaded being at war with Japan without or before the United States. Now I think it is all right.'[64] By the end of that day, Pearl Harbor made it very 'all right' for Britain.

Was there a conspiracy?

We can see that both Roosevelt and Churchill had motives for withholding information on Pearl Harbor.

In FDR's case, if, after the final ultimatum, he had received intelligence about the task force heading towards Hawaii, his miscalculation would have been revealed. But he could not afford the Japanese raid losing the element of surprise and being aborted without firing that all-important 'first shot'. A warning to put the base on high alert might be intercepted or the increased activity noted by Japanese agents on Oahu.

(The general order from Washington to all bases on 28 November specifically demanded that security should only be heightened if it could be done without attracting the attention of the civilian population or the Japanese, to maintain the illusion of a surprise attack.[65] As this sort of obfuscation was impossible at Pearl Harbor, Admiral Kimmel and General Short could not act on that order.)

But even the calculating Roosevelt would hardly sacrifice so many ships and men in order to persuade Congress to approve war with Japan. Even the most radical isolationist could hardly deny that the mere presence of a Japanese strike force so close to Hawaii was anything other than an act of war. However, Roosevelt would almost certainly have assumed that Pearl Harbor would detect the approaching aircraft well before they were a 'clear and present danger'. Indeed, the first wave showed up on radar on Oahu when still 130 miles away, but the inexperienced operators – radar was still very new – refused to believe it. Such human error is hard to work into any conspiracy theory. Had the radar operators sounded the alert, the attack may have been repelled – and Roosevelt would still have had his 'first shot'.

Had Churchill known that the Japanese were heading for Pearl Harbor – and not the expected British or Dutch target – he too would have a motive for not warning the Americans: an attack on US territory would finally 'bring the Americans in'. So *he* wouldn't have wanted the Japanese to abort the raid, either.

However, while both leaders had reasons to withhold the information, is there any evidence that they actually did so? Unquestionably, information relating to Pearl Harbor has been deliberately suppressed. Some American and British documents remain classified on the grounds of national security to this day, but this could simply be because they would reveal straightforward incompetence – perhaps a failure to analyse intelligence that would have saved Pearl Harbor.

The argument for the LIHOP theory revolves around whether the Japanese Navy code had been broken. Although Roosevelt read the *diplomatic* decodes, they would only describe military plans in the broadest terms. More important are the Japanese Navy codes – *Kaigun Ango*, '5-Num' to American cryptanalysts and 'JN-25' to the British. Although they were broken, and contributed to Allied victories in the Pacific, officially this was not until the spring of 1942 – after Pearl Harbor.

Both Stinnett and Rusbridger/Nave present evidence that JN-25 *was* broken on both sides of the Atlantic long before Pearl Harbor (autumn 1939 in Britain and October 1940 in America) and that signals were intercepted by both intelligence services that, if decoded and collated, would have revealed the Pearl Harbor plan several days in advance. In fact, both contentions are now acknowledged by military and intelligence historians – the British government's official history *British Intelligence in the Second World War* (1979) states that the Japanese naval codes had been cracked before 1941[66] – but they maintain that the cover-up was to hide the fact that this information was *not* put together in time: an embarrassing intelligence failure. Advocates of the LIHOP theory are unable to *prove* that these signals were decoded in time, or that they found their way to the President or Prime Minister.

There is other, circumstantial, evidence. On 2 December 1941, the Dutch military attaché in Washington wrote of his visit to ONI headquarters: 'Meeting in Navy Department, the location of 2 Japanese carriers leaving Japan with eastern course [i.e. towards Hawaii] are pointed out to me on map.'[67] Several senior figures in the Dutch military in the Far East stated that their code-breakers had intercepted and decoded Japanese signals indicating a possible attack on Hawaii, and that warnings were passed to Washington and London.[68]

Another warning came from the American passenger liner *Lurline* en route from California to Hawaii, which picked up transmissions indicating the presence of Japanese ships in the north Pacific and duly reported this to naval intelligence in Honolulu on 3 December. In the 1970s, the *Lurline*'s logbook was removed from archives by the US Navy.[69]

Robert Ogg, in 1941 an ONI officer based in San Francisco, stated in the 1980s that in the first days of December 1941 he had the task of plotting the course of Japanese warships based on their position as given by radio direction finding. The ships were heading eastwards, towards the United States, but on 3 or 4 December they turned south – towards Hawaii – after which no more bearings were received. According to Ogg, this information was transmitted to Washington by his superior officer.[70] His claims were dismissed by most historians as being merely anecdotal – until Robert Stinnett tracked down the records of the signals that Ogg said had been received . . .[71]

Then there is the testimony of leading figures in British intelligence. In 1975, the writer Constantine FitzGibbon described how Victor Cavendish-Bentinck, wartime Chairman of the Joint Intelligence Committee (JIC), told him two days before Pearl Harbor:

> Mr Cavendish-Bentinck has informed this writer privately that the British at least knew when the Japanese fleet changed course [towards Hawaii]. His statement is so important that I quote him directly. Referring to a Joint Intelligence Sub-Committee meeting held on the Friday before Pearl Harbor [5 December], he writes: 'We knew that they had changed course. I remember presiding over a JIC meeting and being told that a Japanese fleet was sailing in the direction of Hawaii, asking "Have we informed our transatlantic brethren?" and receiving an affirmative reply.'[72]

The MP Sir Julian Ridsdale – in 1941 a Captain liaising between military intelligence's Far Eastern section, MI6 and the JIC – told historian Robert Aldrich not only that he recalled a JIC meeting at which it was agreed to warn Washington that the Japanese fleet might be heading towards Pearl Harbor, but also that several years after the war he had discussed this episode with Cavendish-Bentinck, who confirmed that the warning *had* been sent.[73] This was also corroborated by William Casey, then a US intelligence officer in Europe, later Director of the CIA, in *The Secret War Against Hitler* (1989). He acknowledges that Donovan in Washington received such a warning, writing: 'The British had sent word that a Japanese fleet was steaming east towards Hawaii.'[74]

But despite the weight of evidence, the case for conspiracy is still not watertight. In fact, defenders of the official version agree that while there were many clues that Pearl Harbor was about to happen, they were ignored, and *this* is the reason for the cover-up. Significantly, however, they claim that one of the most important reasons why the warnings were ignored was because Washington was so firmly fixed on the belief that the Japanese would attack British or Dutch territory.[75]

But even considering what is *not* disputed, the implications are still astonishing. Unlike the Pearl Harbor task force, there is no doubt that a huge Japanese invasion force was being tracked southwards, posing a threat to Malaya, the Netherlands East Indies, Thailand and the Philippines. Initially, it was not known which it would attack. In the final days before it struck, however, its target became more and more apparent. As Michael Smith explains in *The Emperor's Codes* (2000):

> For the past two months, the airwaves had been full of Japanese radio transmissions and the codebreakers had identified every ship in the Japanese armada. They had also deciphered a message from the Japanese Ambassador in Bangkok to Tokyo revealing that the ships were to land an invasion force at Kota Bharu in north-eastern Malaya.[76]

On 29 November, the Americans intercepted a signal from the Japanese Ambassador in Bangkok to Tokyo, which indicated an attack on the Kra Isthmus (the border between Malaya and Thailand). Roosevelt personally passed this warning on to Halifax the same day. At 14.00 hours on 6 December 1941, a Royal Australian Air Force plane from Kota Bharu spotted a Japanese convoy in the Gulf of Thailand.[77] As the historian Robert J. Aldrich comments: 'Japan's landward attack on Malaya, far from being an intelligence disaster, ranks as one of the most widely predicted operations of the Second World War.'[78]

Yet, although a general alert was issued to British and American bases, including Pearl Harbor, on 28 November, when the invasion finally struck it disastrously caught out the British in Malaya. Two days before, the British Commander-in-Chief in the Far East, Air Chief Marshal Sir Robert Brooke-Popham, announced, 'There are no signs that Japan is going to attack anyone'[79] – which was ludicrous: the Japanese build-up had been monitored for over a month and a substantial fleet was being tracked towards Malaya.

About three hours after the attack on Kota Bharu – while the Pearl Harbor raid was still under way – Japanese bombers struck at Singapore. Military bases were alerted, their sirens blaring. However, because it was a weekend, nobody was on duty in the civilian Air Raid Precautions Unit, and so the city's sirens remained quiet. One British intelligence officer, watching from the surrounding hills, later recalled 'sitting there and seeing Japanese aircraft flying overhead and dropping bombs on parts of Singapore which were still brilliantly lit up. You would not believe it but that was how unprepared Singapore was.'[80] But why were the British so unprepared, given the amount of intelligence? Michael Smith puts it down to their commanders' arrogance, and dismissal of the warnings as 'defeatist'. They simply refused to acknowledge that the Japanese had any chance of winning.

Aldrich claims: '. . . warnings were ignored not only in Singapore. In London the principal culprit was Churchill',[81] arguing that the Prime Minister did nothing because, at that time, his mind was fixed on the Middle East as he did not believe that Japan would come into the war if there was a risk of American involvement. However, none of this fits the facts.

Churchill was *very* interested in the Far East. Since the breakdown of the US–Japanese negotiations, he focused on the Pacific, it being *certain* that Japan would strike. The code-breakers in Bletchley Park, Singapore and Hong Kong were working overtime to piece together information about Japanese fleet and troop movements. And

Churchill was kept fully informed, Bletchley Park's Malcolm Kennedy writing on 6 December:

> . . . the All Highest [his term for Churchill] is all over himself at the moment for latest information and indications re Japan's intentions and rings up at all hours of day and night, except for the four hours of each 24 when he sleeps.[82]

There was no excuse for British unpreparedness in Malaya – any more than Admiral Kimmel's at Pearl Harbor – but this time there is no controversy about the fact that they knew the Japanese attack was imminent. Clearly, Churchill was also 'letting them fire the first shot'. If Japan was *seen* as the aggressor it might persuade the Americans to support the British. The attacks on Malaya and Singapore had to *appear* to come out of the blue.

In other words, the controversy over American foreknowledge of Pearl Harbor has distracted attention from a much more glaring example of the leaders' 'let it happen on purpose' policy.

The last day of American peace

On Sunday, 7 December 1941, a family lunch was arranged at the White House, but at the last minute Roosevelt announced he would be lunching alone in his study with Hopkins, where they were when news of the attack on Pearl Harbor reached them at 1.40 p.m. Washington time. The usual story is that Roosevelt was planning a 'leisurely afternoon' with his stamp collection when the news came through.[83] This is manifest nonsense. He and Hopkins had spent the previous night contemplating an intercepted Japanese signal that meant that war would almost certainly break out within the next 24 hours. But instead of being closeted in top-level emergency meetings, Roosevelt chose to be alone with Hopkins. Obviously, the homely 'stamp collection' spin is intended to reinforce the idea that even the President was taken by surprise. The months of make-or-break negotiations and the fact that war was imminent had been carefully withheld from the American people.

Officially, news of Pearl Harbor reached Churchill after he had Sunday lunch with Averell Harriman and Ambassador John G.

Behind the Infamy

Winant at Chequers. Arriving late, Winant was greeted by the agitated Prime Minister pacing up and down outside the front door waiting for him. Churchill immediately asked whether he thought that there would be war with Japan. When Winant replied in the affirmative, he declared 'If they declare war on you, we shall declare war within the hour' – and then asked if America would do the same. Winant, naturally, replied that only Congress could decide, writing later:

> He did not say anything for a minute, but I knew what was in his mind. He must have realised that if Japan attacked Siam or British territory it would force Great Britain into an Asiatic war, and leave us out of the war. He knew in that moment that his country might be 'hanging on one turn of pitch and toss'.[84]

Only Winant and Harriman remained until the evening. At nine o'clock, Churchill suggested they listen to the news on the radio, which included the first sketchy details about an attack on American shipping in Hawaii. According to his memoirs, it took his butler, Sawyers, to make them aware of the enormity of the situation, exclaiming: 'The Japanese have attacked the Americans!'[85]

According to Winant, Churchill jumped up and announced, 'We shall declare war on Japan!' to which the Ambassador replied, 'Good God, you can't declare war on a radio announcement.'[86] Winant then called Roosevelt to confirm the news. Because FDR was prevented from giving details of losses over the phone, he failed to grasp the significance of the disaster, saying, 'That's fine, Mr President, that's fine.'[87] He then passed the phone to Churchill. When FDR told him that the next day he was going to ask Congress for a declaration of war, the Prime Minister growled that Britain's 'would follow within the hour'.

Although post-war accounts by Churchill, Winant and John Martin (Churchill's secretary) broadly agree, inconsistencies suggest the Prime Minister was stage-managing events to some extent. As Winant points out, the attack on Pearl Harbor had happened two hours before (and the Japanese attack on Malaya two hours before *that*[88]), and although the news had reached the BBC, apparently no one had thought to inform the Prime Minister.[89] And Roosevelt telephoned Lord Halifax with the news at 2.15 (7.15 London time), while the attack was still under way.[90] Surely it is inconceivable that Halifax failed to pass this on to London with the greatest urgency – and yet Churchill professed to be surprised by the news nearly two hours later!

Declaring war on Germany

Considering that Roosevelt had certainly provoked Japan into war, the elusiveness of the Pearl Harbor 'smoking gun' hardly matters. But even so, why would he take such a momentous step? Was he, as has been suggested, using Japan as a circuitous way of bringing the United States into the war against Hitler? Hopkins' account of the White House conference that followed news of Pearl Habor seems to suggest as much:

> The conference met in not too tense an atmosphere because I think that all of us believed that in the last analysis the enemy was Hitler and that he could never be defeated without force of arms; that sooner or later we were bound to be in the war and that Japan had given us an opportunity.[91]

But was this true?

Following Pearl Harbor, there was a frenzy of war-declaring: the United States on Japan on 8 December, followed by Britain. Japan declared war on Britain. China, after four years fighting Japan, formally declared war on 9 December. Then Germany and Italy declared war on the US on 11 December, after which the US declared war on them. But there was one conspicuous absentee from this mass war dance. Despite Churchill's commitment to Russia and Roosevelt's vital Lend-Lease aid, the Russian leader stayed aloof, deciding to honour his non-aggression pact with Japan. (In fact, the Soviet Union only joined in the Pacific conflict in the very last days of the Second World War, even though the US and Britain effectively kept the Japanese off Stalin's back for three and a half years.)

A disgusted Breckinridge Long recorded Ambassador Litvinov's statement on 10 December: 'Russia has no quarrel with Japan now – Japan had not attacked her.' Long added:

Hitler's Deputy, Rudolf Hess.
(© National Archives)

The secrets behind the peace mission of Rudolf Hess in 1941 reveal Britain's real relationship with its soon-to-be Allies. Churchill used American fears that Hess's mission heralded an armistice to persuade President Roosevelt to step up its support for Britain, then standing alone against the Nazis, and suffering horrifically from the Blitz (above). He also used the Hess factor to ensure that Germany went ahead with its attack on the Soviet Union, thus turning away from Britain. (© Wandsworth Museum)

Above left: the treaty that caused the war. German Foreign Minister Joachim von Ribbentrop signs the notorious Nazi–Soviet Pact on 23 August 1939, watched by Vyacheslav Molotov, Soviet Foreign Commissar and Iosif Stalin. The Pact included a secret agreement to jointly invade Poland. However, in June 1941, Hitler turned the full might of his military machine on his Russian allies, precipitating some of the worst carnage of the war as both sides adopted the harshest of scorched-earth policies. Above right: Russian villages burnt on Stalin's own orders before the Germans could reach them. (Both pictures © National Archives)

Above left: President Roosevelt takes a keen interest in the globe. He ruthlessly exploited the war to ensure that America emerged as a superpower – at Britain's expense. But could he have achieved this without the extraordinary machinations of his *éminence grise*, Harry Hopkins (pictured to the left of Roosevelt in the photo above right)? (Both pictures © Franklin D. Roosevelt Library)

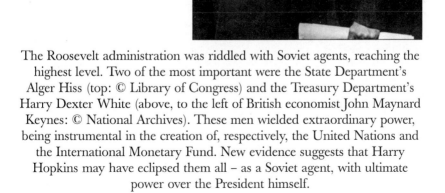

The Roosevelt administration was riddled with Soviet agents, reaching the highest level. Two of the most important were the State Department's Alger Hiss (top: © Library of Congress) and the Treasury Department's Harry Dexter White (above, to the left of British economist John Maynard Keynes: © National Archives). These men wielded extraordinary power, being instrumental in the creation of, respectively, the United Nations and the International Monetary Fund. New evidence suggests that Harry Hopkins may have eclipsed them all – as a Soviet agent, with ultimate power over the President himself.

Under spy chief William Stephenson ('Intrepid') – and on Churchill's specific orders – British Intelligence mounted a major covert operation in America designed to undermine Roosevelt's opponents and bring the US into the war on Britain's side. Above: OSS head 'Wild Bill' Donovan presents Stephenson with the Medal for Merit in 1946 (© National Archives). Remarkably, in 1941 Stephenson's team gave Roosevelt a map purporting to prove Nazi designs on both South America and the US itself (right: Franklin D. Roosevelt Library). A British Intelligence fake, it swayed US public opinion in favour of war.

Contrary to popular belief, there was back-door communication between German and British Intelligence actually during hostilities. The head of the Abwehr (German Military Intelligence) Admiral Wilhelm Canaris (above) – who opposed Hitler – remained in contact with MI6 chief Sir Stewart Menzies until the former's disgrace in 1944. (© Ullstein Bilderdienst)

The devastation of the shock Japanese attack on Pearl Harbor that famously ended American neutrality. But was it really a surprise to both Churchill and Roosevelt? (© Library of Congress)

Hitler was jubilant at the fall of Paris (above), capital of his hated France, but the Nazi occupation was relatively short-lived. (© National Archives)

On 26 August 1944, General Charles de Gaulle triumphantly headed the liberation of Paris. But behind this now legendary image lay great intrigue and hostilities among the Allies: Roosevelt was opposed to his leadership – and Churchill even wanted him 'eliminated'. (© National Archives)

According to Major George Racey Jordan, Harry Hopkins was personally responsible for passing atomic secrets and materials to the Soviet Union under the guise of Lend-Lease aid. Here, Jordan receives the rank of Major, tellingly from Russian Lend-Lease administrator Colonel Kotikov – but on American soil.
(© US Army Corps)

Churchill rallies the British troops in Egypt. Although a legend for his courage and historic rhetoric, his war-time leadership was by no means without controversy. Roosevelt and Stalin were often openly contemptuous of him.
(© Broadwater Collection)

American and Soviet troops meet at the River Elbe on 25 April 1945 (above right). Their advance into Germany had been carefully coordinated with post-war spheres of influence in mind: the Americans – against Churchill's protests – allowed the Russians to capture Berlin (above left), even though the Western Allies could have seized that prize first.
(Both pictures © Library of Congress)

The 'Big Three', Churchill, Roosevelt and Stalin, at the Yalta Conference in February 1945, which confirmed the Soviet domination of Eastern Europe – ironically, including Poland, the Nazi/Soviet threat to whose independence started the Second World War – and set the scene for the Cold War.
(© National Archives)

> The interference [*sic*] was easy that Russia and Japan had an
> understanding – non aggression – and Russia would take all the
> assistance she could get against Germany, but give no help
> other places . . . She is not fighting for 'liberty', for 'democracy',
> for the 'freedom of others' – but only for Russia, and will use
> her power only to advance the selfish ambitions of the leaders
> of Russia.[92]

Rather than using the Japanese atrocity to rush to Britain's aid, the
day after Pearl Harbor Roosevelt only asked Congress to endorse a
declaration of war on Japan. But three days later, it was *Hitler* who
declared war on America – and suddenly, there was no longer any
excuse: America was in the European conflict after all.

Hitler's move seems peculiar. Although the Tripartite Pact bound
Germany, Japan and Italy to mutual defence, it did not apply when
one of them struck the first blow (after all, Japan had chosen not to
join in after Barbarossa). Hitler's advisers told him he was not
obliged by the Pact to declare war on the USA – and that America
would probably not declare it on them.[93] Surely the smart move
would have been to try to squeeze some concessions out of Japan in
exchange for help – such as support against Russia. This was what
Washington believed Hitler would do.[94]

But although it is often assumed that FDR realised that Hitler
would settle the matter without having to risk crossing the
isolationists, as Eric Larrabee writes:

> As to involvement in the European war, if this is what the
> President intended war with Japan to accomplish, then his
> own actions cannot be said to have brought it about. After
> Pearl Harbor he did not ask Congress to declare war on
> Germany. It was Germany some days later – obligingly, if you
> like, but also puzzlingly – that declared war on the United
> States. For the President to have been certain in advance that
> this would happen is impossible. It is difficult enough even
> now to know why Hitler did it, why he deliberately
> minimized Roosevelt's difficulties when by simply doing
> nothing he could have maximized them.[95]

This has long been considered one of the great puzzles of the Second World War: why did Hitler declare war on the USA? Had he no fear history would repeat itself? Historians are deeply perplexed; Richard Lamb, calling Hitler's declaration his 'crowning folly', stated bluntly, 'We do not know why he did it,'[96] while A.J.P. Taylor writes: 'Indeed, it is difficult to see how the Americans could ever have become involved in the European war on a fighting basis, if Hitler had not gratuitously done it for them.'[97] Intelligence historians W.R. Corson and R.T. Crowley, discussing the 'curious fact' of Hitler's declaration of war, agree: 'On 11 December, Hitler made the still inexplicable decision to declare war on the United States . . . No rational explanation has been advanced that adequately accounts for Hitler's action.'[98] Yet the explanation is simple – and breathtaking . . .

As Charles Higham points out in *American Swastika* (1985), Hitler himself spelled out the reasons in a lengthy speech justifying his declaration of war: it was partly because of 'neutral' America's provocation, but also 'With no attempt at an official denial there has now been revealed in America President Roosevelt's plan by which, at the latest in 1943, Germany and Italy are to be attacked in Europe by military means.'[99] Clearly it was this – and not the Tripartite Pact – that prompted him to plunge Germany into the abyss.

Hitler was referring to an event that, had it not been eclipsed by Pearl Harbor, would be considerably better known today – and which marked the crowning achievement of William Stephenson's intelligence operation in the United States: in his words, 'Hitler helped us achieve what Congress might have prevented or delayed.'[100] Stevenson explained that 'Roosevelt's plan' (or the 'Victory Program'), like the secret map touted by the President a few weeks earlier, had actually been created by BSC – 'The Political-Warfare Division of BSC concocted the Victory Program out of material already known to have reached the enemy in dribs and drabs, and added some misleading information.'[101] As negotiations with the Japanese broke down and war looked imminent, BSC leaked the invented plan, specifically because of the effect it would have on Hitler.

The motivation was made clear by a BSC source quoted by Stevenson: 'Instinct warned Churchill that his friend the President would turn his attention and energies to the Pacific.'[102] The leaking of the Victory Program was intended to ensure that he didn't forget Germany. Richard Lamb writes:

> There were grave doubts in the Foreign Office as to whether the USA would declare war on Germany, and it was well on the cards that she would be at war with Japan but not with Germany or Italy. Most American historians believe that, if Roosevelt had immediately asked Congress to declare war on Germany, he would have faced strong opposition because the only real enemy that had attacked the United States was Japan.[103]

The BSC plan was insurance against this eventuality.

The leak was orchestrated in two ways – first, through the leading isolationist Senator Burton Wheeler, who since the start of the war had been approached by several senior military figures who disagreed with Roosevelt's policies, including an anonymous Army Air Force captain worried by FDR's exaggerated claims of the military's strength. In September 1941, this source revealed the existence of a plan for a 'gigantic American Expeditionary Force' to be sent to Europe. When Wheeler asked him for a copy, on 3 December the captain handed over a bulky document labelled 'Victory Program', one of only five copies.[104] Wheeler then arranged for details of Roosevelt's 'secret war plan' to be published in the isolationist *Chicago Tribune*, and the affiliated *Washington Times-Herald*, the next day. On the same day that Wheeler received his copy, the plan was also leaked to the German Embassy in Washington, which despatched details to Berlin in advance of the newspaper articles – although how they got them remains a mystery.[105]

This massive BSC triumph provoked Hitler into declaring war on America – a concerted effort with the Japanese now might prevent the build-up detailed in the Victory Program – and achieved Churchill's dream of 'bringing the Americans in'. The scheme was also a masterpiece of timing: it could only work if Japan was about to go on the offensive.

But there is an added twist. William Stevenson was being less than straight about the 'bogus' BSC plan: it was *absolutely authentic*. Not only does Leonard Mosley acknowledge this in his 1982 biography of General Marshall,[106] but the man responsible for the army's contribution, Colonel Albert C. Wedemeyer, confirmed that the media extracts were from the genuine plan.[107]

Over the Rainbow

The 'Victory Program' was part of the War Department's overall war plan 'Rainbow Five', a detailed analysis of how to beat both Germany and Japan. This, the fifth revision of the original 1939 'Rainbow' plan, in September 1941 called for a defensive war in the Pacific and an offensive war in Europe.[108] The part leaked to Wheeler and the German Embassy analysed the manpower, production and financial requirements needed. Not surprisingly, Higham calls Rainbow Five 'the most important single document in the possession of the chiefs of staff and of the White House'.[109]

Rainbow Five called for a massive build-up of the US Army – a five-million strong force for the final offensive against Germany in July 1943. Before this, Germany would be encircled and relentlessly bombed from Britain. Globally, the plan envisaged an army of eight million, also considering American forces being deployed in North Africa and the Middle East. The Victory Program set out how this was to be achieved, at a cost of $150 billion.

Like ABC-1, Rainbow Five was essentially a contingency plan, forecasting how the United States would win a potential war against Germany and Japan. The Administration and even the military were divided about the likelihood – not to mention the desirability – of such an eventuality. Roosevelt's views are especially unclear. But to many, the plan's very existence implied that the Americans were secretly planning to attack Germany . . .

The newspaper exposés caused a sensation – the *Washington Times-Herald* selling out almost as soon as it hit the streets. Despite Roosevelt's promises the year before that 'our boys' would not be sent overseas, here was a document that apparently said he was planning to do just that:

Germany and her European satellites cannot be defeated by

the European powers now fighting against her . . . If our
enemies in Europe are to be defeated it will be necessary for
the United States to enter the war, and to employ a part of its
armed forces defensively in the western Atlantic and in Europe
and Africa.[110]

Roosevelt refused to comment, and although Stimson claimed it was
just a contingency plan, in doing so he tacitly admitted it was
genuine. Curiously, Roosevelt's Press Secretary, Stephen Early, not
only omitted to condemn the leak but actually upheld the press's
right to publish such stories.[111] The Victory Program was set to blow
up into a major scandal – but within three days the conflagration in
Hawaii would give America something more pressing to worry
about.

The implications of the leaking of Rainbow Five are staggering.
British intelligence orchestrated the theft and leaking of America's
most highly secret and sensitive document – not just to the
isolationist press but also to the Nazis . . . And with breathtaking
cheek and daring, they did it to trick Hitler into declaring war on the
US, thus dragging the American people into a war that most of them
had never wanted.

It could have gone terribly wrong. Had Pearl Harbor not virtually
obliterated the Rainbow Five scandal, it would have seriously
damaged Roosevelt's standing and undermined his covert support
for Britain's war effort, not to mention handing over US secrets to
the Nazis. And Wheeler himself had been used. At any other time,
his exposure of the Victory Program would have destroyed
Roosevelt's plans. However, Wheeler had no idea that Roosevelt and
Churchill knew hostilities were to break out with Japan within a
matter of days: publicising the plan would have the opposite effect,
pushing Hitler into declaring war and landing America at its centre,
the very outcome Wheeler had been so keen to prevent. (Like most
isolationists, he became an 'Asia-firster' after Pearl Harbor.)

There is more. Even at the time, many in Washington believed
that Roosevelt himself was ultimately behind the leak, such as the
anti-war Colonel Wedemeyer – at first, one of the prime suspects as
the 'mole'.[112] Burton Wheeler himself believed that someone higher

up the chain of command had authorised the leak. Of course, the notion of presidential approval makes no apparent sense – until seen in the context of an impending attack by Japan.

Once again, Roosevelt had manipulated a war while appearing to keep his own hands clean. But even without an obvious smoking gun, the provocation of Japan had backfired: the truth is that the 3,500 mangled casualties of Pearl Harbor were the victims of their own government's 'friendly fire' – aided and abetted by Winston Churchill.

CHAPTER NINE

The End of the Beginning

'We must just KBO.' (Keep Buggering On)
Winston S. Churchill's favourite
advice to his wartime staff[1]

On the day of Pearl Harbor, Churchill immediately insisted on going to Washington to confer with Britain's new Ally. Overjoyed, he wrote later: 'So we had won after all!'[2] Naively, he thought that Britain would be an equal partner in the alliance, as Chief of the Imperial General Staff, Field Marshal Sir Alan Brooke (later Lord Alanbrooke), explains:

> At one of our meetings shortly after the USA had come into the war, someone was still adopting the careful attitude that had been necessary before the entry of the USA to ensure that we did not let ourselves into a war with Japan without the USA being in it. Winston turned to him, and with a wicked leer in his eye, said: 'Oh! That is the way we talked to her while we were wooing her, now that she is in the harem we talk to her quite differently!'[3]

Egos in Arcadia

The Prime Minister and his entourage arrived in Washington on 22 December 1941 for a three-week conference ('Arcadia'), thrashing out how to defeat their enemies.

Arcadia's first major outcome was the historic United Nations Declaration of New Year's Day 1942, signed by the United States, Britain, the Soviet Union and China, with many other nations (or governments-in-exile) also signing during the war, committing their 'full resources, military and economic' to the defeat of the Axis countries, and pledging not to make a separate peace. The declaration ultimately formed the basis of today's United Nations Organisation, inaugurated in 1945, although – confusingly – the term 'United Nations' was also used by the Allies to refer to themselves during the war.

But all eyes were on the new intimacy between Britain and America: 'Never before in the history of warfare had two nations agreed to such a meshing of their military efforts.'[4] After Arcadia, the Anglo-American war effort was overseen by a Combined Chiefs of Staff: in each theatre of war, the army, navy and air force of both countries were under a single supreme commander. Broadly, America would be responsible for the Pacific, the British for the Middle East (and, potentially, India). They would work together in Europe.

They found it harder to agree on details. Churchill had his own grand three-phase design to beat the Germans, which he called 'closing the ring'. First, Germany and Italy would be encircled: the Russians were already restraining them in the east, and if the Western Allies could control the Atlantic and expel the Axis from North Africa the 'ring' would be complete. Next would come economic strangulation: blockade with morale-eroding air raids – as well as orchestrated subversion and sabotage in the occupied countries, for which Churchill had created SOE to 'set Europe ablaze'. This would pave the way for Allied liberation. He assumed that Italy would surrender, oust Mussolini and come over to the Allied side. Finally, Churchill envisaged an 'assault on the German citadel' – a steady advance on a country worn down by the bombing and blockade. Fighting all the way to Berlin might not even be necessary: perhaps the Germans might simply sue for peace, if necessary, overthrowing the Führer.[5]

The building of the ring relied on seizing control of North Africa from Morocco to Egypt, forcing Hitler and Mussolini to defend Europe's lengthy Mediterranean coastline. As Churchill expected French North Africa to actually invite the Allies in, he had cultivated General Weygand, although unfortunately the latter had been recalled to France.

The Prime Minister's grand strategy clashed with the US War Department's Rainbow Five planned build-up in Britain for a massive offensive beginning in mid-1943 (which, thanks to British intelligence, Hitler was now expecting). But even though Roosevelt had tacitly approved Rainbow Five, it still made him uneasy, as it entailed sending 'our boys' to Europe, despite his promises to the contrary. Still hoping to limit America's involvement to sea and air, he told the conference it would be a 'mistake' to send troops to England or Scotland, while there was a 'great deal to be said' for establishing USAAF bases in Britain to bomb Germany.[6]

Churchill's plan, as the least-risk for American troops, appealed to the President. Although siding with the Prime Minister against his own chiefs, Roosevelt ensured the Arcadia Conference broadly agreed to focus on North Africa. (However, as we will see, FDR soon changed his tune.) He also backed Churchill's suggestion that American troops be confined to Northern Ireland, freeing British garrisons for action elsewhere. (Despite protests in Eire, by June 1942 there were 32,000 GIs in the province.) Churchill jubilantly relayed to the War Cabinet Roosevelt's reassuring: 'Trust me to the bitter end.'[7]

The demise of BSC

Predictably, the first casualty of the Anglo-American alliance was William Stephenson's British Security Coordination. Now that Roosevelt had used it for his own ends, it was too dangerous to be allowed to survive in the United States.

The official reasons for its demise[8] are that at the end of January 1942 the McKellar Act transferred responsibility for monitoring all foreign agencies in the US from the State to the Justice Department, also prohibiting foreign agents operating within the United States. BSC's operations would no longer be scrutinised so tolerantly: when Stephenson complained, Donovan unsurprisingly supported him, lobbying Roosevelt to veto the Act, or to at least give BSC immunity.

This brought Stephenson into conflict with Adolf Berle of the State Department (Roosevelt's security adviser) who was already worried about a backlash, particularly over the forged 'Nazi map'. As the row with Stephenson exploded, Berle wrote, 'a British espionage service functioning here . . . might at any time be turned not to espionage on the enemy, but to operations within the United States'.[9] He also urged FDR not to be swayed by Donovan's close relationship with Stephenson and British intelligence. Predictably, Stephenson assigned agent Denis Paine to dig up enough dirt on Berle to get him sacked from the State Department, but when the FBI found out, J. Edgar Hoover ordered the agent out of the country.

At the end of February, Hoover, Berle and the Attorney General, Francis Biddle, met to discuss how BSC could have built up such an extensive operation inside the US, admitting it probably happened because of 'an informal agreement between Churchill and the President before the war'.[10] (This suggests that they knew of some intelligence-related deal involving Churchill even before he became Prime Minister.)

A week later, Berle, Hoover and Biddle took their suspicions to Lord Halifax – who professed surprise: according to Stephenson, the FBI had approved all BSC's operations. When Hoover denied it, Roosevelt ordered that BSC should be reduced to the innocuous liaison organisation it was supposed to be, and that Stephenson should leave the country – although he was reprieved by Menzies, who maintained that the Stephenson–Donovan partnership was vital. It was still the end of BSC as a significant operation in America.

That is the official story, but just after America's entry into the war, the timing seems a little too pat. Having got Roosevelt his third term and backing for Britain, BSC had become a liability: it had to go. Did Berle and Hoover engineer the downfall – using Stephenson's own methods of discrediting the opposition?

Significantly, some of the Americans who had cooperated with BSC shrewdly shifted their focus after Pearl Harbor, such as Walter

Lippmann, who had advocated that the United States should support Britain. Now he argued it was a war of liberation from the British Empire.[11]

Another result of BSC's demise was the creation of America's first 'central intelligence' organisation, the OSS – effectively the forerunner of the CIA – in June 1942. Bill Donovan's appointment as its head was actually Roosevelt's way of clipping his wings.[12] In July 1940, as 'Coordinator of Information' (COI) Donovan headed 'America's first national intelligence entity'[13] – which was not only a British idea, but even British-controlled. Stephenson had enlisted certain of those close to Roosevelt and Churchill, including Robert Sherwood and Desmond Morton, to lobby for it, and it was he who suggested Donovan ('our man') for the post. Donovan was effectively a British agent, the set-up actually run by Stephenson's assistant, Dick Ellis.[14] But now, as head of OSS, he had to report directly to the Joint Chiefs of Staff.

Munitions make millions

The day after Pearl Harbor, the War Department cancelled all Lend-Lease, to howls of outrage. Consequently, in January 1942 the War Production Board was set up to guarantee the massive increase in production that would keep both Lend-Lease customers and the US Army and Navy happy – the final stage of the United States' conversion to all-out military production. The Board took control of all American industry, deciding quotas and schedules. The power behind the War Production Board was Harry Hopkins.

Predictably, 'After Pearl Harbor, Hopkins became in every respect except for the title the chief of staff to the President,'[15] Churchill describing him as the link between the President, the Secretaries of State, War and the Navy (Hull, Stimson and Knox), and Army Chief of Staff Marshall – making Roosevelt almost entirely dependent on him. And soon, his control of Lend-Lease also involving him in Treasury decisions, he had become the indispensable link between every branch of the government.[16]

On the military side, General Marshall – Hopkins' appointee back in 1939 – had efficiently metamorphosed the small and poorly trained US Army into a fighting machine numbering millions. In

1942, the symbol of this new abrasiveness was the construction of the Pentagon. The largest building in the world, its message was clear: not even Allies could mess with the United States.

Inconvenient Allies

The weaker Allies became very anxious at the posturing of the 'Big Three'. What would their alliance mean for those who simply wanted the Axis out of their countries? Would they be trodden underfoot – either in the mad dash for victory or afterwards? To the Big Three it soon became clear that the lesser Allies were inconvenient, embarrassing – or even downright hostile.

A perennial problem was France, particularly the role of the Free French, as Roosevelt's government still upheld Vichy as the legitimate French government. On learning about Pearl Harbor, de Gaulle said: 'Well, this war is over. Of course there will be more operations, battles and combats. But the war is over since the outcome is known. In this industrial war, nothing can resist the might of American industry. From now on, the British will do nothing without Roosevelt's agreement.'[17]

An even greater worry was Sikorski's Free Polish government. Until Hitler had driven them out, the Soviets had occupied half of Poland, which Stalin clearly expected to get back when Germany was defeated – also expecting that Britain and the United States would recognise Soviet sovereignty.

Sikorski realised that the Grand Alliance would seek to placate Stalin – sacrificing Poland yet again. At the beginning of 1942, relations between his government in exile and the Soviet Union were tense but still manageable. After Barbarossa, Stalin had ordered that Polish prisoners of war be released to fight alongside the Red Army under the command of General Władysław Anders, himself freed from Moscow's Lubianka prison. Officially the 2nd Polish Corps, 'Anders' Army' was eventually 70,000-strong. (A few months later, the Soviets reneged on the amnesty, claiming it referred only to ethnic Poles, and refusing to free other Polish nationals, such as Ukrainians and Jews.[18]) Stalin also refused to arm and supply the Polish Corps. Eventually, in the summer of 1942, Anders evacuated his men – 'the only large group of prisoners ever allowed to leave the

USSR'[19] – along with 40,000 Polish civilians, into Iran, where they fought alongside the British. After the war, Anders was stripped of Polish citizenship by the Soviet-backed Polish government and was never allowed to return home.

Western governments had chosen to ignore rumours about the gulags for years, and were now keen to prevent the sudden flood of personal testimony from Anders' Army reaching the press and public – for example, one of 436 Poles sent to Kolyma reported that by March 1941 only 46 remained alive[20] – which caused particular outrage in certain American circles, although the government kept publicity to the minimum until after the war. But there should have been no more excuses for turning a blind eye to the inequities of Stalin's regime, Ally or not.

Britain had been working on the terms of its alliance with Stalin before America's entry into the war. He demanded an alliance for the duration, and a treaty to regulate Anglo-Soviet relations after victory. Incredibly, Stalin proposed to include a secret protocol that recognised the Soviet Union's borders as they had existed the day before Barbarossa – i.e. including the half of Poland and the Baltic states he won from his other secret protocol with *Hitler*! Even more unbelievably, Anthony Eden agreed in principle, although cautioning it would need the approval of the British and – now – American governments. Churchill would have none of it, declaring that Stalin's demands opposed the principles of the Atlantic Charter, to which the USSR had subscribed, and arguing that all territorial issues should wait until after victory.[21] However, his principles soon deserted him . . .

Stalin then turned the screws on the Allies, alarming them with his speech to the Red Army on 23 February 1942, in which he mentioned neither them nor their aid, and blaming the Russia–Germany conflict specifically on a 'Hitler clique', recalling Hitler blaming a 'Churchill clique' for the Anglo-German conflict (a coded overture to a British 'peace group').[22] At around the same time, the US army intelligence agency, G-2, reported to Hopkins the 'distinct possibility' that Stalin might make a separate peace.[23]

But was peace between Germany and the Soviet Union really likely at that time? Given Hitler's obsession with beating Stalin, perhaps not, but Roosevelt and Churchill were in no position to take the risk. (And who could be sure about *anything*, after the Nazi–Soviet Pact of 1939?) Clearly, peace between Russia and Germany would be disastrous for Britain and America, freeing Hitler's vast Eastern Front resources (and making it impossible to 'close the ring' around Germany). Stalin had to be kept in the war – he must neither make peace nor be defeated. Undergoing a sea change, Churchill wrote to Roosevelt:

> The increasing gravity of the war has led me to feel that the principle of the Atlantic Charter ought not to be construed so as to deny Russia the frontiers she occupied when Germany attacked her. This was the basis on which Russia acceded to the Charter, and I expect that a severe process of liquidating hostile elements in the Baltic States, etc., was employed by the Russians when they took those regions at the beginning of the war. I hope therefore that you will be able to give us a free hand to sign the treaty which Stalin desires as soon as possible.[24]

Poland, barely two years before a cause for war, is now a mere 'etc'.

Singapore – and other disasters

Despite the Grand Alliance, things were grim. On 10 December 1941, battleships HMS *Prince of Wales* and *Repulse* were sunk by Japanese aircraft 200 miles off Malaya, with over 700 dead. On the same day, the island of Guam and its American base were captured, and Japanese troops landed on the Philippines, followed by Borneo, prompting the Dutch and British to set fire to the oil wells. Hong Kong fell on Christmas Day.

The inexorable Japanese advance was fast becoming a rout. On 19 January, Churchill learned from General Archibald Wavell, chief of the newly formed ABDA (American-British-Dutch-Australian) Command, that Singapore's fixed fortifications faced seaward, utterly useless against a land invasion. Singapore surrendered to the Japanese on 15 February 1942 – 80,000 prisoners of war were taken. The first Japanese air raid on Australia took place on Darwin on 19 February 1942, a profound shock to the British dominions. On 8 March, the Japanese took the Burmese capital Rangoon, beginning the longest fighting retreat in the history of the British Army as it fell back to India. With Burma almost entirely in enemy hands by May, India was exposed to attack. Another 60,000 prisoners were taken with the ABDA surrender in Java on 9 March. A month to the day later, the American-Filipino army in the Philippines followed suit – the largest surrender in American history, with 35,000 troops and 25,000 civilians taken prisoner. When the last remaining US forces in the Philippines surrendered on 6 May, Japan controlled the whole of the Pacific.

It was only in May and June that the US Pacific Fleet's victories in the Battles of the Coral Sea and Midway stemmed the Japanese advance. Even so, Tojo's men were still the unquestioned masters of the Pacific west of the Midway Islands.

Matters were not much better elsewhere in spring 1942. On the Eastern Front, the Soviet counterattack had halted, the two sides preparing to renew fighting in the summer. And in the Atlantic, U-boats were sinking more shipping than ever before.

FDR's vision

Roosevelt could now pursue his long-held plans for restructuring the world order – America's economic expansion, the end of colonialism and his 'world police' idea of 20 years before. Obviously, this brought him into a head-on collision with Churchill – and so roused the Prime Minister's passions that he almost resigned in the middle of the war.

Although ardently devoted to destroying colonialism as a point of principle, FDR's plan was not entirely divorced from America's economic ambitions, as Allan M. Winkler of the University of Oregon explains:

> Opposition to imperialism was a major factor in American policy during the Second World War. Based in part on the conception of a system in which the older European powers played a less powerful role than before, in part on the vision of an order in which American enterprise was free to expand . . . [25]

During the Arcadia Conference, when he suggested that Churchill make an immediate commitment to full Indian self-government, the result was a 'violent explosion'.[26] In his memoirs, Churchill wrote: 'I reacted so strongly and at such length that he never raised it verbally again.'[27] But the Prime Minister was being disingenuous: Roosevelt did raise the issue again – in writing and through intermediaries. Several times.

Roosevelt must have known how Churchill felt about India: indeed, his refusal to countenance any moves towards self-government was largely responsible for his 'wilderness years', also rebelling against his own party on the subject in 1935. Not only did the Prime Minister see Roosevelt's nagging as blatant interference in Britain's business but also as a worrying sign that the United States now had the status to do so.

Even during Churchill's Washington visit, Roosevelt kept up the pressure by suggesting that India should be one of the signatories to the United Nations Declaration – revealing that the United States considered it a separate, sovereign nation. After much discussion, the Prime Minister gave way.

Realising that Britain needed Indian goodwill, raw materials and manpower – as well as sending a signal to Roosevelt – the Cabinet despatched Sir Stafford Cripps for discussions with the Indian National Congress (the main independence group). Appalled, Churchill told the Cabinet on 7 March that, if the talks resulted in Indian independence, he would resign. Two days before, he had told Anthony Eden he would advise the King to make him Prime Minister in his place.[28]

Determined to show the world that this *was* very much the United States' business, Roosevelt sent 'personal representative' Louis Johnson to India at the same time as Cripps. But despite the latter offering concessions that virtually guaranteed post-war independence, the talks broke down, prompting Churchill to dance around the Cabinet room, declaring, 'No tea with treason, no truck with American or British Labour sentimentality . . . !'[29]

He threatened to resign yet again in April when Harry Hopkins personally passed on the President's warnings of American outrage if India was invaded by the Japanese. Churchill hit the roof again, largely because of the implication that he should be swayed by American public opinion – telling Hopkins sharply that he was 'quite ready to retire to private life if that would do any good in assuaging public opinion'.[30] Hopkins reported to FDR 'the string of cuss words lasted for two hours in the middle of the night.'[31] In fact, Churchill got as far as drafting his resignation on 12 April 1942[32] – one of two occasions during the war.

At this, Roosevelt backed down: obviously, it was better to have Churchill rather than a less controllable newcomer in 10 Downing Street – although he would return to the subject after the Japanese threat to India had subsided. Until then, he shifted his attention to French Indo-China.

'American Lebensraum'

Roosevelt's commitment to the decolonisation of the European empires did no harm to his plan for America's domination of the world's economy, which was furthered by entering the war. The Americans mounted a two-pronged attack: first, continuing the pressure on Britain to remove the trade barriers around the Empire. The second was to impose controls on Britain's gold and dollar reserves – eliminating the Old Country's economic rivalry and replacing sterling with the dollar as the world's dominant currency.

However, Britain had two particular allies, Dean Acheson, Under-Secretary of State, and John J. McCloy of the War Department, who put up a strong, but ultimately unsuccessful, battle against the Treasury. Acheson wrote: 'McCloy and I would accuse the Treasury of envisaging a victory where both enemies and allies were prostrate – enemies by military action, allies by bankruptcy.'[33]

Sentiments were just as blunt on the British side. Leo Amery, Secretary of State for India, wrote that the American demands for free trade were 'a policy for breaking up the British Empire and reducing it to an American Lebensraum'.[34] But in the end, as John Charmley explains: 'The Roosevelt administration, like its successor, possessed the economic muscle and the will to make the economic structures which supported the British Empire and the social system it underpinned conform to the desires of the economic and social liberalism of those who wanted to internationalise the "New Deal".[35]

The business end of the first prong was Lend-Lease, which at the end of 1941 had yet to be formalised. The core of the disagreement was the controversial 'Article Seven', which related to *post-war* trade. This linked Lend-Lease to the dismantling of imperial preference, by agreeing to eliminate 'discriminatory treatment in international commerce' – i.e. Britain had to allow the Americans equal opportunities in Empire countries.[36]

The US government had included Article Seven in the Lend-Lease draft in July 1941, and the two governments had been haggling over it ever since. John Maynard Keynes, head of the British delegation, was quick to condemn the 'lunatic proposals of Mr Hull'.[37] For most of 1941, the talks went nowhere, mainly because Britain had more pressing concerns. But when both agreement and Article Seven reappeared on the Arcadia agenda, the Prime Minister resolutely refused to give way.

Selecting the perfect moment, with disasters in the Far East making Britain needier than ever, in early February Roosevelt urged Churchill to settle swiftly. The Prime Minister replied that the Cabinet was against linking Lend-Lease to ending the imperial preference system – casually adding that its opponents in both countries might even think that America was taking unfair advantage of Britain's predicament. Roosevelt murmured smoothly that nothing was further from his mind.[38]

After Churchill reassured the Cabinet he had a 'definite assurance' from the President that Article Seven did not commit Britain to abolishing imperial preference, the Agreement – including the controversial clause – was finally signed on 23 February 1942 as the Mutual Aid Agreement. The US government launched a PR campaign to impress the public with the deal America had struck in return for Lend-Lease, specifically because of Article Seven. In Britain, there was virtually no publicity at all.[39] As Professor Richard J. Overy writes: 'The British feared that this [giving up imperial preference] would mean the collapse of the Empire, and a dominant America. Only when Roosevelt insisted in February 1942 that the British sign the Lend-Lease Agreement or risk harmful consequences was their hand forced.'[40]

Did Churchill and his government realise exactly what they had signed? In April 1944, he stated to the House that Article Seven had not committed Britain to abandoning imperial preference, although Richard Gardner calls this 'somewhat misleading', writing: 'There can be little doubt that the State Department intended "discriminatory treatment" to embrace Imperial Preference and made this clear to their British counterparts.'[41]

The Mutual Aid Agreement – a resounding triumph for Roosevelt and Henry Morgenthau – effectively meant that Britain had agreed to fall in with America's economic plans, something that successive British governments had fought for years to avoid and had nearly brought the two nations to war in the 1920s. Britain had relinquished its pride as the most powerful nation in the world to the United States.

The Mutual Aid Agreement also provided for 'Reverse Lend-Lease' – officially 'Reciprocal Aid' – seldom mentioned today, but highly significant. The principle was that Britain and its dominions were to supply materials and services for America's war effort free of charge. By 1945, the US had received Reverse Lend-Lease of about $5.7 billion from Britain alone, and a further $2 billion from Commonwealth/Empire countries.[42] The idea seems fair until the details are considered: as we have seen, in practice Britain had to pay for Lend-Lease aid through trade concessions and the like, while Reverse Lend-Lease was simply given away to America. Both cost Britain dearly.

The major American negotiator on the Mutual Aid Agreement – presiding over the economic dismantling of the British Empire – was, predictably, the controversial Harry Dexter White, whose role in undermining Britain's international standing will become even more central.

The Second Front

An uncomfortable pattern soon became apparent within the Triple Alliance: the President throwing his support behind the Soviet Premier to Britain's cost – utterly astounding to the Prime Minister, who believed the 'English-speaking nations' should stick together.[43] Wasn't the USSR opposed to the very capitalist foundation of both

Britain and America? And hadn't Stalin not only jointly caused the war, but also, until Barbarossa, repeatedly blamed Britain and France for starting it?

Given the putative 'virtual armistice' between Britain and Germany, the Prime Minister was keeping his own guilty secret from both his allies – he was effectively letting Stalin's forces fight Germany on Britain's behalf. Even though that tacit agreement was now crumbling, the Russians would continue to do all the real work in Europe for some time. The British Chiefs of Staff's report in October 1942 concluded, 'The Russian Army is, today, the only force capable of defeating the German Army or, indeed, containing it.' Churchill noted in the margin, 'I hope Stalin will not see this.'[44]

From the beginning of their alliance, Roosevelt had been desperate to meet Stalin face to face – but without Winston Churchill. He first suggested it to Stalin in April 1942,[45] whose '*niet*' was apparently implacable: despite several more invitations, FDR would have to wait until November 1943 for his meeting.

In 1942, the Second Front would become the major bone of contention among the three Allies, as the President sided with Stalin. The strategy agreed at Arcadia – 'closing the ring', with North Africa first – was forgotten, as Roosevelt began to back his own chiefs' preference for direct engagement with Germany in Europe through a cross-Channel invasion. In *The Politics of the Second Front* (1977), American historian Mark A. Stoler argues that this was driven by politics, not military wisdom.

At first, support in America for the Second Front originated with the US Army because it was essentially a return to Rainbow Five, and with Harry Hopkins, who swiftly sold the idea to Roosevelt. Another key figure was beginning to make his mark: deputy chief of the War Plans Division, Colonel Dwight D. Eisenhower – Marshall's protégé – now promoted to Major-General and head of the new Operations Division. As his avowed priority was keeping the Soviet Union in the war, the Germans had to be diverted from the Eastern Front. In late February, his team developed a 'second front' plan, but – predictably – it was Hopkins who convinced the President to abandon the Arcadia agreements, telling the army he was sure FDR would come round to it. Just three days later, it had Presidential approval.[46]

The End of the Beginning

Within days, Roosevelt cabled Churchill that the invasion of North Africa would have to be 'temporarily shelved'[47] – a terrible blow to both his strategy and ego. At the end of March, Marshall rolled out the new plan: as the Anglo-American efforts were to be concentrated on the cross-Channel invasion (Operation Roundup), they would have to act defensively *everywhere* except in the Atlantic, so that US forces could be amassed in Britain for Roundup in spring or summer 1943 – essentially a return to Rainbow Five. But the plan also included the contingency of launching a limited assault, Operation Sledgehammer, in northern France in autumn 1942 if the defeat of the Soviet Union seemed imminent. As insufficient forces would have been assembled in Britain, this stood little chance of success, being merely a 'sacrifice' to the higher purpose of keeping Russia afloat.[48] However, Hopkins soon set about persuading Roosevelt that the 1942 operation should be the *main* plan, writing to him a week after the President had agreed to Marshall's plan: 'I doubt if any single thing is as important as getting some sort of a front this summer against Germany.'[49] Hopkins could hardly have done a better job for the Kremlin.

However, there were other benefits for Roosevelt. There was a growing public clamour for some kind of American action – and mid-term Congressional elections were due in November, so waiting until spring 1943 for a big push was not an option. Naturally, the public would prefer to see Pearl Harbor avenged, but there seemed little immediate prospect of a Pacific triumph. The Second Front was the perfect solution – satisfying both his fellow Americans and Stalin – but he wanted it in 1942, preferably before the elections. With no time for a major American build-up in Britain: '. . . the 1942 assault depended almost entirely on British willingness to risk their troops in what could easily prove to be another Dunkirk.'[50] Whatever the reason, Marshall's 'sacrifice' contingency was now Roosevelt's preferred option. The Americans would be happy their boys were doing their bit, while the British paid the price. Media spin would certainly help: as we will see, in the Dieppe raid in August only 50 of the 6,000 troops were American – yet from the US headlines one would scarcely know any other nation was involved.

Now a total convert to the plan, Roosevelt despatched Hopkins and Marshall to London to persuade Churchill, cabling ahead: 'What Harry and Geo. Marshall will tell you about has my heart and *mind* in it.' Roosevelt also referred to the importance of the Second Front: 'Even if full success is not attained, the *big* objective will be.'[51] Robert Nisbet responds in *Roosevelt and Stalin: The Failed Courtship* (1989): 'Big objective? What could that be if not the pleasing of Stalin at whatever cost?'[52]

Roosevelt was desperate for a fait accompli. Before Hopkins and Marshall were even in London he had ordered a crash building programme for landing craft, also discussing with his Cabinet the idea of telling Stalin that the Second Front was going ahead in 1942 – before Churchill had even been consulted.[53]

Hopkins and Marshall arrived in London on 8 April with 'Roosevelt's' (actually Marshall's) plan, to which he demanded immediate agreement. Privately, Churchill was not happy that his Arcadia strategy had been rejected. And if Sledgehammer went ahead in 1942 before the American build-up was complete, Britain would have to supply most of the troops – not an attractive thought, especially for an operation described as a 'sacrifice'. However, Churchill cannily cabled Roosevelt, praising 'your masterly document' – while never having the slightest intention of implementing it.[54]

When Foreign Commissar Molotov visited London in May 1942 for talks on the Anglo–Soviet treaty, Roosevelt suggested he travel on to Washington to discuss a 'very important military proposal'. But Molotov brought a startling new demand from Stalin – he now wanted *all* of Poland . . . In fact, he was playing a shrewd game, relying on the British agreeing to a Second Front rather than overturn their whole reason for going to war in the first place. Significantly, Roosevelt took exactly the same line, advising Churchill to agree to the Second Front rather than give in to the territorial demands. Yet again, Roosevelt and Stalin were acting almost in concert for the same agenda.[55]

Eventually, realising that the British were resolutely opposed to a Second Front in 1942, Molotov dropped his demands – first for the eastern part of Poland, then for British recognition of Soviet sovereignty over the Baltic states. Finally, after Ambassador Winant informed him that Roosevelt would back Churchill on the Second Front but not the treaty, Molotov gave in and signed a treaty that effectively deferred the territorial issues until the end of the war.[56]

In Washington in late May and early June, Molotov had several days of meetings with Roosevelt, discussing the Second Front. When he arrived in Washington, Hopkins met the Russian before the President saw him, explaining the military's objections – and coolly advising him what arguments to use to overcome them.[57]

After Roosevelt established from Marshall that the Second Front was technically feasible, and without even consulting Churchill, he authorised Molotov to tell Stalin that the Second Front would happen during 1942 – preferably in August. The President declared he was prepared to sacrifice up to 120,000 men to help relieve the pressure on the Russian front, but failed to mention they would mostly be *British*.[58]

On 3 June, Molotov requested that a communiqué include the statement that 'full understanding was reached with regard to the urgent tasks of creating a Second Front in Europe in 1942'. However, now Marshall demurred, having checked the feasibility with Eisenhower in London. Apparently the whole build-up was such a shambles that a successful cross-Channel operation might not even be possible in 1943. (Eisenhower assessed the chances of Sledgehammer's success as one in five, but considered it worth the risk if it kept the Russians in the war.[59]) Marshall lobbied Hopkins to have the statement dropped from the communiqué, but Roosevelt and Hopkins insisted that it be issued.[60]

Molotov returned to London, triumphantly flourishing the communiqué, which needed Churchill's approval before it could be released. Aghast, the Prime Minister agreed to its release on the basis that it was *misinformation* aimed at Hitler. It was duly issued on 11 June 1942. Churchill told Molotov he could make no promises on the Second Front, but he was now set on shelving the cross-Channel offensive indefinitely.[61]

Before Molotov's intervention, Churchill had already decided to send his new Chief of Combined Operations, Vice-Admiral Lord Louis Mountbatten – the King's near-pathologically arrogant cousin – to explain personally to the President the British reservations about

Sledgehammer, his future command. Their five-hour meeting made the President start to waver – disastrous for Hopkins who, desperate for the operation to go ahead, cabled Churchill asking him to come to Washington urgently.[62] Such was the urgency that for the first time, the Prime Minister crossed the Atlantic by air.

While at the White House, Churchill heard – humiliatingly from the President himself – that Rommel's men had routed the Eighth Army, capturing 32,000 prisoners and 100 tanks. With the fall of Tobruk, Egypt was now exposed to invasion, seriously threatening the whole North African strategy, adding to his deepening anxiety.

Churchill argued that no cross-Channel assault should take place until it stood a chance of establishing a permanent bridgehead. To him, a second Dunkirk with no miracle was 'the only way in which we could possibly lose this war'.[63] Roosevelt, on the other hand, had no problem with a cross-Channel assault that was repelled – even with heavy casualties – provided it diverted German resources from the Eastern Front.

Roosevelt and Churchill finally agreed to continue the troop build-up and review the situation on 1 September – if Sledgehammer was still impracticable, they would return to the Prime Minister's favoured North Africa invasion. At least that way *something* would happen in 1942. It was an awkward compromise: both leaders afraid they would fail to get what they wanted, but at least Churchill could claw back his original strategy.

But another problem loomed. At the beginning of July, the German summer offensive began, centring on Stalingrad, which Hitler was desperate to annihilate and Stalin equally obsessed with defending. As the situation looked bad for Russia, Hopkins, Marshall and Eisenhower began to press for 'sacrificial' Operation Sledgehammer to go ahead, regardless of Washington's wait-and-see decision. On 8 July, Churchill told Roosevelt that his chiefs of staff were unanimously against Sledgehammer, which he no longer considered viable, adding later, 'I have found no one who regards "Sledgehammer" as possible.' Instead, he urged that the North Africa invasion go ahead and that a joint operation with the Russians against Norway be considered – 'All this seems to me as clear as noonday.'[64]

The End of the Beginning

The next day, the British Chiefs of Staff representative in Washington, Field Marshal Dill, cabled Churchill a warning – Hopkins, Marshall and the Chief of Naval Operations, Admiral Ernest J. King, had been ordered to London to convince him to change his mind. Dill wrote ominously:

> Unless you can convince him [Marshall] of your unswerving devotion to it [Sledgehammer] everything points to a complete reversal of our present agreed strategy and the withdrawal of America to a war of her own in the Pacific, leaving us with limited American assistance to make out as best we can against Germany.[65]

Indeed, Roosevelt's next cable stressed that the American people wanted to see action against Japan, not Germany – a not-so-veiled threat.[66] Anthony Cave Brown writes: 'Not before, and not again, would the Grand Alliance be in such danger; not before, and not again, would Hitler appear to be so close to victory – for that must be the consequence of an Anglo-American split.'[67]

When Hopkins, Marshall and King arrived in Scotland on 19 July 1942, Churchill laid on a train for them to join him at Chequers – but incredibly, they simply ordered it to take them directly to London for their meeting with the American military. The Prime Ministerial train had become an American taxi, an astonishing snub, although as protocol demanded, they had persuaded Roosevelt to cable Churchill: 'I really think it better for our friends to go straight to London and not go to resort [Chequers] for a couple of days.' Although Hopkins did travel to Chequers to mollify the furious Prime Minister, Churchill replied pointedly: 'Certainly. Whatever you wish. We are always entirely at your disposal.'[68]

The ensuing three days of heated debate between the British and American chiefs of staff resulted in deadlock. The British were staggered by the Americans' impracticality: essentially administrators and planners, neither Marshall nor Eisenhower had ever directed a battle in their lives or even had any combat experience. As Mark Stoler writes: 'The fact that Marshall had not even begun to think about what to do after the landings took place only strengthened

[Field Marshal Alan] Brooke's belief that the plan was merely a political ploy and the American chief of staff a strategic fool.'[69]

Frustrated, and telling Marshall 'I am damned depressed,' Hopkins was desperate that any major action in 1942 *must* happen in Europe and aid the Russians, even at the sacrifice of British and American lives. On the other hand, Roosevelt was keen that American troops were seen in action *somewhere* before the end of the year, and although he preferred the European operation he would compromise on the alternative of the North Africa operation.

Eventually, Roosevelt as Commander-in-Chief overruled his own Chiefs of Staff, and the Americans agreed to join the British in the invasion of North Africa, Operation Torch.[70] However, as usual Britain had to pay a price: although Torch would have a joint US–British staff, Eisenhower was to be its Supreme Commander. Cave Brown comments, 'it marked the beginning of the end of Britain's domination of the strategy of the war – and her position as a first-rank world power.'[71] Worse was to come.

Although at the time Churchill was naturally gratified to have triumphed over the Americans, he later told Sir Robert Boothby that judged by the long-term political consequences, 'I am not sure I shall be held to have done very well.'[72]

The bulldog and the bear

As Stalin would be unhappy that the Second Front had been abandoned, on 3 August the Prime Minister flew to Moscow for three days to try to convince him of the benefits of the North Africa invasion, after a week in Cairo lambasting his generals about their inability to beat Rommel. He travelled with Cadogan and Field Marshal Brooke, and was also accompanied by Averell Harriman, representing Roosevelt. (Harriman flew with de Gaulle as far as Egypt – the first time Churchill had allowed the Frenchman to leave Britain for nearly a year.)

Almost immediately after arriving, the Prime Minister was vigorously selling Torch to Stalin, who merely accused the British and Americans of being unwilling to take risks. But when Churchill mentioned he planned to step up the bombing of Germany, especially with American help, as Harriman reported to Roosevelt:

> Here came the first agreement between the two men. Stalin took over the argument himself and said that homes as well as factories should be destroyed. The Prime Minister agreed that civil morale was a military objective, but the bombing of working men's houses came as a by-product of near-misses on factories. The tension began to ease and a certain understanding of common purpose began to grow. Between the two of them, they soon had destroyed most of the important industrial cities of Germany.[73]

The ice broken, Churchill then concentrated on Torch, making his celebrated sketch of a crocodile, declaring that he aimed to control North Africa by the end of the year and use it as a base to strike at the 'soft underbelly' of Axis Europe – its weakest points, Italy and Vichy France. Suddenly, Stalin smiled. He even blessed the idea with a most un-Bolshevik, 'May God help this enterprise to succeed.'[74] Unfortunately, on subsequent days he returned to Britain and America's 'broken promise' over the Second Front. At one point, he sneered: 'You British are afraid of fighting. You should not think that the Germans are supermen. You will have to fight sooner or later. You cannot win a war without fighting.'[75] The British leader exploded, reminding Stalin in no uncertain terms who had been an Ally of the Nazis for two years while Britain stood alone.

During their six-hour, vodka-fuelled farewell meal, when Churchill brought up the subject of the kulaks, Stalin admitted that 10 million had died, adding chillingly: 'But we had to do it to mechanise our agriculture. In the end, production from the land was doubled. What is one generation?'[76] But on that last day – 15 August – Churchill was also persuaded to promise that a Second Front would be opened in France during 1943. Meanwhile, just to make sure, Stalin tried to sabotage the North Africa operation and the entire Western strategy. While preparations for Torch were underway in Britain and America, the Soviet Ambassasor to London, Ivan Maisky, brazenly told two reporters about the North Africa operation – almost certainly on Stalin's orders.[77]

Dieppe: a royal cock-up?

When Churchill broke his return journey at Cairo, he received yet more terrible news: the disaster of the Dieppe Raid of 19 August 1942, the controversial operation that remains one of the Second World War's most enduring mysteries, largely because of the fog of secrecy that still shrouds it.

Operation Jubilee aimed to land troops along a ten-mile stretch of the French coast, over 200 warships and landing craft, with fighter cover, carrying across the Channel a force of 5,000 Canadians, 950 British commandos and a token presence of 50 US Rangers – the first American troops to see action in Europe. (Before Dieppe was known to be a debacle, American headlines bragged: 'Yanks in 9-hour Raid on Nazis' and 'US and British Invade France'. When the truth dawned about the fiasco, the raid suddenly became a foreign affair.[78]) Of the 5,000 soldiers who made it to the beaches, 900 were killed and 3,700 captured or wounded. Only 1,400 returned. The RAF lost over 100 aircraft, and a number of brand-new Churchill tanks were left behind – a gift to German intelligence. The Germans lost only 300 dead, with a similar number wounded.

The recriminations still rumble on, although it is now generally agreed that the culprit was its inexperienced, inept and glory-obsessed commander, Lord Louis Mountbatten. In refusing to acknowledge the obvious obstacles 'he permitted himself to be driven by the ageless forces of hunger for power and prestige'.[79] Undoubtedly, a cover-up rapidly buried certain facts about the raid, but was it simply to salve the reputation of the well-connected Mountbatten? As David Reynolds puts it: 'Dieppe was more a cock-up than a conspiracy. But it was such a costly cock-up that it required a major conspiracy to conceal it.'[80]

But the controversy over who was responsible for the 'cock-up' conceals a more central puzzle: what was Jubilee intended to achieve – even if had been successful? When the grim cable reached the Prime Minister in Cairo, stating, 'It is certain that casualties have been heavy and that generally speaking objectives were not attained', he replied: 'Consider it wise to describe Jubilee as quote reconnaissance in force unquote.'[81] At least this confirms that Jubilee was *not* intended for reconnaissance. Nor was it an invasion: dropped leaflets warned the locals, 'This is a raid and not the invasion', advising them not to do anything that would bring German reprisals.[82] Clearly, this was a hit-and-run affair; the troops would not be staying.

The usual explanation is that the raid was intended to test the German defences in order to gather data for future invasion plans. But if the raid was successful, wouldn't the Germans simply strengthen them, putting the Allies back where they started? From the outset, there were rumours that there was more to the disaster than just staggering incompetence: had spies in Britain tipped off the Germans, who simply lay in wait? A later version was that the operation had been *deliberately* leaked by British intelligence to establish the credibility of one of their double agents.

Anthony Cave Brown argues that Jubilee was a deception of another kind – carefully stage-managed for Roosevelt and Stalin's benefit, as evidence of British willingness to open a Second Front while at the same time demonstrating its impossibility.[83] (In fact, Eisenhower's grandson agreed that the British used the raid to make the point that Sledgehammer was impossible.[84]) Indeed, the deceptions and diversions that always accompany such operations were absent in Jubilee – suggesting it was a diversion itself.[85] And Jubilee was a revived version of Operation Rutter, the purpose of which had been, in part, to demonstrate to Stalin that his Western Allies were doing something to relieve his forces.[86]

However, Jubilee was not necessarily *meant* to fail so tragically: a successful hit-and-run raid would have placated Roosevelt and Stalin. But when Mountbatten made it a debacle, the fact that so many lives had been thrown away on what was essentially political posturing could never be admitted.

Warming up to Torch

Back in London, there was even more bad news. Because of the approaching elections, Roosevelt now wanted the North African landings to be an American-only affair. Marshall announced to Eisenhower in London: 'The President pictures the landing of some 80,000 men in the two assault convoys and thinks such a number would be necessary to his political purposes.'[87] Roosevelt also proposed making landings at only two sites, rather than the original three.

On his return from Moscow on 25 August 1942, Churchill invited Eisenhower and his deputy, Major-General Mark Clark, to dinner to discuss Torch. As the President had yet to authorise them to inform the Prime Minister that no British would take part, the embarrassed Americans squirmed throughout the long meal while their cigar-waving host waxed lyrical about it.[88]

Learning of Roosevelt's plan the next day, an over-wrought Churchill and his Chiefs of Staff's flurry of transatlantic cables resulted in an urgent Anglo-American conference at which the three-centre landing plan was restored, but on a smaller scale. And, even though Britain was to supply 40 per cent of the troops and nearly all of the warships, it was to be presented to the world as primarily an *American* operation. Churchill cabled Roosevelt: 'In the whole of TORCH, military and political, I consider myself your Lieutenant asking only to put my viewpoint plainly before you . . . This is an American enterprise, in which we are your help mates.'[89] It may have stuck in his throat, but the alternative was to risk Roosevelt cancelling the entire operation.

Although a successful Torch would certainly redress some of the previous year's humiliations, it would also present another problem – as this was French territory, exactly who would represent France? Whoever it was would, in all likelihood, also assume power when France was liberated. Roosevelt and Churchill agreed from the outset not to involve the egregious loose cannon de Gaulle or even inform him in advance, although the Prime Minister wanted to let him in on the secret the day before the landings, but FDR refused even that.[90] Their favoured candidate was General Henri-Honoré Giraud, a prisoner of war who had courageously escaped from Germany and made his way to Vichy France. Although Hitler had demanded his return, Giraud was eventually allowed to stay after signing a pledge of loyalty to Pétain. But as Roosevelt's representative in French North Africa, Robert Murphy, reported he was held in great esteem by the anti-Vichyites in North Africa – if they could get him there, he would do very nicely.

Lighting the touch paper

November 1942 was the major turning point of the war, with the British victory at El Alamein, the Anglo-American invasion of North Africa and the beginning of the Soviet counter-offensive at Stalingrad that resulted in the surrender of the German Sixth Army within two months.

After a week of sand-blasted and bloody fighting, Montgomery took El Alamein on 2 November: as George VI wrote in his diary, 'A victory at last'.[91] So great was the relief that Churchill allowed church bells to be rung throughout Britain – the first time since June 1940. Six days later came Torch, a huge armada of over 1,500 ships carrying 90,000 men, assembled in Britain and the USA and transported to its target, astonishingly without detection. The cover story – it was for an offensive in Norway – worked: the Germans were completely taken by surprise. It was the last thing they had expected the Allies to do, proving the wisdom of Churchill's strategy.

However, although the operation was presented to the victory-hungry Allies as a sudden success, it was the climax of diplomatic deals going back for months, without which – as this was the American troops' first taste of combat – there is little doubt Torch would have even eclipsed all the earlier disasters of 1942.

One of the main reasons for the delicate diplomacy was that as Roosevelt continued to recognise Pétain's regime as the legitimate government of France, essentially the US was about to fire on a *friend*. It was therefore important that the French authorities in Algeria and Morocco be seen to welcome the 'invaders'. Even after the landings, the President was keen to maintain good relations with Vichy: in fact, it was Vichy that broke off diplomatic relations with Washington as a result of Torch, not the other way round.

Robert Murphy had been busy preparing for a deal that would mean the Allies would be *invited* into French North Africa, cultivating key individuals and working with anti-Vichy conspirators in contact with General Giraud in France. A parallel campaign run by SOE and later the OSS had ensured that small resistance bands – the Corps Francs d'Afrique – were ready to rise up when the Allied offensive began.

It was a complex plan for a complex situation, juggling two

conflicting groups of colonial French – military and civil leaders, who were widely regarded as collaborators by the resistance groups, coming out in support of the Allies, while the resistance fighters took over essential facilities. A central figure in Murphy's game plan was General Alphonse Juin, commander-in-chief of French forces in North Africa, who had indicated he would order his men not to resist the Americans.

But less than three weeks before Torch, there was another twist. Murphy received feelers from none other than Admiral Darlan, vice-Premier of Vichy and commander-in-chief of all its armed forces. Recognising signs of an impending Allied invasion, Darlan announced his willingness to move his base to North Africa and side with the Allies. Although reviled in Britain, America and among the Free French as the arch-collaborator – Darlan had positively welcomed Vichy's cooperation with the Nazis – securing a deal with him appealed to Murphy. To him, the perfect solution for stable North African colonies would be Darlan and Giraud sharing power – keeping both sides happy. (Of course, given their antagonism, it was more likely to make both sides deeply *un*happy.)

In the days before Torch, General Clark came ashore from a submarine on the Algerian coast for a meeting with General Charles Mast, a chief of staff and Giraud supporter, and a British submarine picked up Giraud from France and took him to Gibraltar.

Suddenly, Darlan appeared in North Africa on an inspection tour. Worse, two days before Torch he installed himself in Algiers, the main seat of power in French North Africa. (Although an extraordinary coincidence, he had a legitimate reason for being there – his son was seriously ill with polio in an Algiers hospital.)

Torch began in the early hours of 8 November with Americans landing at Casablanca in French Morocco and Algiers and Oran in Algeria, the British being kept back as reinforcements. As the resistance groups seized key buildings, opposition was light, and although 1,400 American and 700 French troops died, it could have been a good deal worse.

In Algiers, Murphy asked General Juin to order his forces not to resist as promised, but the latter explained that as Darlan had seniority, and he was now in town, *he* would have to give the order.

Murphy made the same request of the Admiral, who wanted to see which way things went before committing himself. It was a curious scenario. An American invasion was happening – yet the French leader was locked in negotiations with the President's representative. Later in the day, Darlan agreed to a ceasefire, but only in Algiers. As fighting continued in the rest of the colonies, Generals Clark and Giraud arrived in Algiers for negotiations. Finally, on 10 November, Darlan ordered all Vichy forces in North Africa to lay down their arms. Torch was a success.

However, Darlan declared: 'I assume authority over North Africa in the name of the Marshal [Pétain]'.[92] But in Vichy itself, Pétain repudiated the ceasefire and ordered French forces to fight off the invasion, also – for the first time – asking for German military assistance, resulting in the Luftwaffe landing at Tunisian airfields. Pétain broke off diplomatic relations with the US, but his time had run out: uncertain about the trustworthiness of its leaders, on 11 November Hitler ordered the occupation of Vichy France.

Hitler also ordered the seizure of the French fleet (still a substantial force, but in accordance with the German armistice, it had never seen action). But when the Germans arrived at the dockyard they were met with resistance, and, honouring a pledge Darlan had made to Churchill in June 1940 that the fleet would never fall into German hands, its commander, Admiral de La Borde, had the ships scuttled. (This was neatly ironic, considering Mers-el-Kébir was proof that Churchill had no faith in Darlan's word.)

There was now the problem of who would control French North Africa. Although the Americans wielded the power, for appearance's sake, a Frenchman would have to be figurehead. Roosevelt cabled Churchill:

> In regard to de Gaulle, I have hitherto enjoyed a quiet satisfaction in leaving him in your hands – apparently I have now acquired a similar problem in brother Giraud. I wholly agree that we must prevent rivalry between the French émigré factions and I have no objection to a de Gaulle emissary visiting KINGPIN [Giraud's codename] in Algiers. We must remember that there is also a cat fight in progress between

KINGPIN and Darlan, each claiming full military command
of French forces in North and West Africa. The principal
thought to be driven home to all three of these prima donnas
is that the situation is today solely in the military field and that
any decision by any one of them, or by all of them, is subject
to review and approval of Eisenhower.[93]

As the difficult de Gaulle was out of the question, and the Allies'
favoured candidate, Giraud, did not enjoy the anticipated support of
the leaders in North Africa, they were left with Darlan. On 13
November 1942, Roosevelt approved Eisenhower's request that
Darlan was to be recognised as the head of government of French
North Africa, with Giraud Supreme Commander of its armed forces.
The decision sent a wave of revulsion through Britain and America,
not to mention the Free French and resistance groups in North
Africa: the Allies were now welcoming the infamous collaborator into
the fold. Would the same apply in other occupied countries – would
Quisling, for example, be allowed to retain power in Norway?

Churchill, too, was deeply unhappy about Darlan's position,
although – having agreed to be America's 'help mate' – he had no
voice in the decision. But he did cable Roosevelt on 16 November:

I ought to let you know that very deep currents of feeling are
stirred up by the arrangement with Darlan. The more I reflect
upon it the more convinced I become that it can only be a
temporary expedient, justifiable solely by the stress of battle.
We must not overlook the serious political injury which may
be done to our cause, not only in France but throughout
Europe, by the feeling that we are ready to make terms with
Quislings.[94]

In fact, in the weeks following the American landings, Darlan
steadily increased his power base, retaining the Vichy administration,
including its rabid new anti-Jewish laws.

So why did Roosevelt choose Darlan? He claimed that there was
simply nobody else to control the colonies, although writing to
Eisenhower – drafted by Hopkins: 'We do not trust Darlan . . . it is

impossible to keep a collaborator of Hitler and one whom we believe to be a Fascist in civil power any longer than is absolutely necessary.'[95] And on 17 November, the President told a press conference that Darlan's dramatic promotion was a 'temporary expedient'.

However, despite these pronouncements Roosevelt sought closer relations with him, flying Darlan's son to America for treatment at his own polio centre at Warm Springs. Darlan, for his part, made it known to General Clark that he considered 'temporary' to mean 'until the liberation of France', and was not told otherwise. Indeed, a month later Admiral Leahy – the former Ambassador to Vichy, now Roosevelt's Chief of Staff – told Field Marshal Dill that Darlan would remain in power 'at least to the end of the war in Europe'.[96]

It seems that keeping Darlan in power suited Roosevelt's long-term plans, as the journalist Anthony Verrier writes:

> . . . Roosevelt is on record as favouring dismemberment of the French Empire; reducing the size of Metropolitan France; denying it membership of the United Nations or any role in a peace settlement and the post-war occupation of Germany. In order to attain these objectives, a complaisant Frenchman had to be found, who would be offered political leadership, of a kind, in post-war France. Darlan filled the bill.[97]

With Vichy's collapse there was a growing feeling in the US that 'an alternative French Government be recognised as existing in Algiers'.[98] If Darlan and his administration could be passed off as the legitimate French government-in-exile, then when France was liberated Darlan would probably be in charge.

However, the problem was solved on Christmas Eve, 1942, when Darlan was shot in his office in the Palais d'Été by a young member of the Corps Francs d'Afrique – SOE-trained Fernand Bonnier de la Chapelle. Shot twice in the stomach, Darlan died in hospital two hours later. (On Giraud's orders, after a summary trial Bonnier de la Chapelle was executed the next day.)

Although the assassination is often portrayed as a local anti-Vichy plot, Anthony Verrier persuasively argues that it was an SOE and

Free French operation. De Gaulle despatched General François d'Astier de la Vigerie to Algiers, whom SOE supplied with $38,000 to organise the killing, on the strict condition that there must be no comebacks on either the British or Free French – being particularly anxious to prevent the Americans from finding out that their Allies were responsible.[99]

Pierre Raynaud, a colleague of Bonnier's in the Corps Francs d'Afrique (who subsequently joined SOE in London), who spoke to the assassin just before his mission, told us that Bonnier said the plan had been worked out by an army padre, the Abbé Cordier, who briefed him – together with Algiers Chief of Police Henri d'Astier de la Vigerie, the General's brother.

Darlan's death was certainly good news for Churchill, sick of constantly tiptoeing on eggshells with Roosevelt, not to mention colleagues appalled by FDR's pro-Darlan policy. Sir Alexander Cadogan echoed the general feeling when he wrote in his diary, 'We shall do no good till we've killed Darlan.'[100] Although Darlan was universally loathed in Britain, his appointment had also revealed a deeply disturbing trend in the Americans' long-term ambitions.

Whether Churchill authorised the killing remains unknown. SOE was quite capable of dispatching him on its own initiative. The Prime Minister wrote that Darlan's assassination 'relieved the Allies of their embarrassment at working with him',[101] but refused to condone it. At the time, only Roosevelt denounced the collaborator's death as 'murder in the first degree'.[102] Certainly, his killing was extremely significant, for not only was it an attempt to change the French factions' balance of power but also relations between Britain and America.

Although Torch and El Alamein combined to turn the tide, speaking on 10 November, the leader who had promised only 'blood, sweat, toil and tears' growled: 'This is not the end. It is not even the beginning of the end. But it is, perhaps, the end of the beginning.'

CHAPTER TEN

Death by Unconditional Surrender

'Je vous liquiderai.'

Winston S. Churchill to
General de Gaulle, January 1943[1]

Eager to exploit Operation Torch, Roosevelt and Churchill hastened to their next summit – 'Symbol' – at Anfa, Casablanca, from 14 to 25 January 1943. Although Roosevelt wanted Stalin to attend, the latter cancelled because the siege of Stalingrad was reaching its desperate culmination. FDR also considered inviting Chiang Kai-shek, another of his 'Four Policemen', but it was decided his involvement would compromise Stalin's neutral status with Japan. Of course, Harry Hopkins was acting as 'the de facto Secretary of State'.[2] Indeed, Roosevelt had chosen to leave his official Secretary of State, Cordell Hull, at home.

Good news filtered in from all fronts. On 18 January, the Soviets broke through the German encirclement of Leningrad. Montgomery pushed on to take the Libyan capital, Tripoli, five days later. The Japanese retreated in New Guinea, while the six-month struggle over the strategically important island of Guadalcanal was drawing to a close, with 30,000 Japanese dead, against 7,000 of the joint US–Australian force.

Although the US Chiefs still favoured a cross-Channel invasion (now Operation Overlord), even they could hardly fault the wisdom of Churchill's 'closing the ring' strategy – first North Africa, then the 'soft underbelly' of Italy, southern France and the Balkans. The Combined Chiefs of Staff decided that Italy was the best option – a successful campaign would remove it from the war and also tie down the Germans. They planned the invasion of Sicily, eventually mounted in July as Operation Husky.

Because of Darlan's prevarication over a ceasefire, the intended swift follow-on from Torch into Tunisia had been held up, giving Pétain's German reinforcements time to dig in. It would take time to dislodge the 17,000 Axis troops on the ground in Tunisia, and their Luftwaffe back-up. Instead of sweeping through to link up with Montgomery, the Allies would not control the whole of North Africa until May: only then could Husky swing into operation.

The US commanders saw the wisdom of weakening Germany first, and as the U-boats were still hampering their build-up in Britain they decided to concentrate on winning the Battle of the Atlantic before making firm plans for the invasion of France.

Total war, total surrender

However, Roosevelt sensationally declared at the 24 January press conference that the war would end only with the '*unconditional surrender* by Germany, Italy and Japan' – and the 'destruction of the philosophies' [political ideologies] of their regimes. This unwillingness to negotiate, rapidly becoming an obsession with the President, was to have major repercussions on the fate of millions. As Robert Nisbet points out, unconditional surrender: '. . . inevitably tends to lengthen a war and is a monumental discouragement to resistance groups working inside the enemy's lines.'[3] Roosevelt was effectively telling Hitler, Mussolini and General Tojo that there was no point in suing for peace. So why was he so insistent, to the point of actually *foisting* it on his British Allies?

The answer lies in what the two countries wanted from the war. Ideally, Britain wanted everything to go back to how it had been in 1939, with its Empire restored to pole position, but as it was becoming increasingly apparent that this was impossible it would have to be content with clinging on to as much as it could. In that sense, Britain was fighting *against* something, but not *for* anything. Roosevelt, on the other hand, was very much fighting *for* a more powerful, recession-free America, that would dominate world trade. Unconditional surrender gave him the golden opportunity to bring in his dream new world order.

At the time, the idea seemed spontaneous – it certainly came as a surprise to Churchill. However, the day before it was announced, Hopkins told the Sultan of Morocco's Grand Vizier that 'the war will be pursued until Germany, Italy and Japan agree to unconditional surrender.'[4] But how could the Americans expect the British simply to acquiesce with such a far-reaching demand, especially without being consulted first?

In fact, the concept had first been mooted in the spring of the previous year, by one of the President's security committees. The idea was to avoid the problems caused by having to negotiate a settlement with the defeated nation.[5] Unconditional surrender would preclude negotiations or territorial settlements, allowing the Allies to do as they wished with their defeated enemies. It appealed to Roosevelt because it allowed him to exploit victory to implement his wider vision for the world. The enemy nations could be occupied and effectively disabled, while the victors would finally become 'world policemen'.

In fact, Roosevelt had even wanted to call Morocco the 'unconditional surrender conference' – the first step to peace on the basis of disarmament and peacekeeping by the major powers. George McJimsey writes: '. . . unconditional surrender would buy time for the United States to establish its world leadership. As usual, whenever he found himself in a group of friends and allies, Roosevelt was all for equality, as long as he called the shots.'[6] However, 'buying time' meant prolonging the war. If Roosevelt had genuinely sought ways to end the suffering swiftly, demanding unconditional surrender made no sense. But with eyes on the future, it made perfect sense.

Victor Cavendish-Bentinck told Sir Alexander Cadogan that, when he heard of the unconditional surrender demand, he thought both leaders had drunk too much Moroccan wine. And in 1984 he declared it had made the Germans fight harder.[7] So why did Churchill agree to it? On 15 January 1944, he wrote to the War Cabinet:

> The expression 'Unconditional Surrender' was used by the President at Casablanca without previous consultation but I thought it right to endorse what he said, and it may be that at that period of the war the declaration was appropriate to the circumstances.[8]

In July 1949, when Churchill was again grilled by the House of Commons, he admitted that Roosevelt had simply announced it without any consultation and explained that, while he knew that the Cabinet would reject it: 'I was there on the spot and I had rapidly to consider whether our condition in the world justified me in not giving support to him.'[9]

Prolonging the war by demanding unconditional surrender was exactly what Roosevelt wanted – as it meant that the war would end with America in the position he wanted, and not before. The demand removed any incentive for the Nazis or Japanese to seek terms, and also Hitler and his henchmen knew that they had no option but to fight to the finish, taking millions with them into the apocalypse. More importantly, since the Allies refused to negotiate under any circumstances – or with any government – it was a massive disincentive to the anti-Hitler groups to risk a coup. The military strategist Basil Liddell Hart states baldly: 'but for the unconditional surrender policy, both they [the German generals] and their troops would have yielded sooner, either separately or collectively'.[10] The anti-Hitler factions in Germany were frankly incredulous, Canaris calling it a 'calamitous mistake'.[11] Indeed, in *Great Mistakes of the War* (1950), Hanson W. Baldwin makes the important point:

> The doctrine of Casablanca was in direct contradiction to the assurances given by the British government in public speeches and private conversations in 1939–40 that a Germany which had rid itself of Hitler and his associates would be an acceptable basis for peace talks.[12]

De Gaulle versus Giraud

Casablanca also saw the continuing struggle for power within – and over – the Fighting French (as the former Free French, the pro-Ally French forces and those liberated from Vichy territories were now called). Who would Roosevelt and Churchill recognise as the true leader of France (and effectively anoint as the post-war head of government) in the wake of Darlan's assassination? Churchill had already backed de Gaulle, while the President now reverted to General Giraud.

Roosevelt's plan was that, in the short term, the US would effectively govern the liberated North African territories, with the civil and military leaders in a subordinate role, and to make separate leadership deals for individual French territories as they fell under Allied control.[13] (This was opposed by Churchill and the American military chiefs.)

Perhaps most importantly, Roosevelt considered that France was no longer in the first rank of nations, and therefore undeserving of any special consideration – and never one of his 'world policemen'. Although the President never made any secret of his deep dislike for de Gaulle, both personally and politically, recently released papers reveal the depth of *Churchill's* antipathy towards the Frenchman, certainly in 1943. The Prime Minister had initially empathised with him as a fellow 'man of destiny', and refused to accept Roosevelt's dismissal of France as an also-ran. But de Gaulle's potential to damage the Alliance was seriously trying his patience.

The other major question that divided Roosevelt and Churchill was the Fighting French's role in the Alliance, particularly in the liberation of France. FDR thought that the liberation should be left to the Americans and British, which hardly endeared him to de Gaulle. Although Churchill fully understood de Gaulle's fierce desire to lead the liberation of his homeland, for the sake of the wider picture once again he acquiesced to Roosevelt.

It was a messy situation. At the beginning of 1943, Giraud (Roosevelt's man) replaced Darlan in French North Africa, as both civilian and military leader, while de Gaulle (Churchill's man) headed the French National Committee in London, also controlling the West and Central African colonies (besides enjoying the support of the resistance in France itself). De Gaulle made overtures to Giraud to find a political settlement: when, on American orders, Giraud refused even to meet him, de Gaulle made the offer public, cannily making Giraud look like the unreasonable one (which indeed he was). This outraged the Americans, who believed de Gaulle was mischief-making against them (which indeed he was).[14]

There was an obvious compromise, Roosevelt telling Churchill, 'We'll call Giraud the bridegroom, and I'll produce him from Algiers, and you get the bride, de Gaulle, down from London, and we'll have a shotgun wedding.'[15] Giraud was duly flown in from Algiers.

De Gaulle – who knew nothing about the conference – received an invitation from Churchill on the third day, promising that if he flew to Morocco, he (Churchill) would arrange the meeting with Giraud. Deeply offended by this flagrant foreign interference, de Gaulle refused to go. Churchill pointed out that the invitation also came from the President of the United States, adding that a refusal to attend might jeopardise de Gaulle's position as leader of the French National Committee. Although de Gaulle again refused, the Committee in London insisted he went.

This was de Gaulle's first meeting with Roosevelt. The President was taken aback but privately amused when de Gaulle announced solemnly, 'I am the Joan of Arc of today'.[16] De Gaulle wrote: '. . . beneath his patrician mask of courtesy, Roosevelt looked at me without goodwill'[17] – indeed, they soon developed a profound mutual loathing. Roosevelt saw de Gaulle as obstinate, dictatorial and comically convinced of his own inflated importance – and that of what FDR considered a second-rate country. De Gaulle saw the President as manipulative and devious, writing, '. . . it was difficult to contradict this artist, this seducer . . . '[18]

De Gaulle was particularly incensed when he discovered that when Roosevelt had outlined his 'world policemen' idea to Molotov, he had stated that because the 'Big Four' (USA, UK, USSR and China) would have a monopoly on military power in the post-war world, France would not even be allowed to have an army.[19]

All attempts to persuade or force de Gaulle and Giraud to come to an accommodation failed, the great obstacle being the role of former Vichyites in the government of the expatriate French: Giraud was already working with them in Algiers and Morocco, but de Gaulle refused to deal with 'traitors'. Roosevelt's and Churchill's proposal for the two generals to take joint presidency of a French National Committee of *all* elements stood no chance. The atmosphere was so explosive that Churchill hissed to de Gaulle: '*Si vous m'obstaclerez, je vous liquiderai!*' ('If you get in my way, I'll liquidate you!')[20] The opposing French leaders were eventually persuaded to issue a joint declaration, but it was simply a statement of desire for French liberation.

Liquidating de Gaulle

There were now two mutually hostile groups of 'fighting French', the de Gaulle and Giraud factions. But Roosevelt's problem was that de Gaulle was much more popular, not only among the French but also in America and Britain. And while Churchill had turned against de Gaulle to placate Roosevelt, with the exception of Anthony Eden the rest of the Cabinet continued to support him. The 'Giraud-versus-de Gaulle' tussle was already threatening the Alliance, particularly because of its implications for the coming liberation of France. But there was worse. Special Branch informed the Foreign Office about an extraordinary speech de Gaulle allegedly made to certain Fighting French officers on his return from Casablanca:

> I have now become a political man and as a politician I am frequently obliged to say the exact opposite of what I actually think and feel; thus when speaking on the BBC, I pretend to be a good friend of Britain in order to create a good impression abroad and keep going the resistance in France. You all remember how, when you joined me, you were told by my Secret Service that England was no friend of ours and that England, like Germany, is our hereditary enemy. This you must always keep in mind. Russia will undoubtedly win the war in the field, so I am obliged to keep on good terms with that country. I am not a communist myself, however, but it is a question of diplomacy. When I am in power in France after the war, I shall ask Russia for time to re-organise without her intervention. Russia will agree to this as she needs a strong

France to balance the power in Europe. I shall then have accomplished what Hitler failed to do – become master of Europe.[21]

Did de Gaulle really say this? As the Foreign Office admitted, the Special Branch only got it second hand, and it certainly has the ring of mischief-making by a rival attempting to discredit him by making him out as the ringleader of a conspiracy against Britain, while seeking to take control of France. On the other hand, de Gaulle had certainly spoken to his entourage about trying to forge an alliance with Stalin and his preference for reconciliation with Germany over any alliance with 'the Anglo-Saxons'. He also believed the next war would be between Europe and America (bracketing Britain with the latter).[22]

Was de Gaulle as an Ally more trouble than he was worth? At the end of February, when he formally requested permission to visit Africa, Churchill snarled to Eden: 'I presume it is quite clearly settled he is not to be allowed to go and that force if necessary will be used to restrain him.' On 10 March, Eden confirmed that MI5 was watching all ports and airports in case de Gaulle tried to leave the country – and was tapping his telephone. The memo confirmed that the American Embassy had also been informed, in case de Gaulle tried to use them to leave the country. The last thing Churchill wanted was for de Gaulle to be 'loose in the world'.[23]

Matters were even worse by the time of the Trident Conference in Washington in May, when Churchill faced immense pressure from Roosevelt over de Gaulle's intransigence. The Prime Minister even asked the Cabinet to consider whether the Frenchman should be 'eliminated as a political force'.[24] Terms such as 'liquidate' and 'eliminate' may be open to radical interpretations, but the most extreme was apparently reinforced in Cadogan's diary: 'Attlee also told Cabinet of telegrams that are coming in from Winston about de G. Former (under American pressure) wants to execute latter.'[25]

In fact, there *is* evidence of an attempt on de Gaulle's life during this nervy period. In 1967, a letter appeared in the *Daily Telegraph* from one William Bonaparte-Wyse, a wartime aide to the Commander-in-Chief of the Fighting French Navy, claiming that on

21 April 1943 an aircraft in which de Gaulle and his staff – including Bonaparte-Wyse himself – were travelling from RAF Heston near London to Glasgow had been aborted on take-off due to mechanical failure. According to Bonaparte-Wyse, 'A few moments later, the General's ADC, very white in the face, told me that an attempt at sabotage had been made.'[26]

Intrigued, controversial author David Irving contacted the RAF, who denied any such incident had taken place. However, besides interviewing Bonaparte-Wyse, Irving interviewed the retired captain, Flight Lieutenant Peter Loat, who confirmed that during the run-up to take-off, the elevator flaps failed to respond and the aircraft was unable to lift off. Had this happened later in the flight, there would have been an historic tragedy. Loat and a maintenance engineer found that the elevator's control rod had been eaten through by what looked like acid. There was a secret RAF investigation, to which Loat gave evidence, and he was told subsequently that the acid-sabotage conclusion had been confirmed. (The ADC mentioned by Bonaparte-Wyse denied saying it was sabotage. De Gaulle himself claimed to have no memory of the event at all – but it is significant that afterwards he would only travel by road or rail in Britain.)[27]

So what – or who – was behind this suspicious episode? What was not widely known in 1967 was the depth of antipathy towards de Gaulle, and his perceived danger to the Anglo-American alliance. A fatal accident would have been good news to some – but who had the most pressing motive for wanting him out of the way? Clearly, the list must include pro-Giraud factions, pro-Churchill elements within covert organisations such as SOE, and similar American organisations such as OSS. The Nazis would not be obvious suspects, enjoying the damage the de Gaulle–Giraud schism was inflicting on the Allies. As for the Soviets, at that stage they probably had no strong feelings one way or the other, although Stalin later backed de Gaulle.

Gomorrah

The Casablanca Conference had approved the Combined Bomber Offensive, in which the RAF and USAAF would destroy German industry and infrastructure: another part of Churchill's grand strategy with which to wear down Germany ready for the liberation of the occupied territories and the final assault on the 'German citadel'.

Although the first of the massive thousand-bomber raids, on Cologne, had happened on 30 May 1942, with others on the Ruhr and Bremen in June, they were largely trial runs, organised by the new head of Bomber Command, Air Chief Marshal Sir Arthur 'Bomber' Harris, to convince sceptics of the potential of such heavy raids.

The Combined Chiefs of Staff issued the 'Casablanca Directive' on 21 January 1943, stating that their objectives were 'the progressive destruction and dislocation of the German military, industrial and economic system, and the undermining of the morale of the German people to a point where their capacity for armed resistance is fatally weakened'.[28] The first daylight raid on Berlin – timed to coincide with the Nazis' tenth anniversary in power – took place nine days later.

Already with a reputation for ruthlessness – after his indiscriminate bombing of villages in Iraq in the 1920s – Harris had been appointed Commander-in-Chief of RAF Bomber Command in February 1942. He was a fervent believer in area or saturation bombing – blitzing civilians – rather than targeting specifics such as factories and military bases. He had also concluded that Germany and Italy could be brought to their knees by bombing alone, without sending in troops – clearly why Churchill chose him for the job. The second part of the Casablanca Directive – the breaking of German morale – was Harris's top priority.

Although the Directive was modified in June – Luftwaffe bases had to be bombed before Overlord could be safely launched – and a month later terror bombing was *officially* dropped, it obviously remained in Harris's mind. As Churchill wrote to the Combined Chiefs of Staff in March 1945: 'It seems to me that the moment has come when the question of the bombing of German cities simply for the sake of increasing the terror, though under other pretexts, should be reviewed.'[29]

After four nights of bombardment – Operation Gomorrah – on 27 July Hamburg became one vast inferno as hurricane-force winds from air sucked into the centre of the conflagration spat flames thousands of feet into the sky. The RAF continued to pound

Hamburg for another week, leaving over 40,000 civilians dead – approximately the same as the *total* of British civilians killed by the Luftwaffe during the Blitz of late 1940/early 1941.[30] Then, in November 1943, Harris launched a five-month campaign to 'wreck Berlin from end to end',[31] resulting in the annihilation of over five square miles of the city centre, leaving over 6,000 blackened corpses and 1.5 million homeless.

British and American attitudes to the bombing differed markedly, particularly during 1943. Harris's RAF favoured morale-sapping area blitzing, while the USAAF concentrated on the precision bombing of factories, oil installations and so on.[32] This largely reflected the conflicting strategies of the two leaders: Churchill aimed to destroy Germany's economy and urban centres, hopefully precluding the need for a large-scale invasion, while the Americans – still set on a grand assault on Germany – were concentrating on weakening the military infrastructure that would otherwise be pitted against them.

Turning points

By spring 1943, the tide had turned. Only a monumental Allied cock-up, or the advent of a new weapon, such as the atom bomb, on the other side, could prevent eventual victory. The major turning point was the fight for Stalingrad during the winter of 1942–3, the most costly battle in history. The day after the last Nazi besieger surrendered on 2 February 1943, an incandescent and incredulous Führer announced the end of the offensive that had begun with Barbarossa. The five-month Battle of Stalingrad had cost nearly a third of a million German lives, and of the 90,000 prisoners of war only 5,000 returned from the hell-camps after the war.[33]

It was not just the turning point of the war but also of the whole of European history, as Christopher Argyll notes:

> The immediate consequences of this change of fortune were the slow, but inexorable advance of the Soviet forces from Stalingrad to Hitler's Bunker in Berlin. But in the longer term it was to lead to the transformation of Eastern Europe into a bloc of satellite states and the brutal division of Germany itself into two separate republics.[34]

Hitler ordered a last throw of the dice – Operation Citadel – against Kursk in mid-July, but was heavily defeated, with 70,000 dead. From then on, the Red Army began its inexorable advance on Germany – a trail of butchery and mass rape – although the Germans fought them every inch of the way.

Another major breakthrough was the Western Allies' victory of the Battle of the Atlantic. Casablanca had made it a priority: without a safe passage across the Atlantic, preparations for the invasion of France were being hampered. Victory was achieved by the middle of 1943 by breaking the German codes and by a vast shipbuilding programme in the US. Faced with mounting losses, on 24 May 1943 Admiral Karl Dönitz suspended U-boat attacks on the convoys: the Allies now controlled the Atlantic.

The German resistance

As the tide turned, the fundamental difference in Roosevelt's and Churchill's attitude to the enemy began to make a serious impact. Churchill was out to defeat the Nazi regime, and was not averse to a deal with a non-Nazi government; his plan was to foster German implosion in order to turn the people against the Nazis, a plan which should have prompted him to encourage internal plots against Hitler. But Roosevelt believed German militarism was the problem, and so bracketed the anti-Hitler conspirators with the Nazis. His imposition of unconditional surrender adroitly spiked Churchill's guns.

As Germany stared defeat in the face, its countrymen began to turn against their Führer. In mid-February 1943, an anti-Nazi demonstration by students in Munich spiralled out of control – and unrest spread to other cities in Germany and Austria.[35] But faced with the prospect of unconditional surrender, what chance did the protesters stand?

Paradoxically, it was only when Germany began to lose that the anti-Hitler conspirators felt strong again. After Torch and Stalingrad, not only were the psychological conditions right for opposition, but their ranks were being swelled by panic-stricken officers. As American spymaster Allen Dulles – in contact with the German conspirators – wrote: 'The battle of Stalingrad, one great turning point of the war, revealed to all but the most fanatical Nazis the absurdity of Hitler's military leadership.'[36]

The effects of FDR's intransigence were soon manifested: in March 1943, Canaris proposed a face-to-face meeting with Menzies at a castle on the Spanish–Portuguese border to discuss the assassination of Hitler and the ending of the war, but although the MI6 chief wanted to accept, the British government had no wish to antagonise Roosevelt.[37]

If the conspirators were to overthrow Hitler and sue for peace, it was important to know what terms the Allies would accept. During 1942, Carl Friedrich Goerdeler had made contact in Sweden with bankers Jacob and Marcus Wallenberg, who had business interests in both Britain and Germany – and who were in contact with Menzies. Goerdeler asked them to establish what terms the Allies would accept if the conspirators assassinated Hitler. Neither Churchill nor Roosevelt had any wish to be bound to a settlement with Germany: the conspirators could ask for terms only *after* they had killed Hitler and removed the Nazis from power.[38] Significantly, it was after these approaches that Roosevelt pushed through his unconditional surrender policy at Casablanca.

Naturally, FDR knew about the Schwarze Kapelle and other anti-Hitler groups, largely through Allen Dulles, who records what Jacob Wallenberg said after he met Goerdeler in February 1943:

> He [Goerdeler] said the decision of the Casablanca Conference for unconditional surrender made his work with the German militarists more difficult since some of the military insisted that if the German forces had to capitulate, they wanted Hitler to bear the responsibility for it.[39]

In May 1943, Goerdeler returned to Stockholm and asked Marcus Wallenberg to contact the British government again for a list of terms that would be acceptable to the post-Hitler regime. Although Wallenberg complied, it was now Allied policy that there could never be any conditions.[40] This was introduced at a time when the anti-Hitler conspirators were adopting a tougher stance. Careful plans were made for Hitler's assassination – Operation Flash – and for wresting control from the Nazis.

Canaris concealed the plan for the takeover of Germany by cunningly suggesting to Hitler that a contingency was needed in case of civil unrest by the four million 'guest' (slave) workers in the country. Hitler authorised the setting up of Operation Valkyrie, in place by October 1942. At the codeword 'Valkyrie', martial law would be imposed, army commanders moving swiftly to 'protect' Nazi institutions.[41]

Still believing that if they got rid of Hitler *surely* Roosevelt and Churchill would negotiate, on 13 March 1943 the conspirators made their first attempt on his life. Canaris arranged for a bomb disguised as a parcel to be on Hitler's plane when he visited the Eastern Front, using British plastic explosives captured from the SOE in France. When the bomb exploded, the codeword 'Flash' would trigger 'Valkyrie', while agents in neutral countries would approach the British and Americans to negotiate a settlement. However, the acid fuse froze at the high altitude, and Hitler's curiously charmed life continued.[42]

The opposition in Italy was also being ignored. This is even harder to understand, as Mussolini was considerably less secure than Hitler, being under such intense pressure that he was virtually unable to govern. Richard Lamb summarises the contradictions:

> In 1941 Churchill was willing to go to great lengths to encourage the anti-Fascists in Italy to end the war – including bribing the Italian fleet to surrender, and offering a non-Fascist Italy a colony in Cyrenaica [part of Libya]. Yet in 1943, when Italy was down and out, no gesture was made by the Allies to the anti-Fascists and monarchists plotting to overthrow Mussolini, and thus a chance was missed to occupy Italy with Allied forces before the Germans poured over the Brenner Pass. This extraordinary and illogical *volte-face* towards the Italian Resistance inside Italy was extremely costly.[43]

Like most war historians, Lamb explains this as a blunder: neither Roosevelt nor Churchill had properly thought through the consequences of demanding unconditional surrender. But surely the likes of Dulles would have pointed them out? A much more plausible, though perhaps unpalatable, conclusion is that the whole *point* was to prevent deals with German and Italian resistance groups ending the war too soon for Roosevelt's long-term plans.

The Big Three

On 12 May 1943, Churchill and Roosevelt's two-week summit 'Trident' took place in Washington (during which 'source 19' informed Moscow about the deliberations over the Second Front). The deferring of Overlord for a year was Trident's major outcome. The taming of Tunisia meant that Husky, the invasion of Sicily, could finally go ahead. To the bafflement of the British Chiefs of Staff, the US army chiefs continued to advocate storming northern France, but reluctantly agreed to wait for another year.[44]

Indeed, although the principle of Husky had been agreed at Casablanca, in April Eisenhower formally asked Churchill to agree to a postponement of the Sicilian invasion, on the grounds that the German presence there – two divisions – was too formidable. Churchill observed that this was odd, as Eisenhower seemed desperate for the Allies to cross the Channel, against far worse odds. A further sign of Eisenhower's eagerness is that he told Churchill that Montgomery agreed with him – which turned out to be completely untrue.[45]

The Prime Minister was pleased at Overlord's postponement, because in the mean time his Mediterranean strategy would be followed, and if successful Overlord might even be cancelled. However, Stalin was furious – worse, reports appeared in the Swedish press, echoed in OSS intelligence, of secret negotiations between German and Russian representatives in Stockholm.[46] Whether these stories were true or deliberately planted is unknown, but of course the OSS was heavily infiltrated by Soviet intelligence.

There is a curious incident mentioned, almost in passing, by Liddell Hart in *History of the Second World War* (1970):

> In June [1943], Molotov met von Ribbentrop at Kirovograd,
> which was then within the German lines, for a discussion

about the possibilities of ending the war. According to German officers who attended as technical advisers, von Ribbentrop proposed as a condition of peace that Russia's future frontier should run along the Dnieper, while Molotov would not consider anything less than the restoration of her original frontier; the discussion became hung up on the difficulty of bridging such a gap, and was broken off after a report that it had leaked out to the Western Powers.[47]

Despite its implications, this story has received surprisingly little attention. If Stalin and Molotov were prepared to discuss terms with Germany while the Western Allies refused to consider conditions at any price, it would be the perfect example of the unequal partnership within the 'Grand Alliance'. But perhaps Liddell Hart is simply perpetuating misinformation put out by Moscow in 1943 – or maybe the talks actually took place but the Russians *intended* them to leak in order to put pressure on their Allies.

To coincide with the conference, Stalin began to make concessions to his Western Allies, clearly hoping that they would relent about the Second Front. On 15 May, he unexpectedly announced the dissolution of the Comintern, and publicly acknowledged for the first time that Russia was benefiting from Western aid – although the Soviet people remained ignorant of this for decades – and agreed to a meeting with the other Allies later that year.[48]

'Marplot and mischief-maker'

Most of Trident's wrangling centred on the problem of de Gaulle – to the frustration of both President and Prime Minister. But just as Churchill realised he had to get rid of him, de Gaulle himself managed to outmanoeuvre both of the despised 'Anglo-Saxons'.

As Churchill headed for Washington on 4 May, de Gaulle made a speech in which he not only denounced the North African settlement but also roundly criticised Giraud, undoubtedly to provoke Roosevelt – and it worked. During the conference, FDR bombarded Churchill with notes complaining about de Gaulle's 'well nigh intolerable . . . continued machinations'.[49] This led Churchill to '. . . ask my colleagues to consider urgently whether we should not now eliminate de Gaulle as a political force . . . When we consider the absolutely vital interest which we have in preserving good relations with the United States, it seems to me most questionable that we should allow this marplot and mischief-maker to continue the harm he is doing.'[50]

But although Churchill had to oppose de Gaulle in order to placate Roosevelt, the Prime Minister's writings also reveal real personal animosity. Unfortunately for him, the Cabinet were on de Gaulle's side, as can be seen from their acerbic reply to him in Washington:

> We suspect that Murphy is becoming impressed by the evidence of rising Gaullism in North Africa which must be reaching him and that he prefers to ascribe this to Gaullist propaganda rather than admit that he was as wrong about Gaullist strength in North Africa as he was about anti-British feeling there.[51]

De Gaulle also had the support of the French resistance, which demanded during Trident that he be appointed head of a provisional government in Algiers while remaining their leader. This prompted Giraud to invite de Gaulle to Algiers to discuss the sharing of power. (Giraud's change of heart may also be partly explained by his discovery that his daughter and grandchildren had been captured in Tunisia and transported to Germany.) Churchill was somewhat mollified when he heard about Giraud's offer of a way out of the mess.

On 30 May 1943, de Gaulle arrived in Algiers – where, to his surprise, he found Churchill, hot-foot from Trident and eager to get Husky moving. After three days, when de Gaulle and Giraud agreed to be joint Presidents of the new French Committee of National Liberation, Churchill cabled Roosevelt with his approval. The composition of the committee would weaken de Gaulle's position – or so they thought. Just days afterwards, when a dispute broke out – most of the committee wanted Giraud to lead the Fighting French – de Gaulle resigned, knowing that the clamour for him to return would strengthen his position. It worked: the committee suddenly had a clear Gaullist majority. Roosevelt and Churchill were apoplectic.

In June, Roosevelt stressed to Churchill that de Gaulle must *not* run the French military, but although the Prime Minister agreed, once again the Cabinet backed de Gaulle. On the same day, Hopkins drafted a new directive for Eisenhower:

> The position of this government is that during the military occupation of North Africa we will not tolerate the control of the French Army by any agency which is not subject to the Allied commander's direction . . . without your full approval no individual civil decision can be made.[52]

But it was too late. On Bastille Day 1943, de Gaulle defiantly addressed the crowd in Algiers:

> Certain people look upon the action of our armies independently of the will and the sentiment of the great mass of our people. They imagine that our soldiers, sailors and aviators of the world, go into battle without caring about the reasons for which they risk death. These theoreticians, claiming to be realists, believe that for France and for Frenchmen alone a nation's war effort can exist apart from national policy and national morale. We declare to these realists that they know nothing of reality.[53]

On 1 August, de Gaulle became President of the French Committee of National Liberation, with Giraud as Commander-in-Chief. At Quebec later that month, Roosevelt and Churchill finally agreed to recognise the Committee's authority over any territories that acknowledged it themselves. Britain also recognised the Committee's responsibility for the French war effort, although the US government pointedly refused to acknowledge it as the provisional government of France.[54] Within six months, when Giraud's job had been subsumed by de Gaulle, 'No one . . . appeared sorry, or even noticed, that he had departed.'[55]

The Sikorski mystery

The discovery of the 4,000 decomposing corpses of Polish officers in

Death by Unconditional Surrender

Katyń Forest precipitated a crisis. When it was announced by Radio Berlin on 13 April 1943, the Kremlin dismissed it as propaganda, and when Sikorski's Polish government-in-exile called for a Red Cross investigation, Stalin simply broke off diplomatic relations with them.

Although Roosevelt authorised a fact-finding mission, even when presented with overwhelming evidence of Russian culpability by his own investigator, once again he closed his ears, saying, 'this is entirely German propaganda and a German plot. I am absolutely convinced the Russians did not do this'.[56] Clearly, Stalin and his regime could do no wrong, no matter how much evidence was stacked against them.

On 4 July 1943, Sikorski 'conveniently' died when his Liberator bomber crashed into the sea shortly after take-off from Gibraltar, while returning from a six-week tour of Polish forces, including Anders' Army, in the Middle East. Although officially an accident, like de Gaulle, the Polish leader had become too hot to handle for the Grand Alliance. Frustratingly, the case for conspiracy has now become indelibly linked with the controversial author of *Accident* (1967), David Irving, all of whose work is automatically dismissed after a sensational 2000 court case. Unfortunately, the baby thrown out with the bathwater is the genuine mystery of Sikorski's death. Less scandalous writers have also smelt a rat: Christopher Argyll, in *Chronology of World War II* (1980), writes that Sikorski was killed 'when his Liberator aircraft mysteriously crashed'.[57]

The plane plummeted into 30-foot-deep sea within seconds of lifting off from the airstrip at Gibraltar, killing 16, including Sikorski and his daughter Zofia Lesniowska. The Czech pilot, Flight Lieutenant Edward Prchal, was the sole survivor. The RAF investigation established that the Liberator crashed because the elevator controls jammed, preventing the aircraft from gaining height, but was unable to ascertain what had caused the jam, concluding that the accident was 'due to the aircraft becoming uncontrollable for reasons which cannot be established'.[58] Bizarrely, the RAF still categorically stated that there was 'no question of sabotage'.[59] But the Polish government-in-exile's review of the inquiry concluded it was impossible to rule out sabotage.[60] In the United States, there was even less doubt. Sumner Welles publicly declared it was 'assassination',[61] based on the uncertain circumstances – and the fact something similar had happened to Sikorski before.

In Canada in November 1942, both engines of his Lockheed Hudson had cut out, forcing an emergency landing, although everybody escaped unhurt. Apparently, the double engine failure was due to the severing of the fuel supply. (Unusually, the pilot had test-fired the engines twice before take-off rather than just once, which saved them.) Although the British investigators originally blamed this on mechanical fault, Sikorski was to write to his deputy:

> The American authorities, and later the British authorities, submitted a theory of German sabotage in regard to the Montreal air accident we know about. Investigations conducted have revealed evidence of this. Please tell Minister [of Information] Stronski to keep the news of this accident a close secret.[62]

In 1967, the play *Soldiers* by the left-wing German playwright Rolf Hochhuth argued sensationally that Sikorski had been murdered on Churchill's orders, claiming his information came from a former member of British intelligence. The ensuing outcry about the attack on the great war-hero's reputation, only two years after his death, even prompted parliamentary questions and led to a flurry of litigation. The furore attracted David Irving to the mystery (who, far from presenting a sensational conspiracy theory, reached an 'open verdict').

Backed by the Churchill family, Edward Prchal (who in the play was party to the murder) sued Hochhuth for libel. Sir Winston's son Randolph sponsored *The Assassination of Winston Churchill* (1969) by Carlos Thompson, in an effort to refute both Hochhuth and Irving, itself the subject of action by Irving and consequently withdrawn. In case it might be asked to release official records to a court, Harold Wilson's government ordered a review of the case (presumably to discover whether it had something to hide – before hiding it).

The Cabinet Office report, only released to the Public Record Office in the 1990s, while clearing Churchill of any involvement, makes some decidedly odd statements, such as: 'The possibility of Sikorski's murder by the British is excluded from this paper. The possibility of his murder by persons unknown cannot be so excluded.'[63] (In other words, we can't say for sure it wasn't murder, but if it was we didn't do it.)

The report discovered that security at the Gibraltar airfield was ludicrously – even implausibly – lax. Witnesses testified that Sikorski's plane remained unguarded during its 24-hour stay, and it was even possible to board it without being challenged. Even more intriguingly, Soviet Ambassador Ivan Maisky's plane had been parked next to Sikorski's for four hours. But even a Russian could only have sabotaged Sikorski's plane in collusion with someone on the British side who had the authority to arrange these events. As the journalist John Coates of *The Times* pointed out in a 2003 article on the 60th anniversary of the crash, in 1943 the head of MI6's counter-intelligence section covering Spain, Portugal and Gibraltar was the Soviet agent Kim Philby.

The inquiry also established that a couple of years previously a Soviet defector had claimed the NKVD was responsible for Sikorski's assassination, but the report warned that even in the 1960s this information was so sensitive that 'no mention of it should be made publicly'.[64]

While the Russians had most to gain from Sikorski's death, the Germans had the least, as the disunity he was causing among the 'United Nations' suited them perfectly: indeed, in order to create mischief among the Allies, in April Himmler had even suggested offering him safe passage to inspect Katyń Forest, but von Ribbentrop vetoed the idea.[65]

Although Sikorski's widow, Madame Helena Sikorska, always believed the Russians were responsible, the fact that his death would satisfy Stalin also gives his British and American Allies a motive for wanting him out of the way. Of course, the British obfuscation about the crash does not necessarily indicate *their* guilt. Evidence of Russian involvement would also have created a terrible dilemma for Churchill. To even *allege* that Stalin had Sikorski killed would have meant the end of the Grand Alliance and totally wrecked its strategy for winning the war. The Prime Minister would have had no option but to remain silent (and, ironically, posthumously be accused of being behind it himself).

Friendly Fire

Oddly, Churchill made no mention of Sikorski's death in his memoirs, suggesting it made him profoundly uncomfortable, which is even odder given his initial reaction to the tragedy – he *wept*.[66] On the day of Sikorski's funeral, 10 July 1943, the Prime Minister said in his broadcast eulogy to Poles everywhere:

> I mourn with you the tragic loss of your Prime Minister and Commander-in-Chief, General Sikorski. I knew him well. He was a statesman, a soldier, a comrade, an ally, and above all a Pole. He is gone, but if he were at my side I think he would wish me to say this – and I say it from my heart: soldiers must die, but by their death they nourish the nation which gave them birth.[67]

Sikorski's death made life much smoother for the Big Three: as events proved, his removal weakened the Free Polish government. Neither his successor Stanisław Mikołajczyk as Prime Minister nor General Kazimierz Sosnkowski as Commander-in-Chief (Sikorski had held both offices) approached the same political stature, and they clashed on policy. Significantly, Mikołajczyk took a much more conciliatory line with Moscow than Sikorski.[68]

But even if the Alliance killed Sikorski, why then? Was it simply a vulnerable moment, when he was away from British soil? However, perhaps *he* wasn't their intended victim at all . . . Also on board was Britain's liaison with the Free Poles, the MP Major Victor Cazalet, who had accompanied Sikorski on his visit to Moscow the previous year, privately circulating a book on his experiences, *With Sikorski to Russia*. Cazalet had become a great devotee to the Polish cause, and – while full of admiration for front-line Russians – had been so appalled by the Soviet system he was fearful for Poland's future.

Researching *The Assassination of Winston Churchill*, Carlos Thompson interviewed General Anders' ADC, Prince Eugene Lubomirski, who said significantly:

> In Cairo, the day before he flew to London, via Gibraltar, accompanying General Sikorski, I sat with Colonel Victor Cazalet in his room in the Shepherd's Hotel. He had just spent

two weeks in Teheran, gathering secret material that proved Soviet bad faith and their unreliability as so-called Allies. I remember being glad to hear him say this, because it was what General Anders and all of us had been trying to get across to the British – in fact, we were constantly frustrated in this, because we were not allowed to write or say any of that publicly, so as not to alienate Soviet friendship. As I was about to say Goodbye, Cazalet pointed to a bulky leather case, almost as big as a valise, and said to me: 'In that suitcase which I am taking back to London, I have enough material indicting Russia to keep the House of Commons busy for the rest of the year![69]

The Prince remarked that as soon as he heard of the crash he thought of that suitcase.

Interestingly, Irving writes after interviewing one of the divers who recovered the bodies, Lieutenant William Bailey (the other, interestingly, being the famed Lionel 'Buster' Crabbe):

> On the surface, Bailey saw a launch flying the Governor's flag come out to meet them, and in it he recognised the stooping figure of [Governor-General of Gibraltar, Lieutenant General Sir Frank] Mason-Macfarlane . . . Macfarlane asked who was in charge of the diving, and what they were looking for. Bailey replied that he was planning to concentrate on bringing up the bodies. The Governor told him to carry on, but that one vital thing he would like Bailey's men to look for was any kind of portfolio or briefcase.
>
> Bailey found a black leather pouch on one of his next dives, and this was sent up. It appears to have been the vital portfolio that the Governor was looking for, because he was not asked to search again.[70]

Was the portfolio the same as Lubomirski's 'leather case'?

Although Anders' Army had informed the British and American governments about the Soviet camps, the latter had kept quiet in the interests of the Alliance. But if ordinary MPs or Congressmen – not to mention the press – discovered the truth about the gulags, that would spell the end of the alliance with the Soviet Union. A crusading spirit like Cazalet would have ensured that the whole world knew, and presumably Sikorski knew of his research – and approved. As the Middle Eastern tour was probably cover for gathering evidence on Stalin's crimes, it would have been imperative that those documents did not reach London.

Unconditional in Italy

Six days after Sikorski's death, Anglo-American forces under Field Marshal Montgomery and Lieutenant-General George S. Patton began the first strike at the 'soft underbelly' of Axis Europe. By the middle of August, Sicily was under an Allied Military Government of Occupied Territories.

Although Churchill anticipated it would be the end for Mussolini, even he must have been surprised at the speedy fall of his one-time hero, after 20 years in power. Since the beginning of the year, Il Duce's leadership had been under mounting pressure from rivals and the Italian people, and for some time Allied agents in Switzerland had been in contact with the anti-Mussolini faction in Italy. During May and June 1943, they established contact with his opponents, including Marshal Pietro Badoglio. The conspirators wanted to negotiate terms in advance of Mussolini's fall, allowing the immediate occupation of Italy, but as one of the British intermediaries, Air Commodore 'Freddie' West, told Richard Lamb, the doctrine of unconditional surrender 'gravely handicapped' their work, quoting one of his colleagues, SOE's John McCaffery: 'The Italians want a peace but they are a proud nation and will not accept *umiliazione* [humiliation]. I am *cento per cento* [hundred per cent] sure that unconditional surrender will wreck our plans.'[71] And so it did.

On 25 July 1943 – 15 days after the first Allied landings in Sicily – the 'palace coup' went ahead, but independently from the Allies, without any agreement about what would happen next. Under pressure from the Fascist Grand Council, Mussolini resigned, and King Victor Emmanuel ordered his arrest. Marshal Badoglio succeeded him and the Fascist Party was dissolved. (In September, Il Duce would be sensationally rescued from the mountain-top castle of

Death by Unconditional Surrender

Gran Sasso in the Apennines by Otto Skorzeny's commandos in gliders sent by Hitler, to set up a Fascist republic in the German-occupied north of Italy.) But the Foreign Office's reaction says it all:

> It is pretty evident that fascism is being liquidated and that the army plus the House of Savoy is making a desperate effort to put itself in a position in which it can obtain what it considers to be 'reasonable terms of surrender' for Italy. But it is equally plain that neither the King nor the army would consider 'our own terms reasonable'.[72]

Churchill was at the Quadrant Conference in Quebec when the Italians' request for terms reached London. But as Anthony Eden simply repeated the mantra 'unconditional surrender', Churchill reminded him sharply: 'Do not miss the bus, and merely harping on unconditional surrender with no prospect of mercy may well lead to no surrender at all.' To which Eden replied: 'I quite understand you wish to sugar the pill for the Badoglio Government [but] . . . I feel that having stated so categorically in public we insist on unconditional surrender we are bound to tell Badoglio's emissary we will require this.'[73]

Lamb sums up the mess caused by the Allies' intransigence:

> The Americans, the Prime Minister and the Foreign Secretary went on arguing about the details of the surrender document, but would not alter the term 'unconditional surrender'. As a result Eisenhower was unable in August to concert plans with Badoglio to land Allied troops in Italy before the Germans were in a position to oppose them. Not until 26 August did Washington send Eisenhower the surrender terms which he was authorized to sign with Italy, and then only because of British insistence.[74]

Because of the danger of a German invasion if Hitler discovered their willingness to surrender, the Italians had to negotiate clandestinely, inevitably delaying the process. For the same reason, speed should have been of the essence for the Allies. Yet it took a month to conclude a deal, while fighting continued in Sicily and air raids smashed Italian cities. Even then it happened in a rush because the first landings on mainland Italy were scheduled: but when the British Eighth Army and the US Fifth Army landed at Salerno on 9 September they faced opposition not only from the Nazis but also the Italians – due entirely to Roosevelt's refusal even to consider terms.

The President and Churchill authorised Eisenhower to sign the 'short terms' of an armistice on 3 September – with Stalin's permission to sign them on his behalf – and a secret negotiating team went to Rome to conclude the full unconditional surrender. Announced on 8 September, it was already too late. On the same day, the Germans (who had tripled their strength in Italy under the excuse of aiding the Italians) took control of strategic locations and disarmed the Italian Army. Although the fatal delay was as much the Italians' fault as the Allies', once again thousands of lives would have been saved if Roosevelt had not insisted on his inflexible dogma.

The battle for mainland Italy would drag on until 1945. Even though it had surrendered, Italy still had to be fought for. This and later disasters are generally ascribed to the Allies being stuck with the policy of unconditional surrender – although we might well suspect that this was no accident. For Roosevelt's endgame to work, the war must not end too soon.

CHAPTER ELEVEN

In Stalin's Pocket

'Harry Hopkins always went to the root of the matter.'
Winston S. Churchill, 1950[1]

The chaos surrounding the Italian surrender had given the Germans the chance to dig in and turned the Allied offensive, moving up from the toe and heel of the Italian 'boot', into a long and costly slog. Hitler had ordered every inch of ground to be contested, and four bitter battles were fought at the mountain-top fortress of Monte Cassino – part of his new defences south of Rome, the Gustav Line – between January and May 1944: the first cost 16,000 Allied casualties for an advance of just seven miles.

These battles were truly collaborative: although under the command of General Clark, the first assault was by the French Expeditionary Corps under General Juin, the second by the Second New Zealand division, the third by the Fourth Indian Division, while Anders' Polish Corps finally took the monastery, at enormous cost, on 17 May. British and Canadian troops also played their part. But as the Allies died, the British and American governments argued over whether they should continue to fight in Italy or abandon it – in favour of Operation Overlord.

A rock and a hard place

Now they were gaining ground, Churchill believed they should concentrate on Italy – even though the 'soft underbelly' was more impenetrable than anticipated. At the week-long Quadrant Conference in Quebec in August 1943, he recommended a revision of the cross-Channel invasion plan – while Harry Hopkins, yet again, kept pushing for Overlord to begin as soon as possible. In the end, they compromised: the invasion of Italy was to continue, but they would also go ahead with a scaled-down version of Overlord – 29 divisions, not 48 – on 1 May 1944. Although Churchill approved, Hopkins still worried that he might try to sabotage the plan later.[2]

The cross-Channel plan was originally meant to draw some of the fire aimed at the USSR, but after Stalingrad that was no longer so important. So why did the Americans – particularly Hopkins – still want to invade France? As there was now little chance of Germany giving in without fighting to the last gasp, the overriding question was which plan would get the Allies to Berlin the fastest? And as the Germans were collapsing in the east, *which* Ally would get to Berlin first – the Soviet Union or the Americans and British?

Churchill believed that not only was it essential to defeat Germany, but the Russians must also be kept as far east as possible, lessening their long-term threat to Europe and pre-empting the Allies' inevitable clash over post-war Poland. The Prime Minister envisaged pushing up through Italy, opening the way for the Western Allies to invade Austria and liberate Czechoslovakia or the Balkans – before the Red Army arrived.[3]

But did the Americans champion the cross-Channel alternative because they believed it would get them to Berlin first? Curiously, the evidence points the other way entirely: that they preferred Overlord – at least politically – because it would mean that the Western Allies would be *slower* in getting there, allowing the Russians to seize most of eastern Europe and even capture the German capital itself. Preposterous though this may seem, this was undoubtedly Roosevelt's and Hopkins' preferred choice once they smelt victory. It was a cornerstone of their post-war projections that Russia would inevitably emerge as the major Eurasian power, counter-balancing the United States. As Dwight Tuttle explains: '. . . Hopkins took the position that the Soviet Union was bound to control much of Eastern and Central Europe and that it was in America's interest to come to terms with this reality.'[4] However, to them this was not necessarily a bad thing. Under Hopkins' influence, the President actively *favoured* the Soviet Union holding the post-war balance of power in Europe. It became a self-fulfilling prophecy: because Hopkins believed Stalin would inevitably control certain parts of Europe, he did what he could to help him – even though it diametrically opposed Churchill's desire to keep the Russians *out* of those territories.

Roosevelt and Hopkins also realised it would be easier to persuade the Allies to agree to the post-war dismemberment of Germany if the Russians controlled a substantial chunk, and if the Americans were already in Europe.[5] The assault on Germany from east and west therefore had to be carefully choreographed so everyone ended up where Roosevelt and Hopkins wanted them to be – even if that meant slowing down the advance. We will see the extraordinary consequences of this in the last stages of the war.

But, again, the question is: did Hopkins persuade Roosevelt to adopt these policies because he believed they were in America's interest, or was he acting under orders from the Kremlin?

The real special relationship

In May, the President sent Joseph E. Davies (former Ambassador to the USSR) to Moscow to arrange a private meeting with Stalin. When Churchill protested, humiliated, using the grounds that German propaganda would make capital out of a meeting from which Britain was excluded, Roosevelt replied, 'I did not suggest to UJ [Uncle Joe] that we meet alone.'[6] He lied.

More strategic conferences took place in November and December 1943, in Cairo and Teheran – the latter being the first time that Churchill, Roosevelt and Stalin met, a moment FDR and Hopkins had long awaited. As Dwight Tuttle writes: 'At the Cairo and Teheran Conferences Hopkins was at the height of his influence.'[7] Roosevelt made it clear he preferred his advice to that of his Secretary of State, Cordell Hull – once again left behind in Washington.

The Cairo Conference, 'Sextant', took place in two blocks (23–26

November and 2–7 December 1943) separated by the Teheran Conference, 'Eureka'. Chiang Kai-shek was present in Cairo because the Japanese war was on the agenda – but as the USSR was not at war with Japan it was inappropriate for Stalin to attend.

In Cairo, Sir Charles Wilson recorded:

> Ran into Harry Hopkins, and found him full of sneers and jibes. He had just come from a meeting of the Combined Chiefs of Staff, who were framing a plan of campaign to put before Stalin at Teheran. According to Harry, Winston hardly stopped talking, and most of it was about 'his bloody Italian war' . . .
>
> Harry made it clear that if the PM takes this line at Teheran and tries again to postpone OVERLORD the Americans will support the Russians.[8]

But it was the Teheran Conference that not only brought about Hopkins' final victory on that score, but also fundamentally changed the course of history. It was here that Roosevelt and Stalin ganged up – there is no other description – on Churchill, pronouncing that Normandy was to be the Allies' focus, even diverting support troops from Italy. Mark Stoler writes: 'For the first time the British were outvoted and overwhelmed by their more powerful Soviet and US allies, who in effect struck a global strategic bargain at the expense of London's indirect approach.'[9]

Roosevelt would deliver the long-awaited invasion of France, with Stalin supporting with a big push from the east. Ironically, the 1942 situation was now reversed: Stalin finally got his 'Second Front' by promising an offensive in the east to draw German forces off. Clearly, he wanted to forestall the threat to his plans for Eastern Europe posed by the Italian campaign. In return for his help, Stalin also undertook to declare war on Japan once Germany was defeated. All his dreams were fulfilled – because of Roosevelt's support. As Robert Nisbet observes: 'At Tehran, FDR played essentially the role Chamberlain had at Munich.'[10]

The outcome was apparent from the beginning. Travelling from Egypt to Iran, Hopkins told Sir Alexander Cadogan bluntly, 'You will find us lining up with the Russians.'[11] Also en route to Teheran, Churchill said to Harold Macmillan: 'Germany is finished, though it may take some time to clean up the mess. The real problem is Russia. I *can't* get the Americans to see it.'[12]

It was far worse than Churchill had anticipated, as Roosevelt's and Stalin's buddy act flagrantly undermined both him and the whole British delegation. After declining the Prime Minister's invitation to stay at the British Embassy, FDR elected to stay at the Soviet Embassy, after Molotov told him that the US legation was not secure and that German agents were plotting to assassinate him. Of course, the President's rooms were bugged.[13] But this arrangement also allowed Roosevelt to have three private meetings with Stalin, at which they agreed some of the major issues in advance of the official sessions. FDR refused Churchill's requests for one-to-one meetings.

When Roosevelt and Stalin discussed Poland's borders, the Russian demanded that they revert to the position defined in the Nazi–Soviet Pact. According to the official US minutes, Roosevelt responded that: 'when the Soviet armies reoccupied these areas, he did not intend to go to war with the Soviet Union on this point'.[14] (Poland could bleed once again without any chance of American first aid.) Although he stood by the Atlantic Charter's principle of a people's right to self-determination, he was sure the people of Poland and the Baltic states would vote to throw in their lot with the USSR. In that, at least, he was right: Stalin ensured that Poles loyal to the government-in-exile did not survive long enough to vote, or were too intimidated to dissent. And Roosevelt knew this.

The President was not only utterly indifferent to the fate of the European Poles, but as Michael Simpson writes: 'Roosevelt secured a delay on Poland until after the 1944 Presidential election, telling Stalin that he dared not face millions of Polish-American voters with an unfavorable agreement (thus implying that a favorable one was unlikely).'[15] He was prepared to sell the Poles (whom he had pushed into war) down the river while ensuring that the Polish Americans voted for him as a champion of freedom. (To a visitor at Hyde Park after the conference, Roosevelt said that he was 'sick and tired' of the Poles, adding: 'Yes, I really think those 1940 frontiers are as just as any.'[16])

Friendly Fire

Privately with Stalin, Roosevelt also pushed his 'Four Policemen' idea, in which France was conspicuous by its absence. In fact, he and Stalin agreed that France deserved *nothing* from the war, and should be stripped of its colonies.[17] FDR also told Stalin he would like to discuss India with him some time, astonishingly saying he preferred to see Indian reform 'somewhat on the Soviet line'.[18] It was just as well Churchill was not present.

Clearly, Roosevelt's main agenda was to ensure that the Soviet Union became the dominant power in Europe. The two leaders agreed that to prevent further German aggression, Germany should be hacked up into its original constituent states after the war. But FDR assured Stalin that France would also be reduced to a 'third-rate power'.[19] There would be nothing to stop the Soviet domination of Europe.

Teheran was a major humiliation for Churchill, not just politically but personally. Even in the official sessions, Roosevelt delighted in insulting the Prime Minister in front of Stalin – signalling that he and bluff Uncle Joe were new best friends.[20] At Stalin's banquet at the Soviet Embassy, Stalin openly taunted Churchill: '. . . in 1919 you were so keen to fight and now you don't seem to be at all. What happened? Is it advancing age? How many divisions do you have in contact with the enemy? What is happening to all those two million men in India?'[21]

During the serial vodka toasts, when Stalin proposed that at the end of the war 50,000 randomly selected German officers should be shot as a lesson to Germany, Churchill was appalled, declaring emphatically that no one, 'Nazi or no', should be dispatched without a proper trial. Pretending to compromise, Roosevelt facetiously proposed to reduce the number to 49,500. As Elliott Roosevelt recorded: 'Americans and Russians laughed. The British, taking their cue from their Prime Minister's mounting fury, sat quiet and straight-faced.'[22]

Although Field Marshal Brooke observed to Cadogan, 'Stalin has the President in his pocket',[23] Roosevelt gave in to him largely because he believed (or had been persuaded by Hopkins) that America would gain by it, preferring a Europe dominated by the USSR to the traditional supremacy of Germany and France.

Churchill had long realised that a weak Germany and France would open the door for the USSR to invade Western Europe. And when the Red Army arrived at the Channel, Britain would effectively find itself back where it was in 1940 – and this time with not even a promise of help from America.[24] He was in an odd frame of mind, telling Wilson, 'I believe man might destroy man and wipe out civilisation. Europe would be desolate and I may be held responsible.' He went on, 'Why do I plague my mind with these things? I never used to worry about anything.'[25] The physician wrote in his diary:

> I lay awake for a long time, frightened by his presentiment of evil. I own that I fear the days that lie ahead. Until he came here, the PM could not bring himself to believe that, face to face with Stalin, the democracies would take different courses. Now he sees he cannot rely on the President's support. What matters more, he realizes that the Russians see this too. It would be useless to take a firm line with Stalin. He will be able to do as he pleases. Will he become a menace to the free world, another Hitler? The PM is appalled by his own impotence.[26]

What Moran did not know was that behind Churchill's dark thoughts was the knowledge that American and British scientists were at that moment working on the ultimate killing machine – the atom bomb.

However, the immediate problems were far-reaching enough. As Dwight Tuttle writes: 'As a result of the conference, Stalin returned to Moscow with a free hand to reorganise Eastern Europe according to his design.'[27] Robert Nisbet puts it more succinctly: 'The Cold War began at the Teheran Conference at the end of November 1943.'[28]

To Russia with love

Throughout 1942 and 1943 Roosevelt had continued aiding the USSR unconditionally, telling Churchill: 'I think there is nothing more important than that Stalin feel that we mean to support him without qualification and at a great sacrifice.'[29] Hopkins followed the same line, in June 1942 promising a Russian Aid rally:

A second front? Yes, and if necessary, a third and a fourth
front . . . We are determined that nothing shall stop us from
sharing with you all that we have and are in this conflict, and
we look forward to sharing with you the fruits of victory and
peace.[30]

Even as late as February 1944, Roosevelt declared: 'We must . . .
continue to support the USSR by providing the maximum amount
of supplies which can be delivered to her ports. This is a matter of
paramount importance.'[31] Why? By that stage of the war, the German
eastern front had collapsed – and the Red Army was back in Poland.
In 1944, some in Roosevelt's administration – such as Marshall –
began to suggest they threaten to withdraw supplies to gain
concessions from the Soviets. After all, it had worked with Britain.
But Hopkins refused to consider putting similar pressure on the
Soviets – and Roosevelt backed him.

In August 1942, the US Ambassador in Moscow, Admiral William
H. Standley, was so appalled by the Soviet government's attitude to
Lend-Lease that he returned to Washington specifically to try to
persuade Roosevelt to change his policy of 'unconditional aid'. Yet
again, the President turned a blind eye. Standley was replaced by
Averell Harriman.[32]

When Harriman became Ambassador to the Soviet Union in
September 1943, he took with him Major-General John R. Deane as
head of the US Military Mission to Moscow, who liaised over Lend-
Lease. Deane's account, *The Strange Alliance* (1947), makes interesting
reading. He sums up his view:

I am convinced that the measure taken by the President [to
speed up Russian Lend-Lease] was one of the most important
decisions of the war and one that was vitally essential when it
was taken. However, it was the beginning of a policy of
appeasement of Russia from which we have never fully
recovered and from which we are still suffering.[33]

Deane cites several examples of how assistance to the USSR not only
deprived the Western Allies of much-needed equipment, but also

how the Russians refused to work as team-members, for the greater good of the Alliance. For example, Overlord's preparations suffered from a severe shortage of diesel engines for the landing craft, although the USSR had stockpiled far more than they could use. Deane was appalled to discover that although 75 were useless because of rust, the Russians had already ordered another 50![34]

One of Deane's major headaches was that although they were supposed to prove a genuine need for what they ordered, the Soviets would only shrug: if we didn't need it, we wouldn't have asked. In January 1944, Anastas Mikoyan, the Commissar of Foreign Trade in overall charge of the Soviet Purchasing Commission (coordinating Russian Lend-Lease), ordered more aluminium, copper wire and other metal products than previously agreed under the Lend-Lease protocols. These commodities were in short supply in the US, so the War Production Board asked Mikoyan to explain his need. As 'short supply' was one of the criteria the Americans used to wring trade concessions out of Britain, it is interesting that, as Deane relates:

> He [Mikoyan] . . . implied that his Purchasing Commission in Washington would have no trouble obtaining approval of the Russian requests regardless of what action I might take. The hell of it was, when I reflected on the attitude of the President, I was afraid he was right.

Deane recommended to the Chiefs of Staff that in future they insist that the Russians fully justify all requests for any items in short supply in the US. He continues:

> I received a reply from General Marshall within a few days approving the recommendations I had made and assuring me of his support in the matter in Washington. Unfortunately Harriman, in reply to a telegram he had sent along the same lines to Harry Hopkins, received what amounted to instructions to attach no strings to our aid to Russia. The Russians on this occasion, as Mikoyan had predicted, received the extra supplies they had requested.[35]

Friendly Fire

Deane comments that it was not until spring 1945 (when Truman came to office) that 'we put some backbone into our relations with the Soviet Union'.[36] He writes of Hopkins and Major-General James H. Burns, head of the Munitions Assignment Board:

> No one did more for the war effort than Harry Hopkins and few did more than Burns . . . With respect to Russian aid, however, I always felt that their mission was carried out with a zeal which approached fanaticism. Their enthusiasm became so ingrained that it could not be tempered when conditions indicated that a change of policy was desirable. In the early days of the program their attitude was not only understandable but essential . . . However, when the tide finally turned at Stalingrad and a Russian offensive started which ended only at Berlin, a new situation was created.[37]

However, contrary to Deane's statement – and what might be expected – both American and Russian historians agree that Lend-Lease made no substantial difference to the Soviet war effort until *after* Stalingrad – and was then cranked up in the last stages of the war. The official Soviet figures show that from the beginning of Barbarossa until the end of 1942 the West's contributions were not substantial.[38] Lydia V. Pozdeeva, Professor of History at the Russian Academy of Sciences, writes: '. . . the blunt fact is that the Lend-Lease Act made no substantial contribution to the victories of the Soviet armed forces at Moscow or Stalingrad.'[39] This echoes the conclusions of official US Army historians of the Second World War, Richard M. Leighton and Robert W. Coakley: 'The impact of US aid to the Soviet Union was as yet insignificant and played no role in the repulse of the German attack before Moscow.'[40]

In fact, it was only from the middle of 1943 – after the breakthroughs of Stalingrad and Kursk – that the supplies began to make a difference. Tellingly, Pozdeeva writes: 'The largest portion of supplies under the Lend-Lease Act was shipped during 1943–44. In other words, it arrived during the turning point in the war and the beginning of the offensive strategy of the Soviet armed forces.'[41] Of course, even after Stalingrad and Kursk, the Red Army still faced the hard, slow push to Germany, and military hardware needed to be replaced. But in that case, why was most of this aid *industrial* – plant and machinery, raw materials, chemicals and transport?

The more one looks at the data, the more obvious it becomes that the bulk of Lend-Lease provided from the beginning of 1944 was given with Russia's post-war needs in mind. Yet this was *illegal*: when Congress had approved the extension of Lend-Lease aid to the USSR, it had specifically stipulated that it was not to be used for post-war reconstruction.[42] The undeclared policy of the Roosevelt administration – set by Hopkins – was clearly to supply goods knowing full well they would be used to regenerate the post-war USSR, while hiding this from Congress.

The US was shipping not just vehicles and commodities, but entire *factories*. Hubert P. van Tuyll, author of *Feeding the Bear: American Aid to the Soviet Union* (1989), cites:

> The Persian Gulf Command transferred two entire truck plants (as well as a quantity of large truck cranes and railroad equipment) to the USSR near the end of the war: little of this material could have been in use before the German surrender. A Ford Motor Company tire plant designed to produce 1 million tires a year was shipped in October 1944 but apparently was not operational during the war.[43]

He also lists 'equipment for several petroleum refineries', power plants and steel mills. The total value of machine tools Roosevelt handed over to the USSR was $306 million, together with material for almost 8,000 miles of railway track and 2,000 locomotives.[44]

Britain's deal may seem better – receiving about 70 per cent of the total Lend-Lease – but it was mainly military supplies and food: the Soviet Union got over half the *industrial* aid, which of course would be useful after the war.[45] In fact, some 40 per cent of goods sent to the USSR via the Far East in 1944 were stockpiled specifically for post-war use.[46] Britain – in many areas one large bomb-site – was allowed to keep back nothing for post-war reconstruction.

The generally agreed figure of Russian Lend-Lease is between about $9 billion and $11 billion, depending on whether services are also taken into account. Writing in 1989, Van Tuyll estimated this as the equivalent of about $75 billion in modern terms.[47] But a huge amount of supplies simply went unrecorded, as Alan Milward writes in *War, Economy and Society* (1977): 'The exact composition of these deliveries has still not been established.'[48]

The Soviet Union also used Lend-Lease logistics as a cover for espionage and intelligence gathering – and the US government either failed to notice or simply didn't care. As W.R. Corson and R.T. Crowley write in their 1986 history of the KGB: 'Now that Congress had approved Lend-Lease, the Soviets could plunge headfirst into the American cornucopia of industrial know-how, an intelligence opportunity of rare and staggering dimensions.'[49]

On Beria's orders, in early 1943 the Lend-Lease Coordinating Group was replaced by the Soviet Purchasing Commission, led by General Leonid Rudenko, consisting of 1,000 'purchasing specialists' dealing with American industry and government departments – *all* of whom were NKVD or GRU agents. (Soviet citizens were forbidden to have contact with a Western country without NKVD supervision.) Incredibly, 1,000 Russian spies were being welcomed into the US and given virtually unhindered access to any factory or military facility, as Corson and Crowley explain:

> Their mission was to buy anything and everything thought necessary to win the Great Patriotic War. Along the way they were to collect, borrow, or steal anything they could carry. As a collateral duty, the Soviet 'buyers' were to bribe and attempt the subornation of any interesting, influential, or powerful American with whom they came into contact. To suggest that this omnivorous approach to intelligence collection was ineffective is to fail to comprehend the scale on which it was carried out. Industrial processes, entire turnkey refineries, strategic raw materials, scientific instruments, radio-manufacturing plants, glass, steel, natural rubber, and thousands of designs, drawings, patents and proprietary secrets sluiced out to the USSR by air and sea. In addition, garnering detailed maps of the United States and aerial photographs of major cities (hardly useful against the

Germans), plus 'inspection' visits to aircraft, tank and weapons manufacturing facilities, rounded out a busy schedule for Rudenko's battalions of foragers.[50]

A senior figure on the American side, Major General Follette Bradley, told the *New York Times* in 1951:

> Of my own personal knowledge I know that beginning early in 1942 Russian civilian and military agents were in our country in huge numbers. They were free to move about without restraint or check and in order to visit our arsenals, depots, factories and proving grounds they had only to make known their desires. Their authorized visits to military establishments numbered in the thousands.
>
> I also personally know that scores of Russians were permitted to enter American territory in 1942 without visa [*sic*]. I believe that over the war years this number was augmented at least by hundreds.[51]

Possibly many more entered the US, particularly through the 'Alsib' (Alaska–Siberia) route – to be discussed below – as the American end had no customs or immigration checks. In any case, even those airfields were largely controlled by Soviet officials.

In bed with the Russians

Although even before the war Roosevelt's administration was riddled with Soviet spies and agents, the alliance with the USSR exacerbated the problem – aided by the US government's naive belief that if they kept their side of the bargain the Russians would keep theirs. Unbelievably, when the OSS acquired an all-important NKVD codebook in 1944, not only did Laughlin Currie, the White House administrator on the NKVD payroll, inform Moscow but when they complained to (newly promoted) Secretary of State Edward Stettinius, he actually ordered Donovan to return it . . .[52]

While neither Western Ally had a single agent in Moscow at the end of the war, the Russians had a great many in Washington and London, working to secure the most advantageous position in what would become the Cold War.[53] And the door was held open for them by Hopkins and Roosevelt. The extent of the damage caused by this extraordinary series of events remains unknown, so much having been swept under the carpet after the war by an astounded Truman administration.

As we have seen, two Soviet agents on Roosevelt's team were particularly influential – the 'number one sources' in the State and Treasury Departments – Alger Hiss and Harry Dexter White. Although identified as agents during Roosevelt's presidency, he not only ignored the allegations but allowed them to further their careers – and play crucial roles in creating the post-war world. (But *if* Hopkins were an agent, in terms of sheer status and power he would eclipse both of them.)

A State Department representative at the Yalta Conference in 1945, which decided on the shape of post-war Europe, Hiss also chaired the 50-nation committee that drew up the United Nations Charter – even becoming its first, albeit temporary, Secretary-General. White was the creator and first Executive Director of the International Monetary Fund and the World Bank. Both are now acknowledged to have been Soviet agents – yet surprisingly little is made of such a massive scandal.

Serving just under four of his five-year sentence for perjury, Hiss maintained his innocence until his death in 1996, insisting he was a loyal and patriotic American. Some believed him, suggesting that he was framed by J. Edgar Hoover, and pointing out that the sole evidence against him was the word of 'turned' Soviet agents. However, in 1993, documents from the 1950s were unearthed in the archives of the Hungarian Interior Ministry on the debriefing of another Communist agent, Noel Field – also Hiss's friend – who stated that Hiss confessed in 1935 to being an NKVD agent.[54]

But even though passing information to the Russians, perhaps Hiss could still be considered a loyal American – if he believed it was to the United States' advantage to cooperate with the USSR on certain matters. Certainly this reasoning seems to have been what drove the other key Soviet agent in the Roosevelt administration, Harry Dexter White.

More equal than others

The day after Pearl Harbor, Henry Morgenthau gave Harry Dexter White equal authority to Assistant Secretary to the Treasury, as 'deputy in charge of international financial problems'.[55] (White was later formally appointed Assistant Secretary of the Treasury, although in real terms his influence was much greater.) White had long wielded influence over the monetary side of foreign policy – such as the final ultimatum given to Japan on 26 November 1941 that precipitated Pearl Harbor.[56] 'Aggressive, irascible, and with a remorseless drive for power,'[57] he was also instrumental in further undermining Britain's position as a major economic force.

The economic historian Alan P. Dobson writes in *US Wartime Aid to Britain* (1986) of the US Treasury's deliberations before the 1942 Mutual Aid Agreement:

> . . . White with typical arrogance and perception said this decision would have a bearing on Britain's reserve position and he suggested that the US really needed to decide the amount of dollars that Britain should be allowed to accumulate. The idea, and later the practice, of America controlling Britain's economic fortunes in this way became a subject of major political controversy . . .[58]

In June 1942, Roosevelt told Congress: 'No nation will grow rich through the war effort of its allies. The money costs of the war will fall according to the rule of equality of sacrifice.'[59] 'Equality of sacrifice' was defined as devoting a similar proportion of national production to the joint war effort. But, like many of the President's apparently even-handed policies, in practice this depended on to whom it was applied. Some were clearly more equal than others.

As a result of White's recommendation, the US Treasury was able to control Britain's gold and dollar reserves, determining how big and how small they were to be. (As the British pointed out, squeezing Britain too hard would damage world trade, which would hardly benefit America.[60]) In January 1943, the US government decided unilaterally that the United Kingdom's gold and dollar balances must not rise above $1 billion or drop below $600 million – a decision that took into account the *post-war* situation. As Dobson writes: 'Neither the State Department nor the US Treasury wanted Britain to be so strong economically that she could act contrary to American economic interests . . .'[61] And as Richard Gardner notes:

> If the philosophy of 'equality of sacrifice' had been literally applied, there should have been no objection to a moderate increase in these [gold and dollar] reserves – in fact, a grant-in-aid might have been positively required in order to make such 'equality' effective. Yet until the very last months of the war the American Government exerted continuous pressure to keep British reserves to a figure not greatly in excess of $1 billion.[62]

Gardner calls this the 'principle of "scraping the barrel" as a condition of eligibility for Lend-Lease materials', partly prompted by Roosevelt's desire to keep the isolationists happy, although Gardner acknowledges '. . . it was prompted also by the same concern with "bargaining power" that we have already noted on the part of some Administration officials. For the lower the level at which British wartime reserves were kept, the greater would be the British dependence on American post-war assistance. And the greater that dependence, it was argued, the greater would be the chances of gaining acceptance for American views on multilateral trade.'[63]

For example, in December 1943 White argued – and gained Morgenthau's approval – that British reserves were now too great, and Lend-Lease should be paid for in cash. Britain should only receive aid while poor – any attempt to get richer and it would have to pay. Adding insult to injury, the Chancellor of the Exchequer, Sir John Anderson, learned of this 'almost accidentally'.[64]

In February 1944, Roosevelt again raised the question of restricting Britain's dollar reserves with Churchill. Anderson wrote to the Prime Minister on 24 February 1944:

> If we were to accept the President's proposal we should have lost our financial independence, in any case precarious, as soon as lend-lease comes to an end, and would emerge from

the war, victorious indeed, but quite helpless financially with reserves far inferior not only to Russia but even to France and to Holland.[65]

A month later, Churchill complained to Roosevelt, 'the suggestion of reducing our dollar balances, which constitute our sole liquid reserves, to one billion dollars would not really be consistent with equal treatment of Allies or with any conception of equal sacrifice or pooling of resources'.[66] But FDR still waited six months before agreeing that British reserves could rise above the $1 billion mark.

By this time, it was obvious that without funds Britain's future was bleak – no end to rationing, shabbiness and despair everywhere and the Empire gone . . . When the Cabinet debated the situation in mid-April, Anderson declared that Britain simply could not afford to antagonise a government from which they would need 'generous assistance' after the war.[67] Britain's post-war future lay entirely in American hands and there was no chance of its being allowed to forget it.

The same situation did not apply to the Soviets. No attempts were made to secure any concessions from *them* or to exploit *their* desperate need. The Russians were never even asked to agree to Reverse Lend-Lease.[68] In November 1943, when Morgenthau threatened to cut off Lend-Lease if Britain's reserves rose above $1 billion, Anderson pointed out to Churchill that although the Soviet reserves were twice those of Britain, no such threat had been made to Stalin.[69] As Leon Martel writes in *Lend-Lease, Loans, and the Coming of the Cold War* (1979):

> The Soviets were not asked to disclose their gold and dollar assets as a condition for material assistance as Britain and other lend-lease recipients were required to do, nor were they required to provide more than the most cursory justification for their requests.[70]

The White Plan

Harry Dexter White's actions against Britain were merely part of a much grander project: from early 1942, as David Rees, author of *Harry Dexter White: A Study in Paradox* (1973), writes, he 'took the leading part in the formulation of American policy for the post-war international financial order'.[71] Morgenthau briefed him on 14 December 1941 (a week after Pearl Harbor) to prepare proposals on the economic relations between the new Allies 'for post-war international monetary arrangements'.[72] A few months later, Morgenthau wrote that: 'the launching of such a plan at this time has tremendous strategic as well as economic bearing. It seems to me that the time is ripe to dramatize our internal economic objectives in terms of action which people everywhere will recognize as practical, powerful and inspiring'.[73] America had been in the war a week and already it was planning to control the post-war world economy.

In fact, after leaving office, Morgenthau declared in a letter to President Truman that since he became Treasury Secretary he had been determined 'to move the financial center of the world from London and Wall Street to the United States Treasury'.[74] (He even wanted to wrest control of the world's finances from *American* banks.)

The result of Morgenthau's brief was the 'White Plan' for economic reconstruction – the subject of much negotiation with the British government in 1942 and early 1943 – focusing on nursing the transition from a global war economy to a workable peacetime system, besides creating an international fund to stabilise the various currencies and a bank to finance post-war reconstruction. This unprecedented worldwide economic transformation was to result in the International Monetary Fund – under Harry Dexter White.[75]

John Morton Blum, the author of a three-volume work based on Morgenthau's papers, writes that White 'sought openly, with the Secretary's approval, to make the dollar the dominant currency in the post-war world ... In that [post-war international economic] cooperation White expected the United States and the United Kingdom to provide the lead, with the United States as the senior partner'.[76]

An alternative plan was proposed by the renowned British economist John Maynard Keynes, and in 1943 the two men negotiated heatedly to try to find a compromise. Although Keynes secured some modifications, essentially the White Plan became the basis of the agreement of the July 1944 Bretton Woods Conference (properly the United Nations Monetary and Financial Conference), which agreed to the creation of the IMF and the World Bank, and authorised a central fund to be used to help countries sort out their economies after the war. This totalled \$8.8 billion, of which the US contributed \$3.2 billion – but in return for certain advantages: the system was to use either gold or dollars, to be freely convertible one to the other. 'The dollar was now the world's leading currency.'[77]

Suddenly, Britain would now have to compete in an economy based on gold and dollars – with the US Treasury controlling its reserves of both during the war. Horrified at the prospect, the British government refused to ratify the Bretton Woods agreement, but was, as we will see, compelled to do so a year later.

The world in his own image

What exactly was White's motive for such draconian control of Britain's economy? What lay behind the White Plan that led to the IMF? Generally, historians are extremely reluctant to consider the implications of White's exposure – just as they are with Hopkins' – which is particularly surprising because they acknowledge that the allegations were true. While happy to admit White's importance, they seem curiously loath to dwell on the unpalatable fact that he was a Soviet agent. *The Oxford Companion to the Second World War*'s entry for the Bretton Woods Conference adds that White 'was, incidentally, a spy of Stalin's'.[78] '*Incidentally*'? Given his influence over the world's financial systems, and particularly his role in undermining Britain's economy, isn't it *crucial* that his affiliations are fully exposed?

Always aiding the Soviets, White proposed in March 1944 to give them a \$5 billion loan with no political conditions attached. Ten months later, when he recommended increasing this to \$10 billion, Morgenthau agreed because it would buy Russian goodwill.[79] (The Soviets never received it – by the time the decision was made, America was in the Truman era.) In November 1945, White wrote in a personal note:

> The major task that confronts American diplomacy – and the only task that has any real value in the major problems that confront us – is to devise means whereby continued peace and friendly relations can be assured between the United States

and Russia. Everything else in the field of international
diplomacy pales into insignificance beside this major task. It
matters little what our political relationships with England
become or what happens in the Balkans or the Far East if the
problems between the United States and Russia can be
solved.[80]

But did he believe this because he was a Soviet agent, or did he
become a Soviet agent because he believed this? Clearly, as an
economist in the US Treasury he was hardly averse to the principles
of capitalism, and yet his social views were decidedly left-wing,
although stopping short of Marxism. So was he really an 'ideological
spy'?

White was exposed by the House Committee on Un-American
Activities – specifically created in 1938 to investigate Communist
penetration of New Deal agencies. Today, the Committee is mainly
associated with the excesses of 'McCarthyism', after the rabidly anti-
Communist Republican Senator Joseph R. McCarthy, in whose
hands it became the instrument of an infamous witch-hunt. However,
before McCarthy rose to prominence in 1951 the Committee had
worked less excitably for several years – sometimes even brushing
potential scandals under the carpet, especially when Roosevelt's and
Truman's administrations were under scrutiny. (McCarthy rose to
dominate the Committee as a direct result of the shock and outrage
caused by the Hiss case.)

The star witnesses of the immediate post-war Committee hearings
were two former agents who had 'turned', Whittaker Chambers and
Elizabeth Bentley, who while informing the Committee in 1948 that
she had acted as NKVD courier, named Harry Dexter White as one
of the agents for whom she had worked. Chambers told the
Committee that White was one of a group of potential 'high fliers'
removed from the Soviet spy network in 1936 to protect them from
risk of exposure.[81] Chambers explained that White's role was not
espionage but the influencing of American economic policy –
provocative stuff, given his remarkable influence over US, British
and the world's economic order. In *Witness* (1952), Chambers
explained:

338

> Harry Dexter White, then the chief monetary expert of the
> Treasury Department, had been in touch with the Communist
> Party for a long time, not only through his close friend,
> George Silverman [another Treasury Department economist
> working for the USSR], but through other party members
> whom he had banked around him in the Treasury
> Department.[82]

Chambers acknowledges that White was not a Communist Party
member, but a 'fellow traveller', meaning, 'I could only suggest or
urge, not give orders.'[83]

The official position was bluntly declared by the Attorney
General, Herbert Brownell, in 1953:

> Harry Dexter White was a Russian spy. He smuggled secret
> documents to Russian agents for transmission to Moscow.
> Harry Dexter White was known to be a Communist agent by
> the very people who appointed him to the most sensitive
> position he ever held in Government service.[84]

– surely one of the most astounding admissions ever made in public
life. Brownell also revealed that previously classified documents
showed that the FBI had briefed the White House on White's
activities in 1945, three years before his exposure to the House
Committee. Despite this, a month later Truman had – successfully –
nominated White as the first Executive Director of the IMF.

However, White has his defenders, most notably (and
unsurprisingly) his brother, Nathan I. White, who points out in *Harry
Dexter White – Loyal American* (1956) that although Chambers' and
Bentley's testimonies about White broadly tally, there are
inconsistencies. He never got the chance to fully defend himself in
court – although he appeared before the Committee on 13 August
1948 to robustly refute the allegations, three days later he suffered a
fatal heart attack. (He had been very ill since his first heart attack a
year earlier and was naturally under great stress.) It is possible he
could still have been the victim of an elaborate frame-up: the
Russians excelled at the technique of destabilising the opposition

through allegations passed on by bogus 'defectors', spreading suspicion and confusion. So what is the evidence against him?

Besides Chambers' and Bentley's testimonies, there is no doubt that the staff White appointed were markedly Communist-friendly – suspicious, but hardly proof.[85] Harder evidence against him – i.e. not the word of reformed Soviet spies – is the so-called 'White Memorandum', a handwritten document found in papers that Chambers hid as 'insurance' when he stopped working for the Russians. According to him, this was one of the regular reports White gave to Colonel Boris Bykov of the Fourth Department; certainly an expert confirmed his handwriting. However, Chambers only showed these papers to the authorities in November 1948 – ten years after he had hidden them and three months after White's death.[86] (Chambers used them in his defence when sued for slander by Alger Hiss, although the case was suspended when the Hiss investigation began.)

Nathan White argues that the 'White Memorandum' was simply his brother's aide-memoire, stolen after his death to incriminate him.[87] And as Richard Gardner points out: 'So far no evidence has appeared to disprove the traditional assumption that White put forward his financial plans in the sincere belief that they would further the interests of the United States.'[88] In fact, the same can be said of Hiss. He and White may have been spies, but what they did certainly benefited the US – and it was entirely in accordance with Roosevelt's own objectives. Whatever White was up to, he had no desire to undermine the economic or social stability of the United States. Indeed, it comes as a shock to realise just how far the interests of the USA and the USSR coincided at that time: both sought to sweep away the old empires, smash Germany and remove Japan as a rival.

The solution to the paradox of Harry Dexter White lies in his personality; his biographer David Rees writes: 'Clearly, the author of the White Plan was a man who wished to remake the world, and it was second nature for him to propose large schemes on a grand scale.'[89] Rees accepts that the White Memorandum is genuine, concluding that White was indeed passing information to Moscow – but only because he believed that the USSR should have it in order to further his *own* plans for reshaping the world. He knew himself to be in the dominant position in the relationship, giving Moscow only what he considered necessary – irrespective of his own government's position.

White considered the ideological rivalries of East versus West to be trivial, and the restrictions of national security and the law as nuisances to be ignored. Like many others – Hopkins being the prime example – he believed that the United States would have to share the world with the Soviet Union, and should prepare itself for the inevitable.

The question of where his real loyalties lay is almost irrelevant: to someone so buoyed up with a Messianic self-belief, clearly his only fundamental loyalty was to himself. Nothing must stand in the way of his ambitions to recast the world economic order, and if that meant keeping up 'back channel' contacts with the Kremlin, then so be it.

Getting inside the head of Harry Dexter White may also provide the key to understanding another putative Soviet agent: the man who effectively ran the Allies' war – Harry Hopkins.

Secrets and lies

Few accounts of Hopkins' wartime role even mention that four years after the war, and three after his death, he was not just accused of aiding the USSR with his Stalin-friendly policies, but of actually passing the Russians classified information about America's greatest wartime secret – the development of the atomic bomb. Even one of the few to discuss it, Henry H. Adams, in *Harry Hopkins* (1977), dismisses it in a sentence or two without any details on the precise nature of the allegations, let alone the supporting evidence.[90]

Before Oleg Gordievsky's bombshell at the end of the 1980s, it was regarded as puerile mischief-making to suggest that Hopkins, who had virtually won the war for America, could possibly have been a traitor. Now, of course, we know that there are serious questions about the extent of his dealings with the Kremlin, so the allegations, first aired in the US media in 1949, of betraying atomic secrets need to be re-examined.

Hopkins was at the forefront in establishing the United States' atomic research project in 1940, but work was slow, mainly because of scepticism that a bomb could be developed quickly enough for the current war. Roosevelt had proposed that atomic fission be developed jointly with Britain, but Churchill rejected the idea, thinking of its industrial potential.[91] The British bomb project, 'Tube Alloys', was initiated in October 1941. It was only after American scientists visited Britain soon afterwards, and found that researchers there were much more optimistic that the weapon could be developed quickly, that the National Defense Research Council recommended all-out US commitment, resulting in the famous Manhattan Project.

The Americans scattered their research among various facilities, collectively known as the Manhattan Engineer District, whose key sites were Los Alamos in New Mexico, where a team under J. Robert Oppenheimer developed the bomb itself; Oak Ridge in Tennessee, which focused on techniques for the extraction of U235 (the rare isotope of raw uranium needed for fission); and Hanford in Washington State, which worked on the production of the alternative energy source, plutonium.

It was not the best time for the British to undertake such an expensive project, but when they asked the Americans for help it was Roosevelt's turn to refuse – why should he aid British post-war exploitation of atomic energy?[92] However, in June 1942, during Churchill's dash to Washington, he and Roosevelt made a dangerously 'unwritten and unrecorded'[93] agreement to pool atomic research, the Prime Minister agreeing that the project be based in the USA.

A few months later, Brigadier-General Leslie R. Groves – the engineer responsible for the Pentagon – was given the Manhattan Project, under the auspices of the Secretary of War, Henry Stimson. The State Department was not informed that the programme even existed (with its gaggle of Soviet spies, this was probably just as well).[94]

The first controlled nuclear chain reaction was achieved on 2 December 1942 by Enrico Fermi's team in a laboratory deep beneath the University of Chicago's football field, with an atomic pile made of graphite blocks, uranium oxide powder and blocks of natural uranium. Not far off creating an atomic bomb, the Americans considered very carefully who else to let in on the secret.

In Stalin's Pocket

Stimson was not only cautious about Britain, but when Roosevelt told Stimson that he was considering an agreement to pool scientific and technological knowledge with the Russians, he remarked, 'I got here just in time.'[95] The American team was instructed only to exchange information with a nation that could exploit the results during the war, which Stimson understood to mean that they should also withhold information from the British. Sir John Anderson, the minister responsible for the British bomb project, wrote to Churchill at the start of 1943 – perhaps the pun was intentional – that this 'has come as a bombshell and is quite intolerable'.[96]

Significantly, the Prime Minister chose to bring the subject up at Casablanca not with Roosevelt, but with Hopkins – who promised it would be 'put right'. Nothing happened. In February, Churchill cabled: 'I should be very grateful for some news about this, as at present the American War Department is asking us to keep them informed of our experiments while refusing altogether any information about theirs.' Hopkins asked for details of his complaint as 'our people here feel no agreement has been breached'. In reply, the Prime Minister sent details of all Anglo-American dealings concerning the bomb since 1940. When Hopkins talked to Roosevelt, Stimson and Vannevar Bush (head of the NDRC), the latter announced that now the project had reached the design and manufacture stage, information should be on a strictly 'need to know' basis.[97]

In March 1943, Churchill warned Hopkins that Britain would go it alone if necessary – clearly no empty threat, as Anderson was already preparing estimates of the costs and manpower. Britain would need its own sources of uranium and heavy water (deuterium, needed to contain the atomic reaction) and although Canada was an obvious and available source, in mid-May 1943 Anderson dropped another bombshell in a memo to Churchill:

> Under a contract which the United States had placed 'with the knowledge' of the Canadian Government, the United States Government have secured entire output of Canadian uranium mines for the next two years. A similar position has also arisen in regard to the Canadian production of heavy water.[98]

Now Britain could no longer go it alone – and the Americans had the monopoly on Canadian uranium and heavy water.

Finally, in late May, Churchill cabled back from the Trident Conference that Roosevelt was prepared to resume the information exchange – clearly believing he had Harry Hopkins to thank for this U-turn.[99] (As with most of Churchill's American 'triumphs', the deal was not quite as it seemed. In August 1946, the McMahon Act prevented American atomic scientists from communicating with foreign governments, abruptly ending Anglo-American cooperation. Congress had no idea about the secret agreements the British had with the Administration – and the Administration wanted to keep it that way. Prime mover Senator Brien McMahon later admitted that if he had known about them he would never have initiated his eponymous Bill.[100] After this, Britian had no choice but to develop its own atomic bomb.)

At Quadrant in August 1943, Roosevelt and Churchill agreed that their nations would not use the atom bomb against each other (hopefully an ongoing arrangement) and would not employ it against their enemies or pass atomic information to another government without the other's consent.[101] Some on the American side were unhappy that this allowed foreigners a veto over their decision to use the bomb. Unsurprisingly, Churchill had to make a significant concession: Britain would not exploit the results of the research commercially after the war. According to Richard Overy:

> Only when Churchill gave a firm guarantee in the 1943 Quebec agreement that Britain would not do so were British scientists brought into the research, though not into the construction of the actual plants involved. Both sides had the post-war situation in mind. Britain was increasingly worried that she might be isolated after the war as the only major power without nuclear weapons, and Americans were anxious about what would happen to their plans for a new world order if other states had the bomb.[102]

Subsequently, in September 1944 in New York, Churchill and Roosevelt signed the 'Hyde Park aide-mémoire' – an agreement that the A-bomb 'might perhaps, after mature consideration' be used against Japan, 'who should be warned that this bombardment will be repeated until they surrender'. They also agreed that, after Japan's surrender, their two nations would cooperatively develop the military and commercial applications of atomic energy. The document specifically assigned Professor Niels Bohr, the Danish refugee physicist who was adviser to the project, as responsible for 'no leakage of information particularly to the Russians'.[103]

Michael Simpson notes that the agreement of the previous year contains an interesting loophole: atomic secrets would not be shared with the USSR 'until her co-operation in Europe was guaranteed'.[104] In other words, they *would* share atomic secrets with the Russians – eventually. Predictably, Churchill was apoplectic at the thought of the 'baboon Bolsheviks' possessing the bomb, but Roosevelt thought very differently. After all, he fully anticipated Russia being one of his 'world policemen' – the only four nations allowed to bear arms.

Following the Yalta Conference in early 1945, Churchill wrote in a draft memorandum to Eden (excised from the final version, along with other less-than-complimentary references to de Gaulle):

> I was shocked at Yalta too when the President in a casual manner spoke of revealing the secret to Stalin on the grounds that de Gaulle, if he heard of it, would certainly double-cross us with Stalin.[105]

'I will call Mr Hopkins'

In fact, it hardly mattered what America's official policy was on the Russians and the bomb. Only now can we fully piece together an extraordinary story of skulduggery – whose implications can still shock – which, of course, involves the unelected President and unsung Soviet hero, Harry Hopkins.

The story centres on the former businessman George Racey Jordan, who joined the US Army in the Second World War, becoming a Lend-Lease expediter and liaison officer with the Russians in May 1942 on the 'Alsib [Alaska–Siberia] Pipeline', a route used mainly for flying Lend-Lease planes into the USSR. Aircraft would arrive at Great Falls in Montana to be 'winterised' for Soviet conditions, then fly on to Alaska, where Soviet pilots would take over for the journey to Siberia. (Stalin refused to allow American pilots to enter the USSR.)

Initially, Jordan was posted as a Captain to Newark Airport, where he worked closely with ace pilot Colonel Anatoli N. Kotikov, head of the Soviet Mission at Great Falls. Jordan was disconcerted by the Russians' power in these American bases, but this soon turned to profound anxiety as he discovered what was going on.

Less than a month after his arrival, a taxiing American Airlines aircraft clipped a Lend-Lease Douglas bomber, but although the damage was minor, Kotikov and his team were outraged – even demanding the American pilot should be shot – and insisting on an assurance it would never happen again. Jordan relates that after a fruitless argument, Kotikov announced, '*I will call Mr Hopkins*.' Jordan wondered why the head of Soviet Lend-Lease should be involved in a relatively inconsequential row. He was even more puzzled when Kotikov added, 'Mr Brown will see Mr Hopkins – no?' The identity of the mysterious Mr Brown was soon to be revealed.

On 12 June, Jordan got two surprises. An order came from Washington banning all civilian airlines from Newark. And the papers revealed the secret visit to Washington by Molotov – travelling as 'Mr Brown'. As Jordan writes wonderingly: 'Would we have to jump whenever Colonel Kotikov cracked the whip?'[106] Deciding to keep his own record of what went on at Newark, and subsequently Great Falls, eventually Jordan amassed two thick binders of notes and documents, a notebook in which he recorded the names of Russians who came and went through the 'pipeline', and, for the last nine months of his posting (up to July 1944), a diary listing daily occurrences.

At the beginning of January 1943, Jordan was transferred to Gore Field at Great Falls in Montana, the next stage in the 'pipeline'. This followed a presidential decree, as reported in a memo from the Air Staff on 1 January:

> The President had decreed that 'airplanes be delivered in accordance with protocol schedules by the most expeditious means'. To implement these directives, the modification,

equipment and movement of Russian planes have been given
first priority, even over planes for US Army Air Forces . . .[107]

The Russians' power was so pervasive that Kotikov not only decided
that Captain Jordan should be promoted to Major but when the gold
oak leaves of his new rank arrived it was he who formally pinned
them on.

Great Falls only increased Jordan's anxieties. As there were no
customs or immigration checks – an open invitation for spies – he set
himself up as an unofficial customs officer, taking details of the
Russians who came and went, eventually listing 418 individuals. He
then turned to the mysterious black suitcases, tied and sealed, that
passed through on their way to Moscow. Allegedly the personal
luggage of Russian flight personnel, at first they went through in
batches of about six, but soon fifty or so were arriving at Gore Field
for onward transfer, accompanied by armed couriers. When trying to
inspect them, Jordan was told peremptorily that they were covered by
diplomatic immunity. Although expressing deep suspicions, he was
unable to interest his superiors, Soviet Lend-Lease being sacrosanct.
When he asked both State and War Departments to confirm that
these items were indeed covered by diplomatic immunity, the former
failed to reply and the latter requested him to be as cooperative with
the Russians as possible.

Eventually, realising that a particularly important batch of cases
was coming through – because Kotikov and his comrades were
obviously desperate to get him out of the way – Jordan arranged a
surprise inspection as the aircraft was about to take off, escorted by
an armed soldier just in case. Despite the frantic attempts of the
Soviet couriers to stop him, he opened some of the cases at random
and made hasty notes of their contents, which began:

> 4-legged-animal book – Tass folders – Amtorg [the Soviet
> trade organisation] – Panama Canal Commission maps – Oak
> Ridge – memos from Sayre & Hiss & others – State dept.
> letters . . .

'Hiss' we know. Francis B. Sayre – Woodrow Wilson's son-in-law –

was an Assistant Secretary of State and Hiss's first boss in the State Department. During the hearings into Chambers' allegations, Sayre cropped up as a possible Communist agent but Chambers denied all knowledge of him.[108] Jordan's note goes on:

> . . . films – reports – 'secret' cut off – large folders on machine tools, electric tools & concrete data – furnaces – White House memo from H.H. about 'hell of a time getting these away from Groves' – bomb powder
>
> [. . .]
>
> Look up words on memo & maps labeled Oak Ridge – Manhattan Engineering Dept. or District I think it was – Uranium 92 – neutron – proton and deuteron – isotope – energy produced by fission or splitting – look up cyclotron – Map of walls 5 feet thick of lead and water to control flying neutrons. Heavy-water hydrogen or deuterons.[109]

According to Jordan, the 'White House memo' was a letter on White House notepaper to 'Mikoyan' (although unknown to Jordan, he was overall head of Lend-Lease in Moscow). The material that 'H.H.' had 'had a hell of a time getting . . . away from Groves [General Groves, head of the Manhattan Project]' was clipped to the letter: a folded map of 'Oak Ridge, Manhattan Engineering District' and a copy of a short report labelled 'Oak Ridge' – the Manhattan Project's facility for research into U235 production – with a note that it was for Harry Hopkins.

Although when Kotikov discovered what Jordan had done he furiously threatened to have him removed from his post, in the end he filed no report. Perhaps he was worried he would be blamed for the lapse. Ironically, the references to atomic research meant nothing to Jordan at the time: he was more upset by the Russians' arrogance and the amount of material they were taking out of the country.

Colonel Kotikov guarded a file labelled 'Experimental Chemicals' especially carefully, which detailed supplies for a 'bomb powder' factory, which Jordan assumed to produce chemicals of some kind. Later, when questioned about this by the Un-American Affairs Committee, he explained:

I saw the word 'uranium' and what he called 'bomb powder' was actually uranium. He had it marked 'uranium'. I did not know what uranium meant and had no inkling at the time it would ever be important. I just knew that that particular shipment I had to expedite.[110]

Shortly after this, in April 1943, another incident demonstrated the priority given to Soviet Lend-Lease. When Kotikov demanded that more American pilots be brought in to fly a backlog of Aircobra fighters to Alaska, a sudden influx arrived from all over the country. The Air Transport Command, supposedly solely responsible for deploying pilots, was furious. Kotikov explained that he was tired of waiting, so had spoken to 'Mr Hopkins'.[111]

A few days later, when the Russian officer wanted an especially heavy consignment of 'experimental chemicals' to be shipped, Jordan refused because it would take up too much of the valuable weight allocation. Kotikov then played his ace: after calling Washington, he handed the phone to Jordan smirking, 'Big boss, Mr Hopkins, wants you.' Astounded, Jordan took the phone. 'Big Boss' Hopkins asked him peremptorily, 'Did you get those pilots I sent you?' After Jordan's hasty thanks Hopkins told him a 'very special' shipment of chemicals was coming through that was not to be discussed with anyone and '*not to go on the records*'. This turned out to be over 1,000 pounds of uranium salts from Canada.[112]

Then, in November 1943, Jordan heard that 'heavy water' was being loaded on a C-47 transport plane. On asking Kotikov the meaning of this peculiar phrase, the reply was 'something for our new chemical plant'.[113] As Jordan pointed out later, although the uranium compounds *could* have had other uses, heavy water only has the one.

Jordan also notes that other industrial material actually documented as Lend-Lease could be used to construct an atomic pile: besides metallic compounds such as cadmium and thorium, over $800,000-worth of graphite was shipped out, plus aluminium tubing – an essential constituent of atomic piles – with a total weight of nearly 14 million pounds.[114]

Finally, in January 1944 Jordan went to Washington to register the flagrant abuses taking place at Great Falls – no censorship, no customs, no immigration controls. The State Department responded by warning him about being 'officious', and assuring him that they were on the case.[115] Consequently, Jordan reported the matter to the Army Counter-Intelligence Corps (CIC), whose report, released in 1949 at the time of the Congressional investigation, reads in part:

> This agent observed that Major Jordan appeared to maintain accurate, detailed files and was very anxious to convey his information through intelligence channels. He requested that he be contacted at a time when the Russian activity could be outlined in minute detail, and was advised that this would be done.[116]

Of course, the very existence of Jordan's CIC report from 1944 undermines criticisms that he invented the whole story five years later, in the wake of the Hiss scandal.

The CIC investigator recommended that Jordan should be interviewed again and the State Department contacted, whose Charles E. 'Chips' Bohlen proceeded to get some action. After meetings with various government departments, he sent a 'reminder' of US customs regulations to the Soviet Embassy, advising that in future they would be enforced. By then, Jordan had left Great Falls, but discovered that as late as September 1944 large quantities of non-diplomatic records were still being shipped to Russia.[117]

When in May 1949 the US media splashed the fact that a tiny quantity of U235 was unaccounted for – lost or stolen – at an Atomic Energy Commission facility, Jordan could only boggle at the irony, remembering the many hundreds of pounds of uranium compounds that had been shipped under his nose. (At that time, he did not appreciate the distinction between uranium compounds and U235.) Although he contacted the broadcaster Fulton Lewis with his story at the time, it was only on 23 September 1949 that it was hot enough news, when Truman shocked America by announcing that the Soviet Union had detonated its first atomic device about a month previously. Lewis brought in Republican Senator Styles Bridges, who promptly called in the FBI. After their investigation, at the beginning of December Lewis broadcast an interview with Jordan. One of the listeners, who worriedly phoned in after the show to verify some of the details, was General Groves.

Jordan was then summoned for two appearances before the House Committee on Un-American Activities, in December 1949 and March 1950. Naturally, his claims caused a furore, but despite the Committee's independent corroboration of much of his testimony, they and the media mounted a concerted campaign to discredit him. In that pre-McCarthy period, the committee was dominated by Democrats, and even some of the Republicans balked at accepting Jordan's claims.[118]

Jordan's reputation was clearly doomed: Representative Francis E. Walter announced to the press that his testimony was 'inherently incredible'.[119] Media reports stated that both the FBI and army intelligence had investigated his claims and found them to be unsubstantiated – but in fact they had done no such thing. One press report attempted to discredit Jordan because his claim to have been a 'United Nations Representative' was denied by the United Nations, but as it turned out, this was a straightforward misunderstanding. Jordan's papers assigning him to Lend-Lease in 1942 stated him to be a 'representative of the United Nations' – i.e. the wartime alliance. But even so, the newspaper declined to print a correction or retraction.[120] In the eyes of the public, he remained a liar and a con-man.

As for the claims about Hopkins – by then dead – Sidney Hyman, who organised his papers for Robert Sherwood's biography, claimed it was nonsense to suggest he had any connection with atomic research, memorably declaring, 'He didn't know the difference between uranium and geranium',[121] which made Jordan look ridiculous. But in fact, Hopkins was deeply involved in America's A-bomb programme (as Sherwood's book acknowledges), and had even helped initiate it. And it was always Hopkins to whom Churchill spoke about the American side of the project.

True or false?

Jordan finally put his side in *From Major Jordan's Diaries* (1952), co-authored with Richard L. Stokes. If he was right, then clearly the implications are staggering. But over half a century later how can we be sure? Does any of this information conflict with the accepted story of the Russians' development of the atom bomb?

According to Professor Lydia Pozdeeva, although the onset of the war with Germany stopped Soviet research into atomic energy, it resumed in February 1942 'after intelligence gave reason to suppose that work on the A-bomb was going on in the West'.[122] Naturally, the Soviet project was backed by a campaign of espionage, and American and British progress would have been a high priority for the swarm of NKVD agents poking around the US in the guise of the Soviet Purchasing Commission.[123] Pozdeeva goes on:

> When President Harry Truman mentioned at the Potsdam conference [July 1945] that the Americans were in possession of a bomb of unusual strength it came as no surprise to Stalin. In any case, by that time a cyclotron was already working in the Kourchatov Laboratory [in Moscow], plutonium – the first in Europe – had been obtained, and construction of an experimental graphite-uranium pile was nearing its end.[124]

So, by the summer of 1945, the Soviets had produced plutonium and were on the point of completing their first atomic pile – a suspiciously impressive achievement, especially for a nation so raw from war. Their first atomic test took place in the last days of August 1949 – over four years after the Americans, but still far more quickly than the West's experts anticipated, suggesting some helping hand, presumably in the form of secret information.

In fact, it is known that the Russians' achievement was the result of information from well-organised NKVD spies within the Manhattan Project, as revealed in September 1949 when the Venona intercepts identified one of the British scientists on the project, Klaus Fuchs, as an agent. There are other suggestive signs: the Americans had adopted a process for producing U235 after exploring several dead ends, whereas the Russian scientists zeroed in on this process immediately, and the Russians' plutonium plant was identical in size and specifications to the Manhattan Project's reactor at Hanford.[125]

Ralph de Toledano, a writer specialising in intelligence matters, particularly Communist penetration of the US government, maintained a correspondence with Whittaker Chambers,[126] and met many of the key figures, including Jordan, whose story, he personally assured us, was true. De Toledano writes of the deliberations by Congress over the US Atomic Energy Act in 1946:

> Key members [of the House and Senate] had been quietly informed by Bernard Baruch – America's representative on atomic matters at the United Nations – of a report he had made to President Truman: The Soviet Purchasing Commission had ordered $1.5 million worth of special equipment in this country, using blueprints and specifications which the experts recognised immediately as coming unmistakably from the MED [Manhattan Engineer District].[127]

Further intriguing evidence comes from the journalist W.L. White, who accompanied a US Chamber of Commerce delegation on a six-week Russian tour in 1944, producing *Report on the Russians*. Visiting the bomb-damaged laboratory where pioneering pre-war work on splitting the atom had been carried out, White's guide said that Russia now had an atomic research centre beyond the Ural mountains, adding, 'We have, like you call in America, Manhattan Project.'[128]

While there is no doubt that atomic secrets reached the Soviet Union from spies in America, Jordan goes further, alleging that US Lend-Lease supplied the USSR with *materials* (most incriminatingly, heavy water) for its atomic project, that Harry Hopkins was behind this – and that he also arranged for the Russians to have crucial technical information (e.g. the 'Oak Ridge' document).

There is no question whatsoever that the first of these allegations is true. Prompted by Jordan's story, the FBI and Congress independently located evidence of the delivery and shipment of the orders, via Lend-Lease, to the Soviet Union: three shipments of uranium salts arrived there in 1943 and 1944.[129] In all, the Soviets received 1,465 pounds of uranium compounds, along with a kilogram of uranium metal – about *half* of the US's total stock at that time. This is actually *more* than Jordan claimed, as he knew only about the first two shipments (and he made a note only of the second).

Although Jordan's testimony is usually ignored or derided, the only part that relies solely on his word is the link between the shipments and Harry Hopkins. And as Hopkins controlled Lend-Lease and all matters concerning Russia, at least he would have been *aware* of Soviet requests for such sensitive material, which could hardly have been supplied without his approval. (Significantly, there were no shipments when Hopkins was ill between January and the beginning of July 1944. The third and final shipment went through immediately after his return to Washington.)

The fact that the uranium compounds came from Canada was another slap in the face for the British. As mentioned earlier, in May 1943 they had to abandon plans to develop an atomic bomb independently because the US government had bought up all Canadian supplies of uranium and heavy water – and then they gave some to *Stalin* . . .

The Congressional investigation also confirmed the order, acquisition and shipment to the USSR of 1,000 grams of heavy water, down to the release certificate number.[130] After the Un-American Activities Committee instructed its special investigator, former FBI agent Donald T. Appell, to examine his story, he was questioned on his findings by Senator Richard Nixon:

> Nixon: On the point of the so-called shipment of uranium . . . the shipment went through. Is that correct?
>
> Appell: Two specific shipments of uranium oxide and uranium nitrate, and shipments of heavy water have been completely documented to include even the number of the plane that flew the uranium and heavy water out of Great Falls.
>
> Nixon: And the final point is the matter of Mr Hopkins having attempted to expedite these shipments. Major Jordan's testimony on that was his notes, written at the time, showed the initials 'H.H.' on one of the consignments which he broke into. Your investigation has shown no correspondence of Mr

Hopkins in which he used the initials 'H.H.' Is that correct?

Appell: That which we reviewed.

Nixon: I understand that. My point is that as far as the investigation you have been able to make is concerned, you as yet have been unable to substantiate Major Jordan's story on that point; is that correct?

Appell: Yes.

Nixon: But you *have* substantiated it on the four other points mentioned?

Appell: Yes.[131]

Representative Harold H. Velde asked Appell: 'Was Major Jordan's story, as far as your investigation was concerned, ever discredited by any of the witnesses whom you contacted?' Appell replied: 'No.'[132]

Two days after Jordan took the stand, General Groves was called before the Committee, confirming that the Soviet Purchasing Commission had put in a Lend-Lease request for 200 pounds of uranium and 220 pounds of uranium nitrate salt, explaining: 'There was a great deal of pressure being brought to bear on Lend-Lease, apparently, to give the Russians everything . . . There was a great deal of pressure brought to give them this uranium material.'[133] In fact, because this request had already been approved before Groves even heard of it, he felt unable to challenge it (oddly, because it might tip the Russians off about the importance of uranium). Several more requests for various forms of uranium were put in during 1943 and 1944, although not all were granted. But in June 1944, the Treasury Department paid for the Soviets to have 45 pounds of uranium nitrate.[134] Groves also testified about equipment urgently needed for the Oak Ridge facility that nearly went to the Russians:

> We were very anxious, in connection with the gaseous diffusion plant to get certain equipment. If it had not been obtained, that plant would have been delayed in its completion. The Russians had a plant on the way. Of course, when I say they had it, you know who paid for it. That plant, some of it was boxed and on the dock when we got it, and I can still remember the difficulties we had getting it. One of the

agreements we had to make was that we would replace that
equipment and use all our priorities necessary to get it
replaced quickly.[135]

Trying to downplay the pressure exerted on him over the uranium
supplies, Groves comments:

> I am sure if you would check on the pressure on officers
> handling all supplies of a military nature during the war, you
> will find the pressure to give to Russia everything that could
> be given was not limited to atomic matters.[136]

'Not limited to' confirms that 'atomic matters' were included – clearly
someone higher up was *in favour* of 'atomic matters' being included
in Soviet Lend-Lease.

The case seems so watertight that one might be forgiven for
wondering why Jordan's credibility should ever have been seriously
questioned. Yet his entire story has been rejected on the quaint
grounds that because Harry Hopkins never signed his letters 'H.H.',
this claim must be false, and if Jordan invented that he must also have
made up the rest. But as he himself pointed out, if a letter from
Hopkins signed 'H.H.' *was* found, this still wouldn't prove his
veracity, so why focus on that issue?[137] The most important point by
far is that Jordan claimed that materials needed to build an atomic
pile, such as heavy water and uranium salts, were shipped to the
USSR – which was confirmed by numerous witnesses and
documents. Surely that is considerably more significant than how
Hopkins might have signed his name?

Presumably, Jordan's testimony has been swept aside because of
the implications that follow from pursuing the logic in the other
direction. The only allegation that rests entirely on Jordan's word is
that Hopkins also sent technical secrets to Moscow. Although there
is no independent confirmation of this, if Jordan's other claims are
found to be true, why should he lie about this one?

What nobody would know for another half-century is that there
was evidence that Hopkins was actively a Soviet agent. Although
Jordan himself only ever alleges that Hopkins' over-zealousness to give

Russia whatever it wanted, no questions asked, led him into very deep water, the main pieces of the jigsaw – seen both separately and together – are damning enough. Hopkins being identified as 'source 19'; his tipping off of Soviet spies that they were being watched by the FBI; his consistent pro-Soviet stance and constant pushing for the US to support the USSR materially and morally (as Ralph de Toledano points out: 'There is no instance on record of a firm United States refusal of a Moscow request once it reached Hopkins'[138]); and now his support for their atomic project . . . But does this make him the American equivalent of Kim Philby or Guy Burgess?

As a card-carrying member of the Socialist Party for a short time in the 1920s, his views were undoubtedly left-wing – extremely so by post-war American standards, although not much he advocated would have shocked the British Labour Party of that era. James Forrestal recorded a conversation in June 1945 when he and Hopkins dined with Lord and Lady Halifax in the British Embassy in Washington, the conversation turning to the recent Labour landslide that had swept Churchill from power:

> Hopkins said that he thought the world was now definitely swinging towards the Left, that we were in the middle of the revolution and that it would be unwise to try to oppose it . . .
>
> Hopkins said that England must inevitably go Socialist and that Churchill did not want the things for England that the Labour people wanted – federal housing, slum elimination, ownership of industries, etc.

Forrestal added 'such a nation could only become Communistic if we, the United States, underwrote the transaction' – and only self-sufficient countries such as the USSR and USA could ever become properly Communist. He continues:

> Harry obviously did not want to pursue this conversation too far, because, I suspect, he did not want to be driven to the position that he was advocating either revolution or Communism for this country. And he turned the talk with discussion of universal military service.[139]

357

However, Hopkins was hardly the archetypal Marxist. His fervent defence of the 'American Way' (even if his own particular interpretation) sits awkwardly with the stereotypical ideological spy, who is not only committed to but *subservient* to the 'just' cause. Hopkins was no political idolater. Like Roosevelt – and Harry Dexter White – he had a vision of a new world order, the 'New Deal universally extended and applied', and an innate Messianic zeal. Like White, he was prepared to do whatever it took to make his vision a reality, but it remained *his* vision.

Again like White, Hopkins regarded the counter-balance of Russian dominance as an unavoidable reality – although he preferred the Soviet system to old Europe's. Whatever the Russians wanted, they could have. Sharing the secret of the atomic bomb with Britain but not the Soviet Union would have made no sense to Hopkins. After all, both were to be 'world policemen'. Like Roosevelt, Hopkins was used to bending or breaking rules, ignoring the law. Indeed, such behaviour is what made him a success. If he decided that the Soviets should also have the bomb, then neither international agreement nor presidential decree would stop him moving heaven and earth to ensure they got it.

The unanswerable question is whether Roosevelt was party to any of this – did Hopkins act behind his back, or did the President actually authorise him to share America's greatest secrets with the Soviet Union?

CHAPTER TWELVE

Overlords

'Wish you were here.'
**Winston S. Churchill, message to President Roosevelt
from the Normandy beachhead, 12 June 1944**[1]

Few today realise that one of the United States' explicit war aims was
directed not at the enemy but at the interests of its Allies: to bring an
end to colonialism and imperialism. As Kathryn E. Brown noted in
Intelligence and National Security in 1998:

> In the last couple of years of the Second World War, President
> Franklin D. Roosevelt was fighting two different wars: a
> military battle in which the defeat of the last of the Axis
> powers was inevitable, and an ideological battle to rid the
> world of Western European imperialism.[2]

And William Roger Louis writes in *Imperialism at Bay* (1977): 'In the
winter and spring of 1943 it became increasingly clear to the British
that *colonial independence* was the explicit American goal.'[3] (His
emphasis.)

After months of stalemate, the American-led Allies in the Pacific
began a two-pronged offensive. Their first big push, from

Guadalcanal in the Solomon Islands into New Guinea and ultimately the Philippines, had begun in June 1943. Under General Douglas MacArthur and Admiral William 'Bull' Halsey, its rapid success was due to 'island-hopping' – isolating the more strongly defended islands to make them easier to capture. Admiral Chester W. Nimitz led the second prong across the central Pacific, beginning with the Marshall Islands in February 1944. It was an apocalypse for the Japanese, instilled with the principle that both surrender and defeat were personal insults to their god-Emperor. Operations on continental South-East Asia were bogged down throughout most of 1943, although both sides were gearing up for offensives in the following spring. The new South-East Asia Command (SEAC) was poised for action, under the vainglorious and inept Mountbatten.

Although the Cairo Conference's final declaration – drafted by Hopkins – had announced that Japan would be stripped of all territories it had occupied in China and the Pacific since 1914, Roosevelt and his colleagues in the State Department reasoned that if the Allies were to liberate, say, Malaya or Borneo, how could they simply be handed back to the British or Dutch after the Japanese had been kicked out? And if *these* places were to be granted independence after Japan's defeat, why shouldn't the same right be extended to all other colonies?

As Sumner Welles declared in his Memorial Day speech in May 1942:

> If this war is in fact a war for the liberation of peoples it must assure the sovereign equality of peoples throughout the world, as well as in the world of the Americas. Our victory must bring . . . the liberation of all peoples. Discriminating between peoples because of their race, creed or color must be abolished. The age of imperialism is ended.[4]

(Fine rhetoric, but five months later Welles declared 'The Negroes are in the lowest rank of human beings.'[5])

Naturally, this idealism was not totally divorced from the potential economic advantage colonial independence would give America. As Robert Nisbet acknowledges in discussing America's improved post-war commercial position: 'Some of these gains were the products of the private war FDR conducted on British and French imperialism during the war against Nazi Germany.'[6]

As Warren Kimball points out, the counterpart to Roosevelt's anti-colonialism was his belief that American political, social and economic ideals were best for everybody. (A similar attitude, of course, prevailed in the British Empire.) But his anti-colonialism was no guarantee of liberalism: referring to his 'distasteful racial notions', Kimball writes, 'Without question, his anticolonialism came with the burdens of paternalism, belief in white and Western supremacy, cultural bias, and ignorance . . .' While FDR believed that colonial independence was inevitable, he considered some areas needed more time for the changeover: to him, India was ready, while French Indo-China needed time to adapt.[7]

However, as ever, political expediency rode roughshod over principle. As William Roger Louis notes: 'Roosevelt in his zeal to bolster French resistance to the Nazis in January 1942 placed himself in the contradictory position of favouring the restoration of the French colonial empire.'[8] On several occasions during 1942, he publicly announced that Indo-China would remain French after the war. It was only after the collapse of his plans to work with Vichy after Torch, the German occupation of Vichy France and the murder of Darlan that he moved in the opposite direction.

At Casablanca, the President had been careful to send out the right signals while he was actually in a colony, whose potentate, Sultan Mohammed V of Morocco, was subservient to France. Hopkins had talks with the Sultan's adviser about Morocco's bright independent future, and in discussions with the Sultan at which Churchill was present, Roosevelt made his support for Moroccan independence so clear that he was 'deliberately provocative'.[9] De Gaulle said later to the Sultan: 'When President Roosevelt jingled the marvels of independence before your Majesty at Anfa, what did he offer you beyond the cash and a place among his customers?'[10] The Fighting French leader agreed with Churchill on one thing: the colonial system should be re-imposed after the war.

Roosevelt favoured 'trusteeships', whereby an independent international body would administer colonies until they could govern themselves. But as Louis writes, 'Since the beginning of the war, Churchill had regarded trusteeship schemes as a cover for American ambitions.'[11] Anthony Eden, too, was sceptical, declaring: 'The American attitude to the Pacific . . . is to give away other people's property . . . to an international committee on which America will be one of three or more.'[12]

However, although FDR has been blamed for the end of the British Empire, there were other reasons for its final demise. Apart from increasingly vocal independence movements within the colonies, many in Britain – particularly among the Labour Party – were uncomfortable imperial masters. And in the end, Roosevelt died before his anti-imperial programme could gather momentum, and the new resident of the White House, President Truman, had very different ideas in that direction – as we will see. But this does not alter the fact that Roosevelt used the war to undermine his Allies, particularly Britain. (And perhaps Roosevelt's charity should have begun at home: what about the civil rights of the United States' own poor blacks in the Deep South – not to mention the Native Americans?)

Even certain American commentators now argue that the US-led move to decolonise was really the beginning of imperialism of a different, but equally pernicious, kind. However, Roosevelt died before the world map could be redrawn to suit him, and less than a month later, 'Wild Bill' Donovan's report to President Truman, 'Problems and Objectives of US Policy', argued:

> . . . the United States should realize . . . its interest in the maintenance of the British, French, and Dutch colonial empires. We should encourage liberalization of colonial regimes in order the better to maintain them, and to check Soviet influence in the stimulation of colonial revolt. We have at present no interest in weakening or liquidating those empires or championing schemes of international trusteeship which may provoke unrest and result in colonial disintegration, and may at the same time alienate from us the European states whose help we may need to balance the Soviet power.

Donovan warned that 'Russia will emerge from the present conflict as by far the strongest nation in Europe and Asia – strong enough, if the United States should stand aside, to dominate Europe and at the same time establish her hegemony in Asia.'[13] Truman immediately declared he supported Indo-China's return to France, over which Roosevelt had engaged in complex plotting. Truman's complete U-turn from Roosevelt's policies tacitly admitted that the latter – yet again – was deliberately aiding the Soviet Union.

'Dirty Donovan'

Despite Donovan's attitude, undoubtedly the OSS was the instrument through which Roosevelt's anti-colonialism and push for increased trade opportunities were to be fulfilled – Donovan approved of reducing European influence where it allowed in American businesses, but not where it opened the door for Communism. At the same time as advocating US support for the European empires to Truman, he was setting up a post-war intelligence network in the Middle and Far East. This radically changed British attitudes: from being 'our man' in 1941, in April 1945 Churchill was writing: 'On the whole I incline against another SOE–OSS duel, on grounds too favourable for that dirty Donovan.'[14]

The difference between British and American attitudes to the colonies was most obvious in the war against Japan, of which Christopher Thorne writes in *Allies of a Kind* (1978):

> . . . of all the parts of the world in which the alliance (or tacit alliance, one should say) was operating, it was very probably South and Southeast Asia and the Far East that constituted the most fertile area for the growth of friction, suspicion and resentment; it was here, in other words, that difficult aspects of the relationship as a whole were most likely to make their mark on the local situation.[15]

In one of the most important recent books on the war in the Far East, *Intelligence and the War against Japan* (2000) – citing recently declassified official documents – Robert J. Aldrich writes:

Secret services quickly became key players in the struggle between Churchill and Roosevelt over post-war Asia. Their initial task was to report on the rival plans and ambitions of Allied governments, headquarters and civil affairs staffs. By 1944 this had translated into a barely disguised 'Great Game' to achieve the upper hand in clandestine pre-occupational strategies across South East Asia. At times the war against Japan appeared relegated to a sideshow.[16]

And in an article on US intelligence operations in India, he writes:

It [recent material] seems to suggest that, from late 1942, William J. Donovan's Office of Strategic Services (OSS) and also British secret services in Asia were increasingly preoccupied, not with the war against Japan, but with mutual competition to safeguard or advance national interests in the fluid situation created in Asia after Japan's dramatic southward expansion of December 1941.[17]

As Aldrich points out, many of the OSS officers in Asia were recruited from companies such as Texaco and Westinghouse, and so 'required little encouragement to gather economic and commercial intelligence' on America's Allies.[18] On the other hand, the British mostly wanted to curb the Americans, so that Britain would be at least restored to its pre-war position after Japan's defeat.

In a Foreign Office briefing in March 1943, MI6's Pacific expert Lieutenant Colonel Gerald Wilkinson warned, 'Wall Street imperialists were causing America to look far more interestedly already at these [post-war] Eastern prospects than ourselves.'[19] Wilkinson was duly transferred to BSC in Washington, officially as Asia liaison with OSS, but also to spy upon the 'Wall Street imperialists'. He complained that while the British had yet to realise Asia's huge commercial potential, the Americans were already considering how best to exploit it. In December 1944, he presented a detailed report on their plans, identifying the companies that posed the 'greatest potential threat' to Britain.[20]

In January 1945, the former head of OSS in India, Colonel John

G. Coughlin, informed Donovan that OSS operations were 'not only important in defeating the Japs but may also be considered in part as cover for an opportunity to serve as a listening post for American interests in Asia'.[21]

Turf wars

The expansion of covert operations from 1942 led to a series of conferences between SOE and OSS to work out 'turf agreements': who would be in charge where, with the other in a supporting role. It was agreed that India was British 'turf' – the OSS could only operate there with their permission – while China, Korea and Manchuria were the Americans'.[22] (Significantly for the British, this put Hong Kong on American turf.) But soon they were flagrantly encroaching on each other's areas.

Early in 1943, Roosevelt appointed his friend William Phillips, a former Ambassador to Italy, as Presidential Representative to India. He was perfect for the job, especially as, having been head of OSS in London the previous year, he possessed some very useful contacts. On Donovan's behalf, he asked the Viceroy of India, Lord Linlithgow, for permission to open an OSS station in Delhi. In March 1943, the Viceroy confided to London he suspected this was 'all part of the American anxiety to dig in this country with a view to the post-war period'. He also said he suspected the Office of Naval Intelligence station in Bombay of gathering intelligence 'in preparation for the post-war commercial penetration by the US'.[23] The British government refused permission for the Delhi station.

As well as spying on the Japanese, the OSS in Calcutta reported to Washington on the political situation in India. A key role in the battle for post-war hearts and minds was played by its sister service, the propagandist Office of War Information (OWI), which had already set up offices in Bombay, Calcutta, New Delhi and Karachi in 1942. The substantial OSS and OWI presence in India worried the British so much they exerted a great deal of energy in keeping them under surveillance. Meanwhile, the OSS and US military delegations suspected that the British were tapping their phones and bugging their offices, although they were never able to prove it.[24]

During Trident in 1943, when William Phillips unwisely brought up the subject of Indian independence, the resulting explosion eclipsed even the Prime Minister's atomic response to Hopkins a year earlier:

> My answer to you is: 'Take India if that is what you want!' Take it by all means! But I warn you that if I open the door a crack there will be the greatest blood-bath in all history; yes, a blood-bath in all history. Mark my words, I prophesied the present war, and prophesy the blood-bath.[25]

Roosevelt hastily removed Phillips from India and posted him to Eisenhower's headquarters in London.

By summer 1943, it was clear that the 'turf agreements' were not working, so the system was revised. When Lord Linlithgow proposed that all intelligence and covert operations in India should be placed under British control, Washington disagreed, though allowing that SOE should be the 'predominant partner' in India, and OSS in China, while either could operate in either country if considered necessary.[26]

Keen to distinguish between American and British prospects for India, the OWI took out newspaper advertisements setting out American policy regarding the Philippines – which Roosevelt had made a Commonwealth in 1935 in preparation for full independence ten years later – pointedly comparing this with the British and India.[27]

When in February 1944 OSS Lieutenant Colonel Sidney S. Rubenstein arrived in India to set up a security and counter-intelligence network, the British Director of Military Intelligence, Brigadier Walter Cawthorn, bristled: 'How would you like it if we came to your country to establish a CE [counter-espionage] system throughout the United States?'

Rubenstein replied, 'That is exactly what you did', and launched into a vivid description of British Security Coordination's activities. Rather sheepishly, Cawthorn admitted defeat.[28]

After D-Day, with the war effectively won, Donovan turned to creating a post-war intelligence organisation to foster US political and commercial interests in colonial territories. OSS in India began organising a US intelligence network for 'a time when the war no longer afforded a pretext for their activities'.[29]

'The Islam show'

The US government was eager to establish American oil companies all over the Middle East, especially as Britain had tried for so long to keep them out. Because Britain more or less had the monopoly of Iran and Iraq's oil supplies, the Americans turned their attention to Kuwait and Saudi Arabia, continuing to negotiate concessions throughout the war.[30]

Although the Saudi king, Ibn Saud, was taking at least a million marks a year from Germany, in July 1941 the American oil company Caltex asked the US government to give him $6 million a year to keep him sweet. Unfortunately, Saudi Arabia was not included on the list of countries approved for Lend-Lease, so in order to bypass Congress, Roosevelt instructed that British Lend-Lease was to be increased, and then Britain could pass the excess on to Ibn Saud. But as Charles Higham points out: 'If it were known that Ibn Saud as Hitler's close ally in Nazi pay was being bribed by the President to protect an oil company, there would have been a major public outcry.'[31]

However, the bribe worked: America was allowed to build an air base at Dhahran – the beginning of a relationship between the United States and the Saudi royal house that has continued ever since.

The Lend-Lease arrangement continued until 1943, when Britain suffered another blow in the Middle East. The Under-Secretary of the Navy, James Forrestal, and his Special Assistant, William Bullitt, considering that British influence in Saudi Arabia was 'becoming excessive', urged Roosevelt to change the system to cut them out as middlemen in the bribing of Ibn Saud. The US government instead invested directly in the Caltex subsidiary Aramco (Arabian-American Oil Company). However, later in the war Aramco was found to be supplying oil to the Axis via middlemen, and realising it was unwise to pour US taxpayers' money into a company caught trading with the enemy, Roosevelt finally declared Saudi Arabia a Lend-Lease country, with the customary declaration: 'I hereby find that the defense of Saudi Arabia is vital to the defense of the United States.' How exactly it was 'vital' remains unexplained – except in protecting US oil concessions.[32]

In 1943, the Anglo-Iranian Oil Company warned the British government that American companies were taking an interest in Iranian oil. Roosevelt had installed a special representative in Teheran, Major-General Patrick Hurley, who, together with the State Department, concentrated on extending American oil concessions while curbing any expansion of British or Russian influence in Iran.[33]

When Donovan began planning post-war espionage in the former colonies, the first territory he turned to was Saudi Arabia. He proposed that the team should pose as an archaeological mission, under the distinguished Harvard anthropologist Carleton S. Coon, a wartime OSS agent. After a few months touring the area to assess American intelligence's military and commercial requirements, Coon recommended that the operation be extended to cover the whole of the Muslim world – what he called the 'Islam show' – and that a separate and self-contained operation, independent of OSS, should oversee it. He also offered to resign from the OSS and return to Harvard to establish his cover. Aldrich writes, 'Whether Donovan acted on this proposal is not known.'[34] Unsurprisingly, the 'Islam show' disappears from the records with Coon's return to America.

The irresistible fall of Mr Hopkins

Teheran may have been Hopkins' greatest achievement, but his star was soon to wane dramatically. Although the immediate cause was another long bout of illness, removing him from the President's side for six months, the real reasons why he never fully regained his previous status are unknown.

Shortly before Teheran – in August 1943 – Hopkins had moved out of the White House into Georgetown with his new wife, the former Paris fashion editor of *Harper's Bazaar*, Louise Macy. On New Year's Day 1944, when he was taken ill with a severe recurrence of his intestinal problems, another operation was recommended – it was feared that his cancer had returned – but he was first sent to Florida for three weeks to build up his strength for the major surgery.

During this time, he was dealt another blow. On 12 February, his

18-year-old son Stephen, from his first marriage, was killed serving with the Marines at Kwajalein Atoll in the Marshall Islands. Some accounts claim he was a victim of what would later be called 'friendly fire'.[35]

The operation found no sign of cancer, and Hopkins began to respond to treatment, although he had a relapse in May which prevented him returning to work until 4 July 1944. Perhaps six months was simply too long to be away from his power-base, but for whatever reason Roosevelt was so chilly towards him that their long-standing friendship was fundamentally undermined. On one occasion, the President even pointedly failed to acknowledge Hopkins when he walked into a meeting late. And where they had once been of one mind over policy, they now began to differ.[36] Perhaps Hopkins' many enemies in the administration had seized the opportunity of his lengthy absence to get their own feet under the presidential table. And the President's own physical and mental health was also in decline, making him easier to influence.

FDR had not been well for some time, his immune system seriously undermined by influenza in mid-1943, leaving him prey to infections. During one dinner at Teheran, he had suffered such severe stomach cramps that he was rushed away for urgent medical attention. Once home, Roosevelt became lethargic and depressed. A full medical check-up at the end of March 1944 revealed heart disease and high blood pressure, which led to anaemia and congestion of the lungs, besides depleting his mental capabilities because of the insufficient blood supply to his brain (secondary metabolic encephalopathy). He found it harder to concentrate, becoming increasingly forgetful, although it was only in early 1945 that this became too obvious to ignore.[37]

After a month's rest, Roosevelt pressed ahead with his fourth-term nomination in July, although it was clearly unwise. Nothing could shake his entrenched belief that only he could lead America at such a crucial time: he still refused to delegate matters of policy and kept even those closest to him in the dark.

Meanwhile, Hopkins was languishing in the wilderness while the final phase of the war was beginning with the Normandy landings, the recapture of the Philippines and the retreat of the Japanese in

Burma. It seemed to be the end of a glittering career – although he was to stage a final comeback, leaving one last indelible mark on history.

The fate of Germany

In early 1944, it was obvious that the defeat of Germany and Japan was imminent. The landings in Normandy were planned for the spring, and the Red Army was poised to cross the (pre-Nazi–Soviet Pact) Polish border. Roosevelt said ominously to Morgenthau: 'We have to be tough with Germany, and I mean the German people not just the Nazis or you have to treat them in such a manner so they just can't go on reproducing people who want to continue the way they have in the past,'[38] speaking of 'castrating' the Germans if they continued to breed aggressive people.[39] In August 1944, Roosevelt declared to Stimson: 'The German people as a whole must have it driven home to them that the whole nation has been engaged in a lawless conspiracy against the decencies of modern civilization.'[40] Yet the draconian measures he envisaged for Germany – breaking it up, depriving its citizens of the means to manufacture arms and the forcible dispersion of the Prussians – flew completely in the face of his much-vaunted Atlantic Charter, not to mention 'the decencies of modern civilization'.

Hopkins – to whom Germany was the major threat to Europe's future – also advocated its dismemberment 'by any means necessary'.[41] He wanted himself, or his protégé Stettinius, to be the United States' high commissioner to post-war Germany, to ensure that the German economy did not revive too rapidly.[42]

In the end, of course, Germany was not dismembered in this way – although disastrously divided for other reasons – but only because by the time the final decisions were made Roosevelt was dead. Had he lived, would he have insisted on grinding Germany down?

Unconditional surrender remained the Allies' policy as D-Day approached, even though they were warned that Goebbels was playing on the anxieties of the German people about their grim fate at the hands of the Allies. (Where the Russians were concerned, he was not far wrong.)

In January 1944, because of the Cabinet's unease about

unconditional surrender (it would inspire the Germans to fight harder on D-Day) Churchill set out Britain's official position, saying that although Roosevelt had announced the idea 'without previous consultation' he had 'thought it right to endorse what he said'. He went on to outline that he believed this meant complete disarmament and removal of the power to rearm; prohibition from any form of aviation; giving up alleged war criminals for trial in the relevant countries; and at least four million Germans as slave labour to rebuild Russia; 'Germany is to be decisively broken up into a number of separate States'; the destruction of the officer class of the army – Churchill adding that to circumvent Stalin's mass executions without trial of the German Army General Staff, a list of 50 to 100 'outlaws of the first notoriety' was to be drawn up for capital punishment. He, too, said nothing about a trial first.[43] The Labour leader Clement Attlee complained, 'I do not recall that we have ever taken so definite a decision' about breaking Germany up into smaller states.[44]

The US commanders were also worried that demanding unconditional surrender would add considerably to the difficulty of the Normandy landings and subsequent liberation of occupied Europe. In late March 1944, the Joint Chiefs petitioned Roosevelt to make it clear that 'unconditional surrender' was aimed at the Nazis and not the German people. Roosevelt responded:

> A somewhat long and personal experience in and out of Germany leads me to believe that German Philosophy cannot be changed by decree, law or military order. The change in German Philosophy must be evolutionary and may take two generations . . .
>
> I think that the simplest way of approaching this whole matter is to stick to what I have already said, (a) that the United Nations are determined to administer a total defeat to Germany as a whole; (b) that the Allies have no intention of destroying the German people. Please note that I am not willing at this time to say that we do not intend to destroy the German nation.[45]

Many historians, politicians and intelligence officers believe the war could have been won at least a year earlier had the Western Allies not been precluded from negotiating the surrender of the opposition in Germany. As Senator Burton Wheeler wrote:

> . . . in the spring of 1944 we had reports that there was a strong movement in Germany to oust Hitler. If FDR had followed the example of Woodrow Wilson and told the German people what the allies wanted instead of insisting on unconditional surrender the German people might have overthrown their dictator. That might have saved the lives of tens of thousands of American boys and avoided tragic political consequences. Our leaders trusted and followed 'good old Joe' Stalin, so today [1960s] we are reaping the global whirlwind.[46]

Richard Lamb agrees:

> What is certain is that if the war had been brought to an end by negotiations with the 'good' Germans in 1944, vast numbers of lives would have been saved both in the Allied forces and among civilians in the German-occupied countries. The Allied Governments were by then well aware of the extermination of the Jews and the wholesale deportations of slave labour. A swift end to the hostilities would have stopped it. The British Government's policy, however, was that it was better to continue the war than to seek peace with the 'good' Germans.[47]

Allen Dulles of the OSS, in close contact with the anti-Hitler conspirators in the lead-up to the bomb plot of July 1944, explains:

> Several of the top generals whom the conspirators approached had been unwilling to take part in the plot and to assume the political responsibility involved because the unconditional-surrender policy, as they understood it, meant that Germany would be treated with the same harshness by the Allies whether the surrender came early by action of the Germans

who dared defy Hitler or at a later date by one of Hitler's henchmen. In April of 1944, before the actual assassination attempt, the conspirators had in fact sent a special emissary to me in Switzerland to see whether there was any hope of getting better terms than unconditional surrender from the West. The answer given was an emphatic no; the Allied position on unconditional surrender could not be changed. The emissary returned with the answer, to the despair of some of the conspirators, many of whom began to feel that the Soviet [*sic*], with a far more flexible attitude, was their main ally against Hitler.[48]

Moscow was clearly *not* adhering to the unconditional surrender demand, although, as we will see, it compelled the Westerners to do so, even complaining vociferously if it suspected that the Americans or British were wavering.

Despite the discouragement, the Schwarze Kapelle still realised they had to get rid of Hitler and the Nazis. Germany was being pounded mercilessly by Anglo-American air raids, while the Red Army was poised to avenge itself barbarously on German civilians. Surely, the Schwarze Kapelle reasoned, the American and British public wouldn't allow their armies to continue fighting if Hitler and his henchmen were removed . . .

Unfortunately, there were serious setbacks after the failed Operation Flash in spring 1943: General Beck was diagnosed with cancer, and others had either been arrested and charged with treason or, like Canaris's deputy General Oster, were under such suspicion that they simply dared not operate. Canaris himself had to lie low. (Despite Gestapo suspicions, in the absence of proof he remained in post until February 1944, when he was given a token position in the new combined Abwehr and SS intelligence organisation, the Sicherheitsdienst, or SD.)

As a result, the conspiracy crystallised around Colonel Claus von Stauffenberg, a dashing young aristocrat and devout Catholic, who had been removed from a major role in the anti-Hitler conspiracy by being posted to Tunisia. Terribly wounded, he became Chief of Staff of the Replacement Army (Ersatzheer) in Berlin, commanded by 'fair-weather' conspirator General Friedrich Fromm.

Before the failed bomb plot of 20 July 1944, there were four other attempts to kill Hitler after Flash. In September 1943, a bomb was planted in his headquarters, but exploded prematurely. A junior officer invited to a staff meeting at Berchtesgaden planned to shoot Hitler, but found himself placed next to a watchful SS bodyguard. In November, when another officer offered himself as a suicide bomber, hiding explosives under the new design of greatcoat he was to model for the Führer, an Allied air raid caused the modelling session to be abandoned. Then, on 26 December, von Stauffenberg made the first attempt to smuggle a bomb in his briefcase into a staff meeting with Hitler, but that, too, was cancelled at the last minute.[49]

Each time, Operation Valkyrie swung into action – disguised as an exercise – in preparation for the army to wrest power from the Nazi Party and SS. A temporary government to run the country and make overtures to the Allies had already been selected.

Without the demand for unconditional surrender, the D-Day landings might well have been unnecessary: by that stage, the anti-Hitler generals were prepared to hand Germany over to the Western Allies. According to Allen Dulles, a month before D-Day his contact in the conspiracy, Hans Bernd Gisevius, received details from Berlin for a German surrender on the Western Front, in which the opposition generals would allow American and British forces to occupy Germany provided they could continue fighting the Russians. Three Allied airborne divisions would be allowed to land in Berlin, with the cooperation of local commanders, together with landings at Hamburg, Bremen and on the French coast. Hitler and his henchmen would be isolated.[50]

Whether Roosevelt and Churchill should have taken up this offer may be debatable, but it shows that there was an alternative in the lead-up to D-Day. And even when the conspirators dropped their demand to be allowed to continue fighting Russia – the West *still* refused to deal with them.

Overlord – at last

Churchill was far from being completely behind D-Day. He still believed that the Western Allies should be concentrating on the

Overlords

Italian campaign, and that focusing on Overlord would open the way for the Russians to capture more of Eastern and Central Europe, perhaps even reaching Berlin first and giving Stalin the all-important head-start in post-war Europe. Whether he would have preferred Overlord to have been postponed or cancelled is uncertain, but he certainly had great reservations about its proposed schedule. He would have preferred Germany to have been worn down further before the Allies even attempted to liberate France.

Even after Overlord was set, Churchill continued to question whether they were doing the right thing. Field Marshal Brooke noted on 19 October 1943:

> COS [Chiefs of Staff meeting] at which we received note from PM wishing to swing round the strategy back to the Mediterranean at the expense of the cross-Channel operation. I am in many ways entirely with him, but God knows where that may lead us to as regards clashes with Americans.[51]

George McJimsey writes: 'Hopkins could not escape the feeling that the British were not to be trusted and that Churchill would come up with some last-minute ploy to scuttle the operation.'[52]

Having decided on an American supreme commander, Hopkins argued for the appointment of his protégé General Marshall, but Churchill vetoed it because he would be too influenced by Roosevelt.[53] But the final choice, Eisenhower ('Ike'), was *Marshall*'s protégé. In February 1944, the Supreme Headquarters Allied Expeditionary Force – SHAEF – was formed under Eisenhower to command Overlord and the subsequent operations in Europe.

On 11 March 1944, Churchill cabled General Marshall in Washington, 'I am hardening very much on this operation as the time approaches',[54] and on 15 May he told the final top-level conference, 'I am hardening toward this enterprise',[55] apparently meaning he was coming round to Overlord – but significantly also implying he was *not* totally committed. Because of the legend of D-Day, there is a general reluctance to admit that Churchill was anything other than four-square behind the operation from the start, but if he had had his way, at the very least Overlord would have been postponed.

After Dieppe, and Dunkirk – not to mention the Dardanelles – one can hardly blame the Prime Minister for suffering near-panic as D-Day approached. The fear of failure certainly played a part: he warned Eisenhower of 'Channel tides running red with Allied blood'.[56] However, Churchill's reservations were not because it was risky but because it seemed to him an *unnecessary* risk.

As history and Hollywood tell, just after midnight on 6 June 1944, 23,000 British and American paratroops were dropped on the flanks of the landing beaches. Under cover of bombardment from sea and air, over 130,000 troops landed at dawn at five points along the coast. Although going smoothly, there were some 10,000 casualties. But only on the notorious 'Omaha' beach, where the 1st US Infantry came ashore under heavy fire and suffered 2,000 casualties (10 times more than 'Utah') was there any significant setback. Once they had established the beachheads, Allied troops – over 850,000 by the end of June – began to pour into France for the next phase, Operation Neptune, the taking of Normandy.

The July plot
The generals plotting to overthrow the Nazis were caught out by Overlord. They had wanted to kick-start their coup before the landings, fearing that otherwise it might look as if they had been panicked into it. However, Overlord was protected by such a successful deception operation – indicating that the invasion would happen later – that the Schwarze Kapelle were fooled. Nevertheless, in their view, they had to try to save Germany. Not only were the Allies remorselessly approaching from east, west and (a little less remorselessly) south – Rome was taken two days before D-Day – but the SD's anti-Nazi arrests were intensifying, and at any moment torture might expose the whole conspiracy. By now, the generals realised they would have to drop their demand to continue fighting the USSR. Dulles writes of the period after the Normandy landings:

> We learned later that the conspirators in Germany began to realize it would have to be unconditional and simultaneous surrender to East and West. This realization, I believe, helped to bring together the Left and the Right, the military and the

civilians, those oriented toward the East and those who wanted to deal only with the West. In any event, the advance of the Allied armies forced the conspirators to bury their ideological differences.[57]

In early July, a messenger from Berlin briefed Gisevius on the bomb plan ('Breakers' to the Americans), who told Dulles, who in turn informed Washington. Meanwhile, MI6's contacts in Sweden gave them advance warning of the plot. Both governments knew about it.[58]

Despite official British acquiescence to unconditional surrender, there are clear signs that they were trying to undermine it by encouraging the conspirators, while trying not to upset Roosevelt. On 6 July, the Deputy Prime Minister, Clement Attlee, announced to the House of Commons:

> So far as His Majesty's Government are concerned, it has repeatedly been made clear in public statements that we shall fight on until Germany has been forced to capitulate and until Nazism is extirpated. It is for the German people to draw the logical conclusion. If any section of them wants to see a return to a regime based on respect for international law and for the rights of the individual, they must understand that no one will believe them until they have themselves taken active steps to rid themselves of their present regime.[59]

Six days later, Churchill made a similar statement in the House. Reminded in a question about his previous call for the Germans to throw out the Nazis, he replied:

> I am very glad to be reminded of that statement, to which I strongly adhere. I think it has been repeated in other forms by the Foreign Secretary and other Ministers. At any rate, it would certainly be a very well-advised step on the part of the Germans.[60]

This seems to be clear encouragement to the German plotters.

(When the coup failed, Churchill and the Cabinet hastily declared that even overthrowing the Nazis wouldn't help the Germans.) Perhaps this was because things were not going well in Normandy. Bad weather had delayed the build-up, and the Allies had managed to advance only about 20 miles since the landings a month before. Until the situation improved, even the spectre of Dunkirk was beginning to loom rather ominously. And the British Isles themselves suffered a new menace, the V-1 'flying bomb' ('doodle-bug'), the first of which hit London on 13 June, followed by a wave of over 10,000, causing over 6,000 deaths. If a speedy end could be brought about by a regime change in Germany, now would be an ideal time. Unfortunately, Roosevelt – and Stalin – had other plans.

Allen Dulles writes of Attlee's and Churchill's statements: 'I urged that some similar statement be made from America as I was convinced that whatever the result of "Breakers" might be, the fact that an attempt was made to overthrow Hitler, whether or not successfully, would help to shorten the war. Nothing of this nature was done.'[61] Presumably this was because Roosevelt had no wish to shorten the war, as it would upset his plans for the division of Europe – in which the Soviet Union would hold the balance of power.

The anti-Hitler cabal certainly wanted the war to end. On 19 July, when von Stauffenberg was summoned to Hitler's 'Wolf's Lair' at Rastenburg in East Prussia, yet again Operation Valkyrie was dusted off. The next day, he placed the briefcase-bomb under the table where Hitler was receiving his daily briefing, before leaving the room.

Having witnessed the explosion, von Stauffenberg made the fatal error of assuming the Führer was dead, returning to Berlin to initiate Operation Valkyrie. A few hours afterwards, as scheduled, Hitler met Mussolini off a train, telling him: 'After my miraculous escape from death today I am more than ever convinced that it is my fate to bring our common enterprise to a successful conclusion.'[62]

Yet, unknown to the slightly battered Hitler, Valkyrie was swinging into action. It called for a state of emergency, the arrest of pro-Hitler officers and Nazi and SS leaders, and the army to take over the rank and file. The formation of a new, non-Nazi government would then be announced.

The news that Hitler was still alive reached the conspirators' headquarters in the General Staff Building in Berlin before von Stauffenberg's message arrived claiming he was dead. Panic and confusion reigned. The Valkyrie order was given, only to be rescinded four hours later. Fatally, the officer in charge of communications from the headquarters – poised to relay instructions to the army throughout the Reich – waited until he could confirm the true situation. Drama meeting farce, Major Otto-Ernst Remer, sent to arrest Goebbels, had the telephone handed to him and found himself talking to the 'dead' Hitler, who promoted him to Colonel and ordered him to suppress the coup.[63]

That night, Berlin was electric with tension. Remer's troops surrounded the Staff headquarters where the coup leaders, including General Beck and von Stauffenberg (still convinced he had killed Hitler), were trying to retain control of the uprising. Dispatching tanks to besiege the SS headquarters, a battle on the streets of Berlin seemed inevitable.

As the coup crumbled, General Fromm, to cover up his own role on the fringes of the conspiracy, ordered the immediate executions of von Stauffenberg and other plotters, but allowed the elderly and respected General Beck the option of suicide. (Despite his subterfuge, Fromm was imprisoned until his execution in March 1945.)

Ironically, Valkyrie went smoothly in Paris: all 1,200 SS officers in the city were arrested. But when the coup fell apart in Germany itself, there was no point in going it alone, and they were freed.

Although Moscow radio appealed for the Germans to rise up against Hitler – clearly the NKVD also had advance warning of the coup – as Dulles asks: 'And what came from Washington and London? The attempt on Hitler's life was dismissed as of no consequence. Churchill suggested that it was merely a case of dog-eat-dog.'[64] Whether British and American encouragement would have persuaded more Germans to join the overthrow of Hitler's regime, it is impossible to say. But it is quite incredible that they didn't even try.

Dulles and his team were disconsolate. As one of his agents in Germany said later: 'They had always hoped that through a sudden downfall of Hitler, the war would be ended before the Soviet Russians entered Berlin. A quick peace agreement with a democratic

German regime would have prevented that. But now all was lost; the continuation of the war would provide the Russians with a pathway to the Elbe in the heart of Europe. American policy had suffered a terrible defeat.'[65] But while this might have been OSS or even State Department policy, it was not Roosevelt's. He would have counted it a failure even if a new German regime had agreed to unconditional surrender.

The British War Cabinet agreed their official stance about the plot before the Commons debate on 2 August: they would discourage any remaining anti-Hitler plotters, reinforcing the message that unconditional surrender was required from *any* German government.[66] So near to victory, they needed the Americans.

It was the end of the anti-Hitler cabals, as their leaders suffered torture to reveal more names. Goerdeler was arrested a few weeks later and executed in February 1945, as were Ulrich von Hassell, Ewald von Kleist-Schmenzin and Adam von Trott zu Solz. The trail even led to Rommel, who had been flirting with joining the conspiracy: he chose to commit suicide. Although not directly involved in the July plot, when Canaris's role in the wider conspiracy emerged during the subsequent investigation he was arrested, and was hanged in the last month of the war.

The 'Jeanne d'Arc complex'

The time had finally come for Roosevelt and Churchill to address the role of de Gaulle and his French Committee of National Liberation in post-war France. In November 1943, Churchill wrote to Duff Cooper (British representative to de Gaulle's Algiers Committee) that de Gaulle was: 'Fascist-minded, opportunist, unscrupulous, ambitious to the last degree and his coming to power in the new France would lead to great schisms there and also to a considerable estrangement between France and the Western democracies.'[67]

In December 1943, angered by de Gaulle's arrest of three prominent former Vichyites in Algeria, Roosevelt wrote to Churchill: 'It seems to me this is the proper time to eliminate the Jeanne d'Arc complex and return to realism.'[68] At around this time, FDR reluctantly replaced Robert Murphy with a more pro-de Gaulle ambassador to Algiers, Edward C. Wilson, in whose instructions the

President specifically pointed out that the Committee's attempts to promote itself as the provisional government of France were not recognised by the US.[69]

Although the personal antagonisms among the three leaders at times verged on the childish (Cadogan wrote: 'Roosevelt, PM and – it must be admitted – de G. all behave like girls approaching the age of puberty'[70]), at the heart lay the serious issues of France's status in the post-war world. De Gaulle may seem to have suffered from an apparently hypersensitive *amour-propre*, but he realised that if he failed to fight France's corner, it would be left nowhere. His fear was fully justified.

There was a fundamental difference in Churchill's and Roosevelt's antagonism towards de Gaulle: the Prime Minister respected France as a great nation but considered the man a complete pain, while Roosevelt detested both man and country. But their personal clashes boiled down to important questions such as whether France would have a permanent seat on the United Nations Security Council.

In Algiers, de Gaulle was even kept out of the D-Day plans. Save for General Jacques Leclerc's Second Armoured Division – included to provide emotive PR at the liberation of Paris – French forces were not to be involved, although they were to be allowed to take part in an invasion of southern France in the wake of Overlord. So who was to be France's leader, when its '*jour de gloire est arrivé*'?

In November 1943, at Cairo, angered that de Gaulle was openly declaring that *he* would appoint France's new government, Roosevelt had written to Cordell Hull, 'The thought that the occupation, when it comes, should be wholly military is one to which I am increasingly inclined.'[71] He declared that until France had 'recovered its balance' the country would be run regionally – effectively making Eisenhower the government. As military governor, he was to appoint civil authorities on a local basis, in collaboration with whichever political group he deemed appropriate – perhaps de Gaulle's Committee, perhaps another body (the only exception being the Vichyites, the Big Three having agreed to have no dealing with the Vichy government 'except for the purpose of liquidating it'[72]).

Without a central French government, the Americans wanted to withhold all overt signs of French sovereignty – the State Department would even print the new French currency. Although a profoundly offended de Gaulle protested and tried to organise his own currency, the post-liberation 'francs' were printed in the US – and were accepted by the French population.[73]

Although Churchill told Eden he was opposed to giving the French Committee civil authority in liberated France, as D-Day approached, practicalities – and the usual Cabinet pressure – made it obvious that ignoring de Gaulle and his Committee was a bad idea. Just three days before Overlord, Churchill invited de Gaulle to join him in the special railway train he used as his mobile headquarters, where he finally briefed him on the operation on 4 June. When the Prime Minister repeatedly attempted to raise post-liberation French administration, de Gaulle refused even to consider it – it was France's business. He always replied: '*C'est la guerre, faites-la, on verra après.*' ('This is war, let's get on with it, we will see afterwards.'[74])

At a meeting with Churchill and de Gaulle, Eisenhower announced that when the invasion began he would broadcast to the French, instructing them to follow his orders until elections could be held. Although de Gaulle was told he could amend Eisenhower's draft, when he did submit his version he found the original was already poised for leaflet-drops over France.[75] As Raoul Aglion, the French Committee's representative in Washington, wrote, 'De Gaulle was furious. The invasion of France that he had expected for years would be done without him, and finally the strategy of Roosevelt was going to eliminate him at the last hour.'[76]

There were other humiliations. As the invasion began, one by one the exiled heads of state or government were to broadcast to their nations from the BBC. The scheduled order, set by protocol, was King Gustav V of Norway, followed by Queen Wilhelmina of the Netherlands, the Grand Duchess of Luxembourg, the Prime Minister of Belgium, Eisenhower and – last and by all means least – de Gaulle. The Frenchman refused to speak after the American, and when Eisenhower also refused to budge, he withdrew the French liaison officers who were to assist the Allied forces after the landings.[77]

Desperate and daring, in his own separate broadcast on the BBC several hours after the landings, de Gaulle declared: 'The directions issued by the French Government and by the French leaders who have been delegated to issue them must be followed to the letter.'[78] He made no mention of the American and British Allies – and no longer spoke of his government as 'provisional'. Churchill and Roosevelt were furious but had no option but to negotiate with the French Committee about civil administration.

In the two weeks following the invasion, de Gaulle's Committee was recognised as the provisional government of France by Belgium, Luxembourg, Norway, Poland, Czechoslovakia and Yugoslavia. On 14 June, he crossed the Channel on a French destroyer and for the first time in four years stepped onto French soil. The enthusiastic welcome demonstrated his support in his beloved homeland, while the rapturous American press coverage showed Roosevelt how his own people also took the Free French leader to their hearts. De Gaulle told one of his commanders, 'You see, we just had to present the Allies with a *fait accompli*. Our administration is now in place. You'll see that they will say nothing.'[79]

After spending a month in France, de Gaulle returned to London, going on to Rome and the Vatican, where he was accepted as a head of state. He delayed visiting Washington until he could confront Roosevelt as an equal, not a supplicant, whatever the US President thought. As a result, Roosevelt agreed to recognise the French Committee, in carefully chosen words, as the 'de facto authority' in France.[80]

De Gaulle continued to put the Americans on the spot. Eisenhower's liberation of Paris had to be brought forward because of a popular uprising, Allied tanks, including Leclerc's, entering the city on 24 August. The dramatic figure of de Gaulle followed the next day amid enormous rapture – declaring that the French Committee of National Liberation was the continuation of the Republic and that he was its President. Much as this annoyed Roosevelt, as Raoul Aglion explains: 'Eisenhower . . . acted independently of the President because he was convinced that only General de Gaulle could prevent disturbances by local factions and the communists and guarantee a calm population at the rear of his army.'[81]

Roosevelt's and Churchill's awkward position was exacerbated when Stalin announced he was prepared to recognise de Gaulle as President of France. Although at Quebec in September 1944 the

President and Prime Minister refused to recognise de Gaulle's government, Churchill wavered afterwards, telling Roosevelt in mid-October that he was now in favour of it – clearly angling for a joint announcement. But FDR stole a march: while cabling Churchill twice to urge further delay, on 23 October the US Ambassador in Paris was instructed to formally recognise de Gaulle's provisional government. Now that Britain was the only nation not to have done so, it had to rush out its own announcement, as if slavishly following the Americans. When an embarrassed and irritated Churchill complained to Roosevelt, he was told that, because FDR had been away campaigning, the State Department had taken 'more precipitate action' than he had intended.[82] Aglion gloats: 'The facts spoke for themselves and Roosevelt was finally forced to give in. In doing so, he tacitly admitted four years of error in his foreign policy towards France.'[83]

However, there was a dividend for Roosevelt. The US elections were to be held on 7 November, and de Gaulle had always been popular with the American people. So by agreeing to recognise him as French leader just a few days before they went to the polls, FDR at least managed to squeeze some advantage from it.

Morganthau's hell

As if looking for a greater incentive for the Germans to fight on than even unconditional surrender, Roosevelt and his team invented the 'Morgenthau Plan', unveiled at the Second Quebec Conference ('Octagon') in mid-September 1944.

Days before, Lord Halifax warned that Morgenthau advocated that Germany should receive no aid to rebuild its industry, deliberately intending to create the kind of runaway inflation that devastated Germany after 1918 – which would have a 'salutary effect' on its people.[84] In fact, the Morgenthau (officially 'Treasury') Plan proposed nothing less than the wholesale de-industrialisation of Germany.[85] Its plant and machinery would go to the Allies – mainly Russia – and the nation transformed into a 'primarily agricultural and pastoral' economy, to make the Germans dependent on the US and other nations for supplies such as steel, machinery and chemicals. No reparations would be demanded – but only because payment would rely on possessing some kind of industry – and no other kind of funding would be forthcoming. The Germans would be left to fend for themselves, with few means of support, their country thrust back into the nineteenth – or even the eighteenth – century. Besides stripping Germany of the Nazis' new acquisitions, the nation itself would be divided into two states, north and south. Morgenthau also called for the summary executions – without trial – of Hitler and his henchmen, and the use of German forced labour to rebuild the nations they had attacked. It was a document of which Stalin would have been proud. Perhaps he *was* – the Plan owed much to Harry Dexter White.[86]

On 11 September, while Churchill was en route to Quebec, the Cabinet discussed the plan and – with the exception of the Minister of Labour, Ernest Bevin – opposed it. But by the time Anthony Eden cabled the Prime Minister with this news, Churchill had already put his initials to the document.

A week later, when details of the Morgenthau Plan were leaked to the *Wall Street Journal* and splashed in America's media, it caused a sensation. Most Americans were appalled: some because it would make them seem no better than the Nazis; others realised if they could read it, the Germans could also read it, and as the perfect propaganda opportunity it could only prolong the war. It was blindingly obvious that even those Germans who would have accepted unconditional surrender would fight all the harder to prevent their nation's enslavement and their families' starvation.

What were Churchill's views on this draconian proposal? Did he genuinely approve or was he pushed into it, as he had been with unconditional surrender? In the same 1949 House of Commons quizzing in which he admitted being caught out over that announcement, Churchill said he had felt similarly constrained to lend his support to the Morgenthau Plan, 'about which I do not feel so confident in my conscience about the judgement of my actions'.[87] Later, he claimed he had been 'violently opposed' to it but was compelled to give in to Roosevelt, only agreeing subject to the approval of the War Cabinet, but according to John Colville and others he never seriously objected, and continued to support it even after the Cabinet's near-unanimous opposition, presumably because the Americans had 'cunningly linked' a desperately needed $6 billion credit to the Plan.[88] And Churchill also realised the potential to British industry of supplying Germany with goods it would be unable to produce itself.[89]

Roosevelt's own attitude is something of a puzzle. Clearly he approved of the Plan at the conference, and with his entrenched prejudice against Germans it was no secret that he was sympathetic to its principles. He *did* favour German dismemberment, disarmament and de-industrialisation, and was not overly concerned about its population. Yet within two weeks he was writing to Hull: 'No one wants to make Germany a wholly agricultural nation again, and yet somebody down the line has handed this out to the press. I wish you could catch and chastise him.'[90] But this *was* what the Morgenthau Plan advocated. Presumably badly rattled by the horrified reaction to the press reports – such a gift to his rivals – he thought it wisest to distance himself from the proposals.

Did the Allies ever seriously intend to subject the Germans to such harsh treatment? If not, what was the Morgenthau Plan all about? A clue may lie in the fact that (unlike alternative plans considered for Germany) it *was* leaked to the media . . . Of course, Goebbels was quick to take advantage – after the Normandy landings he had already hammered home the terrifying prospect that the Allies planned to 'exterminate us root and branch as a nation'.[91] The Morgenthau Plan appeared to prove him right. A report on German propaganda by the British Political Warfare Executive in October 1944 stated:

> Greatest prominence given to Morgenthau alleged proposals for the economic subjugation of Germany. Newspapers report, under many headings. Morgenthau surpasses Clemenceau who claimed there were 40 million Germans too many . . .[92]

Morgenthau was described as the leader of the agitation 'who sings the same tune as the Jews in the Kremlin and demands complete annihilation of the German industry, dismemberment of the country and extermination of half the population'. Never one to miss a trick,

Goebbels triumphantly pointed out that Morgenthau was Jewish.

The Germans believed him about the Plan, because they saw with their own eyes what the Allies were capable of. Following the Normandy landings, 'Bomber' Harris had switched Bomber Command's priority to attacks on factories, believing that their most vital component was the workers – and they were easier to hit. And at the beginning of 1945, the Allies instigated Operation Thunderclap, an air offensive against Berlin and other cities, which notoriously culminated when at least 50,000 people were killed in the historic city of Dresden in February. As the Supreme Allied HQ's report stated: 'The Dresden raid was designed to cripple communications. The fact that the city was crowded with refugees at the time of the attack was coincidental and took the form of a bonus.'[93] (At a press briefing, it slipped out that Thunderclap had actually set out to destroy civilians – to widespread horror. Churchill also wrote that 'the destruction of Dresden remains a serious query against the conduct of Allied bombing'.[94]) By the end of the war, the bombing offensive had killed between 750,000 and a million Germans.[95]

As Richard Lamb writes:

> There is incontrovertible evidence that indiscriminate bombing and the policy of unconditional surrender immeasurably stiffened the German people's will to resist and appalling damage and casualties from British and American bombing were interpreted to the German people by Goebbels as an integral part of the Morgenthau Plan.[96]

The Germans were already expecting dire treatment from the Russians – but now it seemed the Western Allies would be just as brutal. The Morgenthau Plan achieved what should have been impossible at that stage of the war, actually *reviving* pro-Hitler sympathies.[97] In retreat since the Normandy invasions, in October 1944 the German military began to resist the Allied advance with renewed vigour. A month later, Eisenhower worriedly informed Washington and London that unless unconditional surrender was reconsidered he could not say how long the war might last. And, although not specifically mentioning the Morgenthau Plan, he also recommended a propaganda counter-offensive to combat Goebbels' successes in rebuilding German morale and to convince the defeated Germans they would be treated fairly. But although Roosevelt had repudiated the Plan in the press (unlikely to be reported by Goebbels) he 'failed to take any steps to halt the adverse propaganda about it in Germany'.[98]

In mid-December, the German counter-offensive in the Ardennes – the Battle of the Bulge – recaptured a large part of Belgium, holding up the Allied advance for a month. If the Allies were truly interested in finishing the war as quickly as possible, then in this instance alone the Plan was a massive setback.

Although, in the end, some territory was confiscated from Germany and its inhabitants kicked out, obviously the full Plan was never put into practice; the dismemberment idea was abandoned (the Cold War division into East and West Germany came about for other reasons) and the industrial decimation never happened. The Nuremberg war crimes trials took the place of summary executions. But was this simply because, by the time the final decisions were made, Roosevelt was dead and Morgenthau out of office?[99] The Plan, having been agreed by Roosevelt and Churchill, was neither formally repealed nor even discussed again. But because of the silence, the world – especially the Germans – continued to believe that Morgenthau's proposals would be put into practice. But as Lamb asks: 'Why did no one grasp that the Morgenthau Plan could only strengthen German resolve?'

However, we believe that the Plan's *whole point* was to 'strengthen German resolve'. That it would do so was so patently obvious – especially when Goebbels began to exploit it – that it is hard to believe it was only ever an enormous diplomatic blunder. Whether there was ever a serious intention to act on it is beside the point: the Germans *believed* it would be carried out, ensuring that they would fight on to their last breath, until the Allies took their country by force – even an unconditional surrender was precluded now – justifying the ongoing blitz of German industry. There was no longer any possibility of Hitler being overthrown (who would lead a coup now?) and the Allies would have to fight every inch of the way to Berlin.

Overlords

It all hinged on the ambitions of Roosevelt and Morgenthau for the post-war world order, particularly in Europe. FDR and Hopkins wanted a significant Soviet presence on the Continent, but the dismemberment and occupation of Germany and Austria also provided justification for a post-war *American* presence. They wanted Europe split between American and Soviet spheres of influence, removing any future threat from Germany and also keeping the old European powers down. Accepting an early surrender from Germany would jeopardise these plans, as it would be easiest to carry them through if the war ended with Eastern and Western Allies already occupying the Reich. If Hitler was overthrown and a new government offered to surrender, there would be pressure from the public and their representatives in Congress and Parliament to accept the offer. In other words, while the war could hardly end too soon for most people, it *could* end too soon for Roosevelt.

CHAPTER THIRTEEN

Exits and Betrayals

'Once you are a Bolshevist you are apparently immune. All past crimes are forgiven and forgotten; all past sentences are remitted and all debts are forgiven; all territory that you want to have is restored to you. You may fight anybody you like and nobody may fight against you.'

Winston S. Churchill, 1919[1]

The Allies' hidden agendas explain many apparent puzzles about some of their decisions – usually ascribed to miscalculations – such as scaling down the Italian campaign, just as it seemed to be achieving success.

The lengthy stalemate in Italy was finally over in May 1944 when Monte Cassino was taken and the German lines breached. Two days before D-Day, Rome fell to General Clark – surely the perfect time to achieve Churchill's goal of opening the way to Central Europe. But, to Churchill's chagrin, the Americans halted the offensive, diverting forces to southern France in support of Overlord. They were then to push northwards to link up with the army of liberation.

Churchill was so angry at the diversion of resources that again he drafted his resignation, though he never used it – possibly because, at this stage of the war, Roosevelt might have called his bluff.[2] Sir Charles Wilson recorded:

> The American landings in the south of France are the last straw. He can see 'no earthly purpose' in them: 'sheer folly,' he calls them. He had fought tooth and nail, he said, to prevent them. If only those ten divisions could have been landed in the Balkans . . . but the Americans would not listen to him: it was all settled, they said.[3]

When the doctor murmured soothingly that the war would soon be over, Churchill exploded: 'Good God, can't you see that the Russians are spreading across Europe like a tide; they have invaded Poland, and there is nothing to prevent them marching into Turkey and Greece!' (Churchill named the southern France operation, launched in mid-August, 'Dragoon', because he'd been dragooned into accepting it.[4])

When we discussed this with Eric Taylor, a veteran of the Sicilian and Italian campaigns and author of a number of books on the Second World War, he agreed that the decision was odd, as the Allied forces could have done far more good where they were – the way was now open to Austria and the Balkans, and a potential fatal blow against Germany before the Russians arrived. There were many excuses – the need to get Juin's forces into action in France, problems getting over the Alps – but fundamentally the Americans preferred full commitment to Overlord. But as General Clark wrote after the war:

> There was no question in my mind that day [on which they took Rome] that we could soon destroy the enemy in Italy and drive him beyond the Alps, and then go on to whatever objective was set for us. The Fifth Army, it seemed to me, had at last become a tremendous fighting machine, and its horizons were unlimited.
>
> That, however, was not the way it worked out. For various reasons . . . our team was broken up, and the Fifth Army was sapped of a great part of its strength. A campaign that might

391

have changed the whole history of relations between the Western world and the Soviet Union was permitted to fade away, not into nothing, but into much less than it could have been. These were decisions made at a high level and for reasons beyond my field and my knowledge . . .

[. . .]

Not alone in my opinion, but in the opinion of a number of experts who were close to the problem, the weakening of the campaign in Italy in order to invade Southern France, instead of pushing on to the Balkans, was one of the outstanding mistakes of the war.[5]

The British commander Field Marshal Sir Harold Alexander believed it was still possible to push into Austria and capture Vienna. The Americans considered this over-ambitious, and in February 1945 the Combined Chiefs of Staff told him simply to pin down as many German divisions as possible. Despite all the problems, he managed to bring about the surrender of the remaining million-strong German Army in Italy at the end of April, vindicating Churchill.[6] Clearly, had the Allies remained in Italy in greater force, this would have happened sooner.

Diverting resources from the Italian campaign was a political decision – specifically to ensure that the Western Allies didn't get in the Russians' way. As Nisbet comments: '. . . the President couldn't be diverted by anyone from his central objective which was that of winning Stalin's total confidence and goodwill for the remaking of the world once the war was over.'[7] It is hard to avoid the conclusion that Roosevelt scaled down the Italian campaign not because it wouldn't work, but because he feared it *would*. Incredible though this may seem, as we will see in the final stages of the advance on Berlin there is no question that Roosevelt deliberately held American and British forces back to allow Stalin to take what he wanted.

Again, there is an element of self-fulfilment. After the decision to transfer resources to Dragoon, Roosevelt told Cordell Hull:

In regard to the Soviet government, it is true that we have no idea as to what they have in mind, but we have to remember

392

that in their occupied territory they will do more or less what they wish. We cannot afford to get into a position of merely recording protests on our part unless there is some chance of some of the protests being heeded.[8]

FDR's acceptance of the Russians being able to 'do what they wish' in their captured territory is particularly repugnant given what Stalin did to Warsaw.

The Warsaw Uprising

The Red Army had entered Polish territory in January 1944 – although Stalin considered it already Soviet, according to the Nazi–Soviet Pact. A Polish National Council had also been set up in Moscow, which announced it was going to form a new government – a major challenge to the Allies, who had recognised the government-in-exile in London since 1939. And the unresolved issue of how much the Soviets would receive of the former Poland had great potential to create fatal divisions within the Alliance.

Churchill told Prime Minister Mikołajczyk that Britain had gone to war to defend Poland's *independence*, stating bluntly, 'You must understand this, Mr Mikołajczyk. Great Britain and the United States will not go to war to defend the eastern frontiers of Poland.'[9]

In March, when Churchill informed Stalin that he would defer the territorial issue until the end of the war, and that 'in the meantime we can recognise no forcible transferences of territory,' Stalin replied, 'should you make a statement of this nature I shall consider that you have committed an unjust and unfriendly act in relation to the Soviet Union.'[10] With D-Day just over two months away, Churchill could hardly take such a risk (especially knowing whose side Roosevelt would take).

The resistance movement, the Polish Home Army, which had pledged its loyalty to the government in London, rose up against the Nazis as the Russians advanced. From London, General Sosnkowski ordered them to cooperate with the Red Army. On 22 July, the Soviets crossed the border defined by the Nazi–Soviet Pact into Poland proper. Four days later, a civil administration, the Polish Committee of National Liberation, made up of Polish

Communists and led by former Comintern agent Bolesław Bierut, was set up in the town of Lublin ('the Lublin Committee') – a more serious challenge to the Poles in London. Mikołajczyk went to Moscow in the forlorn hope that he might be able to compromise with Stalin.

As the Red Army advanced westwards, Moscow radio urged the Home Army in Warsaw to rise up, promising to link up with them. On 1 August, the Poles went into action, fighting so hard that by the time the Red Army arrived, they already controlled most of the city. But when they reached the river Vistula, on the outskirts of Warsaw, the Soviets halted, and waited . . . There was to be no link-up with the Polish freedom fighters. German reinforcements entered Warsaw and, after 63 days of fighting and the deaths of 15,000 members of the Polish resistance and between 200,000 and 250,000 civilians (besides 17,000 Germans), at the beginning of October the Home Army surrendered. When the British and American governments asked Stalin for permission to drop weapons, food and medical supplies to the beleaguered fighters, he refused.

When Churchill drafted a complaint to be signed jointly by himself and Roosevelt – which might have had some effect on Stalin – the President replied: 'I do not consider it advantageous in the long range general war prospect for me to join with you in the proposed message to UJ.'[11] Shocked, many in Roosevelt's administration, such as Harriman, began to question his policy of Soviet appeasement.[12]

It must be remembered that Roosevelt was on the campaign trail, ready for the elections in November. And, as he had told Stalin in their private meeting in Teheran, he had already made up his mind to agree to Stalin's demands over Poland, but would not reveal this until after the elections, for fear of losing the Polish-American vote.

The Polish question
In the midst of a war, with a familiar and trusted incumbent, the result of the election was a foregone conclusion. FDR won against Thomas E. Dewey with 54 per cent of the popular vote and 432 Electoral College votes against 99, returning to office for a fourth term. Significantly, the Republicans chose not to fight on an isolationist platform, not only supporting America's war but also its

involvement in post-war international organisations. American isolationism was dead.

Two weeks after his re-election – and three months after the crushing of the Warsaw Uprising under the studied indifference of the Red Army – on 22 November, Roosevelt finally came off the fence about Poland, declaring to Mikołajczyk that its borders and government were issues for them and the USSR alone. There would be no intervention from the United States. Two days later, Mikołajczyk resigned, and a new Polish government was created in London, headed by the Socialist Tomasz Arciszewski.

Six years earlier, Roosevelt had pressed a reluctant Chamberlain to give such a guarantee of protection to Poland, criticising him for not having done so over Czechoslovakia. But now he was in the same position, Roosevelt withheld such a guarantee.

On the last day of 1944, the Lublin Committee declared itself the provisional government of Poland and was recognised by Stalin. Churchill was deeply worried by this and the situation in the Balkans, which – as he had anticipated – were falling under Stalin's sway.

In Nazi-occupied Yugoslavia, the resistance leader Tito appealed to Stalin for help – resulting in his Communist-dominated coalition government in March 1945, which fell under Soviet control. In August 1944, the Romanian King Michael ordered the arrest of the pro-Axis government, allowing the Red Army into Romania; the Allies agreed that Soviets could preside over the country until the end of the war. Bulgaria fell to a Communist coup when the Russians arrived. And Stalin installed a provisional government in Hungary when it was taken by the Red Army in December. Only in Greece had the British presided over the liberation – although even that dissolved into a three-year civil war against Communist rebels.

Faced with overwhelming Soviet domination, Churchill finally confronted the issue of Poland, calling for a meeting of the Big Three. This was set for Yalta in the Crimea in February (with a preliminary US/British meeting in Malta).

Twilight of the gods
After his fall from grace, Harry Hopkins staged a dramatic comeback

in the final months of the war, wielding even more influence than before (although his friendship with FDR never recovered). As with his decline, the reason for this eleventh-hour resurgence remains unclear. Dwight Tuttle suggests he had used 'his knowledge of the White House political intrigues' to fight his way back to power.[13]

Hopkins was dispatched to Europe on a 'fence-mending' mission to improve America's relations with her Allies on the eve of the conference. In London, he discussed the formation of the United Nations Security Council with the Foreign Office, in Paris he met de Gaulle and his Cabinet, and in Rome, besides meeting government representatives, he had an audience with the Pope. The main reason for Hopkins' Paris trip was to smooth over the embarrassment that de Gaulle had not been invited to Yalta. When the conference had first been mooted in 1944, Churchill and Stalin were in favour of elevating France to a new 'Big Four' – but Roosevelt had vetoed it. Stalin had since cooled on the idea and Churchill's sole support had not been sufficient to secure an invitation for de Gaulle.[14]

The conference ('Argonaut') was held in a dilapidated villa, 80 miles of bad roads from the nearest airfield. While US medics were sent ahead to de-louse the President's rooms, Churchill felt he could 'survive it by bringing an adequate supply of whisky'.[15]

Today, the Yalta Conference is notorious for handing Stalin Eastern Europe on a plate and agreeing to the Soviet-friendly division of the continent, which Churchill later famously called the 'Iron Curtain'. But after all, Stalin was surrounded by friends. He was faced with an ailing President whose major adviser, Hopkins, had been fighting his corner for years. Moreover, Stettinius brought Alger Hiss, whose main brief was dealing with issues of decolonisation and trusteeship, and although Harry Dexter White was not present, his economic ideas and recommendations significantly influenced the proceedings.[16] At times, the Soviet delegation must have felt as if it was negotiating with itself, with the British presence merely a minor inconvenience.

The delegates were shocked by the President's appearance. His hands trembled, and his mental faculties were alarmingly depleted. As an American doctor observed just before the conference: 'If anything was brought up that wants thinking out he would change the subject.'[17] By the beginning of 1945, FDR was sleeping 14 hours a day – surely not the most efficient way to run the war.[18] In fact, around the time he was sworn in for his fourth term in January 1945, Roosevelt was told that he might have only three more months to live.[19] As Robert H. Ferrell points out in *The Dying President* (1998), FDR's insistence on going for a fourth term, even though he knew he was swiftly declining, constituted almost criminal neglect of his obligations. Making no contingency plans for dying in harness, he kept Truman as much in the dark as any of his previous Vice-Presidents.

Churchill's physician Sir Charles Wilson commented:

> To a doctor's eye, the President appears a very sick man. He has all the symptoms of hardening of the arteries of the brain in an advanced stage, so that I give him only a few months to live. But men shut their eyes when they do not want to see, and the Americans here cannot bring themselves to believe that he is finished.[20]

Wilson reports British table talk:

> Everyone seemed to agree that the President had gone to bits physically . . . He intervened very little in the discussions, sitting with his mouth open. If he has sometimes been short of facts about the subject under discussion his shrewdness has covered this up. Now, they say, the shrewdness has gone, and there is nothing left. I doubt, from what I have seen, whether he is fit for his job here.[21]

Wilson noted: 'The President seems to have no mind of his own.'[22] (But did it really matter? He certainly still possessed Hopkins' mind.)

Roosevelt's mental state is often cited as the reason he let Stalin get away with so much at Yalta, but, in fact, the President had pursued the same policies at Teheran 15 months earlier, and even before that.

The conference began on 4 February 1945 with a private meeting of Roosevelt and Stalin. Apparently joking, the President reminded Stalin about his idea of executing 50,000 German officers,[23] perhaps to remind him how this had irritated Churchill in order to re-establish their buddy act. Not all the Americans were happy to be in Uncle Joe's pocket, however. Harriman, Stimson and Marshall, now being deeply mistrustful of Stalin (largely because of Warsaw), urged the President to try to wring some concessions from him, but – as ever – Roosevelt flatly refused.[24]

Hopkins, Special Assistant to the President, was also gravely ill. Wilson noted: 'Physically he was only half in this world. He looked ghastly – his skin was a yellow-white membrane stretched tight over the bones – but he began to talk with his old verve.'[25] But Hopkins, at least, still had his wits about him. As Tuttle remarks: 'Despite his illness, Hopkins clearly emerged as FDR's most important adviser. This result was inevitable since the entire foreign policy apparatus had been established around Roosevelt and Hopkins.'[26] Particularly in the early sessions, Roosevelt seemed to be little more than Hopkins' ventriloquist's dummy, Hopkins frequently passing him notes giving very specific advice. For example, when Churchill objected to the idea of the 'dismemberment' of Germany, he scribbled to FDR:

> I would suggest that you say this is a very important and urgent matter and that the three foreign ministers present a proposal tomorrow as to the procedure by which a determination as to dismemberment can be arrived at an early date.[27]

Roosevelt duly said exactly that. It took until the fifth day of the conference for him to assert himself, becoming less reliant on Hopkins.[28]

For the British, Yalta – one official called it a meeting of the 'Big Two and a Half'[29] – was yet another frustrating and humiliating experience. Of course, the hot issue was Poland, which Britain had gone to war to protect: now its fate would set the pattern for future East–West relations. But what sort of government would Poland have? What about its borders?

The conference agreed that the Polish borders could return to the 'Curzon Line', a demarcation proposed (but not accepted) in 1920 as a settlement of the Polish–Soviet war, which gave the USSR slightly less territory than the Nazi–Soviet Pact, although Stalin managed to tweak the Curzon Line to grab extra territory in the south that included the important city of Lwów.

In short, Stalin was allowed to keep nearly everything he got from Hitler – and now, following the Allies' shameful agreement to recognise the puppet Lublin government, the whole of Poland was also effectively in his grasp. Initially, Roosevelt supported Churchill's refusal to recognise Lublin – but when he reversed his decision, Churchill was compelled to do so, betraying the Free Polish government he had dealt with in London for five years, not to mention Sikorski's memory.[30] Although Stalin agreed to include Poles from abroad in the new government and to hold democratic elections (but without independent observers), Churchill signed the declaration with great reluctance. Events proved him right – Stalin soon blatantly reneged on these pledges.

Since the beginning of the war, Poland's representatives had been flagrantly betrayed – their nation handed over wholesale to one of the invaders. The Poles wondered what it had all been for, having come full circle with only enormous suffering to show for it.

Although many believe it was at Yalta that Eastern Europe and the Baltic states were handed over to Stalin, this had already been accomplished by secret agreement with Roosevelt at Teheran. The major change in the mean time was that Stalin now also had physical possession of those countries – Yalta merely legitimised his claims.[31]

With huge irony – and some desperate cynicism – the conference ended with the issuing of the Declaration on Liberated Europe, reaffirming the Atlantic Charter's principle of the right of a people to choose their own government, and making a commitment to hold free and democratic elections in the liberated countries.[32]

At Yalta, Stalin reaffirmed that once Germany was defeated he would join in the war against Japan, but not in order to repay the Allies for all their help: he still demanded a reward of territory lost to Japan by Tsarist Russia in 1905. Roosevelt simply agreed to everything. (Churchill elected not to attend these sessions.[33])

Astonishingly, Hopkins wrote to Roosevelt afterwards:

> The Russians have given us so much at this conference that I
> don't think we should let them down. Let the British disagree
> if they want to, and continue their disagreement in [the
> forthcoming talks in] Moscow.[34]

This is an incredible statement; Stalin had conceded *nothing* at Yalta.

Less than a month after signing the Declaration on Liberated
Europe, when Stalin imposed an unelected Communist government
on Romania, neither Britain nor the US so much as complained.
Then the Soviets began the mass arrest and deportation of
intellectuals, professionals, priests and others in Poland and the Baltic
states. When in early March 1945 Churchill again proposed a joint
complaint, again Roosevelt refused.[35] He even refused to intervene
when his own countrymen were involved; American prisoners of war
being 'liberated' by the Russians were often terribly mistreated. At
the end of March when an outraged Harriman asked him to
complain, FDR responded: 'It does not appear appropriate to me to
send another message now to Stalin.'[36]

More betrayals

Although Allied successes in the Far East mirrored their progress in
Europe, there was much more to do. MacArthur's and Nimitz's
advances were going well and US submarines were taking a heavy
toll on Japanese shipping, causing a severe fuel shortage. The US had
also captured the Marianna Islands in June 1944, bringing mainland
Japan within range of their bombers and causing Tojo Hideki's
government to fall. Responsible for the failure of their fightback, he
was forced to resign in July. (He was hanged as a war criminal in
December 1948.) He was replaced by Lieutenant-General Koiso
Kuniaki, the Governor-General of Korea.

On 21 October, MacArthur and the President of the Philippines,
Sergio Osmena, returned to the islands from which they had been
driven out. Although MacArthur famously declared: 'People of the
Philippines, I have returned' in front of the newsreel cameras, it was
to take four months of bitter fighting before Manila was back in
American hands. The Japanese clung on in some areas until the final
surrender in August. It was as they were being beaten back that the

kamikaze – suicide-bomber – campaign appeared, attacking US and Australian ships in the Philippines.

Nimitz's next target was Iwo Jima, its three airstrips perfect for attacks on Japan, which was just 650 miles away. After 72 days of aerial bombardment, on 19 February 60,000 US Marines landed, expecting the island to fall within two weeks. It took over a month, taking a third of a million US personnel to uproot 22,000 Japanese troops, who fought to the bitter end. One-third of the Marines were casualties, with 6,000 dead.

In March 1944, the Japanese had begun an offensive at Imphal in Burma, intending to sweep beyond into India. Instead, it was the greatest defeat ever suffered by the Japanese Army – and by the end of the year the Allied (chiefly Indian) forces were slowly but surely pushing them back into Burma.

Confidence in the defeat of Japan was so ebullient that in August the French Committee of National Liberation and the Dutch government-in-exile began to formulate a joint policy for their former colonies, with an eye to repossessing them. To Roosevelt, his long-held fear that the old imperial powers would collude as the war drew to a close was confirmed.[37]

Although while courting Vichy FDR had consistently maintained that Indo-China would remain in French hands, after he broke with them, he made Indo-China 'one of the most important focuses of his campaign against Western European imperialism in his desire to oversee the coming of a post-imperial world'.[38] Roosevelt told the Pacific War Council in July 1943: 'Indo-China should not be given back to the French Empire after the war.'[39] And at Cairo, he proposed it should be given to China – but Chiang Kai-shek refused to take it.[40]

By speaking of Indo-China being 'given back' to France, FDR seems to have assumed that Indo-China would end up in Japanese hands – but when he made the statement in July 1943 it was still French, albeit technically Vichyite. Because of its relations with Japan's Nazi allies, Tokyo had no intention of occupying Indo-China while it remained Vichyite. However, in spring 1944, French officials and military commanders in Indo-China initiated contact with de Gaulle's French Committee of National Liberation. (From intercepted signals, it appears that both the Japanese and – even

worse for de Gaulle – Roosevelt knew about this.) Even so, the
colony's leadership remained loyal to Vichy until the Normandy
landings, after which it seemed wise to reconsider their position. But
if Indo-China went over to de Gaulle, it was likely that the Japanese
would invade – so the Free French planned to send reinforcements.

Roosevelt backed neither the Vichyites nor the Free French – as
either would recolonise – decreeing in February 1944 there would be
no US aid to French forces liberating Indo-China, followed by an
Executive Order in October expressly forbidding it.[41] In fact, until
March 1945 – when Churchill presented him with a fait accompli –
Roosevelt scrupulously kept the Free French out of *any* Allied
operations in the Far East.

The Allies – largely SOE – had worked with the Free French to
prepare to defend Indo-China through a campaign of subversion
called Operation Belief. But following Roosevelt's directive, the
Americans were conspicuous by their absence. Instead, ironically in
view of later events, the OSS threw its support behind the
Communist nationalist organisation led by Ho Chi Minh, the Viet
Minh, forerunners of the Viet Cong[42] – not the last time US
intelligence created a problem for the future by building up a guerrilla
leader who would turn against them – which provoked serious
deception and infighting between the British and Americans,
sometimes with tragic consequences. For example, in July 1944 SOE
tricked the Americans into letting them use one of their bases in
southern China for dropping Free French agents into Indo-China.
When the US Joint Chiefs complained to Roosevelt, American air
facilities in southern China were abruptly withdrawn from SOE. As
a result, supplies for the resistance had to be flown in from Burma by
the RAF – a long and hazardous journey. SOE also decided not to
tell the Americans about these missions, even though the RAF flew
over American-controlled airspace. Several British aircraft were shot
down by US fighters.[43]

With the liberation of France, at the beginning of 1945 the colony
became subject to de Gaulle's new Free French Council of Indo-
China. For a year, Roosevelt had vetoed an SOE request to allow a
1,200-strong French special force to be moved from the Middle East
to Asia for deployment in Indo-China in the event of a Japanese

attack. But soon after Yalta, Churchill gave SEAC his unilateral approval for the move.[44]

Japan finally began its military occupation of Indo-China on 9 March 1945, and the French guerrilla campaign went into action. Roosevelt would not aid the French but the OSS did arm and supply the Viet Minh; FDR preferred to see his *enemies* drive all the *Allied* French out of the country, while positioning native Communist independence groups to take over. As Kathryn E. Brown points out: 'This decision [not to aid the French] clearly indicates that Roosevelt had by this time made the war against imperialism a greater priority than the war against the Axis.'[45]

From a detailed analysis of the 'Magic' intercepts seen by the President – released in the late 1990s – Brown has established that Roosevelt had been watching Japanese plans for a military takeover for at least a month before it happened. And yet a month *after* fighting began the French were complaining they still had no help from the US.[46] Refusing to help one of his Allies against a common enemy is invidious enough, but there is evidence that Roosevelt had already done considerably worse than that, having actively *provoked* the Japanese invasion in the first place.

In autumn 1944, the US propaganda organisation OWI concentrated on convincing the Japanese that a US-led land invasion was planned in Indo-China as the first step to re-conquer mainland Asia. In fact, there were no such plans.[47] Under the circumstances, the purpose of OWI's misinformation can only have been to encourage Japan to take over Indo-China completely in order to set up defences against the 'invasion' – and drive out the French.

The theory was first put forward by Stein Tonnesson in a paper to the Society for Historians of American Foreign Relations at a conference in, of all places, Roosevelt's home of Hyde Park in 1992.[48] Although hugely controversial, it has attracted support from others, such as the University of California's David Marr, who believes it is entirely possible that FDR might have used air raids and OWI deceptions 'as a device to trigger Japanese elimination of the French in Indo-China'.[49] And it is known that in the weeks before the Japanese invasion, Roosevelt and his top brass were discussing a secret and sensitive plan – but its nature has never been revealed.

Roosevelt was also paying special attention at that time to Gaullist signals intercepted by US intelligence.[50] The theory is taken relatively seriously because there is no other plausible explanation for the OWI misinformation campaign, and Roosevelt's desire to have Indo-China free of French influence is well attested.[51] It was only after the French complaints that Roosevelt grudgingly authorised US air support for their ground forces.

Given the *White Book*, and the fact of Roosevelt goading Japan into war in the first place, it should no longer surprise us that he should not only encourage Japan to attack the possessions of one of his Allies (he recognised de Gaulle's government by this time) but also then withheld assistance.

The race for Berlin

Although it had been agreed to push on to Berlin, Eisenhower held his forces back, allowing Soviet troops to get to the German capital first. He always maintained that this was because there was no military reason for the Western Allies to fight for those cities. In terms of winning the war against Hitler, this was true, but from the post-war perspective it was staggeringly naive and short sighted – not to mention callously disregarding of the masses who would find themselves under Soviet rule. And in those tumultuous days, many other decisions were made with the post-war situation in mind, as in Indo-China; if Eisenhower had no wish to enter those cities in triumph it was because his political masters had decided Russia should have them.

The major problem was that the Western Allies were advancing more swiftly than the Russians (battling desperate Germans on the Eastern Front). Montgomery and Patton both believed they could have reached Berlin before the end of 1944 – if they had been allowed to. As Montgomery wrote later: '. . . if we had run the show properly, the war could have been finished by Xmas 1944. The blame for this must rest with the Americans.'[52] But as it had been agreed at Yalta that eastern Germany was to be in the Soviet zone of occupation, the Red Army had to be allowed to take it.

In fact, Yalta had deemed the coordination of the Allied advances so important that – incredibly – it was agreed for the last stages of the war Eisenhower should take his orders *direct from the Kremlin*. The official US minutes state:

> The President said that he felt that the armies were getting close enough to have contact between them and he hoped General Eisenhower would communicate directly with the Soviet Staff rather than through the Chiefs of Staff in London and in Washington, as in the past.[53]

The final phases of the fall of Germany were to be coordinated between Eisenhower and the Soviet Chiefs – without any input from the British and American Chiefs of Staff. And now Roosevelt could prevent Churchill from winning the Berlin race.

Eisenhower even cabled Stalin directly to outline his strategy of pushing south, towards Dresden, saying nothing about Berlin – implying that he was handing it over with the President's blessing. Churchill thundered that Eisenhower had 'ceded Berlin to Stalin without notifying, much less consulting, in advance the Combined Chiefs to whom the Supreme Commander was responsible in military matters and had been since the creation of SHAEF'.[54] The Prime Minister then tried to persuade Eisenhower to countermand his cable – but predictably Marshall backed his protégé. Churchill then urged Eisenhower to push on to Berlin, making the same plea to Roosevelt the next day. But Eisenhower ignored him, telling Marshall: 'Berlin itself is no longer a particularly important objective.'[55] Years later, Marshall himself admitted that it was primarily a political decision: 'I do not think we should have gone into Berlin at that time . . . However it must be remembered that all this time we were trying to do business with the Russians' and 'we were trying very hard to find a basis of negotiation to go along with the Russian government'.[56]

Perhaps a better 'basis of negotiation' would have been for America and Britain to have *held* Berlin. In his *Stalin, Churchill, and Roosevelt Divide Europe* (1990), Remi Nadeau argues that the US government *should* have made Berlin a political pawn precisely because Stalin was already flagrantly in breach of his Yalta agreements in Romania and Poland.[57]

In fact, there is no question that the Western Allies could have got to Berlin first had they wanted to. Although they were further away than the Soviets, the Germans were not resisting as strongly on the Western Front.[58] When on 11 April the 9th US Army under Lieutenant-General William Simpson reached the Elbe, 60 miles from Berlin, Eisenhower ordered him not to cross the river. Although once again Churchill complained, Simpson's army was told to stay put. After the war, various egregious lies obscured the conscious decision not to take Berlin. As Simpson said:

> Harry Hopkins later made a statement that we'd outrun our supplies and all that sort of thing. Well, he didn't know what he was talking about because my army was in good shape, the supplies were in good shape, and we could have gone right on to Berlin and put up a darned good show . . . So I think we could have ploughed across there within twenty-four hours and been in Berlin in twenty-four to forty-eight hours easily.[59]

Surely there can no longer be an argument when, according to Nikita Khrushchev: 'Stalin said that if it hadn't been for Eisenhower, we wouldn't have succeeded in capturing Berlin.'[60]

The Red Army only set foot in Germany five days after Simpson's halt, finally entering Berlin two weeks later. The day after US and Soviet forces first met at the village of Stehla on the Elbe on 24 April, Soviet tanks from Marshal Georgi Zhukov's army completed the city's encirclement, and the street-by-street battle for the Nazi capital began.

VE Days

Meanwhile, as Italy fell, British intelligence and the OSS searched desperately for Mussolini. In *Circles of Hell* (1993), political and defence analyst Eric Morris writes: 'Mussolini was known to have had some papers with him which would have proved extremely embarrassing had they ever seen the light of day. He was carrying two briefcases of papers, believed to include evidence that would help him in the event of a trial.'[61] It is an open secret what those embarrassing papers included, as Richard Lamb reveals: 'When

Mussolini was captured and assassinated by the partisans in 1945 he was carrying letters from Churchill for use if he was tried as a war criminal. They have not survived.'[62] Such was the success of Churchill's personal reinvention as the epitome of British democracy that his previous admiration for Il Duce would have been a shocking revelation to most British and Americans.

Together with his mistress Clara Petacci and other Fascist leaders, Mussolini was fleeing from Milan to Austria in a German truck convoy with an SS escort when, on 27 April, they were seized by Communist partisans, who (surprisingly) let the Germans go. After an overnight delay, awaiting orders from their headquarters in Milan, Communist Party member Walter Andisco and two companions executed the Fascist leader and his mistress, their bodies soon afterwards hung by their ankles in the streets of Milan. But what happened to the documents and Churchill's letters? Were they destroyed, or did they fall into the hands of the NKVD? It is unlikely we will ever know.

The day after Mussolini's ignominious end, German forces in Italy surrendered – a week before Germany itself. In fact, as Allen Dulles writes:

> Unknown to the outside world, since the end of February, 1945, emissaries and messages had been passing secretly between the OSS mission in Switzerland, of which I was in charge, and German generals in Italy. For two crucial months the commanders of contending armies locked in battle had maintained secret communications through my office in Bern seeking the means to end the fighting on the front in Italy, hoping a Nazi surrender there would bring in its wake a general surrender in Europe.[63]

When Stalin accused Roosevelt of betraying the Alliance by negotiating without a Soviet presence, for once FDR was furious, replying that he rejected his 'vile representations of my actions or those of trusted associates'.[64]

The day after the first surrender of his troops and SS elite, the Führer, too, was dead. On 30 April, as the Red Army was storming the Reichstag a quarter of a mile away, Hitler committed suicide in his bunker (with his very new wife Eva Braun). The Russians were particularly thrilled to hoist the hammer and sickle flag over the Reichstag on their all-important May Day. The next day, Berlin surrendered.

Grand Admiral Karl Dönitz succeeded Hitler as the second and last Führer of Germany – Göring, Hitler's heir, having been dismissed four days earlier for proposing peace feelers. Dönitz wanted to give German forces in the east time to escape westwards, through a series of area-by-area surrenders. On 4 May, he surrendered north-west Germany, the Netherlands and Denmark to Montgomery.

On 5 May, as the Soviets and Patton's Third Army advanced towards Prague, the population rose up against the 'master race'. When the Czech government-in-exile and resistance in Prague appealed for help from the Western Allies, the Soviet General Staff urgently requested Eisenhower to leave Prague to them – and, despite his entreaties, Patton was ordered to halt, even though his Third Army was just 40 miles from the city and the Germans were slaughtering the insurrectionists.[65] This is even more astonishing given what had happened in Warsaw, although the Czech government–in-exile under Beneš had made it clear that they saw their future with the Soviet Union.

At 2.41 a.m. on 7 May 1945, the Allies finally got their unconditional surrender. General Alfred Jodl, representing Dönitz, signed the document at Eisenhower's HQ in Rheims, ordering all German forces to lay down their arms at 11 p.m. the next day. Characteristically suspicious, Stalin refused to accept the agreement, demanding that another signing ceremony take place in Berlin the next day (which is why the Russians celebrate VE-Day a day later than everyone else).

The death of the President

Roosevelt did not live to see any of these triumphs. The day after General Simpson's troops were stopped from advancing on Berlin, he was dead. In his last weeks, one issue above all had preyed on his mind: after all those years of appeasing Stalin, he finally worried he was untrustworthy, telling a friend on the last day of his life: 'We've taken a great risk here, an enormous risk, it involves the problems of Russian intentions.'[66]

On 12 April 1945, at Warm Springs, Roosevelt suffered a fatal brain haemorrhage – long feared by his doctors – in the company of Lucy Mercer Rutherfurd, the lover who had nearly cost him his marriage in 1918. At about 1 p.m., FDR said, 'I have a terrific headache', and slumped forward. He was declared dead at 3.35 p.m.

It was Eleanor Roosevelt who summoned the Vice-President to the White House and told him he was now the leader of what had become, thanks to her husband, the most powerful nation on earth. A stunned Truman asked Eleanor, 'Is there anything I can do for you?' to which her reply was, 'Is there anything we can do for *you*? For you are the one in trouble now.'[67]

Yalta had also taken its toll on Hopkins, who on his return had to be taken back into the Mayo Clinic, suffering from pneumonia and a low blood count. While he was in hospital, the State Department's liaison with the White House, 'Chips' Bohlen, broke the news by telephone: 'There was a long silence at the other end of the phone. Then Hopkins said, "I guess I better be going to Washington."'[68]

In London, Churchill gave a glowing tribute to the President in the House of Commons, stressing his respect, affection and gratitude for his friendship with Britain. However, his eulogy concentrated on the years before Pearl Harbor: he covered the subsequent period in a single paragraph.[69] And was his absence from Roosevelt's funeral a deliberate snub? Admittedly, it was a critical time, and he had his own name to stamp on history, but perhaps he could have made the time to attend the funeral of the American President.

From Moscow, Harriman reported that Stalin appeared genuinely upset at the news, but typically made an official request for a post-mortem, suspecting that the President might have been poisoned.[70]

After a funeral service in the White House – Roosevelt's home for 12 years – his coffin was taken to his estate at Hyde Park, where he was buried in the rose garden. He had died on the brink of his greatest triumphs: in three weeks, Germany would surrender; in just two, the United Nations would be inaugurated.

Hopkins' swansong

As for Harry Shippe Truman, as Robert Aldrich notes wryly: 'Publicly he vowed that he would continue Roosevelt's policies, but privately he was not certain what these policies were.'[71] No lover of Stalin or the Soviet Union, he soon abandoned Roosevelt's policy of 'Soviet courtship',[72] adopting a 'doctrine of containment' towards the Soviet Union that was diametrically opposed to Roosevelt's championing of Russian expansion. The containment policy also changed US attitudes to Britain – Truman needed the UK as an ally to stop Soviet expansion in Europe.[73]

Almost immediately after the German surrender, tensions surfaced between the two new superpowers, particularly when Stalin blatantly ignored the Yalta agreement on Poland. One brazen breach particularly shocked the Americans: 16 leaders of the Polish underground visited Moscow for talks about the new government, on a guarantee of safe conduct – but once there they were arrested and charged with treason. The nervous Polish government-in-exile in London wanted the mess sorted out before they became involved in the Moscow talks.

In May 1945, Averell Harriman and Chips Bohlen proposed that Truman ask Hopkins – inevitably the continuity between the two Presidents' foreign policy[74] – to visit Moscow to try to resolve matters with Stalin. Hopkins duly left on his last major adventure on 23 May: as Christopher Andrew and Oleg Gordievsky write: 'A number of historians, though unaware that the NKVD/NKGB regarded Hopkins as a Soviet agent, have nonetheless been struck by his pro-Soviet approach to the negotiations.'[75]

Hopkins stated the US position: 'We would accept any government in Poland which was desired by the Polish people and was at the same time friendly to the Soviet government.'[76] Of course, Stalin achieved this simply by ensuring that any Poles who sought any other form of government were eliminated, deported or intimidated into inaction. He proposed that the new government in Warsaw could include up to four non-Communists (out of twenty) – provided he could nominate them. George McJimsey writes – clearly with no sense of irony:

The Yalta accords had also provided for a consultation in Moscow between communist and noncommunist Poles to begin the process of establishing a provisional government. In order to show good faith Hopkins offered to remove from the list any Pole whom Stalin considered hostile to the Soviet Union.[77]

Bizarrely, McJimsey calls this a 'brilliant stroke'. Hopkins then urged Truman and Churchill to approve the purged list.

The other major controversy in the West concerned the arrested underground leaders, which Hopkins discussed with Stalin privately, assuring him that the United States government did not support the London Poles.[78] The talks were inconclusive. Bohlen, who had accompanied Hopkins, wrote of the journey home:

> . . . on the way across the Atlantic, Hopkins, in private talks with me, began to voice for the first time serious doubts as to the possibility of genuine collaboration with the Soviet Union, saying he thought our relations were going to be stormy. He based his views primarily on the absence of freedom in the Soviet Union. He felt that the American belief in freedom might lead to serious differences over affairs in third countries.[79]

Others agree that in the last months of his life, Hopkins came to have severe doubts about Stalin and the Soviet system, his faith having been shaken by the treatment of the Polish underground leaders (10 of the 16 were to die in Soviet prisons) and the Russian government's disdain for world opinion. Of course, these doubts contradict the concept of him as an ideological Soviet spy, but they do suggest that he was driven to help the Russians because of the role he believed they should play in reshaping the world order. Like Roosevelt, as he faced death, he seemed suddenly stricken with a crisis of belief about the Frankenstein's monster he had helped to create.

Terminal

The final conference of the war, 'Terminal', was held at Potsdam,

Germany, from 17 July to 2 August 1945. (Hopkins was absent, having resigned from government service because of his disagreements with the new administration's policies.)

The talks were interrupted after nine days by the dramatic results of the British general election. The first general election to be fought on party lines since 1931 – coalitions had governed ever since – swept Churchill and the Conservatives from power with a massive Labour landslide, bringing in the first ever majority socialist government. Not only does this show what Britons really thought about the prospect of 'Good Old Winnie' as a peacetime leader, it also confirmed the worst fears of the pre-war peace movement that the war would shift Britain to the left. As a shattered Churchill had to hand over the proceedings to Clement Attlee midway through the conference, only Stalin remained of the original war leaders.

The question of the Polish–Soviet border having been decided at Yalta, the Polish–German border was defined at Potsdam, although less controversially, as members of the provisional Lublin government were allowed to participate. The border would follow the rivers Oder and Neisse, hiving off land from Germany to recompense Poland for its losses to the USSR agreed at Yalta. Not only was the Polish border moved some 125 miles west but the 3.5 million Germans there were also expelled, to resettle in the new, smaller Germany. Poles living in the areas now belonging to Stalin were also evicted, to settle the areas taken from Germany – but soon found themselves under Soviet control anyway.

The Soviet Union now controlled Central and Eastern Europe, the Baltic and the Balkans. The new western border added 21 million people to its population, and the governments of all the adjacent nations were now acceptable to Moscow, becoming even more amenable as the Iron Curtain clanged shut on huge tracts of Europe. The Baltic states were quietly re-absorbed into the USSR as 'Soviet Republics'; as Polish specialist Norman Davies points out, this 'clearly breached international law; but it passed without challenge'.[80]

The Free Poles in Britain, Italy, the Middle East and part of Germany agonised over whether to return to a Soviet-dominated home or stay where they were – if they could.

Set up in June 1945, the new government – a Cabinet of 21, 16

Lublin Communists and 5 from the government-in-exile, including Mikołajczyk as Deputy Prime Minister – was formally recognised by Britain and the US a month later. Elections in 1947 unsurprisingly resulted in an overwhelming victory for the Communist Party; a few months later, Mikołajczyk fled to Britain, in fear of his life.

Nearly six years previously, the British had gone to war in order to keep Poland free; now they allowed it to be handed back to one of the original invaders. Poland was both first victim of the Second World War and first victim of the Cold War. Although the war had switched from being about the sovereign rights of nations to an all-out attack on Nazism, and making Poland's sovereignty an issue again in 1945 risked another war, this time with the Soviet Union, what about the *principle* involved? If it was worth fighting for in 1939, why wasn't it still worth fighting for in 1945? As John T. Flynn said in 1948: 'Chamberlain appeased Hitler and averted war. Churchill got for England both a war and appeasement.'[81]

'Little Boy' and 'Fat Man'

Terminal's other major issue was Japan. By the time of the conference, it was clear that an Allied victory was inevitable – even without the atomic bomb: it was just a question of how long it would take and how many lives it would cost.

In Burma, Japanese forces continued to be pushed back steadily. Rangoon was recaptured by Indian troops on 3 May 1945, just as the European war was coming to an end. The Japanese attempt to break out of the Arakan region produced one of the most mismatched battles of the war, with 17,000 Japanese casualties to just 95 on the Allied side. The assault on Okinawa, just 350 miles from the Japanese mainland, began on 1 April, but there was ferocious resistance, even from the local children. Of 77,000 Japanese troops on the island, less than 10 per cent were taken prisoner. The land resistance and kamikaze attacks cost 12,500 US lives and the loss of 36 US warships before the island was fully in Allied hands in June – a grim foretaste of what would happen if they attempted to invade mainland Japan. Also in April, the Australians began the re-conquest of the Netherlands East Indies, with US support.

The Japanese government and establishment was not composed

413

solely of aggressive warriors. There always had been an active peace movement, although because of the military caste's grip on the government during the war it remained unobtrusive. But as the tide turned, it began to re-emerge, led by General Koisi's Deputy Prime Minister, Admiral Yonai Mitsumasa. There was another change of leadership in Japan in April 1945. Koisi had made a bumbling attempt to persuade Chiang Kai-shek's government to break away from the Alliance, but when this was leaked he was forced to resign. He was succeeded by the 78-year-old Admiral Suzuki Kantaro, who had the backing of the peace lobby.

By the end of July, Japan was under siege, heavy bombardment and blockade causing economic chaos and food shortages. The government and military was split between those who believed that Japan should defend its honour to the last breath and those who wanted to save it by suing for peace. Under Suzuki, the first tentative peace feelers were put out. Navy Secretary James Forrestal noted on 13 July 1945:

> The first real evidence of a Japanese desire to get out of the war came today through intercepted messages from Togo [Shigenori], Foreign Minister, to Sato, Jap Ambassador in Moscow, instructing the latter to see Molotov if possible before his departure for the Big Three meeting [Potsdam], and if not then, immediately afterward, to lay before him the Emperor's strong desire to secure a termination of the war.[82]

Before Potsdam, Emperor Hirohito had already made it clear that although he was prepared to talk peace, unconditional surrender was not acceptable. On 26 July, the Potsdam Proclamation reiterated the demand and those of the Cairo Declaration, that all territory outside Japan itself would be removed from Japanese control. A more democratic system would be introduced, Japan being occupied until this was done.

Both sides believed the Pacific war would run at least for another year, because even very few Americans knew about the atom bomb. The first – 'Trinity' – was exploded at Alamogordo, New Mexico, on 16 July 1945, the day before the Potsdam Conference. In advance of the test, Churchill cabled to Truman: 'Let me know if it's a flop or a plop.'

Truman replied, 'It's a plop.'[83]

As we have seen, the tentative decision to continue bombing until Japan surrendered was made by Roosevelt and Churchill in September 1944, although ironically it was their successors who were faced with the terrible responsibility. The first of only two atomic bombs ever to have been used in war was dropped on the city of Hiroshima at 8.15 a.m. on 6 August 1945. To convince the Japanese how awesome a weapon this was, a city as yet unscathed by Allied bombing was chosen, which would also make it easier for the Allies to assess the WMD's damage. The bomb was nicknamed 'Little Boy' after Roosevelt, presumably ironically, as he was 6 ft 2 in. tall. Less ironically – but more cruelly – the Nagasaki bomb was 'Fat Man', after Churchill.

Five square miles of city were flattened. Of the 350,000 people in Hiroshima, besides the 92,000 destroyed by the searing flash and blast, others were to experience a slow death, sometimes many years later, from the after-effects of the heat and radiation. Within a year, over 118,000 deaths had been recorded, the eventual total being approximately 140,000. Through the genetic damage caused by the radiation, the horror was also visited on mutated unborn children.[84]

The next day, when the Japanese Ambassador in Moscow asked Molotov to act as a mediator for peace talks, he received instead a declaration of war – the million-man Russian offensive on Manchuria and northern Korea beginning just two hours later. Soviet forces also attacked southern Sakhalin (the large island off the Siberian coast that had been divided between the two nations since 1905) and the Kurile Islands. There is little doubt that Stalin only joined the war so late in the day because Japan's surrender was imminent, and if he stood aloof from the Allies he would never get the territory he wanted. But despite promising to join in once Germany was defeated, he 'still delayed joining the war against Japan, preferring to let his allies expend their energies in the Far East while he consolidated his position in Europe'.[85]

When the Japanese rejected Truman's demands to surrender, the second atomic bomb was dropped on 9 August. The target was the city of Kokura, but because of heavy cloud the aircraft was diverted to Nagasaki, whose population of 270,000 lost 74,000.

As the Japanese hawks and doves were still deadlocked, Suzuki appealed to the Emperor to make the final decision: on 10 August, the Japanese informed the Allies that they accepted the terms, except for one condition, 'that it does not comprise any demand which prejudices the prerogatives of the Emperor as sovereign ruler'. As Truman accepted, technically it was not actually unconditional surrender after all. On 14 August, Hirohito broadcast to his people – despite an armed attempt to prevent the broadcast – telling them hostilities had ceased. Predictably, Stalin only ordered his forces to lay down their arms when they had taken everything he wanted in China, Sakhalin and the Kuriles, prolonging hostilities by another two weeks. The formal surrender took place on 2 September, bringing Britain's involvement in the Second World War to an end just one day short of its sixth anniversary.

Undoubtedly, according to international law, dropping the bombs on Japan was a war crime pure and simple – the Geneva and Hague Conventions forbid the deliberate targeting of civilians in order to put pressure on their government. Its apologists argue that it saved lives – mostly American – as an attempt to invade Japan would have been the most savage battle yet, while many others argue that such apocalyptic carnage could never be justified.

However, between the stark choices of these two evils lies the spectre of unconditional surrender. Had peace talks and some form of compromise been possible to save Japan's face, neither invasion nor the Bomb would have been necessary. Yet the unconditional-surrender policy remained unyielding to the last. The Allies' priorities were curious, to say the least: faced with a choice between vaporising thousands and an invasion of carnage beyond imagining, they still considered backing down on unconditional surrender less acceptable than either.

After Japan surrendered, close to two-thirds of a million soldiers and civilians in Manchuria, Korea, Sakhalin and the Kuriles were deported to the Soviet gulags, mostly in Siberia. Within a decade, one in ten was dead, buried in unmarked graves in nearly 800 burial grounds, the location of some still uncertain. With grim irony, the

Russians set the Japanese to work on building Siberian railways; exactly how many died during their construction is unknown, but according to *The Oxford Companion to the Second World War* under every sleeper lies a Japanese body.[86]

Stalin had been extraordinarily successful. In Europe, he had conspired with Hitler to start a war in order to win coveted territory, and despite ending the conflict on the other side he still got everything he wanted – indeed more, as now he controlled all Central and Eastern Europe and the Balkans. It may have cost the lives of some 20 million Soviet citizens, but that meant nothing to him – as he said to Churchill, what is one generation? In Asia, after letting his Allies do the fighting for the best part of four years, Stalin's forces fought for just eight days to gain all the territory he wanted there as well.

Picking up the pieces

Shattered Britain felt the shockwaves from the Japanese surrender in very immediate terms, for as David Dimbleby and David Reynolds explain: 'Eight days after the war ended with Japan's surrender, President Truman cancelled Lend-Lease . . . The British Food Mission, despatching tons of supplies from the United States, only learnt about it when one of their ships was refused permission to sail. Next day, the official announcement was made.'[87] Keynes aptly called the decision a 'financial Dunkirk'.[88]

To be fair to Truman, this was not his initiative, but that of Congress. As the Lend-Lease Act gave the President unprecedented control over the terms of supplies, Congress had no wish for this to continue into the phase of post-war reconstruction. Wanting to control the aid and its conditions, they stuck rigidly to the letter of the law: Lend-Lease applied only while a state of war existed.[89]

However, the terms for the final settlement of Lend-Lease were surprisingly generous. Of the $15 billion (£3.75 billion) difference between the value of the goods received and the value of Reverse Lend-Lease given in return, Britain was asked to repay only $650 million (£162.5 million). But as American businessman General Robert E. Wood said in November 1945: 'If you succeed in doing away with the Empire preference and opening up the Empire to

United States commerce, it may well be that you can afford to pay a couple of billion dollars for the privilege.'[90]

Even so, the abrupt ending of Lend-Lease still left serious questions over Britain's ability to feed and clothe itself, not to mention rebuilding its cities and industry – especially as its dollar and gold reserves were now vastly diminished, and a huge amount of its export trade had vanished across the Atlantic. And, unlike the USSR, Britain had been given no copious amounts of aid to help its post-war recovery.

By 1945, Britain had a balance-of-payments deficit of around $3 billion and had sold off a huge amount of its assets. War production had diverted 1.5 million workers from export industries – which meant they were unable to carry out the export drive necessary for economic recovery. Britain also needed *imports* for its reconstruction, and, as the only industrial nation left intact, the United States was the only real source of what it needed – but, thanks to Harry Dexter White and Morgenthau, the British dollar reserves were insufficient to buy it.[91]

In order to survive, once again Britain had to go cap-in-hand to the US Treasury. Keynes was sent to Washington to negotiate a loan, asking for $5 billion and eventually getting $3.75 billion (and $1.25 billion from Canada), repayable with 2 per cent interest in 50 annual instalments, beginning in 1951.

As we write in 2004, Britain is still paying it off – but not for much longer. Although on six occasions the country's economy has been in such a parlous state that it defaulted on the repayments, in June 2002 the Blair government announced that (barring some major financial disaster) the final instalment will be paid on 31 December 2006. Finally, the United Kingdom will be out of debt to the United States, financially at least.[92] (Unless it will need yet another loan for yet another war . . .)

However, the generous settlement of Lend-Lease and the loan came at the price of British endorsement of the Bretton Woods agreement – which the government had steadfastly refused – by the end of 1945. By agreeing to end exchange controls and allowing sterling to be freely converted into dollars, this effectively acknowledged that the dollar was now king. The vote to endorse this agreement caused pandemonium in the House of Commons, and although many MPs accepted the inevitable and voted in favour, 100 voted against and 169 abstained – even including Winston Churchill.[93] There was some poetic justice in the humbling of once-mighty Britannia; as Dimbleby and Reynolds write: 'Having imposed terms on others for two centuries, the British were discovering what it was like to be on the receiving end.'[94]

Nothing was going right for the British. Even the loan caused another financial crisis. Forced to approve the Bretton Woods agreement, in July 1947 they had to end exchange controls, and businessmen and investors with large amounts of sterling seized the opportunity to convert it to the golden new global currency, causing sterling to collapse. In five weeks, Britain lost $900 million – and had to use much of the remainder of the loan to plug the gap.[95]

Once again, the terms extended by the US to the USSR were rather different. On their side, the Soviet Union refused to give anything in exchange for Lend-Lease until 1951, when it offered $300 million on a 'take it or leave it' basis.[96] (Somehow, even after Japan's surrender – and the abrupt termination of Lend-Lease – the USSR managed to squeeze another $76 million out of Uncle Sam.[97])

Seemingly oblivious that so much Lend-Lease had already been supplied for post-war use, the US Treasury had long pondered on how to help the Soviet Union with its reconstruction. The idea of extending a loan had been mooted as far back as 1943, when it was intimated to the Kremlin that a post-war application was likely to be favourably received.[98] In January 1945, Molotov requested a $6 billion loan at 2.25 per cent interest in exchange for substantial orders for capital equipment from American companies. Harry Dexter White's response was telling: he proposed that the US offer $10 billion at 2 per cent for the purchase of American goods, and Morgenthau approved it – without any conditions.[99] (However, by the time the decision was made the harder-line Truman was in office, so in the end there was some proper bargaining.)

The ravages of war really began to hit Europe hard in 1947: damage to industry, shattered economies and population upheavals were too great – millions were sliding into starvation. In May 1947, the US Under-Secretary of State, Will Clayton, toured Europe and concluded: 'Without further prompt and substantial aid from the United States, economic, social and political disintegration will overwhelm Europe.' However, this aid must come from the United States, not via the United Nations or the International Monetary Fund – 'the United States must run this show'.[100] And run it the Americans did, in the form of General George Marshall, whom Truman had appointed Secretary of State in 1947, and who enthusiastically took up the challenge.

Responding to an overture by Marshall, 16 Western European nations – the Soviet Union refused to be involved, or allow its satellites to take part – met in Paris to assess their requirements. The final assessment, made in September 1947, amounted to $29 billion, but Marshall trimmed this to $17 billion, payable over four years.

Congress approved the Marshall Plan in March 1948, but largely because of events that had prompted fears of a Soviet takeover in Europe. In February 1948 came the first great crisis of the Cold War – when it seemed it was about to become very hot – with a Communist takeover in Czechoslovakia. The American commander in Germany reported that war 'may come with dramatic suddenness'.[101] In response to this threat, Truman urged Congress to approve the Marshall Plan, as well as re-introducing the draft.

The crisis also led to the Brussels Defence Pact of March 1948, in which Britain, France, the Netherlands, Belgium and Luxembourg undertook a mutual defence agreement, and to the first discussions with the United States that culminated in the formation of NATO in April 1949.

Roosevelt's and Hopkins' division of Europe, creating a menace that now required Truman's doctrine of containment, meant that, unlike the First World War, this time the American GIs did not go home; this time, they stayed in Europe – in case hostilities flared up with the Soviet Union.

The legacy

On 4 September 1945, Hopkins was awarded the Distinguished Service Medal by Truman, only just in time. Besides his intestinal ailments, he was diagnosed with cirrhosis of the liver – as he wrote to Churchill on 22 January 1946 (the last letter he ever wrote), 'not due, I regret to say, from taking too much alcohol'.[102] He died on 29 January 1946, aged 56.

With the demise of both Roosevelt and Hopkins, a chapter ended in American – and world – history that is only now being fully understood. It was only as death stood in the wings that both men independently realised that the Russian they had made a demi-god was just as bad, if not worse, than the Nazi monster they had annihilated. If they had realised this years before, today's world would be unrecognisable.

Although not many people today even know his name, Hopkins' legacy was of truly epic proportions. This sickly and inconspicuous man – unelected and holding no official post in the US administration – actually shaped the world according to his own grand design. The greyest of grey eminences, he outshone the most honoured household name, and for a time his star seemed unquenchable. But despite his grand vision, his immediate and enduring legacy was a world riven with fear and paranoia.

EPILOGUE

Guilty Secrets and Secret Agendas

The Second World War is seen today as totally different from all other wars. Although questions are readily asked, for example about the real reasons for the invasion of Iraq in 2003, to most people there is no debate about the 1939–45 global conflict: it was purely and simply a moral crusade against the evils of Nazism. End of argument. But in reality, some actions were taken that had no connection with the defeat of Nazism, and certain actions that should have been necessary to overthrow Nazism were *not* taken. None of the main wartime governments emerges with much credit from the events described in this book, as they struggled to dig political, financial and military advantage out of the rubble.

The Second World War in Europe was not caused solely by Hitler's aggressive ambitions: one of the most crucial of the other interlocking factors was Stalin's endorsement of the Nazi–Soviet Pact, guaranteeing war between Britain, France and Germany. Another vital factor was Roosevelt pressing Britain to take a hard line over Poland and giving worthless guarantees to the Poles, whom he then left high and dry when the Nazis marched in. In our view, the evidence suggests that Roosevelt played fast and loose with Poland because he wanted an economically beneficial war in Europe, giving him a way out of the 'Roosevelt Recession' and an opportunity to establish the United States as the most powerful economic power on the planet. With the same long-term objectives, he craftily engineered the appointment of the uncompromisingly bellicose Winston Churchill as Britain's Prime Minister, to ensure there would be no swift negotiated peace.

Because, for their own reasons, both leaders wanted the war against Germany to continue after the fall of France in June 1940, Churchill and Roosevelt ignored opportunities to end the war, for example by avoiding negotiating with anti-Hitler groups within Germany. For his part, Churchill fooled Roosevelt, his opponents in Parliament and the British people into believing in a non-existent invasion threat, to maintain American aid and prevent his opponents pressing for peace talks. In return for Roosevelt's support, Churchill effectively lent him British intelligence, which then mounted operations to discredit, undermine and neutralise Roosevelt's political opponents in the US, and to secure his re-election for a third term. The result was that British intelligence hijacked the 1940 US Presidential elections and created 'straw-man' candidate Wendell Willkie. British intelligence also supplied fake 'Nazi documents' that Roosevelt used to further his own political ends.

In return, often flouting the US constitution and law, and certainly making a nonsense of America's ostensible neutrality, Roosevelt pushed through deals for aid to Britain – such as Lend-Lease, the shamelessly named Bill 1776 – which, while appearing to be magnanimous gestures of moral and practical support, in fact exacted a very heavy price. Britain was required to do away with the trade barriers that protected its position within the Empire, opening the markets up to US business on conditions so advantageous as to constitute submission to American post-war supremacy, and allowing the dollar to replace sterling as the world's strongest currency and the US Treasury to take complete control of Britain's gold and dollar reserves for the duration of the war.

The contrast could hardly be greater with Roosevelt's attitude to the USSR. When Hitler's troops attacked the Soviet Union in June 1941, propelling Stalin into the Allied camp, FDR – again, often with borderline legality – offered him 'unconditional aid'. Roosevelt and his alter ego Harry Hopkins supplied and built up Russia not simply to defeat the Nazis but also because they believed it was not only inevitable but desirable that the USA and USSR would become the two post-war superpowers, and the Soviet Union should hold the balance of power in Europe in order to neutralise the old imperialists.

The peculiar policies created by Roosevelt and foisted upon Churchill – first unconditional surrender and then the Morgenthau Plan – were designed to ensure that the war continued until the US and USSR were where he wanted them to be. Together, Roosevelt and Stalin out-voted Churchill to carry through strategies that ensured the Western Allies did not encroach on Stalin's intended sphere of influence, even deliberately slowing down the Western Allies' advance, and carefully coordinating the final assault on Germany to ensure that the Russians captured Berlin.

Churchill, too, had his guilty secret: he had exploited Rudolf Hess's peace mission in order to reach an understanding with Hitler, even a de facto truce, that diverted German forces to the Soviet Union, letting the Red Army – not to mention millions of ordinary Russians – deal with the worst of the Wehrmacht and Luftwaffe's might while buying Britain precious time.

As for the war against Japan, once again Roosevelt was far from the injured party he always liked to portray. He pursued an aggressively provocative and uncompromising policy that strengthened the 'war party' in Japan – and then goaded it into attacking. He wanted to further American trade and influence by killing off the European Empires in the Far East, creating a vacuum that the US could fill. He believed that the Japanese would strike against British, or perhaps Dutch, territories, but the plan backfired when Pearl Harbor was attacked. When Japan did attack, Roosevelt did not intend to declare war on Germany – but British intelligence tricked Hitler into doing it for him, by leaking top-secret US war plans, thereby pushing the United States into a war against the wishes of the majority of its people.

Of the Big Three, the United States and the Soviet Union were the victors in the Second World War: not only were they on the winning side but they actually gained substantially from the conflict, emerging as the two global superpowers. It was not a status that could be claimed by the United Kingdom for much longer. It might have entered the conflict a proud imperial superpower but it emerged blinking feebly from its battered Anderson shelter much diminished – even humiliated – by having to beg for handouts. As John Charmley writes '. . . if 1945 represented "victory", it was, as Chamberlain had foreseen, for the Soviets and the Americans'.[1]

In the last 60 years, the feeling on both sides of the Atlantic that Britons should be eternally grateful for American aid during the Second World War has become set in stone. To challenge it is to be ungrateful, even unpatriotic – yet the impression that Britain never repaid either a dime or a dime's worth of goods could hardly be further from the truth. In terms of giving away its overseas commercial advantages, Britain has paid several times over.

Britain's economic usurpation was not an accidental, or incidental, consequence of war. All of it was *calculated*, as A.J.P. Taylor explains:

> Great Britain became a poor, though deserving, cousin – not to Roosevelt's regret. So far as it is possible to read his devious mind, it appears that he expected the British to wear down both Germany and themselves. When all independent powers had ceased to exist, the United States would step in and run the world. Despite talk of liberating or even restoring Europe, Roosevelt really assumed that there was no Europe. The United States would engross all the power in the world, with Europe and indeed everywhere else as their grateful dependants.[2]

At the very least, Roosevelt and other major figures such as Henry Morgenthau – and Harry Dexter White – took advantage of Britain's plight and then its subordinate position in the Grand Alliance. However, we believe that the evidence shows that Roosevelt actively worked to *engineer* the war, specifically in order to save America's economy.

To the victor the spoils

As Mark Stoler writes: '. . . the United States ended the war with fewer deaths than any other major belligerent, fought no major battles on or even near its own soil, and was the only power to emerge with an economy stronger than when the war had begun'.[3] This is even more remarkable as the American economy was on a knife-edge in 1939. Years of throwing federal money at New Deal projects had merely staved off the day of disaster, and America was sliding into another depression that, this time, looked likely to be a bottomless pit. But, miraculously, Roosevelt not only found something else to throw money at but also actually succeeded in spending his way out of financial disaster. Between 1941 and 1945, the US government spent $317 billion on the war, but as a result America's gross national product more than doubled, and unemployment plummeted from 14.6 per cent of the workforce in 1940 to under 2 per cent in 1945. Predictably, the war gobbled up the available workforce: in 1939 the United States had 11 million unemployed, and an army of just a quarter of a million; by 1945 the US armed forces employed almost 12 million people (8.2 million in the army and 3.4 million in the navy).[4]

There could be no question of reverting to isolationism now the war was won – it would wreck the economy. US industry was now supplying the world, so it had to continue to do so, if not with weapons (although they still represent a significant proportion of America's exports) then with consumer goods. And through deals with Britain in return for Lend-Lease, the world was now open for American exports. As David Reynolds writes: 'The USA enjoyed both guns and butter, and her wartime boom not only pulled her out of the Depression but laid the foundations for her quarter-century or so of post-war industrial supremacy.'[5]

This tactic of using defence spending to prop up or regenerate the economy has also been used by Roosevelt's successors – ironically, mainly Republicans. One economic correspondent wrote of the recession-hit 1980s:

> Ronald Reagan famously resorted to deficit spending, using
> talk of the Evil Empire and communist threats from Central

America as his excuse to rachet up the military budget. In 1984, the deficit rose to a whopping 6.2 per cent of GDP [gross domestic product]. Consequently, the economy grew by more than 7 per cent that year, and he was re-elected by a landslide.[6]

In his second term, Reagan turned to the Strategic Defense Initiative (or 'Star Wars') programme as a means of boosting military spending, even though the Cold War threat was diminishing.

And in January 2004, it was reported that George W. Bush's War on Terror and the invasion of Iraq was bringing about a major economic boost. In the second quarter of 2003, as the invasion was in progress, no less than 60 per cent of the growth in the US's GDP was due to military spending. As Robert Pollin, Professor of Economics at the University of Massachusetts, explains:

> It may be very inefficient and obviously not fair, but it is nevertheless causing almost 5 per cent more money to be pumped into the economy than is being taken out in tax revenues. At the same time, it fits into the broader ideological goals of his administration because they can paint it as part of a national emergency, the fight against terrorism, the fight against Saddam Hussein and so on.[7]

Is this a coincidence, or is George W. Bush following FDR's well-established precedent?

Roosevelt also exploited the war to fulfil his greatest ambitions for America and the world. It presented him with the opportunity to realise his 20-year dream of a new organisation to replace the tired and discredited League of Nations, building upon the Atlantic Charter and the United Nations Declaration to transform the 'United Nations' of the anti-Axis alliance into the United Nations Organisation. The UN's inaugural meeting was held in San Francisco under the sombre pall of Roosevelt's death just two weeks before. The major modification to FDR's scheme related to the Security Council, supposed to consist of his 'Four Policemen' with the monopoly on military strength. A fifth member, France, was added to his global elite, and as there would be six other non-permanent seats elected by the General Assembly it was possible for the rest of the world to curb the Big Five's power.

Was Roosevelt's original idea of world policemen with a monopoly on arms better than what the world actually got? We suggest that it depends on who polices the policemen, assuming that they would cooperate on the same global agenda. As events were soon to show, this was an idealistic fantasy.

The most significant aspect of the new organisation was that the US played such a central role – unthinkable in the isolationist climate when Roosevelt came to office. This transformation was perhaps his greatest achievement. For most of his Presidency, even up to the brink of war, most Americans refused to countenance their nation becoming embroiled in international affairs; yet by the time of his death, the United States was setting the global agenda. Today, few could even conceive of the US in any other role. Seldom has a politician pursued a line that is so out of step with his country's deepest instincts – and ended by persuading the people that he was right.

Since the war, the US military's massive presence around the globe has mushroomed, with air, naval and army bases scattered across the face of the world. We have seen how the first of these bases were secured in return for wartime aid. At the end of the war, America had a presence in Europe and Japan – and, until very recently, never went home. This was the result of Roosevelt's doctrine of 'defence at a distance', being prepared to meet any perceived threat to US interests as far away from America as possible.

At the end of 1943, at his behest, the US Joint Chiefs completed a wide-ranging study of American requirements for military bases and operating rights in other countries. To avoid problems over sovereignty – and allegations of imperialism – the bases would be leased from the various host nations. The report, which FDR embraced enthusiastically, called for a massive number scattered throughout the world, from the Arctic to the Azores and Mexico, West Africa and the Middle East, and throughout the Pacific.[8]

On 12 March 1947, President Truman enunciated to Congress what became known as the 'Truman Doctrine': '. . . the policy of the

United States is to support free people who are resisting attempted subjugation by armed minorities or by outside pressure'.[9] It was the final end of American isolationism and of the Monroe Doctrine.

Roosevelt left another legacy: he changed the role of US President – not necessarily in particularly noble ways. Roosevelt established the principle that deceiving the people is a legitimate tactic of foreign policy. As history has judged that the ends (defeat of the Nazis and Japan) justified these means, he set a precedent. However, discussing the Vietnam War, Senator William Fulbright declared in 1971: 'FDR's deviousness in a good cause made it easier for LBJ to practice the same kind of deviousness in a bad cause.'[10]

Of course, Churchill was as adept at spin and manipulation as FDR, and also blithely rewrote history, so successfully that his self-justificatory version is still the best known. Unlike Roosevelt, who seems to have been as concerned about his nation's future as his place in its history, Churchill was primarily motivated by self-aggrandisement. To him, Britain was fighting to maintain its golden status quo, not to make enormous gains in the post-war world. He assumed that once he had saved his nation, it would return to its glory days. Despite the warnings of those around him such as Chamberlain and Lord Halifax, in his early premiership, he persisted on the path that would fulfil his own destiny, which he believed to be Britain's destiny, too.

Churchill thought he could cleverly out-manoeuvre Roosevelt, getting the aid he wanted to win the war while giving little or nothing back. He couldn't. It must have dawned on him quite quickly that he was sacrificing the Empire and even Britain's independence. In the end, Churchill was the man who sold Britain and its Empire to the USA, for the sake of his own glory.

Frankenstein's monster

However, if Roosevelt screwed the British, he was, in his turn, screwed just as much by Stalin. The Soviet Premier was no doubt hugely amused at the naivety of the American President, who thought that giving in to whatever he wanted – *'noblesse oblige'* – would make him soften his regime. Of course, in reality the Soviet dictator was gleefully rubbing his hands as he squeezed even more concessions out of Roosevelt. And Churchill could only shake his head in disbelief.

With a grotesque irony, Britain, the United States, France and the other Allies fought in partnership with a regime that equalled that of the Nazis' in brutality, repression and totalitarianism, whose alliance with Germany had caused the war in the first place – and even participated in the invasion of Poland that had exploded the war into being. It was also a regime that explicitly sought the downfall of its Allies – indeed, it boasted a political creed with world domination at its very core.

And yet at the end of the conflict the Soviet Union was handed nearly half a century's domination of eastern and central Europe. Millions of people who had been promised liberation were enslaved by a brutal totalitarianism – with the blessing of the British and American governments. And, much to the disgust of those who knew the truth about his regime, Stalin and his henchmen were elevated to the same moral high ground as the other victors: witness the presence of Soviet judges on the International Military Tribunal that tried the Nazi leaders in Nuremberg on charges of conspiracy to wage war, war crimes and crimes against humanity. Stalin was just as guilty of all three.

Stalin was also treated as an equal when the victors divided up Germany and Europe. The original plan was that the 'four victorious powers' would draw up a peace treaty, set up a new democratic government in Germany and then withdraw. However, disagreements soon set in between the three Western Allies and the Soviet Union, and in 1948 Britain, France and the USA began to create a new state in their zones of occupation, while the Soviet Union set up its own regime in its zone. The division into East and West Germany would last for nearly half a century. Stalin also quickly tightened his grip on the nations that had fallen into his sphere of influence – including Poland, Czechoslovakia, Hungary and Bulgaria – until they were nothing more than Soviet puppets.

Not only did the USSR gain territorially but Roosevelt also supplied it with a vast amount of material for its post-war regeneration through Lend-Lease, contrary to the Lend-Lease law. Essentially, Roosevelt and Hopkins were funding the Cold War.

We would argue that this division of the world between East and West was the result of a deliberate policy by Roosevelt and Hopkins, the logical extension of their pre-war geopolitical ideas, when the idea of splitting the world into two power blocs, each dominating a hemisphere, was not as crazy as it seemed later. What they failed to anticipate was the development of the atomic bomb and the means to deliver this new weapon between continents, in the shape of the long-range bomber and, later, the Inter-Continental Ballistic Missile. (Even when the atomic bomb was fast becoming a reality they seemed to think Stalin could be persuaded to be reasonable over it.) Their grand design backfired badly, creating the Cold War and the threat of nuclear annihilation that chilled the lives of generations. It is easy to forget just how close this came, and that the Cold War blew exceedingly hot for many millions of people.

Foothold for the future

As the Allies were locked in a struggle for post-war supremacy, the conflict was deliberately and cynically extended as each player battled for prime position for after the dust settled. Lives were lost and terrible destruction visited on Allies and Axis alike to an extent that was unnecessary had victory been the only goal. The devastation of Europe need never have happened, yet without it, there would have been no necessity for the United States to step in again with the Marshall Plan.

How much sooner could the war have ended? What opportunities were missed? The choices open to the Allies are usually depicted as either fighting to total victory or ignoble surrender followed by abject enslavement. However, there were several other options, but history has been deliberately distorted in order to make it appear that those alternatives never existed.

After the fall of France, it was possible to negotiate a settlement with Germany that would *not* have meant humiliation for Britain. Hitler had made his principles clear – if Britain stayed out of Europe, Germany would not interfere with its Empire. Rudolf Hess brought the same terms to Britain in May 1941. Of course, few would advocate today that peace should have been made on those terms knowing the full horror of Nazism. It would have meant abandoning the nations of Europe either to Nazi rule or, at the very least, to alignment with Nazi ideology and policies; one shudders to think what that might have meant in practice. But at the time such a course of action was at least feasible, and those who advocated it – at one point a majority in the Cabinet – were not lily-livered cowards or closet Hitlerites. (And we must remember that the full horrors of the Final Solution still lay, unguessably, in the future: indeed, it is possible that the failure to reach a peaceable solution in 1941 led directly to the Holocaust.[11]) Had that option been taken, it is impossible to say what would have happened when Germany turned east – who would have won then, without Allied support – or, given the level of opposition to Hitler within the German Establishment, how long Germany would have stayed Nazi.

There were other options that may well have brought the war in Europe to an end much earlier – had the policy of unconditional surrender not been adopted at the beginning of 1943. Swifter advantage could have been taken of Mussolini's fall in September 1943, perhaps bringing Allied troops into the Greater Germany by the end of that year and avoiding hellishly costly battles such as those at Monte Cassino. Advantage could have been taken of the anti-Hitler conspirators' offers to arrest the Nazi leaders and allow Allied troops into Germany before D-Day. In both scenarios, the costly operation of liberating Europe and pushing into Germany itself would have been unnecessary. The Normandy campaign may have been a success, but it cost some 37,000 American, British and Canadian lives: disasters such as Omaha Beach and the abortive assault at Arnhem in September 1944 could have been avoided. And, of course, hundreds of thousands in the Nazis' extermination camps, which maintained their grim daily routine of gassing and cremation until the last months of 1944, would have been saved. The reign of terror on Germany that was Operation Thunderclap, culminating in the Dresden firestorm, would have been unnecessary. And there were Hitler's final desperate attempts to use his new V-weapons to undermine the morale of the British people, bringing a new Blitz on London. All this could have been spared.

The West has been too long in denial about the real motives and hypocrisy of the Allied leaders, too intent on building up the image of legendary leaders and just nations. There were indeed heroes and noble deeds, too often unsung and unknown, contrasting with profoundly evil and inhuman regimes. But unless we acknowledge the double-dealing and private agendas, and challenge the near-holy veneration of the likes of Roosevelt and Churchill, the lessons learnt in that hardest of schools will pass us by, and we will be condemned to learn them all over again.

Notes and References

Introduction: The More Things Change . . .
1 Quoted in *The Independent*, 7 February 2004.

Chapter One: The Hess Predictions
1 Stuart, p. 96.
2 In *Double Standards*, we examine the surprisingly persuasive doubts that the person who emerged from captivity in 1945 really was Hess, or a double who had replaced him in the intervening period. We also present evidence that the real Hess may have died in a plane crash in Scotland in August 1942. However, this is only relevant to the present discussion in that – in contrast to other researchers who follow the 'doppelgänger theory' – we believe that it was the real Rudolf Hess who arrived in Britain on 10 May 1941.
3 UK National Archives, file FO 898/14, memo from S. Voight to SO1 Director Rex Leeper, 12 May 1941.
4 UK National Archives, file PREM 2/219/4.
5 Howe, p. 133.
6 UK National Archives, PREM 3/219/7, memo from Eden to Churchill, 27 May 1941.
7 See *Double Standards*, pp. 300–4.
8 A translated transcript of the meeting is in the UK National Archives, file FO 1093/1.
9 A copy of the original and a translation is in the House of Lords Record Office, Beaverbrook Papers, file D/443.
10 UK National Archives, FO 1093/1: 'Record of an Interview with Herr Rudolph Hess, May 13'; 'Record of a Conversation with Herr Hess on May 15th, 1941'.
11 See *Double Standards*, pp. 120–3.
12 Cadogan, p. 374.
13 See *Double Standards*, chapter 9.

Notes and References

14 Roberts, *Eminent Churchillians*, pp. 207–8.

15 See *Double Standards*, chapters 12 and 13.

16 Quoted in Gilbert, *Winston S. Churchill*, vol. VI, p. 616.

17 E.H. Carr, *Britain*, p. 190.

18 Argyll, p. 6.

19 Watt, *How War Came*, p. 448.

20 Goebbels, p. 424.

21 UK National Archives, PREM 3/219/7, cable from British Consul to Ministry of Information, 19 June 1941.

22 Sherwood, vol. I, p. 294.

23 Kimball, *Churchill and Roosevelt*, vol. I, pp. 187–9.

24 Cadogan, p. 389.

Chapter Two: The Unthinkable

1 Quoted in Watt, *Succeeding John Bull*, p. 59.

2 Quoted in E.H. Carr, *International Relations since the Peace Treaties*, p. 281.

3 Quoted in Basil Collier, p. 11.

4 *Ibid.*, p. 24.

5 *Ibid.*, p. 52.

6 See *ibid.*, pp. 27–9.

7 E.H. Carr, *International Relations since the Peace Treaties*, p. 86.

8 Calvocoressi, Wint & Pritchard, vol. II, p. 45; Basil Collier p. 50.

9 See: Calvocoressi, Wint & Pritchard, vol. II, pp. 48–51; Tansill, pp. 80–2.

10 Calvocoressi, Wint & Pritchard, vol. II, p. 65.

11 Dimbleby & Reynolds, p. 84.

12 Quoted in *ibid.*, p. 78.

13 Gallagher, p. 108.

14 Hastings, 'Britain's Last Warrior'.

15 See Basil Collier, pp. 60–1.

16 E.H. Carr, *Britain*, p. 44.

17 Watt, *Succeeding John Bull*, p. 54.

18 Wheeler-Bennett, *Disarmament and Security since Locarno*, p. 142.

19 Quoted in Dimbleby & Reynolds, p. 81.

20 On the Geneva Conference and its consequences, see Roskill, vol. I, chapters XII and XIV.

21 See Watt, *Succeeding John Bull*, pp. 56–60.

22 Quoted in *ibid.*, p. 50.

23 Quoted in *ibid.*

24 Quoted in Dimbleby & Reynolds, p. 82.

25 Quoted in Watt, *Succeeding John Bull*, p. 60.

26 *Ibid.*, pp. 61–2.

27 Larkin, p. 262.

28 E.H. Carr, *Britain*, p. 45.

29 *Ibid.*, p. 44.

30 See our *Double Standards*, pp. 53–4.

31 Anthony Cave Brown, *Treason in the Blood*, p. 177.

32 Hitler, *Hitler's Secret Book*, p. xxiv. See also Calvocoressi, Wint & Pritchard, vol. I, pp. 59–61.

33 Quoted in Shepherd, pp. 33–4.

34 *Ibid.*, p. 30.

35 Horrie.

36 Anthony Cave Brown, *Treason in the Blood*, p. 182.

37 E.H. Carr, *Britain*, p. 151.

38 Newton, p. 4.

39 Quoted in Hargrave, p. 116.

40 See Newton, pp. 58–9.

41 Hargrave, p. 221.

42 *Ibid.*, pp. 221–2.

43 *Ibid.*, p. 221.

44 Newton, p. 66.

45 *Ibid.*, p. 94.

46 *Ibid.*, p. 112.

Chapter Three: New Orders

1 Enright, p. 82.

2 Quoted in E.H. Carr, *International Relations since the Peace Treaties*, p. 284.

3 Quoted in Andrew, *Secret Service*, p. 264.

4 Larkin, p. 279.

5 Quoted in *ibid.*, p. 312.

6 *Ibid.*

7 Watt, *How War Came*, pp. 109–10; Lamb, *The Ghosts of Peace*, p. 90.

8 To be strictly accurate, the NKVD was the Soviet foreign ministry, espionage being the province of one of its departments, the GUGB (Main Administration of State Security, the forerunner of the KGB), but to avoid confusion caused by the department's later name changes it is customary to call it by the name of the overall ministry.

9 Quoted in Blum, vol. I, p. 56.

10 Tansill, pp. 128–30.

11 *Daily Mail*, 4 October 2003.

12 Applebaum, p. 19. The following overview of the history and working of the gulag system is drawn mainly from Applebaum, the most up-to-date study.

13 Bullock, *Hitler and Stalin*, p. 293.

14 *Ibid.*, p. 294.

15 Applebaum, p. 104.

Notes and References

16 *Ibid.*, p. 518.

17 Figures from Johannes Tuchel, writing in Dear, p. 260.

18 Bullock, *Hitler and Stalin*, p. 1056.

19 Applebaum, pp. 20–1.

20 *Ibid.*, p. 388.

21 Bullock, *Hitler and Stalin*, pp. 1036–8; pp. 1049–50.

22 Applebaum, pp. 74–5.

23 Simpson, p. 21; Buhite & Levy, p. 5; Heale, p. 18.

24 Watt, *How War Came*, p. 124.

25 Quoted in Israel, p. 13.

26 Quoted in Shogan, p. 27.

27 Schlesinger, vol. II, p. 520.

28 Quoted in Kimball, *The Juggler*, p. 7.

29 Lasky, p. 143.

30 *Ibid.*, pp. 160–1.

31 Dallek, pp. 289–90.

32 Maney, p. 201.

33 See Flynn, *The Roosevelt Myth*, pp. 237–42.

34 Simpson, p. 2.

35 Murray, pp. 85–6.

36 Eleanor Roosevelt, p. 273.

37 Simpson, p. 7.

38 Alsop, p. 52.

39 Range, pp. 164–6.

40 *Ibid.*, pp. 172–7.

41 Watt, *Succeeding John Bull*, p. 79.

42 Range, p. 8.

43 *Ibid.*, p. 2.

44 *Ibid.*, p. 184.

45 *Ibid.*, p. 177.

46 *Ibid.*, pp. 1–2.

47 *Ibid.*, p. 178.

48 *Ibid.*, p. 81.

49 David Reynolds, 'Power and Superpower', in Kimball, *America Unbound*, p. 13.

50 Buhite & Levy, p. 141.

51 Watt, *Succeeding John Bull*, p. 67.

52 *Ibid.*, p. 66.

53 Arnold, pp. 278–9.

54 Heale, p. 22; Sherwood, vol. I, p. 55.

55 Simpson, p. 25.

56 Schlesinger, vol. III, p. 191.

57 Sherwood, vol. I, p. 44.

58 *Ibid.*, vol. I, p. 3.

59 Flynn, *The Roosevelt Myth*, p. 140.

60 Baruch, *The Public Years*, p. 144.

61 Sherwood, vol. I, p. 296.

62 *Ibid.*, pp. 16–18.

63 *Ibid.*, p. 107.

64 e.g. Tuttle, p. v.

65 Sherwood, vol. I, p. 17.

66 McJimsey, *The Presidency of Franklin Delano Roosevelt*, p. 203.

67 Quoted in Sherwood, vol. I, p. 49.

68 Quoted in Tuttle, p. 26.

69 Quoted in Sherwood, vol. I, p. 28.

70 Quoted in *ibid.*, vol. I, p. 112.

71 McJimsey, *The Presidency of Franklin Delano Roosevelt*, p. 202.

72 Heale, p. 19.

73 Sherwood, vol. I, pp. 50–2.

74 Maney, p. 55.

75 Sherwood, vol. I, pp. 63–4.

76 Tuttle, p. 18.

77 Quoted in Adams, p. 65.

78 Quoted in Tuttle, p. 35.

79 Quoted in Schlesinger, vol. III, p. 191.

80 E.H. Carr, *International Relations since the Peace Treaties*, pp. 247–8.

81 Simpson, p. 41; see also McJimsey, *The Presidency of Franklin Delano Roosevelt*, p. 75.

82 Simpson, p. 42.

83 Heale, p. 37.

84 Buhite & Levy, pp. 124–5; Adams, p. 135.

85 Adams, p. 133.

86 On Hopkins' presidential ambitions, see Sherwood, vol. I, pp. 91–7 and Lash, *Eleanor and Franklin*, p. 503.

87 Lash, *Eleanor and Franklin*, p. 204.

88 Sherwood, vol. I, p. 102.

89 On Eleanor Roosevelt and Communism, see Lash, *Eleanor and Franklin*, chapter 48.

90 Quoted in Schlesinger, vol. III, p. 620.

91 Quoted in Sherwood, vol. I, pp. 139–40.

92 For example, Abbot Simon of the Communist-dominated American Youth Congress, who, to the alarm of staff, was given a bedroom in the White House for two weeks (Flynn, *The Roosevelt Myth*, p. 255).

93 A.J.P. Taylor, *From Sarajevo to Potsdam*, p. 129.

94 Andrew & Gordievsky, p. 184.

95 The notes taken by Berle at the meeting, with the agents named, are

reproduced in Chambers, pp. 466–9.

96 *Ibid.*, pp. 28–9.

97 Hayden B. Peake, 'Soviet Espionage and the Office of Strategic Services', in Kimball, *America Unbound*, p. 111.

98 Andrew & Gordievsky, p. 227.

99 Hayden B. Peake, 'Soviet Espionage and the Office of Strategic Services', in Kimball, *America Unbound*, pp. 115–17.

100 Andrew & Gordievsky, p. 228.

101 Andrew & Mitrokhin, p. 146.

102 De Toledano, *Notes from the Underground*, p. 55.

103 Lash, *Eleanor and Franklin*, p. 591.

104 *Ibid.*, pp. 702–3.

105 Quoted in *ibid.*, p. 596.

106 Andrew & Gordievsky, p. 233.

107 Mark, p. 24.

108 Andrew & Gordievsky, p. 233.

109 Andrew & Mitrokhin, p. 162.

110 Tuttle, p. 206.

111 Although Akhmerov was the NKVD 'resident' in the US, the codename suggests '19' was Fourth Department, which used numbers to identify agents and sources rather than the NKVD's names.

Chapter Four: War

1 Winston S. Churchill, *Great Contemporaries*, p. 261. (Although published in 1937, the article was written two years earlier.)

2 Adams, p. 140.

3 Haight, pp. 16–17.

4 *Ibid.*, p. 53.

5 Quoted in Sherwood, vol. I, pp. 97–8.

6 Tuttle, p. 38; Sherwood, vol. I, pp. 75–6.

7 Maney, p. 117.

8 Sherwood, vol. I, p. 77.

9 *Ibid.*, p. 99.

10 McJimsey, *The Presidency of Franklin Delano Roosevelt*, p. 203; Sherwood, vol. I, p. 99.

11 Simpson, pp. 43–4; Adams, p. 122; Buhite & Levy, p. 10.

12 Adams, pp. 127–8.

13 Simpson, p. 46.

14 Flynn, *The Roosevelt Myth*, p. 171.

15 *Ibid.*, p. 174.

16 Shogan, p. 30.

17 Tuttle, p. 37.

18 Watt, *How War Came*, pp. 126–7.

19 Watt, *Succeeding John Bull*, p. 81; *How War Came*, p. 612.

20 Shepherd, p. 124.

21 Elliott Roosevelt, p. 24.

22 Watt, *How War Came*, p. 127.

23 David Reynolds, *The Creation of the Anglo-American Alliance*, p. 195.

24 Watt, *Succeeding John Bull*, p. 82.

25 Sherwood, vol. I, p. 125.

26 *Ibid.*, p. 189.

27 See Shogan, pp. 41–3, for examples of Roosevelt's support for isolationist policies.

28 Tansill, p. 212; Dimbleby & Reynolds, p. 94.

29 Tansill, pp. 212–13.

30 See Shogan, pp. 213–14, for other examples of the profits reaped by US businesses.

31 Dallek, p. 102.

32 Flynn, *The Roosevelt Myth*, p. 170.

33 Divine, p. 168.

34 Dallek, pp. 135–6. See also Divine, pp. 168–72 and 223–8.

35 Rauch, p. 34.

36 Divine, p. 172.

37 *Ibid.*, p. 218.

38 Range, p. 24.

39 Calvocoressi, Wint & Pritchard, vol. II, p. 247.

40 Tansill, p. 421; Adams, p. 141.

41 Maney, p. 116.

42 Watt, *How War Came*, pp. 260–2.

43 *Ibid.*, pp. 553–6.

44 Stafford, *Roosevelt and Churchill*, p. 27; Lash, *Roosevelt and Churchill*, pp. 20–2.

45 Watt, *How War Came*, pp. 256–8.

46 This and the following quotes are from Lash, *Roosevelt and Churchill*, pp. 25–7.

47 Quoted in Watt, *How War Came*, p. 129.

48 *Ibid.*, pp. 129–30.

49 Quoted in James, p. 166.

50 Blum, vol. I, pp. 514–15.

51 Haight, pp. 8–9.

52 *Ibid.*, pp. 31–7.

53 Adams, pp. 141–2; Charmley, *Churchill's Grand Alliance*, p. 14.

54 Blum, vol. II, p. 48.

55 Watt, *How War Came*, pp. 132–5; Shogan, p. 49; Haight, p. 96.

56 Watt, *How War Came*, p. 135.

57 *Ibid.*, pp. 135–7.

Notes and References

58 Haight, pp. 69 and 225.

59 *Ibid.*, pp. 225–31.

60 See Kaiser, pp. 192–3.

61 Calvocoressi, Wint & Pritchard, vol. I, p. xvi.

62 Quoted in Wark, p. 126.

63 Shepherd, pp. 35–6; Peden, pp. 109–10; Wark, pp. 28–31.

64 UK National Archives, PREM 1/345, memo from Churchill to Chamberlain, 27 March 1939.

65 Quoted in Calvocoressi, Wint & Pritchard, vol. II, p. 272.

66 Quoted in *ibid.*, p. 247.

67 Dallek, p. 89.

68 Calvocoressi, Wint & Pritchard, vol. II, p. 213.

69 *Ibid.*, p. 246.

70 *Ibid.*, pp. 248–9.

71 *Ibid.*, pp. 249–50.

72 Watt, *How War Came*, p. 133.

73 UK National Archives, CAB 24/287.

74 Quoted in Cookridge, p. 62.

75 *Ibid.*

76 Lamb, *The Ghosts of Peace*, p. 108.

77 Anthony Cave Brown, *Bodyguard of Lies*, p. 166.

78 Lamb, *The Ghosts of Peace*, pp. 70–3; see also Watt, *How War Came*, pp. 103–5 and von Klemperer, pp. 105–10.

79 Dulles, *Germany's Underground*, pp. 41–9.

80 Anthony Cave Brown, *Bodyguard of Lies*, p. 168.

81 *Ibid.*, p. 146.

82 *Ibid.*, p. 139.

83 *Ibid.*, pp. 146, 153–6; Dear, p. 190.

84 Anthony Cave Brown, *Bodyguard of Lies*, p. 234.

85 Von Klemperer, pp. 115, 189, 229–30.

86 Quoted in Sherwood, vol. I, pp. 139–40.

87 Norman M. Davies, vol. II, p. 430.

88 Keynes, p. 272.

89 Quoted in Howe, p. 57.

90 Quoted in Shepherd, p. 40.

91 Quoted in Jenkins, p. 159.

92 Newton, pp. 110–11.

93 Quoted in Calvocoressi, Wint & Pritchard, vol. II, p. 268.

94 *Ibid.*, vol. II, p. 270.

95 Lamb, *The Ghosts of Peace*, p. 108.

96 *Ibid.*, pp. 76–7.

97 *Ibid.*, pp. 103–4.

98 Quoted in Howe, p. 38.

99 For the full text of the Pact and secret protocol, see Sontag & Beddie, pp. 76–8.
100 Lamb, *The Ghosts of Peace*, p. 110.
101 Watt, *How War Came*, p. 257.
102 Quoted in Lamb, *The Ghosts of Peace*, p. 116.
103 Quoted in Tansill, p. 552.
104 *Ibid.*, pp. 554–5.
105 Quoted in *ibid.*, p. 555.
106 Millis & Duffield, p. 129.
107 Kessler, pp. 207–8.
108 Long, p. 105.
109 Farnsworth, pp. 155–6.
110 Tansill, p. 556.
111 Watt, *How War Came*, p. 132.
112 Kessler, p. 197.
113 Long, p. 148.
114 Farnsworth, p. 175.
115 The formal title of the *White Book* is *Polnische Dokumente zur Vorgeschichte des Krieges* (*Polish Documents on the Origin of the War*).
116 Long, p. 74.
117 *Polnische Dokumente zur Vorgeschichte des Krieges*, Document 4. (All translations are the authors'.)
118 *Ibid.*, Document 6.
119 *Ibid.*, Document 9.
120 *Ibid.*, Document 15.
121 Quoted in Tansill, p. 406.
122 Kessler, p. 209.
123 De Bedts, p. 144.
124 Herzstein, p. 320.
125 Tansill, p. 557.
126 See, for example: Sherwood, vol. I, pp. 127–8; McJimsey, *The Presidency of Franklin Delano Roosevelt*, pp. 188–9.

Chapter Five: The Odd Couple

1 Quoted in Stafford, *Roosevelt and Churchill*, p. xxiii.
2 Kimball, *Churchill and Roosevelt*, vol. I, p. 24.
3 Kimball, *Forged in War*, p. 39.
4 Leutze, p. 54.
5 Kimball, *Forged in War*, p. 35.
6 Quoted in Stafford, *Roosevelt and Churchill*, p. xvi.
7 Lamb, *Churchill as War Leader*, pp. 75 and 164.
8 Kimball, *Churchill and Roosevelt*, vol. I, p. 4.
9 Schlesinger, vol. I, p. 367.

Notes and References

10 Stafford, *Roosevelt and Churchill*, p. xvii.

11 Quoted in *ibid.*, p. 28.

12 Kimball, *Churchill and Roosevelt*, vol. I, p. 23.

13 Quoted in Enright, p. 14.

14 See our *War of the Windsors*, pp. 156–8.

15 Hastings, 'Britain's Last Warrior'.

16 Moran, p. 277.

17 *Ibid.*, p. 147.

18 Gilbert, *In Search of Churchill*, pp. 95–6.

19 Winston S. Churchill, 'Fantastic Trial at Moscow'.

20 Gilbert, *In Search of Churchill*, p. 215.

21 Randolph S. Churchill, vol. I, p. 351.

22 *Ibid.*

23 Quoted in Charmley, *Churchill*, p. 85.

24 Quoted in *ibid.*, p. 136.

25 Quoted in Roberts, '*The Holy Fox*', p. 1.

26 See our *War of the Windsors*, pp. 157–8.

27 Quoted in Lamb, *Churchill as War Leader*, p. 4.

28 Rose, p. 144.

29 Winston S. Churchill, *Great Contemporaries*, p. 265.

30 *Ibid.*, p. 261.

31 Kimball, *Forged in War*, p. 22.

32 Quoted in *ibid.*

33 See Gilbert, *Winston Churchill: The Wilderness Years*, pp. 119–23.

34 Basil Collier, p. 104.

35 Gilbert, *Winston Churchill: The Wilderness Years*, p. 128.

36 Calvocoressi, Wint & Pritchard, vol. I, p. 114.

37 Lamb, *The Ghosts of Peace*, p. 124.

38 Cowling, p. 361.

39 Quoted in Howe, p. 47.

40 Sontag & Beddie, p. 91.

41 Hobley, p. 18.

42 Howe, p. 67.

43 Lamb, *The Ghosts of Peace*, pp. 126–7.

44 Sontag & Beddie, p. 107.

45 Watt, *How War Came*, p. 110.

46 Dear, p. 646.

47 Bullock, *Hitler and Stalin*, p. 709.

48 Applebaum, p. 382.

49 *Ibid.*, p. 383; Bullock, *Hitler and Stalin*, p. 710.

50 Bullock, *Hitler and Stalin*, p. 710.

51 See, for example, Anthony Cave Brown, *Treason in the Blood*, p. 336.

52 Charmley, *Churchill*, p. 2.

53 Sontag & Beddie, p. 134.

54 Charmley, *Churchill*, pp. 434–5.

55 See Lamb, *The Ghosts of Peace*, pp. 126–9.

56 Lamb, *Churchill as War Leader*, p. 16.

57 Quoted in Lamb, *The Ghosts of Peace*, p. 126.

58 Dimbleby & Reynolds, p. 123; see also Range, pp. 24–5; Tansill, pp. 561–2.

59 Range, p. 24.

60 Quoted in Sherwood, vol. I, p. 127.

61 Dimbleby & Reynolds, p. 123.

62 Michel, p. 69.

63 Warren F. Kimball, 'US Economic Strategy in World War II', in Kimball, *America Unbound*, pp. 142–3.

64 Quoted in Blum, vol. II, p. 101.

65 See Rauch, pp. 162–5.

66 Quoted in Blum, vol. II, p. 102.

67 See Tansill, pp. 558–61.

68 Newton, p. 155.

69 Lockhart, vol. II, p. 748.

70 Ponting, *1940*, pp. 62–3.

71 Colville, *The Fringes of Power*, vol. I, p. 141.

72 Winston S. Churchill, *The Second World War*, vol. I, pp. 522–4.

73 Quoted in Roberts, *'The Holy Fox'*, p. 204.

74 *Ibid.*

75 Halifax's account is reproduced in *ibid.*, p. 205.

76 Cadogan, p. 280.

77 Colville, *The Fringes of Power*, vol. I, p. 141.

78 Gilbert, *Winston S. Churchill*, vol. VI, p. 22, quoting a memo written by Churchill on 10 September 1939.

79 Ickes, vol. III, p. 196.

80 Quoted in David Reynolds, *The Creation of the Anglo-American Alliance*, p. 114.

81 Quoted in Costello, p. 50.

82 See Davis, pp. 498–500; McJimsey, *The Presidency of Franklin Delano Roosevelt*, p. 20; Schwarz, pp. 279–80.

83 Schwarz, p. 353. On Churchill's friendship with Baruch, see Colville, *The Churchillians*, pp. 86–8; Lamb, *Churchill*, p. 9.

84 Schwarz, p. 354.

85 Coit, p. 467. These are Churchill's words as reported by Baruch to his biographer Margaret L. Coit and others in the 1950s. In his own autobiography, Baruch changed that last sentence to a more modest – or perhaps more prudent – 'You'll be in the forefront of it over there, and I'll be on the sidelines here.' (Baruch, *The Public Years*, p. 273).

Notes and References

86 Gilbert, *Winston S. Churchill*, vol. VI, p. 358, citing memoirs dictated by Randolph Churchill in 1963.
87 Shepherd, p. 297.
88 Roberts, *Eminent Churchillians*, pp. 149–50.
89 Sherwood, vol. I, p. 125.
90 *Ibid.*, p. 11.
91 *Ibid.*, p. 279.
92 *Ibid.*, p. 163.
93 *Ibid.*, p. 159.
94 Quoted in *ibid.*, pp. 156–7.
95 Whalen, p. 311.
96 For a detailed study of the intricacies of the Tyler Kent affair, see Bearse & Read.
97 Shogan, p. 129.
98 Whalen, p. 309.
99 Quoted in Shogan, p. 68.
100 Quoted in Goodhart, pp. 1–2.
101 Kimball, *Churchill and Roosevelt*, vol. I, pp. 37–8.
102 *Ibid.*, pp. 38–9.
103 Beard, pp. 15–16.
104 David Reynolds, *The Creation of the Anglo-American Alliance*, p. 109.
105 Sherwood, vol. I, p. 151.
106 *Ibid.*, vol. I, p. 51.
107 Shogan, pp. 82–3.
108 Tuttle, pp. 46–7.
109 Shogan, p. 75.
110 Kimball, *Churchill and Roosevelt*, vol. I, p. 40.
111 Leutze, p. 77.
112 Quoted in Editors' note to Moffat, p. 310.
113 *Ibid.*
114 Charmley, *Churchill*, p. 429.
115 See David Reynolds, *The Creation of the Anglo-American Alliance*, p. 104; Lamb, *Churchill as War Leader*, p. 50.
116 For a more detailed discussion see our *Double Standards*, pp. 116–19.
117 Lamb, *The Ghosts of Peace*, pp. 140–2.
118 Quoted in David Reynolds, *The Creation of the Anglo-American Alliance*, p. 104.
119 UK National Archives, CAB 65/13, Minutes of War Cabinet meeting, 4.30 p.m., 27 May 1940.
120 Lamb, *Churchill as War Leader*, p. 51.
121 Quoted in Gilbert, *Winston S. Churchill*, vol. VI, p. 468.
122 David Reynolds, *The Creation of the Anglo-American Alliance*, p. 105; Ponting, *1940*, p. 111.
123 Charmley, *Churchill*, p. 431.

124 See our *Double Standards*, pp. 287–8.

125 Gilbert, *Winston S. Churchill*, vol. VI, p. 18; Argyll, p. 19.

126 Quoted in *ibid.*, p. 341.

127 Quoted in Hobley, p. 27.

128 Charmley, *Churchill's Grand Alliance*, p. 16.

129 Sherwood, vol. I, pp. 145–6.

130 Winston S. Churchill, *The Second World War*, vol. II, pp. 180–3.

131 Gilbert, *Winston S. Churchill*, vol. VI, p. 10.

132 See Ponting, *1940*, pp. 189–95.

133 UK National Archives, CAB 65/13, Minutes of War Cabinet meeting, 28 May 1940.

134 Ponting, *Churchill*, pp. 476–7.

135 Ponting, *1940*, pp. 188–9.

136 Anthony Cave Brown, *Treason in the Blood*, p. 233.

137 Welles, p. 47.

138 Howe, p. 102.

139 Lamb, *Churchill as War Leader*, p. 68.

140 Quoted in Berthon, p. 21.

141 On Halifax and Butler's peace initiatives, see Newton, pp. 172–9; Lamb, *Churchill as War Leader*, pp. 75–6; Ponting, *1940*, pp. 112–13. For a defence of Halifax, see Roberts, *'The Holy Fox'*, pp. 234–7.

142 See Anthony Cave Brown, *Bodyguard of Lies*, pp. 178–85.

143 Lamb, *The Ghosts of Peace*, p. 132.

144 Bryans, p. 103.

145 Quoted in Ponting, *1940*, p. 124.

146 Charmley, *Churchill's Grand Alliance*, p. 25.

147 Howe, p. 80.

148 Argyll, p. 42.

149 Dobson, p. 20.

150 Quoted in Howe, p. 99.

151 See our *Double Standards*, pp. 120–3.

152 See, for example, Anthony Cave Brown, *Bodyguard of Lies*, p. 38.

153 Tuttle, pp. 47–8; Stafford, *Roosevelt and Churchill*, pp. 52–3.

Chapter Six: Lost Empire

1 Quoted in Charmley, *Churchill*, p. 431.

2 Strictly speaking, the name BSC was given to Stephenson's operation in January 1941. Before this, it does not appear to have had any formal name, Stephenson's official position being the hoary MI6 cover of 'passport control officer'.

3 Quoted in Mahl, p. 48.

4 Charles Howard Ellis, 'A Historical Note', in Stevenson, p. xviii.

5 Mahl, p. xi.

6 Troy, p. 163.

7 Mahl, p. vii.

8 *Ibid.*, p. 1.

9 *Ibid.*, p. 47.

10 *Ibid.*, p. 186.

11 Troy, p. 33.

12 *Ibid.*, pp. 148–9.

13 Hyde, p. 28.

14 Quoted in Mahl, p. 206.

15 *Ibid.*, p. 9.

16 Troy, p. 41.

17 Colville, *The Churchillians*, p. 61.

18 Troy, pp. 179–80.

19 *Ibid.*, p. 191.

20 *Ibid.*, p. 41.

21 *Ibid.*, p. 184.

22 *Ibid.*, p. 183.

23 Quoted in Mahl, p.16.

24 Stafford, *Roosevelt and Churchill*, p. 78.

25 Mahl, p. 133.

26 Quoted in Troy, p. 185.

27 Quoted in Mahl, p. 7.

28 *Ibid.*, p. 58.

29 See *ibid.*, chapter 2.

30 British Security Coordination, p. 20. See also Mahl, pp. 54–6.

31 Hayden B. Peake, 'Soviet Espionage and the Office of Strategic Services', in Kimball, *America Unbound*, p. 115.

32 Mahl, p. 49.

33 British Security Coordination, p. 17. See Mahl, pp. 58–9.

34 Mahl, pp. 56–7.

35 See *ibid.*, chapter 6.

36 *Ibid.*, p. 87. This was confirmed to Mahl by the Foreign Office's SOE adviser, Duncan Stuart, in 1997.

37 *Ibid.*, chapter 4. See also British Security Coordination, pp. 222–3.

38 Mahl, pp. 73–4.

39 Except where noted, the following material on the Willkie affair is from *ibid.*, chapter 8.

40 *Ibid.*, p. 157.

41 Stafford, *Roosevelt and Churchill*, p. 77.

42 Mahl, p. 164.

43 Quoted in Gilbert, *Winston S. Churchill*, vol. VI, p. 960.

44 For example, Breckinridge Long reveals it in a diary entry on 24 June 1940 (Long, pp. 113–14).

45 See Maney, p. 123; Flynn, *The Roosevelt Myth*, p. 214.

46 Adams, p. 177.

47 Lasky, pp. 145–6.

48 Sulzberger, pp. 627–8.

49 Quoted in Stevenson, p. 71.

50 Quoted in Troy, p. 3.

51 Stafford, *Roosevelt and Churchill*, p. 40.

52 *Ibid.*, p. 55.

53 Anthony Cave Brown, *The Last Hero*, p. 33.

54 Mahl, p. 169.

55 Stafford, *Roosevelt and Churchill*, p. 56; Shogan, p. 132.

56 Kimball, *Churchill and Roosevelt*, vol. I, pp. 58–9.

57 See Mahl, pp. 164–7.

58 Shogan, p. 82, citing Morgenthau's diaries in the Franklin D. Roosevelt Presidential Library, Hyde Park, New York.

59 Sherwood, vol. I, p. 274.

60 Quoted in Mahl, p. 166.

61 Quoted in *ibid.*, p. 165.

62 See Goodhart, Appendix A.

63 Shogan, p. 17.

64 Sherwood, vol. I, pp. 175–6; see also Kimball, *Churchill and Roosevelt*, vol. I, pp. 56–69.

65 David Reynolds, *The Creation of the Anglo-American Alliance*, p. 132.

66 Quoted in Range, p. 16.

67 *Ibid.*, pp. 15–16.

68 Kimball, *Churchill and Roosevelt*, vol. I, pp. 65–6.

69 Dimbleby & Reynolds, p. 127.

70 Basil Collier, p. 181.

71 David Reynolds, *The Creation of the Anglo-American Alliance*, pp. 121 and 131.

72 Buhite & Levy, p. 163.

73 Stafford, p. 48; David Reynolds, *The Creation of the Anglo-American Alliance*, p. 131.

74 Ponting, *1940*, pp. 187–8.

75 Lamb, *Churchill as War Leader*, p. 151.

76 Quoted in Berthon, p. 106.

77 *Ibid.*, p. 72.

78 Quoted in *ibid.*, p. 109.

79 *Ibid.*

80 Quoted in *ibid.*, p. 29.

81 Ponting, *1940*, p. 5.

82 *Ibid.*, p. 213.

83 See Eduard Kubu, 'Czechoslovak Gold Reserves and their Surrender to

Notes and References

Nazi Germany', in Foreign & Commonwealth Office, *Nazi Gold*.
84 Dobson, p. 24.
85 *Ibid.*, p. 26.
86 *Ibid.*
87 Kimball, *Churchill and Roosevelt*, vol. I, pp. 121–3.
88 Dobson, p. 27.
89 Charmley, *Churchill*, p. 431.
90 Adams, pp. 186 and 193.
91 Quoted in *ibid.*, p. 184.
92 Kimball, *Churchill and Roosevelt*, vol. I, p. 81.
93 *Ibid.*, pp. 83–4.
94 Sherwood, vol. I, p. 223.
95 Buhite & Levy, pp. 164–73.
96 *Ibid.*, p. 164.
97 Sherwood, vol. I, p. 224.
98 *Ibid.*, p. 227.
99 Quoted in Beard, p. 14.
100 See *ibid.*, pp. 24–8.
101 *Ibid.*, p. 30.
102 Quoted in *ibid.*, p. 17.
103 Quoted in Flynn, *The Roosevelt Myth*, p. 295.
104 Kimball, *The Most Unsordid Act*, pp. 151–2.
105 Quoted in Sherwood, vol. I., p. 237.
106 Hopkins' account of the meeting is reproduced in *ibid.*, pp. 238–40.
107 Berthon, pp. 101–4.
108 Quoted in Sherwood, vol. I, p. 244.
109 *Ibid.*, p. 262.
110 Quoted in Gilbert, *Winston S. Churchill*, pp. 1009–10.
111 Stafford, *Roosevelt and Churchill*, p. 56.
112 *Ibid.*, p. 57.
113 *Ibid.*, p. 45.
114 Sherwood, vol. I, p. 269.
115 *Ibid.*, p. 264.
116 Quoted in Dear, p. 677.
117 Sherwood, vol. I, p. 281.
118 *Ibid.*, p. 280.
119 *Ibid.*, p. 265.
120 Adams, p. 216.
121 Dear, pp. 679–80.
122 Adams, p. 220.
123 Harriman & Abel, p. 3.
124 *Ibid.*, p. 21.
125 Sherwood, vol. I, pp. 268–9.

126 Stafford, *Roosevelt and Churchill*, p. 77.

127 All quotes are from Richard Collier, p. 22.

128 Range, p. 11.

129 Quoted in Richard Collier, p. 6.

130 Quoted in Ponting, *1940*, p. 212.

131 David Reynolds, *The Creation of the Anglo-American Alliance*, p. 162.

132 Charmley, *Churchill*, pp. 437–8.

133 David Reynolds, *The Creation of the Anglo-American Alliance*, p. 163.

134 Quoted in Richard Collier, p. 22.

135 Harold Ickes, quoted in *ibid.*

136 David Reynolds, *The Creation of the Anglo-American Alliance*, p. 163.

137 Dobson, pp. 127–8.

138 Figures from: David Reynolds, *The Creation of the Anglo-American Alliance*, p. 167; Milward, p. 271.

139 Gardner, pp. 171–2.

140 *Ibid.*, pp. 55–6.

141 Quoted in *ibid.*, p. 64.

142 David Reynolds, *The Creation of the Anglo-American Alliance*, p. 273.

143 See Dobson, pp. 131–3 for details.

144 Gardner, p. 144.

145 Theodore A. Wilson, 'The United States: Leviathan', in Reynolds, Kimball & Chubarian, p. 213.

146 Theodore A. Wilson *et al.*, 'Coalition: Structure, Strategy and Statecraft', in *ibid.*, p. 81.

147 Quoted in Theodore A. Wilson, 'The United States: Leviathan', in *ibid.*, p. 214.

148 Quoted in *ibid.*, p. 221.

149 Quoted in Richard Collier, p. 22.

150 Quoted in *ibid.*

151 Quoted in Dobson, p. 53.

152 *Ibid.*, p. 127.

153 Quoted in Elliott Roosevelt, p. 24.

154 The document is reproduced in Tuttle, pp. 41–2.

155 Hopkins, pp. 1–2.

Chapter Seven: Hell

1 Colville, *The Fringes of Power*, vol. I, p. 480.

2 Sherwood, vol. I, p. 292.

3 Quoted in Richard Collier, p. 25.

4 Ickes, vol. III, p. 470.

5 Quoted in Harriman & Abel, p. 32.

6 Millis & Duffield, p. 20.

7 Sherwood, vol. I, pp. 157–9.

Notes and References

8 Maney, p. 121.

9 David Reynolds, *The Creation of the Anglo-American Alliance*, p. 212.

10 Simpson, p. 59.

11 Flynn, *The Roosevelt Myth*, p. 295.

12 Range, p. 26.

13 Langer & Gleason, *The Undeclared War*, p. 735.

14 Sherwood, vol. I, pp. 367–8.

15 Tuttle, p. 45.

16 Sherwood, vol. I, pp. 273–4.

17 Quoted in *ibid.*, p. 271.

18 David Reynolds, *The Creation of the Anglo-American Alliance*, pp. 183–5.

19 Quoted in Sherwood, vol. I, pp. 258–9.

20 Quoted in *ibid.*, p. 259.

21 Lamb, *Churchill as War Leader*, p. 151.

22 Basil Collier, p. 194.

23 David Reynolds, *The Creation of the Anglo-American Alliance*, p. 198.

24 Sherwood, vol. I, p. 291.

25 *Ibid.*, p. 293.

26 See our *Double Standards*, pp. 155–6.

27 Quoted in Langer & Gleason, *The Undeclared War*, p. 455.

28 Quoted in Burns, pp. 91–2.

29 David Reynolds, *The Creation of the Anglo-American Alliance*, p. 198.

30 *Ibid.*, p. 201.

31 Ickes, vol. III, p. 523.

32 Sherwood, vol. I, p. 297.

33 Buhite & Levy, p. 177.

34 Sherwood, vol. I, pp. 298–9.

35 Tansill, p. 612.

36 David Reynolds, *The Creation of the Anglo-American Alliance*, p. 203.

37 Sherwood, vol. I, p. 299.

38 David Reynolds, *The Creation of the Anglo-American Alliance*, p. 203.

39 Sherwood, vol. I, p. 290.

40 Corson & Crowley, p. 208.

41 Calvocoressi, Wint & Pritchard, vol. I, p. 224.

42 See Hastings, *Bomber Command*, p. 116.

43 Terraine, p. 295.

44 See Levine, pp. 30–1; Terraine, pp. 291–4; Hastings, *Bomber Command*, pp. 108–9; Middlebrook & Everitt, pp. 220–1.

45 Terraine, p. 461.

46 Dear, p. 1269.

47 Richard Collier, p. 28.

48 Quoted in Berthon, p. 105.

49 Paxton, p. 113.

50 See Dear, p. 1272.

51 Quoted in Berthon, p. 136.

52 Quoted in *ibid.*, p. 137.

53 Quoted in *ibid.*, p. 140.

54 *Ibid.*, pp. 141–2.

55 Quoted in *ibid.*, p. 144.

56 Whaley, p. 80.

57 Beevor, p. 5.

58 Quoted in *ibid.*

59 Howe, p. 136.

60 Beevor, p. 45.

61 Maney, pp. 132–3.

62 Quoted in Howe, pp. 137–8.

63 *Ibid.*, p. 139.

64 Quoted in Adams, p. 239.

65 Tuttle, p. 102.

66 Harriman & Abel, p. 74.

67 Harriman's foreword to Adams, p. 17.

68 Stettinius, *Lend-Lease*, p. 111.

69 David Reynolds, *The Creation of the Anglo-American Alliance*, p. 206.

70 Stettinius, *Lend-Lease*, p. 113.

71 Kimball, *The Juggler*, p. 194.

72 David Reynolds, *The Creation of the Anglo-American Alliance*, p. 211.

73 Gaddis, p. 180.

74 McJimsey, *Harry Hopkins*, p. 263.

75 Corson & Crowley, p. 447, citing their interview with Henderson in 1982.

76 Andrew & Mitrokhin, p. 784.

77 Buhite & Levy, p. 140.

78 Harriman & Abel, pp. 73–4; see also Simpson, p. 61.

79 Buhite & Levy, p. 140.

80 Farnsworth, p. 175.

81 Tansill, p. 42.

82 Joseph E. Davies, p. 276.

83 Farnsworth, p. 1, quoting an article written by Bullitt for *Life* in 1948.

84 Quoted in Kimball, *Churchill and Roosevelt*, vol. I, p. 421.

85 A.J.P. Taylor, *From Sarajevo to Potsdam*, p. 182.

86 Quoted in Applebaum, pp. 382–3.

87 *Ibid.*, p. 383.

88 Quoted in Bullock, *Hitler and Stalin*, p. 707.

89 Corson & Crowley, pp. 204–5.

90 Kimball, *The Juggler*, p. 100.

91 Maney, p. 133.

Notes and References

Chapter Eight: Behind the Infamy

1 Lamb, *Churchill as War Leader*, p. 161, quoting Churchill's memo to Sir Robert Craigie, September 1943.
2 Stafford, *Roosevelt and Churchill*, p. 67.
3 Elliott Roosevelt, p. 36.
4 *Ibid.*, pp. 41–2.
5 *Ibid.*, p. 38.
6 *Ibid.*, p. 25.
7 Dimbleby & Reynolds, p. 135.
8 See Lippman, appendix V, for the full text of the Atlantic Charter.
9 See Dobson, chapter 3, and Gardner, chapter III.
10 Allan M. Winkler, 'American Opposition during World War II', in Jeffrey-Jones, pp. 84–5.
11 Quoted in Range, p. 106.
12 Dear, p. 890.
13 Quoted in Dallek, pp. 299–300.
14 Sherwood, vol. I, pp. 367–8.
15 Beard, pp. 121–3.
16 Quoted in Heale, p. 50.
17 Stafford, *Roosevelt and Churchill*, p. 72.
18 Buhite & Levy, p. 188.
19 Quoted in *ibid.*, p. 189.
20 Quoted in Beard, p. 143.
21 Quoted in Mahl, p. 55.
22 *Ibid.*, pp. 55–6.
23 Quoted in Tansill, p. 614.
24 Larrabee, p. 94.
25 Howe, p. 152.
26 Calvocoressi, Wint & Pritchard, vol. II, p. 335.
27 *Ibid.*, pp. 336–7.
28 Maney, p. 137.
29 Calvocoressi, Wint & Pritchard, vol. II, p. 337.
30 *Ibid.*
31 McJimsey, *The Presidency of Franklin Delano Roosevelt*, p. 211.
32 Howe, p. 157.
33 See Lamb, *Churchill as War Leader*, pp. 155–8; Adams, p. 255.
34 Lamb, *Churchill as War Leader*, p. 158.
35 Baruch, *The Public Years*, pp. 288–91.
36 Quoted in Lash, *Eleanor and Franklin*, p. 646.
37 Quoted in Stinnett, p. 180.
38 Calvocoressi, Wint & Pritchard, vol. II, p. 347.
39 Lamb, *Churchill as War Leader*, p. 161, citing UK National Archives, FO 371/35957.

40 McCollum's report is reproduced in facsimile in Stinnett, Appendix A.

41 Stinnett, p. 9.

42 Quoted in Dallek, p. 307.

43 Quoted in Stinnett, p. 172.

44 Quoted in Beard, p. 12.

45 Calvocoressi, Wint & Pritchard, vol. II, pp. 360–1.

46 Quoted in Adams, p. 257.

47 *Ibid.*, p. 257.

48 Stinnett, p. 228.

49 Tansill, p. 651.

50 Dear, p. 711; Calvocoressi, Wint & Pritchard, vol. II, pp. 358–60.

51 McJimsey, *The Presidency of Franklin Delano Roosevelt*, p. 212.

52 Larrabee, p. 91.

53 Editor's note to Long, p. 226.

54 Quoted in Flynn, *The Truth about Pearl Harbor*, p. 31.

55 *Ibid.*, pp. 31–2.

56 Calvocoressi, Wint & Pritchard, vol. II, p. 347.

57 McJimsey, *The Presidency of Franklin Delano Roosevelt*, p. 212.

58 Calvocoressi, Wint & Pritchard, vol. II, p. 337.

59 Gilbert, *Winston S. Churchill*, vol. VI, p. 1262.

60 Flynn, *The Truth about Pearl Harbor*, p. 30.

61 Gilbert, *Winston S. Churchill*, vol. VI, p. 1265.

62 *Ibid.*

63 *Ibid.*, p. 1266.

64 Quoted in *ibid.*

65 Stinnett, p. 172.

66 Hinsley, *et al.*, vol. I, pp. 52–3; see also Michael Smith, *The Emperor's Codes*, pp. 120–1.

67 Quoted in Stinnett, pp. 43–4.

68 Toland, pp. 317–18.

69 *Ibid.*, p. 316; Stinnett, pp. 197–8.

70 Toland, pp. 280–2 and 286. Ogg appears in Toland's book under the name 'Seaman First Class Z', but Stinnett reveals his true identity.

71 Stinnett, pp. 194–5.

72 Constantine FitzGibbon, p. 255.

73 Aldrich, *Intelligence and the War against Japan*, p. 87.

74 Casey, p. 7.

75 See, for example, Aldrich, *Intelligence and the War against Japan*, pp. 88–91.

76 Michael Smith, *The Emperor's Codes*, p. 24.

77 Aldrich, *Intelligence and the War against Japan*, p. 59.

78 *Ibid.*

79 Quoted in Michael Smith, *The Emperor's Codes*, p. 23.

80 Sergeant John Burrows, quoted in *ibid.*, p. 27.

Notes and References

81 Aldrich, *Intelligence and the War against Japan*, p. 57.

82 Quoted in Michael Smith, *The Emperor's Codes*, p. 129.

83 See, for example, McJimsey, *The Presidency of Franklin Delano Roosevelt*, p. 213.

84 Winant, p. 197.

85 Winston S. Churchill, vol. III, p. 475.

86 Winant, p. 199.

87 Gilbert, *Winston S. Churchill*, vol. VI, p. 1268.

88 The attack lasted from a few minutes before 8 a.m. to 10 a.m. Hawaii time, which was 1–3 p.m. Washington time (Roosevelt got the news at 1.40) and 6–8 p.m. London time.

89 Winant, p. 198.

90 Rusbridger & Nave, pp. 192–3.

91 Quoted in Adams, p. 258.

92 Long, p. 236.

93 Lamb, *Churchill as War Leader*, p. 161; Miller, p. 469.

94 Buhite & Levy, pp. 196–7.

95 Larrabee, p. 83.

96 Lamb, *Churchill as War Leader*, p. 161.

97 A.J.P. Taylor, *From Sarajevo to Potsdam*, p. 181.

98 Corson & Crowley, pp. 207–8.

99 Quoted in Higham, *American Swastika*, p. 135.

100 Quoted in Stevenson, pp. 299–300.

101 *Ibid.*, p. 298.

102 Quoted in *ibid.*, p. 302.

103 Lamb, *Churchill as War Leader*, p. 160.

104 Wheeler & Healy, pp. 32–6.

105 Stevenson, p. 328.

106 Mosley, pp. 156–7.

107 Wheeler & Healy, p. 35.

108 See Mark A. Stoler, 'The United States: The Global Strategy', in Reynolds, Kimball & Chubarian, pp. 57–9.

109 Higham, *American Swastika*, p. 137.

110 Quoted in *ibid.*, p. 142.

111 Wheeler & Healy, p. 36.

112 Higham, *American Swastika*, p. 144; Wheeler & Healy, p. 36.

Chapter Nine: The End of the Beginning

1 Gilbert, *Winston S. Churchill*, vol. VI, p. 1273.

2 Winston S. Churchill, *The Second World War*, vol. III, p. 477.

3 Alanbrooke, p. 209.

4 Mark A. Stoler, 'The United States: The Global Strategy', in Reynolds, Kimball & Chubarian, p. 61.

5 See Winston S. Churchill, *The Second World War*, vol. III, pp. 506–15.

6 David Reynolds, *Rich Relations*, p. 14.

7 Gilbert, *Winston S. Churchill*, vol. VII, p. 43.

8 See Andrew, *For the President's Eyes Only*, pp. 128–30; Stafford, *Roosevelt and Churchill*, pp. 159–60.

9 Quoted in Andrew, *For the President's Eyes Only*, p. 128.

10 *Ibid.*, p.129, quoting Berle's diary for 26 February 1942.

11 Louis, pp. 134–5.

12 Stafford, *Roosevelt and Churchill*, pp. 160–1.

13 Hayden B. Peake, 'Soviet Espionage and the Office of Strategic Services', in Kimball, *America Unbound*, p. 111.

14 Mahl, pp. 19–21.

15 Adams, p. 262.

16 McJimsey, *The Presidency of Franklin Delano Roosevelt*, pp. 239–42.

17 Quoted in Berthon, p. 147.

18 Applebaum, p. 407.

19 *Ibid.*, p. 409.

20 Dear, p. 519.

21 Stoler, pp. 21–3.

22 *Ibid.*, p. 37.

23 *Ibid.*, p. 31.

24 Kimball, *Churchill and Roosevelt*, vol. I, p. 394.

25 Allan M. Winkler, 'American Opposition during World War II', in Jeffrey-Jones, p. 77.

26 Moran, p. 47.

27 Quoted in Kimball, *The Juggler*, p. 27.

28 Charmley, *Churchill*, pp. 494–5.

29 Quoted in Kimball, *The Juggler*, p. 134.

30 Quoted in Charmley, *Churchill's Grand Alliance*, p. 53.

31 Quoted in Aldrich, 'American Intelligence and the British Raj', p. 138.

32 Lamb, *Churchill as War Leader*, p. 164.

33 Acheson, p. 28.

34 Quoted in Charmley, *Churchill*, p. 485.

35 Charmley, *Churchill's Grand Alliance*, p. 97.

36 On the negotiations over Article Seven, see Gardner, chapter VI.

37 Quoted in *ibid.*, p. 57.

38 Kimball, *Churchill and Roosevelt*, vol. I, pp. 344–6, 351 and 357–8.

39 Gardner, pp. 63–4.

40 Richard J. Overy *et al.*, 'Co-operation: Trade, Aid and Technology', in Reynolds, Kimball & Chubarian, p. 214.

41 Gardner, p. 66.

42 Richard J. Overy *et al.*, 'Co-operation: Trade, Aid and Technology', in Reynolds, Kimball & Chubarian, p. 211.

Notes and References

43 Nisbet, p. 19.

44 Alex Danchev, 'Great Britain: The Indirect Strategy', in Reynolds, Kimball & Chubarian, p. 4, citing UK National Archives, PREM 3/499/6.

45 Nisbet, p. 39.

46 Stoler, pp. 31–2.

47 Kimball, *Churchill and Roosevelt*, vol. I, pp. 398–9.

48 Stoler, p. 35.

49 Quoted in *ibid.*, p. 33.

50 *Ibid.*, p. 39.

51 Kimball, *Churchill and Roosevelt*, vol. I, p. 441.

52 Nisbet, p. 32.

53 Stoler, p. 42.

54 Charmley, *Churchill*, pp. 495–6.

55 See Stoler, p. 43.

56 *Ibid.*, pp. 44–5.

57 Andrew & Mitrokhin, p. 784.

58 Nisbet, p. 35.

59 Stoler, pp. 56–7.

60 *Ibid.*, pp. 48–9.

61 *Ibid.*, p. 50.

62 *Ibid.*, p. 49.

63 Quoted in Sherwood, vol. II, p. 594.

64 Quoted in Anthony Cave Brown, *Bodyguard of Lies*, p. 79.

65 Quoted in *ibid.*

66 Stoler, p. 40.

67 Anthony Cave Brown, *Bodyguard of Lies*, p. 79.

68 Kimball, *Churchill and Roosevelt*, vol. I, p. 536.

69 Stoler, p. 34.

70 Mark A. Stoler, 'The United States: The Global Strategy', in Reynolds, Kimball & Chubarian, p. 64.

71 Anthony Cave Brown, *Bodyguard of Lies*, p. 82.

72 Quoted in *ibid.*, p. 82.

73 Harriman & Abel, p. 153.

74 *Ibid.*, p. 154.

75 Nisbet, p. 30.

76 Moran, p. 82.

77 Anthony Cave Brown, *Bodyguard of Lies*, p. 538.

78 Atkin, p. 255.

79 Dear, p. 763.

80 David Reynolds, *Rich Relations*, p. 128.

81 Quoted in Atkin, p. 254.

82 *Ibid.*, p. 263.

83 See Anthony Cave Brown, *Bodyguard of Lies*, pp. 80–91.

84 David Reynolds, *Rich Relations*, p. 128.

85 Anthony Cave Brown, *Bodyguard of Lies*, p. 81.

86 Lamb, *Churchill as War Leader*, p. 171.

87 Quoted in Berthon, p. 184.

88 *Ibid.*, pp. 184–5.

89 Kimball, *Churchill and Roosevelt*, vol. I, p. 594.

90 *Ibid.*, pp. 660–2.

91 Quoted in Alex Danchev, 'Great Britain: The Indirect Strategy', in Reynolds, Kimball & Chubarian, p. 4.

92 Quoted in Verrier, p. 167.

93 Kimball, *Churchill and Roosevelt*, vol. I, p. 669.

94 *Ibid.*, vol. II, p. 7.

95 Quoted in Adams, p. 298.

96 Verrier, p. 222.

97 *Ibid.*, p. 21.

98 Quoted in *ibid.*, p. 214.

99 *Ibid.*, pp. 230–1; see also Stafford, *Roosevelt and Churchill*, p. 194.

100 Cadogan, p. 493.

101 Winston S. Churchill, *The Second World War*, vol. IV, p. 578.

102 Quoted in Verrier, p. 247.

Chapter Ten: Death by Unconditional Surrender

1 Quoted in Berthon, p. 245.

2 Tuttle, p. 183.

3 Nisbet, p. 43.

4 Quoted in McJimsey, *Harry Hopkins*, p. 277.

5 *Ibid.*, p. 264.

6 McJimsey, *The Presidency of Franklin Delano Roosevelt*, p. 222.

7 Lamb, *The Ghosts of Peace*, p. 223.

8 Quoted in *ibid.*, p. 226.

9 Quoted in Baldwin, pp. 18–19.

10 Quoted in *ibid.*, p. 20.

11 Quoted in von Klemperer, p. 241.

12 Baldwin, p. 21.

13 Berthon, p. 229.

14 See *ibid.*, pp. 226–8.

15 Quoted in *ibid.*, p. 234.

16 Quoted in *ibid.*, p. 243.

17 De Gaulle, vol. II, p. 84.

18 *Ibid.*, p. 242.

19 Tuttle, p. 183.

20 Berthon, p. 245.

Notes and References

21 Quoted in *ibid.*, p. 253.

22 *Ibid.*, p. 252.

23 Quotes from *ibid.*, pp. 255–7.

24 *Ibid.*, p. xii.

25 Cadogan, p. 532.

26 *Daily Telegraph*, 11 May 1967.

27 Irving, *Accident*, p. 163.

28 Quoted in Dear, p. 253.

29 Quoted in Hastings, *Bomber Command*, p. 343.

30 Dear (p. 140) gives the total British civilian losses in the Blitz as approximately 43,000.

31 Quoted in Argyll, p. 144.

32 Dear, p. 1072.

33 Argyll, p. 122.

34 *Ibid.*

35 See Argyll., p. 121.

36 Dulles, *Germany's Underground*, p. 67.

37 Anthony Cave Brown, *Treason in the Blood*, p. 312.

38 Anthony Cave Brown, *Bodyguard of Lies*, pp. 239–40.

39 Quoted in Dulles, *Germany's Underground*, p. 144.

40 *Ibid.*, pp. 144–6.

41 Anthony Cave Brown, *Bodyguard of Lies*, pp. 236–7.

42 *Ibid.*, pp. 240–2.

43 Lamb, *The Ghosts of Peace*, p. xi.

44 Mark A. Stoler, 'The United States: The Global Strategy', in Reynolds, Kimball & Chubarian, p. 69.

45 Nisbet, p. 37.

46 Tuttle, pp. 206–7.

47 Liddell Hart, pp. 510–11.

48 Stoler, p. 102.

49 Berthon, p. 262.

50 Quoted in *ibid.*, p. xii.

51 Quoted in *ibid.*, p. 267.

52 Quoted in Viorst, p. 168.

53 Quoted in *ibid.*, p. 172.

54 Berthon, p. 288.

55 Dear, p. 488.

56 Quoted in Perlmutter, p. 121.

57 Argyll, p. 134.

58 Quoted in Irving, *Accident*, p. 178.

59 Quoted in *ibid.*, p. 118.

60 *Ibid.*, p. 134.

61 *Ibid.*, pp. 134–5.

62 Quoted in *ibid.*, p. 148.
63 Quoted in Coates.
64 *Ibid.*
65 Irving, *Accident*, pp. 31–2.
66 Quoted in Gilbert, *Winston S. Churchill*, vol. VII, p. 426.
67 Quoted in Irving, *Accident*, p. 102.
68 Dear, p. 898.
69 Quoted in Thompson, pp. 126–7.
70 Irving, *Accident*, pp. 77–8.
71 Lamb, *The Ghosts of Peace*, p. 183.
72 Quoted in *ibid.*, p. 193.
73 Quoted in *ibid.*
74 *Ibid.*

Chapter Eleven: In Stalin's Pocket
1 Churchill, *The Second World War*, vol. III, p. 34.
2 McJimsey, *Harry Hopkins*, p. 295; p. 130.
3 See Nisbet, p. 60.
4 Tuttle, pp. 216–17.
5 See McJimsey, *Harry Hopkins*, pp. 283–4.
6 Kimball, *Churchill and Roosevelt*, vol. II, p. 283.
7 Tuttle, p. 214.
8 Moran, pp. 151–2.
9 Mark A. Stoler, 'The United States: The Global Strategy', in Reynolds, Kimball & Chubarian, p. 69.
10 Nisbet, p. 12.
11 Cadogan, p. 581.
12 Quoted in Nisbet, p. 50.
13 Andrew & Gordievsky, pp. 271–2.
14 Nisbet, p. 46, quoting from the official notes taken by the US delegation.
15 Simpson, pp. 69–70; see also Nisbet, p. 60.
16 Quoted in Nisbet, p. 47.
17 *Ibid.*
18 Quoted in *ibid.*, p. 48.
19 *Ibid.*, p. 49.
20 See *ibid.*, pp. 49–51.
21 Quoted in Stoler, p. 149.
22 Elliott Roosevelt, pp. 188–9.
23 Cadogan, p. 582.
24 Nisbet, p. 51.
25 Moran, p. 162.
26 *Ibid.*
27 Tuttle, p. 231.

Notes and References

28 Nisbet, p. 102.

29 Kimball, *Churchill and Roosevelt*, vol. I, p. 625.

30 Quoted in Jordan & Stokes, p. 31.

31 Quoted in Martel, p. 48.

32 Nisbet, pp. 30–1.

33 Deane, p. 89.

34 *Ibid.*, p. 96.

35 *Ibid.*, p. 98.

36 *Ibid.*, p. 98.

37 *Ibid.*, p. 90.

38 Lydia V. Pozdeeva, 'The Soviet Union: Phoenix', in Reynolds, Kimball & Chubarian, p. 160.

39 *Ibid.*, p. 161.

40 Quoted in Martel, p. 38.

41 Lydia V. Pozdeeva, 'The Soviet Union: Phoenix', in Reynolds, Kimball & Chubarian, p. 163.

42 Gaddis, pp. 178–9.

43 Van Tuyll, p. 25.

44 Milward, p. 73.

45 Van Tuyll, p. 25.

46 Richard J. Overy *et al.*, 'Co-operation: Trade, Aid and Technology', in Reynolds, Kimball & Chubarian, p. 209.

47 Van Tuyll, pp. 23–4.

48 Milward, p. 72.

49 Corson & Crowley, p. 209.

50 *Ibid.*, pp. 209–10.

51 Quoted in Jordan & Stokes, pp. 66–7.

52 Andrew & Gordievsky, pp. 230–1.

53 *Ibid.*, p. 271.

54 Tanenhaus, pp. 518–19.

55 Gardner, p. 4.

56 Rees, p. 9.

57 Gardner, p. 73.

58 Dobson, p. 130.

59 Quoted in Gardner, p. 167.

60 David Reynolds, *The Creation of the Anglo-American Alliance*, p. 166.

61 Dobson, p. 6.

62 Gardner, p. 174.

63 *Ibid.*

64 Charmley, *Churchill's Grand Alliance*, p. 94.

65 Quoted in *ibid.*, p. 95.

66 Kimball, *Churchill and Roosevelt*, vol. III, p. 35.

67 Charmley, *Churchill's Grand Alliance*, pp. 99–100.

68 Lydia V. Pozdeeva, 'The Soviet Union: Phoenix', in Reynolds, Kimball & Chubarian, p. 165.

69 Charmley, *Churchill's Grand Alliance*, p. 94.

70 Martel, p. 59.

71 Rees, p. 9.

72 Quoted in *ibid.*, p. 137.

73 Quoted in *ibid.*, p. 140.

74 Quoted in *ibid.*, p. 138.

75 On the White Plan, see Gardner, pp. 71–7; Rees, chapter 10.

76 Blum, vol. III, p. 123.

77 Dimbleby & Reynolds, p. 166.

78 Dear, p. 158.

79 Gardner, pp. 10–11.

80 Quoted in *ibid.*, p. 7.

81 Rees, pp. 12–13.

82 Chambers, p. 383.

83 *Ibid.*

84 Quoted in Rees, p. 420.

85 Blum, vol. III, p. 90.

86 Rees, p. 418.

87 See Nathan I. White, pp. 81–115.

88 Gardner, p. 73.

89 Rees, p. 426.

90 Adams, p. 318.

91 Richard J. Overy *et al.*, 'Co-operation: Trade, Aid and Technology', in Reynolds, Kimball & Chubarian, p. 220.

92 *Ibid.*

93 Gilbert, *Winston S. Churchill*, vol. VII, p. 415.

94 Sherwin, p. 101.

95 *Ibid.*, pp. 100–1.

96 Gilbert, *Winston S. Churchill*, vol. VII, p. 416, quoting UK National Archives, PREM 3/139/8A.

97 Sherwood, vol. II, pp. 700–1.

98 Gilbert, *Winston S. Churchill*, vol. VII, p. 418, quoting UK National Archives, PREM 3/139/8A.

99 *Ibid.*, pp. 418–19.

100 Dimbleby & Reynolds, p. 168.

101 Gaddis Smith, pp. 165–6.

102 Richard J. Overy *et al.*, 'Co-operation: Trade, Aid and Technology', in Reynolds, Kimball & Chubarian, p. 220.

103 Sherwin, Appendix C.

104 Simpson, p. 76.

105 Sherwin, p. 290.

Notes and References

106 Jordan & Stokes, p. 25; on Molotov's 'Mr Brown' alias, see Sherwood, vol. II, p. 572.

107 Quoted in Jordan & Stokes, p. 44.

108 Tanenhaus, pp. 380–1.

109 Jordan & Stokes, pp. 82–3.

110 Quoted in de Toledano, *The Greatest Plot in History*, p. 104.

111 Jordan & Stokes, pp. 88–90.

112 *Ibid.*, pp. 92–5.

113 *Ibid.*, p. 110.

114 *Ibid.*, pp. 32–3.

115 *Ibid.*, pp. 193–4.

116 Quoted in *ibid.*, p. 195.

117 *Ibid.*, pp. 195–6.

118 On the political and media reactions to Jordan's claims, see de Toledano, *The Greatest Plot in History*, chapter VII.

119 *Ibid.*, p. 106.

120 Jordan & Stokes, pp. 42–3.

121 De Toledano, *The Greatest Plot in History*, p. 107.

122 Lydia V. Pozdeeva, 'The Soviet Union: Phoenix', in Reynolds, Kimball & Chubarian, p. 155.

123 Dear, p. 71.

124 Lydia V. Pozdeeva, 'The Soviet Union: Phoenix', in Reynolds, Kimball & Chubarian, p. 155.

125 De Toledano, *The Greatest Plot in History*, p. 43.

126 Published as *Notes from the Underground* in 1997.

127 De Toledano, *The Greatest Plot in History*, p. 250.

128 *Ibid.*, p. 112.

129 Jordan & Stokes, pp. 95–6.

130 See *ibid.*, pp. 112–13.

131 Reproduced in *ibid.*, pp. 8–9.

132 *Ibid.*, p. 9.

133 Quoted in de Toledano, *The Greatest Plot in History*, p. 108.

134 *Ibid.*, pp. 108–9.

135 Quoted in *ibid.*, p. 111.

136 Jordan & Stokes, p. 85.

137 *Ibid.*, p. 10.

138 De Toledano, *The Greatest Plot in History*, p. 38.

139 Millis & Duffield, pp. 84–6.

Chapter Twelve: Overlords

1 Quoted in Enright, p. 154.

2 Kathryn E. Brown, p. 109.

3 Louis, p. 225.

4 Quoted in *ibid.*, p. 154.

5 Quoted in *ibid.*, p. 170.

6 Nisbet, p. 12.

7 Kimball, *The Juggler*, p. 130.

8 Louis, p. 155.

9 Harold Macmillan, quoted in *ibid.*, p. 72.

10 Quoted in Kimball, *The Juggler*, p. 72.

11 *Ibid.*, p. 457.

12 Quoted in Aldrich, *Intelligence and the War against Japan*, p. 123.

13 Quoted in *ibid.*, pp. 304–5.

14 Quoted in *ibid.*, p. 1.

15 Thorne, *Allies of a Kind*, pp. 701–2.

16 Aldrich, *Intelligence and the War against Japan*, p. xv.

17 Aldrich, 'American Intelligence and the British Raj', p. 132.

18 *Ibid.*, p. 135.

19 Aldrich, *Intelligence and the War against Japan*, p. 129, quoting Wilkinson's diary.

20 *Ibid.*, p. 130.

21 Quoted in *ibid.*, pp. 140–1.

22 Aldrich, 'American Intelligence and the British Raj', pp. 141–2.

23 Quoted in *ibid.*, p. 143.

24 Aldrich, *Intelligence and the War against Japan*, pp. 152–3.

25 Quoted in Venkataramani & Shrivastava, p. 150.

26 Aldrich, 'American Intelligence and the British Raj', p. 144.

27 Aldrich, *Intelligence and the War against Japan*, p. 148.

28 *Ibid.*, p. 153.

29 Aldrich, 'American Intelligence and the British Raj', p. 156.

30 Charmley, *Churchill's Grand Alliance*, pp. 92–3.

31 Higham, *Trading with the Enemy*, p. 81.

32 E.g., see Dear, p. 977.

33 Charmley, *Churchill's Grand Alliance*, p. 97.

34 Aldrich, 'American Intelligence and the British Raj', pp. 154–5.

35 See Tuttle, p. 232.

36 *Ibid.*, p. 235.

37 Ferrell, p. 37; Kimball, *The Juggler*, pp. 14–15; Buhite & Levy, p. 145.

38 Blum, vol. III, p. 342.

39 Kimball, *The Juggler*, p. 199.

40 Quoted in Rossi, p. 14.

41 McJimsey, *Harry Hopkins*, p. 283.

42 *Ibid.*, p. 362.

43 Churchill's note is reproduced in Lamb, *The Ghosts of Peace*, pp. 226–7.

44 Quoted in *ibid.*, p. 228.

45 Quoted in Anthony Cave Brown, *Bodyguard of Lies*, pp. 588–9.

Notes and References

46 Wheeler & Healy, p. 31.

47 Lamb, *The Ghosts of Peace*, p. xi.

48 Dulles, *The Secret Surrender*, p. 30.

49 Anthony Cave Brown, *Bodyguard of Lies*, pp. 315–16.

50 Dulles, *Germany's Underground*, p. 139.

51 Alanbrooke, p. 461.

52 McJimsey, *Harry Hopkins*, p. 299.

53 *Ibid.*, p. 298.

54 Quoted in Lewin, p. 243.

55 Quoted in David Reynolds, *Rich Relations*, p. 360.

56 Quoted in Alex Danchev, 'Great Britain: The Indirect Strategy', in Reynolds, Kimball & Chubarian, pp. 3–4.

57 Dulles, *Germany's Underground*, p. 139.

58 Anthony Cave Brown, *Bodyguard of Lies*, p. 739.

59 Quoted in *ibid.*, pp. 740–1.

60 Quoted in *ibid.*, p. 741.

61 Dulles, *Germany's Underground*, p. 140.

62 Bullock, *Hitler and Stalin*, p. 911.

63 *Ibid.*, p. 913.

64 Dulles, *Germany's Underground*, p. 172.

65 Quoted in Anthony Cave Brown, *Bodyguard of Lies*, p. 769.

66 See Lamb, *The Ghosts of Peace*, pp. 299–300.

67 Quoted in Berthon, pp. 294–5.

68 Quoted in Viorst, pp. 186–7.

69 Rossi, pp. 121–2.

70 Cadogan, pp. 634–5.

71 Quoted in Viorst, p. 184.

72 Rossi, p. 122.

73 Aglion, pp. 165–6.

74 *Ibid.*, pp. 166–7.

75 *Ibid.*, pp. 167–8.

76 *Ibid.*, p. 168.

77 *Ibid.*, pp. 168–9.

78 Quoted in *ibid.*, p. 169.

79 Quoted in Berthon, p. 314.

80 Aglion, p. 171.

81 *Ibid.*, p. 194.

82 Kimball, *Churchill and Roosevelt*, vol. III, pp. 367 and 369.

83 Aglion, p. 195.

84 Lamb, *The Ghosts of Peace*, p. 236.

85 See McJimsey, *Harry Hopkins*, pp. 344–7.

86 See Rees, chapters 15 and 16.

87 Quoted in Baldwin, pp. 18–19.

88 Lamb, *The Ghosts of Peace*, p. 238; Nisbet, p. 56.

89 Lamb, *The Ghosts of Peace*, p. 237.

90 Quoted in Sherwin, p. 285.

91 Quoted in Lamb, *The Ghosts of Peace*, p. 305.

92 Quoted in *ibid.*, p. 239.

93 Quoted in Larkin, p. 403.

94 Quoted in Dear, p. 312.

95 *Ibid.*, p. 1073.

96 Lamb, *The Ghosts of Peace*, p. 240.

97 *Ibid.*, p. 305.

98 *Ibid.*, pp. 241–2.

99 Morgenthau resigned soon into Truman's presidency, leaving office on 22 July 1945.

Chapter Thirteen: Exits and Betrayals

1 Quoted in Gilbert, *Winston S. Churchill*, vol. IV, p. 277.

2 Lamb, *Churchill as War Leader*, p. 164.

3 Moran, p. 181.

4 Mark A. Stoler, 'The United States: The Global Strategy', in Reynolds, Kimball & Chubarian, p. 71.

5 Clark, pp. 347–8.

6 See Nisbet, p. 67.

7 *Ibid.*

8 Quoted in Sherwin, p. 286.

9 Quoted in Nadeau, p. 123.

10 Quoted in *ibid.*, pp. 124–5.

11 Kimball, *Churchill and Roosevelt*, vol. III, pp. 295–6.

12 Charmley, *Churchill's Grand Alliance*, p. 125.

13 Tuttle, p. 236.

14 Viorst, pp. 230–1.

15 Quoted in Rossi, p. 147.

16 On Hiss's role at Yalta, see Louis, pp. 453 and 458; Andrew & Gordievsky, pp. 273–4. On White's influence, see Andrew & Gordievsky, pp. 274–5.

17 Dr Roger Lee, in a letter to Sir Charles Wilson just before the conference, quoted in Moran, p. 250.

18 Buhite & Levy, p. 145.

19 Perlmutter, p. 179.

20 Moran, p. 250.

21 *Ibid.*, p. 249.

22 *Ibid.*, p. 251.

23 Tuttle, pp. 249–50.

24 Nisbet, p. 70.

Notes and References

25 Moran, p. 251.

26 Tuttle, p. 249.

27 Quoted in *ibid.*, p. 250.

28 *Ibid.*, p. 258.

29 Edmonds, p. 453.

30 Nisbet, p. 72.

31 *Ibid.*, pp. 70–1.

32 See Edmonds, Appendix V.

33 Nisbet, p. 75.

34 Quoted in *ibid.*, p. 77.

35 See Kimball, *Churchill and Roosevelt*, vol. III, pp. 547–51.

36 Quoted in Nisbet, p. 81.

37 Kathryn E. Brown, pp. 120–1.

38 *Ibid.*, p. 110.

39 Quoted in Louis, p. 277.

40 *Ibid.*, p. 279.

41 Aldrich, *Intelligence and the War against Japan*, p. 208; Kathryn E. Brown, p. 112.

42 Aldrich, *Intelligence and the War against Japan*, pp. 292–4.

43 *Ibid.*, pp. 208–11.

44 *Ibid.*, p. 211.

45 Kathryn E. Brown, p. 110.

46 *Ibid.*, p. 117.

47 Aldrich, *Intelligence and the War against Japan*, p. 341.

48 For a discussion of the theory, see *ibid.*, pp. 340–1.

49 Quoted in *ibid.*, p. 341.

50 *Ibid.*

51 Complete acceptance of Tonnesson's theory requires also accepting that the Japanese would not otherwise have invaded Indo-China, which is virtually impossible to prove. But at the very least Roosevelt did nothing to discourage an invasion, and this must have been a factor in the Japanese decision.

52 Quoted in Larrabee, p. 472.

53 Quoted in Nisbet, p. 84.

54 Quoted in *ibid.*, pp. 84–5.

55 Quoted in Nadeau, p. 154.

56 Quoted in Pogue, *George C. Marshall: Organizer of Victory*, p. 571.

57 Nadeau, pp. 152–3.

58 Nisbet, p. 85.

59 Quoted in *ibid.*, p. 86.

60 Quoted in Nadeau, p. 163.

61 Morris, p. 429.

62 Lamb, *Churchill as War Leader*, p. 4.

63 Dulles, *The Secret Surrender*, p. 3.

64 Quoted in Nisbet, p. 80; on the Soviet objections, see Dulles, *The Secret Surrender*, pp. 146–7.

65 Hogg, p. 147; d'Este, pp. 727–8.

66 Quoted in Tuttle, p. 265; see also Nisbet, p. 81.

67 Lash, *Eleanor and Franklin*, p. 721.

68 Bohlen, p. 209.

69 Stafford, *Roosevelt and Churchill*, p. 298.

70 Harriman & Abel, p. 441; Kimball, *Churchill and Roosevelt*, vol. III, p. 631.

71 Aldrich, *Intelligence and the War against Japan*, p. 303.

72 Nisbet, pp. 107–8.

73 Watt, *Succeeding John Bull*, p. 118.

74 Adams, pp. 385–6.

75 Andrew & Gordievsky, p. 286.

76 Quoted in *ibid.*, p. 287.

77 McJimsey, *Harry Hopkins*, p. 384.

78 *Ibid.*, p. 385.

79 Bohlen, p. 222.

80 Writing in Dear, p. 108.

81 Flynn, *The Roosevelt Myth*, p. 392.

82 Millis & Duffield, pp. 86–7.

83 Quoted in Aldrich, *Intelligence and the War against Japan*, p. 307.

84 Dear, pp. 530–1.

85 Arnold, p. 260.

86 Akashi Yogi, Norman Davies & Robert Service, writing in Dear, p. 519.

87 Dimbleby & Reynolds, p. 164.

88 Quoted in Arnold, p. 369.

89 Gardner, pp. 175–6.

90 Quoted in *ibid.*, p. 197.

91 Charmley, *Churchill's Grand Alliance*, pp. 98–9.

92 Smith & Morgan.

93 Dimbleby & Reynolds, pp. 166–7.

94 *Ibid.*, p. 167.

95 *Ibid.*, pp. 175.

96 Van Tuyll, p. 39.

97 *Ibid.*, pp. 23–4.

98 Gaddis, pp. 175–6.

99 *Ibid.*, pp. 190–2.

100 Quoted in Dimbleby & Reynolds, p. 173.

101 *Ibid.*, p. 176.

102 Quoted in McJimsey, *Harry Hopkins*, p. 397.

Notes and References

Epilogue: Guilty Secrets and Secret Agendas

1 Charmley, *Churchill*, p. 2.

2 A.J.P. Taylor, *From Sarajevo to Potsdam*, pp. 178–9.

3 Mark A. Stoler, 'The United States: The Global Strategy', in Reynolds, Kimball & Chubarian, p. 56.

4 *Ibid.*, p. 55; Theodore A. Wilson, 'The United States: Leviathan', in *ibid.*, pp. 180–3.

5 Reynolds, *The Creation of the Anglo-American Alliance*, p. 284.

6 Gumbel.

7 Quoted in *ibid.*

8 See Louis, pp. 271–2.

9 Quoted in Dimbleby & Reynolds, pp. 172–3.

10 Quoted in Dallek, p. 289.

11 See our *Double Standards*, pp. 496–9.

List of Abbreviations

ABDA	American-British-Dutch-Australian (Command)
BBC	British Broadcasting Corporation
BSC	British Security Co-ordination
CE	counter espionage
CIA	Central Intelligence Agency
CIC	Counter-Intelligence Corps
COS	Chiefs of Staff
FBI	Federal Bureau of Investigation
FDR	Franklin Delano Roosevelt
FECB	Far East Combined Bureau
FERA	Federal Emergency Relief Administration
GCCS	Government Code and Cipher School
GCHQ	Government Communications Headquarters
COI	Coordinator of Information
GRU	*Glavnoye Razvedyvatelnoye Upravlenie* (Main Intelligence Administration)
GUGB	*Glavnoye Upravlenie Gosudarstvennoy Bezopasnosti* (Main Administration of State Security)
IIC	Industrial Intelligence Centre
IMF	International Monetary Fund
JIC	Joint Intelligence Committee
KGB	*Komitet Gosudarstvennoy Bezopasnosti* (Committee of State Security)
LBJ	Lyndon Baines Johnson
LIHOP	'Let it Happen on Purpose'

List of Abbreviations

MED	'Manhattan Engineer District'
NATO	North Atlantic Treaty Organisation
NDRC	National Defense Research Council
NKGB	*Narodnyi Kommissariat Gosudarstvennoy Bezopasnosti* (People's Commissariat for State Security)
NKVD	*Narodnyi Kommissariat Vnutrennikh Del* (People's Commissariat for Internal Affairs)
NSA	National Security Agency
ONI	Office of Naval Intelligence
OSS	Office of Strategic Services
OWI	Office of War Information
RAF	Royal Air Force
SA	*Sturmabteilung* (Storm Section)
SD	*Sicherheitsdienst* (Security Service)
SEAC	South East Asia Command
SHAEF	Supreme Headquarters Allied Expeditionary Force
SIO	Security Intelligence Organisation
SOE	Special Operations Executive
SS	*Schutzstaffel* (Guard Squadron)
USAAF	United States Army Air Force
WPA	Works Progress/Project Agency

Bibliography

Entries are for the editions cited in the text. If this is not the first edition, details of first publication (where known) follow in brackets.

Acheson, Dean, *Present at the Creation: My Years in the State Department*, Hamish Hamilton, London, 1970

Adams, Henry H., *Harry Hopkins*, G.P. Putnam's Sons, New York, 1977

Aglion, Raoul, *Roosevelt and de Gaulle: Allies in Conflict – A Personal Memoir*, Free Press, New York, 1988 (revised, translated edition of *De Gaulle et Roosevelt*, Librarie Plon, Paris, 1984)

Alanbrooke, Field Marshal Lord, (ed. Alex Danchev and Daniel Todman), *War Diaries 1939–1945*, Weidenfeld & Nicolson, London, 2001

Aldrich, Richard J., 'American Intelligence and the British Raj: The OSS, SSU and India, 1942–1947', *Intelligence and National Security*, vol. 13, no. 1, Spring 1998
Intelligence and the War against Japan: Britain, America and the Politics of Secret Service, Cambridge University Press, Cambridge, 2000

Friendly Fire

Alldritt, Keith, *The Greatest of Friends: Franklin D. Roosevelt and Winston Churchill 1941–1945*, Robert Hale, London, 1995

Allen, Martin, *The Hitler/Hess Deception: British Intelligence's Best-Kept Secret of the Second World War*, HarperCollins, London, 2003

Alsop, Joseph, *FDR 1882–1945: The Life and Times of Franklin D. Roosevelt*, Thames & Hudson, London, 1982

Andrew, Christopher, *Secret Service: The Making of the British Intelligence Community*, Heinemann, London, 1985
For the President's Eyes Only: Secret Intelligence and the American Presidency from Washington to Bush, HarperCollins, London, 1995

Andrew, Christopher and Oleg Gordievsky, *KGB: The Inside Story of its Foreign Operations from Lenin to Gorbachev*, Hodder & Stoughton, London, 1990

Andrew, Christopher and Vasili Mitrokhin, *The Mitrokhin Archive: The KGB in Europe and the West*, Allen Lane/Penguin Press, London, 1999

Applebaum, Anne, *Gulag: A History of the Soviet Camps*, Allen Lane, London, 2003

Argyll, Christopher (ed.), *Chronology of World War II*, Marshall Cavendish, London, 1980

Arnold, David, *Britain, Europe and the World 1871–1971*, revised edition, Edward Arnold, London, 1973 (*Britain, Europe and the World 1870–1955*, Edward Arnold, London, 1966)

Atkin, Ronald, *Dieppe 1942: The Jubilee Disaster*, Macmillan, London, 1980

Avon, The Earl of, *The Eden Memoirs: Facing the Dictators*, Cassell, London, 1962
The Eden Memoirs: The Reckoning, Cassell, London, 1965

Baldwin, Hanson W., *Great Mistakes of the War*, Alvin Redman, London, 1950

Baruch, Bernard M., *My Own Story*, Henry Holt & Co., London, 1957
Baruch: The Public Years, Holt, Rinehart & Winston, New York, 1960

Beard, Charles A., *President Roosevelt and the Coming of the War, 1941: A Study in Appearances and Realities*, Yale University Press, New Haven, 1948

Bearse, Ray and Anthony Read, *Conspirator: The Untold Story of Churchill, Roosevelt and Tyler Kent, Spy*, Macmillan, London, 1991

Bibliography

Beevor, Antony, *Stalingrad*, Penguin Books, London, 1999 (Viking, London, 1998)

Bentley, Elizabeth, *Out of Bondage*, Rupert Hart-Davis, London, 1952

Benz, Wolfgang and Walter H. Pehle (eds), *Encyclopaedia of German Resistance to the Nazi Movement*, Continuum, New York, 1997 (*Lexikon des Deutschen Widerstandes*, S. Fischer Verlag, Frankfurt-am-Main, 1994)

Berthon, Simon, *Allies at War*, HarperCollins, London, 2001

Blum, John Morton, *From the Morgenthau Diaries, Vol. I: Years of Crisis, 1928–1938*, Houghton Mifflin Company, Boston, 1959; *Vol. II: Years of Urgency, 1938–1941*, Houghton Mifflin Company, Boston, 1965; *Vol. III: Years of War, 1941–1945*, Houghton Mifflin Company, Boston, 1967

Blumenson, Martin, *Mark Clark*, Jonathan Cape, London, 1986

Bohlen, Charles E., *Witness to History 1929–1969*, W.W. Norton & Co., New York, 1973

Bond, Brian, *British Military Policy between the Two World Wars*, Clarendon Press, Oxford, 1980

Brissaud, André,(trans. and ed. Ian Colvin), *Canaris: The Biography of Admiral Canaris, Chief of German Military Intelligence in the Second World War*, Military Book Society, London, 1973 (*Canaris: Le 'petit amiral', prince de l'espionnage allemand, 1887–1945*, Librairie Académique Perrin, Paris, 1970)

British Security Coordination (ed. Nigel West), *British Security Coordination: The Secret History of British Intelligence in the Americas 1940–45*, St Ermin's Press/Little, Brown & Co., London, 1998 (originally produced for the UK government, 1946)

Brown, Anthony Cave, *Bodyguard of Lies*, Star, London, 1977 (W.H. Allen, London, 1976)

The Last Hero: Wild Bill Donovan, Michael Joseph, London, 1982

The Secret Servant: The Life of Sir Stewart Menzies, Churchill's Spymaster, Michael Joseph, London, 1988

Treason in the Blood: H. St John Philby, Kim Philby and the Spy Case of the Century, Robert Hale, London, 1995

Brown, Archie (ed.), *The Soviet Union: A Biographical Dictionary*, Weidenfeld & Nicolson, London, 1990

Brown, Kathryn E., 'The Interplay of Information and Mind in

Decision-Making: Signals Intelligence and Franklin D. Roosevelt's Policy-Shift on Indo-China', *Intelligence and National Security*, vol. 13, no. 1, Spring 1998

Bryans, J. Lonsdale, *Blind Victory (Secret Communications, Halifax-Hassell)*, Skeffington & Son, London, 1951

Buhite, Russell D. and David W. Levy (eds), *FDR's Fireside Chats*, Penguin, New York, 1993 (University of Oklahoma Press, Norman, 1992)

Bullock, Alan, *Hitler, A Study in Tyranny*, revised edition, Pelican, Harmondsworth, 1962 (Odhams, London, 1952)
Hitler and Stalin: Parallel Lives, revised edition, Fontana Press, London, 1993 (HarperCollins, London, 1991)

Burleigh, Michael, *The Third Reich: A New History*, Pan Books, Macmillan, London, 2000

Burns, James MacGregor, *Roosevelt: The Soldier of Freedom 1940–1945*, Weidenfeld & Nicolson, London, 1971

Cadogan, Sir Alexander (ed. David Dilks), *The Diaries of Sir Alexander Cadogan O.M., 1938–1945*, Cassell, London, 1971

Calder, Angus, *The Myth of the Blitz*, Jonathan Cape, London, 1991

Calvocoressi, Peter, Guy Wint and John Pritchard, *Total War: The Causes and Courses of the Second World War*, revised edition, 2 vols, Penguin Books, London, 1989 (Allen Lane, London, 1972)

Campbell, John P., *Dieppe Revisited: A Documentary Investigation*, Frank Cass, London, 1993

Carr, E.H., *Britain: A Study of Foreign Policy from the Versailles Treaty to the Outbreak of War*, Longmans, Green & Co., London, 1939
International Relations since the Peace Treaties, revised edition, Macmillan & Co., London, 1941 (first edition 1937)

Carr, William, *Arms, Autarky and Aggression*, Edward Arnold, London, 1972

Casey, William, *The Secret War against Hitler*, Simon & Schuster, London, 1989

Cazalet, Major V.A., *With Sikorski to Russia*, privately published, London, 1942

Chambers, Whittaker, *Witness*, Random House, New York, 1952

Charles, Searle F., *Minister of Relief: Harry Hopkins and the Depression*, Syracuse University Press, Syracuse, 1963

Bibliography

Charmley, John, *Chamberlain and the Lost Peace*, Hodder & Stoughton, London, 1989

Churchill: End of Glory, Hodder & Stoughton, Sevenoaks, 1993

Churchill's Grand Alliance: The Anglo-American Special Relationship 1940–57, Hodder & Stoughton, London, 1995

Chisholm, Anne and Michael Davie, *Beaverbrook: A Life*, Hutchinson, London, 1992

Churchill, Randolph S., *Winston S. Churchill, Vol. I: Youth, 1874–1900*, William Heinemann, London, 1966; *Vol. II: Young Statesman, 1901–1914*, William Heinemann, London, 1967

Churchill, Winston S., 'Fantastic Trial at Moscow: Soviets' Appeal to the Organised Ferocity of the Mob', *Daily Telegraph*, 4 December 1930

Great Contemporaries, Thornton Butterworth, London, 1937

Step by Step: 1936–1939, Thornton Butterworth, London, 1939

The Second World War, Vol. I: The Gathering Storm, Cassell & Co., London, 1948; *Vol. II: Their Finest Hour*, Cassell & Co., London, 1949; *Vol. III: The Grand Alliance*, Cassell & Co., London, 1950; *Vol. IV: The Hinge of Fate*, Cassell & Co., London, 1951; *Vol. V: Closing the Ring*, Cassell & Co., London, 1952; *Vol. VI: Triumph and Tragedy*, Cassell & Co., London, 1954

Ciano, Count (ed. Malcolm Muggeridge), *Ciano's Diary 1939–1943*, William Heinemann, London, 1947

Clark, General Mark, *Calculated Risk: His Personal Story of the War in North Africa and Italy*, George G. Harrap & Co., London, 1951

Coates, John, 'Sikorski: Was it Murder?', *The Times*, 4 July 2003

Coit, Margaret L., *Mr Baruch*, Victor Gollancz, London, 1958

Collier, Basil, *Barren Victories: Versailles to Suez (1918–1956)*, Cassell, London, 1964

Collier, Richard, *1941: Armageddon*, Hamish Hamilton, London, 1981

Colville, John, *The Churchillians*, Weidenfeld & Nicolson, London, 1981

The Fringes of Power: Downing Street Diaries 1939–1955, Vol. I: September 1939–September 1941, Sceptre, Sevenoaks, 1986; *Vol. II: October 1941–1955*; Sceptre, Sevenoaks, 1987 (first, single-volume edition Hodder & Stoughton, London, 1985)

Cookridge, E.H., *Gehlen: Spy of the Century*, Corgi, London, 1972 (Hodder & Stoughton, London, 1971)

Corson, W.R. and R.T. Crowley, *The New KGB: Engine of Soviet Power*, Harvester Press, Brighton, 1986

Costello, John, *Ten Days that Saved the West*, Bantam Press, London, 1991

Cowling, Maurice, *The Impact of Hitler: British Politics and British Policy 1933–1940*, Cambridge University Press, London, 1975

Dallek, Robert, *Franklin D. Roosevelt and American Foreign Policy, 1932–1945*, revised edition, Oxford University Press, Oxford, 1995 (first edition 1979)

Dalton, Hugh (ed. Ben Pimlott), *The Second World War Diaries of Hugh Dalton, 1940–45*, Jonathan Cape, London, 1986

Davies, Joseph E., *Mission to Moscow*, Victor Gollancz, London, 1942

Davies, Norman M., *God's Playground: A History of Poland*, 2 vols, Columbia University Press, New York, 1982

Davis, Kenneth S., *FDR: The Beckoning of Destiny 1882–1928*, Random House, New York, 1972

Deane, John R., *The Strange Alliance: The Story of American Efforts at Wartime Co-operation with Russia*, John Murray, London, 1947

Dear, I.C.B. (ed.), *The Oxford Companion to the Second World War*, Oxford University Press, Oxford, 1995

de Bedts, Ralph F., *Ambassador Joseph Kennedy 1938–1940: An Anatomy of Appeasement*, Peter Lang, New York, 1985

d'Este, Carlo, *A Genius for War: A Life of General George S. Patton*, HarperCollins, London, 1995

de Gaulle, Charles, *War Memoirs, Vol. I: The Call to Honour 1940–1942*, Collins, London, 1955; *Vol. II: Unity 1942–1944*, Weidenfeld & Nicolson, London, 1959 (*Mémoires de la Guerre*, Librarie Plon, Paris, 1955/56)

de Toledano, Ralph, *Spies, Dupes and Diplomats*, Duell, Sloan & Pearce/Little, Brown & Co., New York/Boston, 1952
The Greatest Plot in History, Arlington House, New Rochelle, 1963
(ed.), *Notes from the Underground: The Whittaker Chambers–Ralph de Toledano Letters, 1949–1960*, Regnery Publishing, Washington DC, 1997

de Toledano, Ralph and Victor Lasky, *Seeds of Treason: The Strange*

Bibliography

Case of Alger Hiss, Secker & Warburg, London, 1950

Dimbleby, David and David Reynolds, *An Ocean Apart: The Relationship between Britain and America in the Twentieth Century*, BBC Books/Hodder & Stoughton, London, 1988

Divine, Robert A., *The Illusion of Neutrality*, University of Chicago Press, Chicago, 1962

Dobson, Alan P., *US Wartime Aid to Britain 1940–1946*, Croom Helm, Beckenham, 1986

Documents on German Foreign Policy 1918–1945, Series D: 1937–1945, 13 volumes, HMSO, London, 1949–64

Dulles, Allen Welsh, *Germany's Underground*, Macmillan & Co., New York, 1947

The Secret Surrender, Weidenfeld and Nicolson, London, 1967 (Harper & Row, New York, 1966)

Edmonds, Robin, *The Big Three: Churchill, Roosevelt and Stalin in Peace and War*, Penguin, London, 1992 (Hamish Hamilton, London, 1991)

Enright, Dominique (ed.), *The Wicked Wit of Winston Churchill*, Michael O'Mara, London, 2001

Farnham, Barbara Rearden, *Roosevelt and the Munich Crisis: A Study of Political Decision-Making*, Princeton University Press, Princeton, 1997

Farnsworth, Beatrice, *William C. Bullitt and the Soviet Union*, Indiana University Press, Bloomington, 1967

Ferrell, Robert H., *The Dying President: Franklin D. Roosevelt 1944–1945*, University of Missouri Press, Columbia, 1998

FitzGibbon, Constantine, *Secret Intelligence in the Twentieth Century*, Hart-Davis, MacGibbon, London, 1976

FitzGibbon, Louis, *Katyn: A Crime without Parallel*, Tom Stacey, London, 1971

Flynn, John T., *The Truth about Pearl Harbor*, The Strickland Press, Glasgow, 1945

The Roosevelt Myth, The Devin-Adair Company, New York, 1948

Foot, M.R.D., *SOE: An Outline History of the Special Operations Executive 1940–46*, BBC, London, 1984

Foreign and Commonwealth Office, *Nazi Gold: The London Conference 2–4 December 1997*, The Stationery Office, London, 1998

Fraser, David, *Knight's Cross: A Life of Field Marshal Erwin Rommel*, HarperCollins, London, 1993

Gaddis, John Lewis, *The United States and the Origins of the Cold War, 1941–1947*, Columbia University Press, New York, 1972

Gallagher, John (ed. Anil Seal), *The Decline, Revival and Fall of the British Empire: The Ford Lectures and Other Essays*, Cambridge University Press, Cambridge, 1982

Gardner, Richard N., *Sterling–Dollar Diplomacy in Current Perspective: The Origins and the Prospects of our International Economic Order*, revised edition, Columbia University Press, New York, 1980 (Oxford University Press, Oxford, 1956)

Garnett, David (ed. Andrew Roberts), *The Secret History of PWE: The Political Warfare Executive 1939–1945*, St Ermin's Press, London, 2002 (*The Political Warfare Executive*, official history written for the Cabinet Office, London, 1947)

Gilbert, Martin, *Winston S. Churchill, Vol. III: The Challenge of War, 1914–1916*, William Heinemann, London, 1971; *Vol. IV: World in Torment, 1917–1922*, William Heinemann, London, 1975; *Vol. V: Prophet of Truth, 1922–1939*, William Heinemann, London, 1976; *Vol. VI: Finest Hour, 1939–1941*, William Heinemann, London, 1983; *Vol. VII: Road to Victory, 1941–1945*, William Heinemann, London, 1986; *Vol. VIII: 'Never Despair', 1945–1965*, William Heinemann, London, 1988
Winston Churchill: The Wilderness Years, Macmillan, London, 1981
Second World War, Weidenfeld & Nicolson, London, 1989
Churchill: A Life, Heinemann, London, 1991
In Search of Churchill: A Historian's Journey, HarperCollins, London, 1994

Goebbels, Josef (trans. and ed. Fred Taylor), *The Goebbels Diaries*, Hamish Hamilton, London, 1982

Goodhart, Philip, *Fifty Ships that Saved the World: The Foundation of the Anglo-American Alliance*, Heinemann, London, 1965

Gordievsky, Oleg, *Next Stop Execution: The Autobiography of Oleg Gordievsky*, Macmillan, London, 1995

Grew, Joseph C., *Ten Years in Japan: A Contemporary Record drawn from the Diaries and Private and Official Papers of Joseph C. Grew, United States Ambassador to Japan 1932–1942*, Hammond, Hammond & Co., London, 1944

Bibliography

Gumbel, Andrew, 'How the War Machine is Driving the US Economy', *The Independent*, 6 January 2004

Haight Jr., John McVickar, *American Aid to France, 1938–1940*, Atheneum, New York, 1970

Harbutt, Fraser J., *The Iron Curtain: Churchill, America, and the Origins of the Cold War*, Oxford University Press, New York, 1986

Hargrave, John, *Professor Skinner alias Montagu Norman*, Wells Gardner, Darton & Co., London, 1939

Harriman, W. Averell and Elie Abel, *Special Envoy to Churchill and Stalin 1941–1946*, Random House, New York, 1975

Hastings, Max, *Bomber Command*, Michael Joseph, London, 1979
Overlord: D-Day and the Battle for Normandy, 1944, Simon & Schuster, London, 1984
'Britain's Last Warrior', *Daily Mail*, 13 July 2002

Haynes, John Earl and Harvey Klehr, *Venona: Decoding Soviet Espionage in America*, Yale University Press, New Haven, 1999

Heale, M.J., *Franklin D. Roosevelt: The New Deal and the War*, Routledge, London, 1999

Henderson, Sir Nevile, *Failure of a Mission: Berlin 1937–1939*, Hodder & Stoughton, London, 1940

Herzstein, Robert Edwin, *Roosevelt and Hitler: Prelude to War*, Paragon House, New York, 1989

Higham, Charles, *Trading with the Enemy: An Exposé of the Nazi-American Money Plot*, Robert Hale, London, 1983
American Swastika, Doubleday & Co., Garden City, 1985

Hinsley, F.H. and C.A.G. Simkins, *British Intelligence in the Second World War, vol. 4: Security and Counter-Intelligence*, HMSO, London, 1990

Hinsley, F.H., with E.E. Thomas, C.F.G. Ransom and R.C. Knight, *British Intelligence in the Second World War: Its Influence on Strategy and Operations*, vols 1–3, HMSO, London, 1979/81/84

Hitler, Adolf, *Mein Kampf*, single-volume edition, Hurst & Blackett, London, 1939 (Munich, 1925/27)
(ed. Raoul de Roussy de Sales), *My New Order*, Angus & Robertson, Sydney, 1942
Hitler's Secret Book, Grove Press, New York, 1961

Hobley, L.F., *The Second World War*, Blackie, Glasgow, 1971

Hogg, Ian V., *The Biography of General George S. Patton*, Hamlyn, London, 1982

Hopkins, Harry L., *What is the 'American Way'?*, Works Progress Administration, Washington, D.C., 1938

Horrie, Chris, 'Revealed: The Fascist Past of the Daily Mirror', *The Independent Review*, 11 November 2003

Howe, Quincy, *Ashes of Victory: World War II and its Aftermath*, Simon & Schuster, New York, 1972

Hull, Cordell, *The Memoirs of Cordell Hull*, 2 vols, Hodder & Stoughton, London, 1948

Hyde, H. Montgomery, *The Quiet Canadian: The Secret Service Story of Sir William Stephenson*, Hamish Hamilton, London, 1962

Ickes, Harold L., *The Secret Diary of Harold L. Ickes*, 3 vols, Weidenfeld & Nicolson, London, 1955

Irving, David, *Accident: The Death of General Sikorski*, William Kimber, London, 1967
The War Path: Hitler's Germany 1933–9, Michael Joseph, London, 1978

Israel, Fred L., *Franklin Delano Roosevelt*, revised edition, Burke Publishing, London, 1988 (Chelsea House Publishers, New York, 1985)

James, Robert Rhodes, *A Spirit Undaunted: The Political Role of George VI*, Abacus, London, 1999 (Little, Brown & Co., London, 1998)

Jeffrey-Jones, Rhodri (ed.), *Eagle against Empire: American Opposition to European Imperialism, 1914–1982*, Groupe de Recherche et d'Études Nord-Américaines/Université de Provence, Aix-en-Provence, 1983

Jenkins, Roy, *Baldwin*, Collins, London, 1987

Jordan, George Racey, with Richard L. Stokes, *From Major Jordan's Diaries*, Harcourt, Brace & Co., New York, 1952

Kaiser, David E., *Economic Diplomacy and the Origins of the Second World War: Germany, Britain, France and Eastern Europe, 1930–1939*, Princeton University Press, Princeton, 1980

Kershaw, Ian, *Hitler, 1889–1936: Hubris*, Allen Lane/Penguin, London, 1998
Hitler, 1936–1945: Nemesis, Allen Lane/Penguin, London, 2000

Kessler, Ronald, *The Sins of the Father: Joseph P. Kennedy and the Dynasty He Founded*, Coronet Books, London, 1997 (Hodder & Stoughton, London, 1996)

Bibliography

Keynes, John Maynard, *The Economic Consequences of the Peace*, Macmillan & Co., London, 1920

Kieser, Egbert, *Hitler on the Doorstep: Operation 'Sea Lion' – The German Plan to Invade Britain, 1940*, Arms & Armour Press, London, 1997 (Bechtle Verlag, Munich, 1987)

Kilzer, Louis C., *Churchill's Deception: The Dark Secret that Destroyed Nazi Germany*, Simon & Schuster, New York, 1994

Kimball, Warren F., *The Most Unsordid Act: Lend-Lease, 1939–1941*, The John Hopkins Press, Baltimore, 1969

(ed.), *Churchill and Roosevelt: The Complete Correspondence*, 3 vols, Princeton University Press, Princeton, 1984

The Juggler: Franklin Roosevelt as Wartime Statesman, Princeton University Press, Princeton, 1991

(ed.), *America Unbound: World War II and the Making of a Superpower*, St Martin's Press, New York, 1992

Forged in War: Churchill, Roosevelt and the Second World War, HarperCollins, London, 1997

Lamb, Richard, *The Ghosts of Peace 1935–1945*, Michael Russell, Salisbury, 1987

The Drift to War 1922–1939, W.H. Allen, London, 1989

Churchill as War Leader: Right or Wrong?, Bloomsbury, London, 1991

Langer, William L. and S. Everett Gleason, *The Challenge to Isolation 1937–1940*, Harper & Brothers/Council on Foreign Relations, New York, 1952

The Undeclared War 1940–1941, Harper & Brothers/Council on Foreign Relations, New York, 1953

Larkin, Maurice, *Gathering Pace: Continental Europe 1870–1945*, Macmillan, London, 1969

Larrabee, Eric, *Commander in Chief: Franklin Delano Roosevelt, his Lieutenants, and their War*, Andre Deutsch, London, 1987

Lash, Joseph P., *Eleanor and Franklin: The Story of their Relationship, based on Eleanor Roosevelt's Private Papers*, André Deutsch, London, 1971

Roosevelt and Churchill 1939–1941: The Partnership that Saved the West, André Deutsch, London, 1977

Lasky, Victor, *It Didn't Start with Watergate*, The Dial Press, New York, 1977

Leahy, William D., *I Was There: The Personal Story of the Chief of Staff to*

Presidents Roosevelt and Truman based on his Notes and Diaries made at the Time, Victor Gollancz, London, 1950

Leutze, James R., *Bargaining for Supremacy: Anglo-American Naval Collaboration, 1937–1941*, The University of North Carolina Press, Chapel Hill, 1977

Levine, Alan J., *The Strategic Bombing of Germany, 1940–1945*, Praegar, Westport, 1992

Lewin, Ronald, *Churchill as Warlord*, B.T. Batsford, London, 1973

Liddell Hart, B.H., *History of the Second World War*, Pan Books, London, 1973 (Cassell & Co, London, 1970)

Lippman, Walter, *U.S. War Aims*, Hamish Hamilton, London, 1944

Lockhart, Sir Robert Bruce (ed. Kenneth Young), *The Diaries of Sir Robert Bruce Lockhart*, 2 vols, Macmillan, London, 1973/1980

Long, Breckinridge (ed. Fred L. Israel), *The War Diary of Breckinridge Long: Selections from the Years 1939–1944*, University of Nebraska Press, Lincoln, 1966

Louis, Wm. Roger, *Imperialism at Bay 1941–1945: The United States and the Decolonisation of the British Empire*, Clarendon Press, Oxford, 1977

Mahl, Thomas E., *Desperate Deception: British Covert Operations in the United States, 1939–44*, Brassey's, Washington, 1998

Maney, Patrick J., *The Roosevelt Presence: The Life and Legacy of FDR*, University of California Press, Los Angeles, 1992

Mark, Eduard, 'Venona's Source 19 and the "Trident" Conference of May 1943: Diplomacy or Espionage?', *Intelligence and National Security*, vol. 13, no. 2, Summer 1998

Martel, Leon, *Lend-Lease, Loans, and the Coming of the Cold War: A Study in the Implementation of Foreign Policy*, Westview Press, Boulder, 1979

McJimsey, George, *Harry Hopkins: Ally of the Poor and Defender of Democracy*, Harvard University Press, Cambridge (Mass.), 1987
The Presidency of Franklin Delano Roosevelt, University Press of Kansas, Lawrence, 2000

Michel, Henri, *The Second World War*, André Deutsch, London, 1971 (*La seconde guerre mondiale*, Presses Universitaires de France, Paris, 1968)

Middlebrook, Martin and Chris Everitt, *The Bomber Command War Diaries: An Operational Reference Book 1939–1945*, revised edition, Midland Publishing, Leicester, 1996 (Viking, London, 1985)

Bibliography

Miller, Nathan, *FDR: An Intimate History*, Doubleday & Co., New York, 1983

Millis, Walter, with E.S. Duffield (eds), *The Forrestal Diaries: The Inner History of the Cold War*, Cassell & Co., London, 1952

Milward, Alan S., *War, Economy and Society 1939–1945*, Penguin Books, Harmondsworth, 1987 (Allen Lane, London, 1977)

Ministry of Foreign Affairs of the USSR, *Stalin's Correspondence with Churchill, Attlee, Roosevelt and Truman 1941–45*, Lawrence & Wishart, London, 1958 (*Correspondence between the Chairman of the Council of Ministers of the USSR and the Presidents of the USA and the Prime Ministers of Great Britain during the Great Patriotic War of 1941–1945*, 2 vols, Foreign Languages Publishing House, Moscow, 1957)

Moffat, Jay Pierrepont (ed. Nancy Harvison Hooker), *The Moffat Papers: Selections from the Diplomatic Journals of Jay Pierrepont Moffat 1919–1943*, Harvard University Press, Cambridge (Mass.), 1956

Montgomery of Alamein, Viscount, *The Memoirs of Field-Marshal the Viscount Montgomery of Alamein, K.G.*, Collins, London, 1958

Moran, Lord, *Winston Churchill: The Struggle for Survival 1940–1965*, Sphere, London, 1968 (Constable & Co., London, 1966)

Morris, Eric, *Circles of Hell: The War in Italy 1943–1945*, Hutchinson, London, 1993

Mosley, Leonard, *Marshall: Organizer of Victory*, Methuen, London, 1982

Murray, Arthur C., *At Close Quarters: A Sidelight on Anglo-American Diplomatic Relations*, John Murray, London, 1946

Nadeau, Remi, *Stalin, Churchill, and Roosevelt Divide Europe*, Praeger, New York, 1990

Neal, Steve, *Dark Horse: A Biography of Wendell Willkie*, University Press of Kansas, Lawrence, 1989 (Doubleday, Garden City, 1984)

Newton, Scott, *Profits of Peace: The Political Economy of Anglo-German Appeasement*, Clarendon Press, Oxford, 1996

Nicholas, H.G. (ed.), *Washington Despatches 1941–45: Weekly Political Reports from the British Embassy*, Weidenfeld & Nicolson, London, 1981

Nisbet, Robert, *Roosevelt and Stalin: The Failed Courtship*, Simon & Schuster, London, 1989

Nixon, Edgar B. (ed.), *Franklin D. Roosevelt and Foreign Affairs*, 3 vols,

The Belknap Press of Harvard University Press, Cambridge (Mass.), 1969

Padfield, Peter, *Hess: The Führer's Disciple*, revised edition, Weidenfeld & Nicolson, London, 1995 (*Hess: Flight for the Führer*, Weidenfeld & Nicolson, 1991)

Parrish, Thomas, *Roosevelt and Marshall: Partners in Politics and War*, William Morrow & Co., New York, 1989

Paxton, Robert O., *Vichy France: Old Guard and New Order, 1940–1944*, Barrie & Jenkins, London, 1972

Peden, G.C., *British Rearmament and the Treasury: 1932–1939*, Scottish Academic Press, Edinburgh, 1979

Peis, Günter, *The Mirror of Deception: How Britain Turned the Nazi Spy Machine against Itself*, Weidenfeld & Nicolson, London, 1977 (*So ging Deutschland in die Falle*, Econ Verlag, Dusseldorf, 1976)

Perlmutter, Amos, *FDR and Stalin: A Not So Grand Alliance, 1943–1945*, University of Missouri Press, Columbia, 1993

Picknett, Lynn, Clive Prince and Stephen Prior, with Robert Brydon, *Double Standards: The Rudolf Hess Cover-Up*, revised edition, TimeWarner Books, London, 2002 (Little, Brown & Co., London, 2001)

War of the Windsors: A Century of Unconstitutional Monarchy, revised edition, Mainstream, Edinburgh, 2003 (first edition 2002)

Pogue, Forrest C., *George C. Marshall: Education of a General 1880–1939*, Viking, New York, 1963

George C. Marshall: Ordeal and Hope 1939–1942, Viking, New York, 1966

George C. Marshall: Organizer of Victory 1942–1945, Viking, New York, 1973

George C. Marshall: Statesman 1945–1959, Viking, New York, 1987

Polnische Dokumente zur Vorgeschichte des Krieges: Erste Folge, Zentralverlag der NSDAP, Berlin, 1940

Ponting, Clive, *1940: Myth and Reality*, Cardinal, London, 1990 (Hamish Hamilton, London, 1990)

Churchill, Sinclair-Stevenson, London, 1994

Armageddon: The Second World War, Sinclair-Stevenson, London, 1995

Range, Willard, *Franklin D. Roosevelt's World Order*, University of Georgia Press, Athens, 1959

Bibliography

Rauch, Basil, *Roosevelt from Munich to Pearl Harbor: A Study in the Creation of a Foreign Policy*, Barnes & Noble, New York, 1967 (first edition 1950)

Rees, David, *Harry Dexter White: A Study in Paradox*, Macmillan, London, 1973

Reynolds, David, *The Creation of the Anglo-American Alliance 1937–41: A Study in Competitive Co-operation*, Europa Publications, London, 1981
Rich Relations: The American Occupation of Britain, 1942–1945, HarperCollins, London, 1995

Reynolds, David, Warren F. Kimball and A.O. Chubarian (eds), *Allies at War: The Soviet, American and British Experience, 1939–1945*, Macmillan, Basingstoke, 1994

Reynolds, P.A., *British Foreign Policy in the Inter-War Years*, Longmans, Green & Co, London, 1954

Roberts, Andrew, *'The Holy Fox': A Biography of Lord Halifax*, Weidenfeld & Nicolson, London, 1991
Eminent Churchillians, Weidenfeld & Nicolson, London, 1994

Roosevelt, Eleanor, *This I Remember*, Hutchinson & Co., London, 1950

Roosevelt, Elliott, *As He Saw It*, Duell, Sloan & Pearce, New York, 1946

Rose, Norman, *The Cliveden Set: Portrait of an Exclusive Fraternity*, Jonathan Cape, London, 2000

Roskill, Stephen, *Naval Policy between the Wars, Vol. I: The Period of Anglo-American Antagonism, 1919–1929*, Collins, London, 1968; *Vol. II: The Period of Reluctant Rearmament, 1930–1939*, Collins, London, 1976

Rossi, Mario, *Roosevelt and the French*, Praeger, Westport, 1993

Rusbridger, James & Eric Nave, *Betrayal at Pearl Harbor: How Churchill Lured Roosevelt into War*, Michael O'Mara, London, 1991

Russell, Francis, *The President Makers: From Mark Hanna to Joseph P. Kennedy*, Little, Brown & Co., Boston, 1976

Salmaggi, Cesare and Alfredo Pallavisini, *2194 Days of War: An Illustrated Chronology of the Second World War*, Windward, London, 1979 (*2194 Giorni di Guerra*, Arnoldo Mondadori, Milan, 1977)

Schlesinger, Jr., Arthur M., *The Age of Roosevelt, Vol. I: The Crisis of the Old Order 1919–1933*, Heinemann, London, 1957; *Vol. II: The*

Coming of the New Deal, Heinemann, London, 1960; *Vol. III: The Politics of Upheaval*, Heinemann, London, 1961

Schwarz, Jordan A., *The Speculator: Bernard M. Baruch in Washington, 1917–1965*, University of North Carolina Press, Chapel Hill, 1981

Shepherd, Robert, *A Class Divided: Appeasement and the Road to Munich 1938*, Macmillan, London, 1988

Sherwin, Martin J., *A World Destroyed: The Atomic Bomb and the Grand Alliance*, Alfred A. Knopf, New York, 1975

Sherwood, Robert E., *The White House Papers of Harry L. Hopkins: An Intimate History*, Eyre & Spottiswoode, London, 2 vols, 1948/49 (*Roosevelt and Hopkins: An Intimate History*, Harper & Brothers, New York, 1948)

Shogan, Robert, *Hard Bargain: How FDR Twisted Churchill's Arm, Evaded the Law, and Changed the Role of the American Presidency*, Scribner, New York, 1995

Simpson, Michael, *Franklin D. Roosevelt*, Basil Blackwell, Oxford, 1989

Smith, David and Christopher Morgan, 'Britain to Pay Off its US War Debt at Last', *Sunday Times*, 2 June 2002

Smith, Gaddis, *American Diplomacy during the Second World War, 1941–1945*, John Wiley & Sons, New York, 1965

Smith, Michael, *Station X: The Codebreakers of Bletchley Park*, Channel 4 Books, London, 1998
The Emperor's Codes: Bletchley Park and the Breaking of Japan's Secret Ciphers, Bantam Books, London, 2001 (Bantam Press, London, 2000)

Snyder, Louis L., *Encyclopedia of the Third Reich*, Robert Hales, London, 1976

Sontag, Raymond James and James Stuart Beddie (eds), *Nazi–Soviet Relations 1939–1941: Documents from the Archives of the German Foreign Office*, Department of State, Washington, D.C., 1948

Stafford, David, *Churchill and Secret Service*, John Murray, London, 1997
Roosevelt and Churchill: Men of Secrets, Little, Brown, London, 1999

Stettinius, Jr., Edward R., *Lend-Lease: Weapon for Victory*, Penguin Books, Harmondsworth, 1944
Roosevelt and the Russians: The Yalta Conference, Jonathan Cape, London, 1950

Bibliography

Stevenson, William, *A Man Called Intrepid: The Secret War*, Harcourt Brace Jovanovich, New York, 1976

Stinnett, Robert B., *Day of Deceit: The Truth about FDR and Pearl Harbor*, Constable, London, 2000

Stoler, Mark A., *The Politics of the Second Front: American Military Planning and Diplomacy in Coalition Warfare, 1941–1943*, Greenwood Press, Westport, 1977

Stuart, James (Viscount Stuart of Findhorn), *Within the Fringe: An Autobiography*, The Bodley Head, London, 1967

Sulzberger, C.L., *The Last of the Giants*, Wiedenfeld & Nicolson, London, 1972 (Macmillan, New York, 1970)

Tanenhaus, Sam, *Whittaker Chambers: A Biography*, Modern Library, New York 1998 (Random House, New York, 1997)

Tansill, Charles Callan, *Back Door to War: The Roosevelt Foreign Policy 1933–1941*, Henry Regnery Company, Chicago, 1952

Taylor, A.J.P., *The Origins of the Second World War*, Hamish Hamilton, London, 1961
From Sarajevo to Potsdam, Thames & Hudson, London, 1966
Beaverbrook, Hamish Hamilton, London, 1972

Taylor, Eric, *Operation Millennium: 'Bomber' Harris's Raid on Cologne, May 1942*, Robert Hale, London, 1987

Terraine, John, *The Right of the Line: The Royal Air Force in the European War 1939–1945*, Hodder & Stoughton, London, 1985

Thomas, Hugh, *Hess: A Tale of Two Murders*, Hodder & Stoughton, London, 1988 (revised edition of *The Murder of Rudolf Hess*, Hodder & Stoughton, London, 1979)

Thompson, Carlos, *The Assassination of Winston Churchill*, Colin Smythe, Gerrards Cross, 1969

Thorne, Christopher, *Allies of a Kind: The United States, Britain and the War against Japan, 1941–1945*, Hamish Hamilton, London, 1978
The Issue of War: States, Societies and the Far Eastern Conflict of 1941–1945, Hamish Hamilton, London, 1985

Toland, John, *Infamy: Pearl Harbor and its Aftermath*, Methuen, London, 1982

Troy, Thomas F., *Wild Bill and Intrepid: Donovan, Stephenson and the Origin of the CIA*, Yale University Press, New Haven, 1996

Tuttle, Dwight William, *Harry L. Hopkins and Anglo-American–Soviet Relations, 1941–1945*, Garland Publishing, New York, 1983

van Tuyll, Hubert P., *Feeding the Bear: American Aid to the Soviet Union, 1941–1945*, Greenwood Press, New York, 1989

Venkataramani, M.S. and B.K. Shrivastava, *Roosevelt–Ghandi–Churchill: America and the Last Phase of India's Freedom Struggle*, Radiant Publishers, New Delhi, 1983

Verrier, Anthony, *Assassination in Algiers: Roosevelt, Churchill, de Gaulle, and the Murder of Admiral Darlan*, W.W. Norton & Co, New York, 1990

Villa, Brian Loring, *Unauthorized Action: Mountbatten and the Dieppe Raid*, updated edition, Oxford University Press, Oxford, 1994 (first edition 1989)

Viorst, Milton, *Hostile Allies: FDR and Charles de Gaulle*, The Macmillan Co., New York, 1965

von Hassell, Ulrich (ed. Hugh Gibson), *The Von Hassell Diaries, 1938–1944*, Hamish Hamilton, London, 1948 (*Vom andern Deutschland: Aus dem nachgelassenen Tagesbüchen 1938–1944 von Ulrich von Hassell*, Atlantis, Zurich, 1947)

von Klemperer, Klemens, *German Resistance against Hitler: The Search for Allies Abroad, 1938–1945*, Clarendon Press, Oxford, 1992

Waller, John H., *The Unseen War in Europe: Espionage and Conspiracy in the Second World War*, Random House, New York, 1996

Wark, Wesley K., *The Ultimate Enemy: British Intelligence and Nazi Germany, 1933–1939*, I.B. Taurus & Co., London, 1985

Watt, Donald Cameron, *Succeeding John Bull: America in Britain's Place – A Study of the Anglo-American Relationship and World Politics in the Context of British and American Foreign Policy-Making in the Twentieth Century*, Cambridge University Press, Cambridge, 1984
How War Came: The Immediate Origins of the Second World War, 1938–1939, Heinemann, London, 1989

Welles, Sumner, *Seven Major Decisions*, Hamish Hamilton, London, 1951

West, Nigel, *MI5: British Security Service Operations 1909–1945*, The Bodley Head, London, 1981
Venona: The Great Secret of the Cold War, HarperCollins, London, 1999

Bibliography

Whalen, Richard J., *The Founding Father: The Story of Joseph P. Kennedy*, Hutchinson, London, 1965

Whaley, Burton, *Codeword BARBAROSSA*, MIT Press, Cambridge (Mass.), 1973

Wheeler, Burton K., with Paul F. Healy, *Yankee from the West: The Candid, Turbulent Life Story of the Yankee-born US Senator from Montana*, Doubleday & Co., Garden City, 1962

Wheeler-Bennett, John, *Disarmament and Security since Locarno 1925–1931*, George Allen & Unwin, London, 1932
Munich: Prologue to Tragedy, Macmillan & Co., London, 1948
(ed.), *Action This Day: Working with Churchill*, Macmillan, London, 1968

White, Nathan I., *Harry Dexter White – Loyal American*, Bessie Bloom, Waban, 1956

White, W.L., *Report on the Russians*, Eyre & Spottiswoode, London, 1945

Winant, John G., *A Letter from Grosvenor Square: An Account of a Stewardship*, Hodder & Stoughton, London, 1947

Young, Desmond, *Rommel*, William Collins Sons & Co, London, 1950

Index

492

Index

Index

Index

Index

of V-weapons, 432
Hoare, Sir Samuel, 99, 150, 185
Hochhuth, Rolf, 312
Ho Chi Minh, 402
Holocaust – see Final Solution
Hong Kong, 210, 239, 253, 270, 365
Hoover, Herbert, 45, 62, 70, 178, 266, 332
Hoover, J. Edgar, 85, 170
Hopkins, Barbara (née Duncan), 74, 78
Hopkins, Ethel (née Gross), 74
Hopkins, Harry L.:
importance to Second World War, 72, 73, 83–6; and New Deal, 73, 75–6; influence over US war effort, 73, 148, 150–1, 151–2, 188, 267; and FDR, 73, 78, 80, 151, 204, 226, 228, 231, 368–70, 396–7, 398; and Stalin, 73, 225, 411; and Churchill, 73, 84, 130, 192–3, 195, 267, 319, 343–4; power in US administration, 73, 122, 188; early life and career, 73–4, 79; character, 74–5; ill health, 75, 78, 90, 150–1, 368–9, 388, 409; tours Europe (1934), 76; and attempted purge of Democrats, 77–8; presidential ambitions, 78; as Secretary of Commerce, 78; as Soviet agent, 78, 79, 83–6, 231, 321, 332, 337, 341, 357–8; and Allied war effort/strategy, 83–4, 276–82, 320–1, 341, 375; and aid to USSR, 84, 325–8, 329, 346, 349; and diversion of New Deal funds into arms industry, 87–8, 92, 102–3; and Marshall, 89, 267; and 1937–38 recession, 90; as Flynn's source, 91; and Sherwood, 95, 174; and Bullitt, 123; and US atomic bomb project, 151–2, 342, 343, 344, 352; and FDR's third-term nomination, 179; and British intelligence, 180,

196; and Lend-Lease, 189–90, 192, 195–6; visit to UK (Jan–Feb, 1941), 192–4, 209–10; world vision, 202–3, 424, 431; on European democracy, 202–3, 228; advocates tough line with Germany, 204, 213, 214; urges renewal of draft, 207; and British policy towards Japan, 209–10; visit to Moscow (1941), 224–5; at Teheran Conference, 225, 321–2, 323, 324; pro-Soviet acts, 226, 228, 231, 332; and US relations with USSR, 226; and Atlantic Conference, 232; suggested as envoy to Japan, 242; and outbreak of war with Japan, 245, 248, 254, 256; visits UK (April 1942), 272–3; and leadership of French North Africa, 291, 310; at Casablanca Conference, 293, 294, 361; wants USSR to hold balance of power in Europe, 321–2, 424; at Cairo Conference, 322, 360; and passing of atomic secrets to USSR, 341–2, 345–6, 348–9, 351–2, 353–5, 356–9; marries Louise Macy, 368; death of son, 368–9; fall from grace, 368–70; and dismemberment of Germany, 370; stages comeback, 395–6; mission to Europe (1945), 396; at Yalta Conference, 396–8, 399–400; on advance on Berlin, 406; and FDR's death, 409; visits Moscow (1945), 410–1; leaves government service, 412; death, 421–2; legacy, 422, 424
Hopkins, Louise (née Macy), 368
Hopkins, Stephen, 369
House, Colonel Edward M., 35, 41, 73, 122
Howe, Quincy, 20
Hull, Cordell, 70, 99, 123, 129, 191, 210, 226, 241,

244, 267, 274, 293, 321, 381, 386, 392
Hungary, 332, 395, 430
Hurley, Major-General Patrick, 368
Husky, Operation, 294, 307, 309
Hussein, Saddam, 12, 13, 14, 427
Huston, John, 76
Hyde, H. Montgomery, 168–9, 170, 171, 173, 181
Hyman, Sidney, 351

Iceland, 214–5, 235
Ickes, Harold, 147, 188, 205, 209, 213
Imperial Defence, Committee of, 42, 116
Imperial Defence Staff, 110
imperial preference, 46, 92, 199, 200, 234, 274–5, 417
India, 106, 132, 133, 239, 264, 271, 272–3, 319, 324, 361, 364–6, 401
Indian National Congress, 272
Indo-China, 161, 209, 240–1, 242, 247, 273, 361, 363, 401–4
Industrial Intelligence Centre (IIC), 135, 170
Industrial Mobilization Plan, 195
Intelligence and National Security, 85
International Monetary Fund (IMF), 332, 336, 337, 339, 420
Iran, 223, 269, 322, 367, 368
Iran-Contra affair, 64
Iraq, 12–13, 182, 217, 218, 302, 367, 427
Irving, David, 301, 311, 312, 315
Ismay, Lord, 116
Italy: FDR on, 13, 67, 104, 125, 144; in North Africa, 25, 192–3, 217; and First World War settlement, 36, 38; and Washington Agreements, 43; in Hitler's thinking, 48; in FDR's global vision, 67; Hopkins in, 76; invades Abyssinia, 96; US embargo on, 96–7; FDR asks for guarantee of non-aggression, 99; and Pact of Steel, 104; and

Index

Index

Index

Rau, Johannes, 56
Raynaud, Pierre, 292
Reagan, Ronald, 182, 426–7
Red Army, 32, 52, 55, 119, 136, 137, 220, 223, 230, 268, 269, 304, 320, 325, 326, 328, 370, 373, 393, 394, 395, 404, 406, 407, 424
Red Cross, 74, 229, 311
Rees, David, 335, 340
Regulation 18b, 26–7
Reichstag, 46, 47, 408
Reid, Helen Ogden, 177
Reith, John (later Lord), 48
Remer, Colonel Otto-Ernst, 379
Representatives, House of (United States), 77, 78, 191, 195, 197, 235
Repulse, HMS, 270
Reuben Jones, USS, 236, 237
Reverse Lend-Lease, 275, 335, 417
Reynaud, Paul, 103, 160
Reynolds, David, 40, 199, 206, 233, 284, 417, 419, 426
Rhineland, 46, 87
Ridsdale, Sir Julian, 251
'Riviera' – see Atlantic Conference
Roberts, Andrew, 26, 146
Roberts, Owen J., 238, 244
Robin Moor, 214
Romania, 38, 395, 400, 405
Rome, 134,164, 217, 318, 319, 376, 383, 390, 391, 396
Rommel, Field Marshal Erwin, 217, 280, 282, 380
Roosevelt, Betsy Cushing, 75
Roosevelt, Eleanor, 66–7, 79, 82–3, 117, 409
Roosevelt, Elliott, 65, 92, 233
Roosevelt, Franklin Delano: exploits Second World War for US's benefit, 13, 89–93, 94, 127, 274–5, 422–3, 425–6; misled by Churchill over invasion, 13, 166, 423; on German threat to US, 13, 31, 214, 215, 228; deceptions of Congress and people, 64, 93–4, 104, 152–5, 235–6; and British intelligence, 14, 169, 170, 173, 174, 175, 196, 266, 423; third-term

campaign/election, 14, 78, 153, 167, 178–80, 188; and declaration of war on Germany, 14, 256, 257–8, 259, 424; and de Gaulle, 14, 184, 186, 297–9, 300, 308–10, 383–4; view of France, 14, 298, 324; post-war legend, 15, 62–3, 433; and Hess affair, 31, 32, 207, 212–4, 215; 'undeclared war' on Germany, 31, 212–5; and US support for Atlantic convoys, 31, 195, 205, 214, 235–6; mobilises US industry for war, 32, 88–90; wants to remove British Empire trade barriers, 46, 69; fears Anglo-German economic co-operation, 51, 92–3; view of/policies on USSR, 55–6, 69–70, 79–80, 108, 214, 223, 227–8, 230–1, 269–70, 311, 392–3, 400, 408–9, 411; and Stalin, 56, 61, 83, 85–6, 275–6, 321, 322–4, 392, 397–8, 407; elected President, 62; character, 63–4, 65; abuses of power, 64–5, 76–8; creates precedents for successors, 64–5, 183, 426–7, 429; life and career to 1932, 65–7; on Germans, 66, 304; 'Grand Design' for world order, 67–70; anti-colonialism of, 68–9, 186, 271–3, 359–64; and independence for Philippines, 69, 366; on Japanese, 69; foreign policy in first term, 70; and Johnson Act, 71; and UK war debts, 71; and New Deal, 71–2, 75, 76–7, 202–3; and Hopkins, 73, 75–6, 78, 84, 150–1, 195, 228, 231, 267, 358, 368–69, 395; second-term election, 77; Communist influence in/Soviet penetration of administration, 78–82, 331–2; on Communism, 79–80, 82–3; and Trident Conference, 85–6, 307–9;

and Czech crisis, 87–8, 98–9, 100–1; diverts New Deal funds into arms industries, 88–9, 127; and aid to UK, 89–90, 93, 94, 140, 141–2, 153–4, 155–6, 157, 160, 423; and aid to France, 93, 94, 102–5, 140, 141–2; and 'Roosevelt Recession', 90, 98; encouragement of European war, 93, 95, 100–2, 109, 119–21, 124–6, 127, 142, 165, 422–3, 424–5; and US involvement in Europe, 94, 188, 206–9, 227, 265; 'defense at a distance' policy, 94, 183, 428; and Neutrality Acts, 95–8, 100, 141–2; and embargo on Italy, 96–7; and Spanish Civil War, 97; and Sino-Japanese war, 97–8; 'quarantine' speech, 98; public stance during 1939 Polish crisis, 99–100; refuses to mediate in Europe, 99–100, 144; and undermining of British economy/trade, 102, 142–3, 187, 199–202, 233–4, 273–5, 334–5; and French reserves, 102, 142; refuses to support UK over Japan, 108; on Nazi invasion of Poland, 113; terminates commercial treaty with Japan (1939), 116; and Kennedy, 122, 143–4, 154; and Churchill, 128, 130, 131, 140, 189, 232–3, 322–3, 324, 391, 409; correspondence with Churchill, 128–30, 153; and Churchill's becoming Prime Minister, 129, 145, 146–9, 423; declares US neutral, 141; extends presidential powers, 143; and Winter War, 143; opposes peace moves, 143–4; and Baruch, 148–9; during phoney war, 150–1; and atomic bomb, 151–2, 342–5, 415; during fall of France, 160; welcomes Mers-el-Kébir,

Index

Shogan, Robert, 91, 94, 153, 182
Short, Lieutenant-General Walter, 238, 249
Siam – see Thailand
Siberia, 39, 41, 57, 116, 211, 239, 240, 331, 345–6, 415, 416–7
Sicherheitsdienst (SD), 373, 376
Sicily, 85, 294, 307, 316, 318, 391
Sikorska, Helena, 313
Sikorski, General Władysław, 137, 224–5, 268, 310–4, 316, 399
Silverman, George, 339
Simon, Abbott, 438
Simon, Lord (Sir John), 21, 27, 50, 108, 150
Simpson, Michael, 63, 72, 77, 90, 206, 323, 345
Simpson, General William, 406, 408
Singapore, 42, 107, 108, 153, 208, 210, 239, 247, 253, 254, 270
Skorzeny, Otto, 317
Sledgehammer, Operation, 277, 278, 279, 280, 281, 285
Smigly-Rydz, Marshal Edward, 114
Smith, Michael, 252, 253
Smith, Moses, 130
Smolensk, 138
Snow, C.P., 135
SO1, 19, 171, 175
Soames, Nicholas, 14
Socialist Party (US), 74
Solomon Islands, 360
Somaliland, 158
Sorge, Richard, 240
Sosnkowski, General Kamierz, 314, 393
'source 19', 85, 307, 357
South Africa, 68, 108, 187, 198
South East Asia Command (SEAC), 360, 403
Soviet Protocol Committee, 226
Soviet Purchasing Commission, 327, 330, 352, 353, 355
Spain, 96, 97, 112, 313
Spanish-American War, 239
Special Branch, 171, 299–300
Special Operations Executive

(SOE), 170, 171, 178, 181, 196, 236, 264, 287, 291–2, 301, 306, 316, 363, 365, 366, 402
Special Senate Committee Investigating the Munitions Industry – see Nye Committee
SS (Schutzstaffel), 138, 164, 221, 230, 373, 374, 378, 407
Stalin, Iosif Vissarionovich: clash with Hitler inevitable, 27, 29, 220; responsibility for outbreak of war, 28, 29, 115, 117, 276; deal with Hitler, 28, 29, 53, 83, 116, 117–8, 422; fears British deal with Germany, 29, 32, 117, 216, 223; views of in Britain, 50; rise to power, 53–4; policies, 54; totalitarianism of, 54–5, 56–61; partnership with USA, 55–6; compared with Hitler, 56, 59–60, 223; as Ally, 56, 61, 424, 269–70, 430; and FDR, 70, 83, 85–6, 227–8, 231, 276, 278, 293, 311, 321, 325, 372, 407, 424, 429–30; and Second Front, 85, 224, 276, 277, 278, 279, 382–3; attempts at alliance against Germany (1938–39), 116–7; territorial ambitions, 118, 127; denounces Britain and France, 137; orders repressive measures in occupied Poland, 138; and Churchill, 140, 282–3; and Barbarossa, 220–1; command of war against Germany, 221, 222, 240, 280; offers Hitler territory, 222; and Hopkins, 224–5, 234, 410–1; approves execution of returned POWs, 230; FDR and Churchill pledge support for, 234; and Japan, 257, 415, 416; orders release of Polish POWs, 269; and Polish sovereignty, 279, 323, 393, 394, 395; tries to undermine Torch?, 283;

Jubilee stage-managed for?, 285; and de Gaulle, 300, 301, 383–4; and postponement of Overlord, 307; seeks peace with Germany?, 308; makes concessions to US and UK, 308; behind Sikorski's death?, 313; and Italian surrender, 318; at Teheran Conference, 321–4; and atomic bomb, 345, 352, 431; and Allied advance on Germany, 378, 392, 405, 406; and Morgenthau Plan, 385; and Warsaw Uprising, 393, 394; Tito appeals to, 395; and Hungary, 395; at Yalta Conference, 397–9; and Romania, 400; breaches Yalta agreements, 405; and German surrender, 408; and death of FDR, 409; Truman's view of, 410; territorial gains, 412, 417
Stalingrad, 280, 287, 293, 303, 304, 320, 328
Standley, Admiral William H., 326
Stark, Admiral Harold R., 183, 200, 208, 215, 236, 238, 244
Station X, 166
Stitt, Admiral Edward R., 150
Steel, Pact of, 104
Steiner, Dr Edward A., 74
Steinhardt, Laurence A., 225, 226
Stephenson, (Sir) William, 168–74, 180–1, 182, 236, 258, 265–7, 446
Stettinius Jr., Edward R., 226, 331, 370, 396
Stevenson, William, 169, 171, 180, 258, 259
Stimson, Henry L., 206, 207, 241, 244, 261, 267, 342, 343, 370, 398
Stinnett, Robert B., 238, 243–4, 250, 251
Stokes, Richard, 159, 166
Stokes, Richard L., 351
Stoler, Mark A., 276, 281, 322, 426
Strategic Defence Initiative, 427

507